# Gender and the Race for Space

# Gender and the Race for Space: Masculinity and the American Astronaut, 1957–1983

Erinn McComb

ANTHEM PRESS

Anthem Press
An imprint of Wimbledon Publishing Company
*www.anthempress.com*

This edition first published in UK and USA 2025
by ANTHEM PRESS
75–76 Blackfriars Road, London SE1 8HA, UK
or PO Box 9779, London SW19 7ZG, UK
and
244 Madison Ave #116, New York, NY 10016, USA

© 2025 Erinn McComb

The author asserts the moral right to be identified as the author of this work.

All rights reserved. Without limiting the rights under copyright reserved
above, no part of this publication may be reproduced, stored or introduced
into a retrieval system, or transmitted, in any form or by any means
(electronic, mechanical, photocopying, recording or otherwise), without the
prior written permission of both the copyright owner and the above publisher
of this book.

*British Library Cataloguing-in-Publication Data*
A catalogue record for this book is available from the British Library.

*Library of Congress Cataloging-in-Publication Data: 2025930283*
A catalog record for this book has been requested.

ISBN-13: 978-1-83998-717-5 (Hbk)
ISBN-10: 1-83998-717-0 (Hbk)

Cover Credit: Robert McCall

This title is also available as an e-book.

# CONTENTS

| | |
|---|---|
| *Acknowledgments* | vii |
| Introduction: Who Can Fly? Gender and the American Astronaut | 1 |
| 1.  Early Cold War Gender Roles in the Public and Private Discourse | 23 |
| 2.  Light This Candle: Project Mercury and Cold War Masculinity | 53 |
| 3.  The First Lady Astronaut Trainees (FLATs) | 87 |
| 4.  Refreshingly Human and Winning: Pilot Control and Project Gemini | 127 |
| 5.  It's Hip to Be Square: Democratic Manhood and the Apollo Program | 157 |
| 6.  What Made It Possible for Sally to Ride?: The Shuttle's Domestication and Democratization of Spaceflight | 199 |
| Conclusion: To Infinity and Beyond | 237 |
| *Bibliography* | 247 |
| *Index* | 285 |

# ACKNOWLEDGMENTS

Writing a manuscript is a challenging and daunting task on the mind and body, and the people below made the life a little easier. I would like to thank the archivists at the NASA History Office in Washington, D.C., the John F. Kennedy Presidential Library and Museum and the Mississippi State University Mitchell Memorial Library. I would be lost without the publications of Dr. Roger Launius, Dr. Margaret A. Weitekamp, Dr. Matthew Hersch, Dr. Debbie Douglas, Dr. David Mindell, Dr. Molly Merryman, Dr. Sarah Parry Myers, Dr. Brian C. Odom, Dr. Michael W. Hankins, Dr. Steven A. Fino, Dr. Amy Bix, Dr. Amy Foster, Lynn Sherr, Amy Shira Teitel and Margaret Lee Shetterly. I would like to thank Dr. Thomas Adam of the University of Arkansas for connecting me with Anthem Press. This manuscript began with my dissertation at Mississippi State University. My advisors, Dr. Alan I Marcus, Dr. Mary Kathryn Barbier, Dr. Jessicca Martucci, Dr. Amy Gangloff and Dr. Richard Damms, provided constructive criticism and amazing direction. I need to give special thanks to my classmates and administrators: Dr. Micah Rueber, Dr. Andi Knecht, Dr. Sean Halverson, Dr. Brian Rumsey, Dr. Alyssa Warrick, Dr. Katie Bruton, Dr. Whitney Snow, Holly Haimes, Dr. Karen Senaga, Dr. Jeff Howell, Dr. Cliff Hutt, Pam and Patsy. A very heartfelt thank-you goes to Dr. Cari Casteel, who spent countless hours with me traveling, in the archives and on the microfilm machine. I would be remiss if I did not acknowledge the encouragement of Dr. Alan Meyer and Dr. Tyler Peterson. You gentlemen rock! The final manuscript would not have been possible without the Johnson Space Center History Office's Oral History Project. I am indebted to Jennifer Ross-Nazzall and Rebecca Wright. I have never met you, but thank you. My colleagues at Del Mar College have been extremely supportive in this grueling task, especially Dr. Bea Alvarado, Christine Muller, Dr. Dawson Barrett, Mendy Meurer-Busby, Korinne Caruso, Dr. Monique Saenz, Dr. Will Rushton, Lucy Medina, Renato Ramirez, Javier Morin, Dr. Paul Gottemoller, Brian Hart, Dr. Bryan Stone, Catherine Albert, Dr. Derek Oden, Dr. Mark Robbins, Dr. Jim Klein, Dr. Teresa Klein, Jennifer Jimenez-Perez, Dr. Stephanie Ding, Dr. Jonathan

Dyen, Lisa Welch and Dr. Leticia Wilson. My first adult job after graduate school was at Texas A&M University-Kingsville. Dr. Brenda Melendy, Dr. Anders Greenspan, Dr. Dean Ferguson, Dr. Abbey Mann, Dr. Alberto Rodriguez, Dr. Christine Reiser-Robbins, Dr. Jeff Glick, Dr. Roger Tuller and Dr. Shannon Baker were very encouraging in turning the dissertation into a manuscript. This adventure would not be possible without my conversations with pilots Lt. Col. Olga Custodio, Lt. Commander Meagan "Rowdy Ronda" Garcia, Lt. Col. Jess Brown, Warrant Officer Jacqlyn Tsao and Lt. Commander Adam Bergman. My fears and emotions were kept in check by the Sisterhood, Dani, Arlean, Peter McComb, Sandra and Mel Valerio, my surrogate mothers Dalia and Silvia, Nami and Vance Fisher, Isaac Garcia, Catherine Wittkower, Laura Commons, J. J. Hart, Veronica and Joe Zamora, Beth Dushman, Erika Locke, Lynn Bradshaw, Crystal, Alejandra Reyes, The Training Room, my students, and dogs Louie, Mickey and Millie. Countless hours of encouraging phone conversations were held with my people, Dr. Ian Aebel and Dr. Jennifer Pearce-Morris. Finally, I would not be here without the visibility of the greatest of all time, the GOATs, women from my grandmother Olga, who was a Pan American stewardess who transfixed me with her stories, to my mother Kim, Amelia, Bessie, Jackie, Jerrie, Wally, Sally, Mae, Ellen and Eileen. Without them, and the historians who uncovered their stories, I may not have had the same self-determination in my lifetime.

# INTRODUCTION: WHO CAN FLY? GENDER AND THE AMERICAN ASTRONAUT

On July 20, 2021, 82-year-old Wally Funk blasted into space aboard *Blue Origin's* first crewed spaceflight. The flight was part of the Federal Aviation Administration's "Commercial Astronaut Wings Program."[1] The craft, *The New Shepard*, named after the first American in space, Alan B. Shepard, reached over sixty-two miles above the Earth's surface. *The New Shepard* crossed the Karman line defined by the Federation Aeronautique Internationale as "space."[2] Jeff Bezos, the founder of Amazon and owner of *Blue Origin*, invited Funk to join the mission, along with his brother Mark and 18-year-old Dutch student Oliver Daemen.[3] Funk became the oldest woman to "fly" into space.[4] Funk waited almost sixty years for her chance for spaceflight.

Funk's fight for spaceflight reminds us that "the past is never dead. It's not even past."[5] For instance, historian Jacquelyn Dowd Hall argues that the United States' modern civil rights movements were not confined to a series of successful events from the 1950s until the late 1960s. Rather, the struggle for civil rights is part of a "long civil rights movement" of individual agency and hidden voices that often conflicted with conservative movements.[6] *Gender and the Race for Space* views the National Aeronautics and Space Administration (NASA) and the American public discourse at the height of the space race as emblematic of progressive and conservative parallel narratives. NASA and the public discourse embraced progress and change in social inequalities, especially in terms of gender and race. Yet, at the same time, the agency highlighted conventionally conservative values pertaining to gender and race. Women and minority voices at NASA reflected "peaks and valleys of human behavior. The tough times they see are just part of a valley. That mountaintop (to co-opt Dr. King's metaphor) is still within sight."[7]

Funk and her fellow First Lady Astronaut Trainees (FLATs) are historical reminders of gender inequalities in American aviation and aerospace technology, or, in other words, those peaks and valleys of human behavior. NASA and the public discourse's more conservative or conventional narrative deemed a

## GENDER AND THE RACE FOR SPACE

woman astronaut a stunt that was too risky and costly. Early manned space-flight's public discourse depicted women's roles as wife and mother, while the male astronaut possessed the ideal American masculinity—rugged individuality, self-determination and control.[8] To differentiate the American space program from that of the Soviets, the United States wanted male jet test pilots as astronauts to demonstrate that American men could control space-flight technology. Unlike in Soviet collectivism, the individual mattered in American masculine constructs. Astronauts as pilots represented American exceptionalism, self-determination and democratic technology in space. The Soviets emphasized the opposite and focused on the sophistication of socialist technology to bring man—and woman—back safely to Earth.

For instance, on June 16, 1963, a working-class textile employee and parachute enthusiast, Valentina "Vayla" Tereshkova, boarded *Vostok 6*, and the Soviet Union launched the first woman into space. Historian Walter McDougall argues that Tereshkova's lack of piloting skills "proved the super-fluousness of the test pilots on the other flights." McDougall maintains that Tereshkova's flight was supposed to demonstrate the "routineness" of Soviet spaceflight.[9] The Soviets did not launch Tereshkova as a symbol of gender equality; rather, her flight symbolized safety and space as motherhood's final frontier.[10]

However, American feminists viewed Tereshkova's flight through their own lens of gender inequality, and the Soviets seized on this moment to prove the lack of gender equality within American democratic technology. Upon her return, both Tereshkova and Soviet Premier Nikita Khrushchev reprimanded American society for not sending American women into space. During her world tour, Tereshkova brazenly announced that her flight confirmed the equality of the sexes in the Soviet Union, but also "the ever-growing superiority of the socialist order of society over capitalism altogether."[11] Tereshkova's first had some Americans asking, "Why Valentina and Not Our Gal?"[12]

The United States had women pilots more qualified than Tereshkova to go into space. In fact, in 1959, while working as a consultant as the Chairman for the Special Advisory Committee on Life Sciences for NASA, Dr. William Randolph "Randy" Lovelace Jr., founder of the Lovelace Foundation for Medical Education and Research in New Mexico, conducted tests to see if women would make viable astronauts. Lovelace believed that sending women into space would be cheaper due to their smaller size and weight. In conjunction with the famed Women's Army Service Pilot (WASP) of World War II, Jacqueline "Jackie" Cochran, Lovelace compiled names of the best women pilots in the United States. At the Lovelace Clinic, nineteen women underwent the same tests that the male astronaut candidates endured. Thirteen

INTRODUCTION 3

of them passed, including 22-year-old Funk. After the medical experiments, Lovelace attempted to put the women through jet piloting tests at the Naval School of Aviation Medicine in Pensacola, Florida. The military prohibited women from flying military aircraft and thus denied his request.

In that same year, 1962, the House of Representatives convened the Subcommittee on the Selection of Astronauts of the Committee on Science and Astronautics to hold a hearing on sex discrimination within NASA's astronaut corps. The subcommittee concluded that even though women could not fly jets for the military, the NASA astronaut jet test-pilot requirement did not indicate that NASA discriminated against women.[13] Until 1963, the United States had answered every Soviet first but not that of Tereshkova's flight. To understand why NASA refused to launch a woman astronaut in the 1960s means unpacking the conventional understanding of gender and technology. NASA did not counter the launch of Tereshkova because Cold War Americans viewed technology—especially aviation and aerospace technology—through a lens of fixed gender roles. Women represented passivity with technology, and women astronauts would have railed against the public discourse's depiction of astronaut pilot control over the spacecraft in this great battle for space.

Margaret A. Weitekamp's *Right Stuff, Wrong Sex: America's First Women in Space Program* (2005) published the first historic work on the FLATs. Her work suggests that Lovelace's conclusions that women were better equipped than men for space travel challenged the American belief that women were passive actors with technology. Lovelace's program attracted attention in the early 1960s because it was on the eve of a "breakthrough in thinking about women's public roles." Weitekamp argues that the pilots and engineers at NASA "brought with them their military culture and its embedded assumptions about women's and men's proper roles. As such, the military ethos of the young civilian agency did not welcome women in the dangerous role of astronauts."[14] Weitekamp's argument is the launching off point for *Gender and the Race for Space.*

*Gender and the Race for Space* is an investigation into the gendered construction of the astronaut image during some of the tensest years of the Cold War era. The book chronicles the history of early spaceflight and asks why the United States did not counter the Soviet launch of Tereshkova. While scholars have pieced together the story of American women's fight for spaceflight, this work adds to the narrative by using a gendered framework that focuses on both masculinity and femininity. The manuscript analyzes the public discourse's gendered construction of the astronaut by focusing on how the astronaut image came to terms with a perceived Cold War masculinity crisis. While NASA argued that it would not answer the 1963 "stunt" of putting a woman into space as it was on an "accelerate timetable for lunar flight," gender also played an important role in the decision.[15] The American construction of the astronaut image was informed by Cold War masculine ideals of rugged individuality, self-determination and control that helped mold a distinctly American (anti-communist) masculinity that appeared—on the surface anyway—to resolve not only an American "crisis of masculinity" but also helped win the Cold War on an ideological and popular level. The space race was as much about beating the Soviets to the moon as it was about reinvigorating masculinity at a time of growing automation, consumerism, collectivism and feminism.

For instance, the end of World War II commenced a technological war between the Soviets and Americans that threatened American democracy at home and abroad. The United States adopted foreign service officer George Kennan's policy of containment to combat the red menace.[16] The launch of the world's first artificial satellite, *Sputnik*, aboard an intercontinental ballistic missile on October 4, 1957, strengthened and focused the United States' ideological resolve to contain communism in space. Bettyann Holtzmann Kevles refers boldly to the successful launch of *Sputnik* as "perhaps the greatest technological and public relations coup of Soviet history."[17] *Sputnik* provided a new frontier to be conquered and democratized. The race in space ushered in an international power struggle that centered on gaining control from the enemy; a battlefield that reinforced gendered meanings of war, flight and technology. Each step that the United States took dealt with projecting an image of masculine control over technology. The glorification of the astronaut's control over spacecraft technology equated the survival of freedom, democracy and separate gender roles.

Much like their predecessors, Cold War Americans viewed sex and gender as fixed.[18] The fact that women could not fly military aircraft partly had to do with—literally at times—their reproductive system as well as American notions of proper gender roles.[19] Post–World War II feminist theorists questioned these fixed gender binaries, arguing for gender as an act as opposed to innate. For instance, in *The Second Sex* (1949), Simone de Beauvoir argues that women were not "born," instead, one "becomes a woman."[20] Gender was an action or performance. Judith Butler has taken this to mean that "gender is in no way a stable identity" but "an identity tenuously constitutive in time—an identity, instituted through a stylized repletion of acts."[21] Similarly, Patricia Cooper argues in *Gender and Technology: A Reader* (2003) that "the term gender is often misused to mean women, but it really refers to the process (and consequences) whereby biological sex become transformed into a socially constructed (as opposed to natural) definition of what it means to be a man or woman."[22]

# INTRODUCTION

However, conventional post–World War II American culture defined the performance of men and women as separate or distinct and thus proof of fixed gender roles, especially military performance. Molly Merryman argues in *Clipped Wings: The Rise and Fall of the Women Air Force Service Pilots (WASPs) of World War II* (1998) that "Because the definitional system that supports the constructions of gender is based on this oppositional categorization, women cannot be allowed to perform in men's spaces, because their performances risk revealing that gender and therefore power are artificial constructions."[23] Cold War Americans understood controlling technology, especially military technology, as masculinity. Controlling a spacecraft was a masculine performance. Tom Wolfe writes in *The Right Stuff* (1979) that pilot control represented "Manliness, manhood, manly courage [...] there was something ancient, primordial, irresistible about the challenge [...]."[24]

The American public discourse viewed women's and men's roles with technology differently. In a world of fixed gender roles, women as pilots or astronauts took away power and control from men, thus feminizing or emasculating men and piloting. Cold War women's technology was limited to domestic technology in the home and technology dealing with women's bodies such as "braziers, birth control, and tampons."[25] American companies marketed domestic technology such as dishwashers, stoves and washing machines as "automatic." [26] Thus, women were passive actors even when using women's technology. Femininity meant inactivity or passivity.[27]

Masculinity depicted control and self-determination. Americans promoted astronaut masculinity through the astronaut's perceived control over the spacecraft while confining femininity to the home. In her 1963 work on women's liberation, Betty Friedan lambasted American culture for embracing female passivity and glorifying masculine activity. Friedan suggested that passivity dehumanized American women, thus only humanizing men.[28] If gender performance with technology continued with male as active and female as passive, gender and sex were fixed. These fixed gender roles fell apart within the public discourse as women fought for spaceflight.

*Gender and the Race for Space* deals with the public discourse to understand what astronaut image Americans and the world consumed from the media, politicians and NASA. I define public discourse as information about spaceflight and the astronauts—whether real or imagined—that was presented to the American public. Through the assumption that the astronaut controlled his craft, his body produced "cultural meanings" of power and control or Cold War masculinity.[29] I use Michael W. Hankins's *Flying Camelot: The F-15, the F-16, and the Weaponization of Fighter Pilot Nostalgia* (2021) to define culture as "assumptions, interpretations, and patterns of thinking that shape behaviors. Most importantly, most of this process is not conscious, 'it is unexamined and unverbalized.'" In other words, "The power of culture is derived from the fact that it operates as a set of assumptions that are unconscious and taken for granted."[30] The "military ethos" and culture that surrounded NASA raise questions concerning the construction of the astronaut's gender, specifically how military pilot control over spaceflight technology helped reinvigorate American masculinity at a time of a perceived masculinity crisis.

The following delves deeper into the construction of early Cold War gender roles by looking at how the language used in the public discourse shaped the early American astronaut image as taking back control from the Soviets and a perceived Cold War masculinity crisis. Using Joan Wallach Scott's work on language and culture, I argue that words mattered and "conveyed the idea of meaning as the patterns and relationships that constitute understanding or a 'cultural system.'"[31] In this case, the "cultural system" were Cold War gender roles. The same language used to combat the perceived crisis of masculinity can also be found in the early space race narrative. The space race was a great adventure, a test of American self-determination and a platform to project an ideal masculinity.

The space race and astronaut image became a microcosm of progressive and conservative gender and gender strife. During NASA's early years, space journalists, politicians and popular culture writers used masculine language such as "conquer," "explore," "dominate," "master[y]," "prestige," "aggressive," "vigor," "strength" and "war" to describe American action in space. This language coupled with images of technological control helped create spaceflight as masculine. The Cold War public discourse championed a return to rugged individualism, self-determination and control as a way for American men to conquer the masculinity crisis and contain Soviet socialism and American feminism.

Recently, historians have seized on aviation and spaceflight's connection to broader themes in American culture and gender. Increasingly, they have shifted their focus from the well-documented programmatic, technological and political history of aviation and spaceflight to the roles that popular culture, the media, propaganda and average Americans played in both shaping and reflecting the pilot and astronaut image.[32] Historian Joseph Corn's seminal work *The Winged Gospel: America's Romance with Aviation* (1983) argues that Americans viewed conquering the sky as a metaphor for the American ability to end social ills and inequalities. Flight was the hope for a better tomorrow.[33] However, access to flying and who could fly reflected American gender culture. While aviation classes were advertised to women, women were largely left out of the flight line in private, commercial and military aviation unless there was a national need.

INTRODUCTION

Linda R. Robertson's *The Dream of Civilized Warfare: World War I Flying Aces and the American Imagination* (2003) argues that the flying pursuit combat ace as a breed apart strengthened the resolve to create piloting as a masculine space.[34] Her work echoes Hall's warning that "remembrance is always a form of forgetting [...]." The romanticized lone-wolf World War I ace removed audiences from trench warfare's horrific realities—even if "air-to-air combat [...] had little, if any, measurable effect on the war's outcome." The military and the public discourse created "heroic images, fighter pilots engaging in exciting aerial duels seemed to revive the possibility of this romantic image of chivalrous warfare."[35]

Despite their presence as interlopers, women were very active in breaking into this masculine space. The 1920s New Woman image created an entering wedge for women pilots. Leslie Haynesworth and David Toomey's *Amelia Earhart's Daughters* (1998) depicted the 1920s New Woman pilot image:

> And in some ways the aviatrix was the perfect icon of the "new" femininity. She was the flapper and the career woman rolled into one: a wild adventuress and a serious, skilled master of a challenging profession. She was participating in the realization of incredible new possibilities. She was brave and she was enterprising. And she did not let traditional notions of what she was "supposed" to do stop her. In short, she was just about everything Americans wanted their heroes to be.[36]

Regardless, gendered stereotypes remained as Americans continued to view flying as not feminine, but rather, dirty and dangerous.[37] The Great Depression created a conservative wave of gender roles in flight, even as Amelia Earhart attempted to be the first woman to fly around the world. Commenting on Earhart's July 1937 disappearance, *Life* insisted that she had undertaken "the kind of dangerous stunt of which the Federal Government now strongly disapproves."[38] Famed author and journalist Bob Considine asked after her flight: "Will women ever fly as well as men? We doubt it." Considine acknowledged women to be better equipped with "timing" and "nicety" with "sensitive" technology that should make them "superior to men." However, "they aren't—and one by one they fall into that mystic abyss that some wrathful Providence seems to have ordained for them."[39]

Despite Considine's beliefs that women were "the bearers of ill-luck, misfortune and disaster," women continued to subvert the 1930s conservative gender stereotypes and flew anyway.[40] For instance, Bendix winner Louise Thaden echoed the New Woman when she argued in her 1940 memoir that being a woman is more than just motherhood. She wrote, "There are always two sides to a woman's life, that of her heart and home, as well as that of her work and profession."[41] Thaden's progressive thinking was not shared by most in American society—even when women proved themselves capable and skilled outside conventional roles.

The public saw women fly military aircraft during World War II, but women's contributions in a masculine space were necessary because of a national need and were to be temporary. Over one thousand WASPs ferried military aircraft across the country. However, unlike the women in the Army, Navy, Coast Guard and Marines, the WASPs were not militarized and thus failed to receive military benefits for their service. Merryman's *Clipped Wings* argues that the government's failure to militarize the WASPs reflected fears of changing gender culture. Merryman writes, "The issue was very clearly not about the WASPs as pilots, but about women who were going beyond culturally constructed normative boundaries of how women were expected to behave, and who were serving in what were constructed to be male roles." After all, women in the Army, Navy, Coast Guard and Marines were militarized, but they filled mostly administrative or "pink-collar" feminine jobs. The WASPs, in contrast, held jobs gendered as masculine—jobs that men wanted. While the Army Air Corps championed the militarization of the women pilots, society was not ready for an upset in gender roles. The congressional Ramspeck Report (1944) argued incorrectly that the Army Air Corps lowered the standards for women pilots and that the social experiment was a waste of government resources.[42] The federal government disbanded the WASPs. The FLATs and the first women astronauts faced the same arguments in the early 1960s and late 1980s.

Sara Parry Myers' *Earning Their Wings: The WASPs of World War II and the Fight for Veteran Recognition* (2023) follows Merryman and argues that the sky acted as a metaphor to demonstrate American masculinity—thus, determining who could and could not fly. Myers builds upon previous works such as Michael Sherry's *The Rise of American Air Power: The Creation of Armageddon* (1987) and Jennifer Van Vleck's *Empire of the Air: Aviation and the American Ascendancy* (2013) that argue for the sky as a frontier or a metaphor for a new American empire.[43] Within Myers' gendered sphere, women entered "a space where fraught debates of gender roles and definitions of the ideal military veteran were contested and reimagined." Giving the WASPs agency, Myers argues that the women "asserted their place as professionals within contested airspace as they confronted male resistance and gendered debates about their abilities" both during and after the war. These very women complicated the role of military service, citizenship, as well as "hero" and veteran.[44] The FLATs and the first women astronauts also confronted the complicated idea that women could be heroes or veterans—especially since they were not combat fighter pilots.

# INTRODUCTION

The public discourse and the military continued to craft the male lone-wolf pilot image during the early Cold War. John Darrell Sherwood writes in *Officers in Flight Suits: The Story of American Air Force Fighter Pilots in the Korean War* (1996) of the post–World War II fighter-pilot image or "flight suit attitude" who flew a "high-performance, single-seat fighter" that embodied the "warrior spirit" or an "attitude [...] of self-confidence and pride that verged on arrogance." The fighter pilot "culture placed a premium on cockiness and informality." Women did not belong in this space other than as "officers' wives" or "bar-room sluts."[45]

Steve Fino's *Tiger Check: Automating the U.S. Air Force Fighter Pilot for Air-to-Air Combat, 1950-1980* (2017) looks at the epitome of American heroism with the F-86 Sabre, the F-4 Phantom II and the F-15 Eagle military fighter pilots. Fino argues that the three essentials of the fighter pilot or "great pilot" myth that emerged from World War I were that: "air warfare represented honorable combat fought by honorable individual warriors; that it was the unique flying skill of the pilot that dictated success; and that the tally of aerial victories recorded by the pilot and recorded in hometown newspapers was an appropriate measure of his success." Increased automation in the 1950s signaled a change in the fighter-pilot archetype that threatened the World Wars' fighter ace romanticized image of Eddie Rickenbacker, Richard Bong, Robin Olds and future astronaut John Glenn. Increased technology meant a lack of individuality, self-determination, a lack of "stick and rudder skill" and an overreliance on computers and automation that would turn the military jet pilot "flying night" into "'long haired' scientists" or "systems managers" or simply another "black box."[46] This debate over male pilot individuality, threatening automation and the dreaded long-haired pilot scientist image played out within the public astronaut image.

Hankins argues in *Flying Camelot* that the fighter-pilot image since World War I was "a collection of ideas that did not always reflect reality—but the romantic, heroic idealization of the fighter pilot meant a great deal to the American public and the pilots themselves." Hankins argues that the "mythic construction of an idealized fighter pilot consists of five core elements: Aggressiveness, Independence, Heroic Imagery, Technology, and Community." American culture did not embrace women who were aggressive, independent, heroic or technologically competent. Thus, these are, as Hankins points out, "concepts of masculinity." The fighter-pilot image reinforced flying as a masculine space, but one that also required the human element—once again reinforcing men as human and women as not yet fully human. In this construction of a fighter-pilot myth, we see that "military technology is not developed solely as a solution to an operational problem, nor does it have a mind of its own. Humans make choices—humans that are

10 GENDER AND THE RACE FOR SPACE

steeped in specific cultures, with specific beliefs, assumptions, behaviors, and values."[47] The astronauts and the public discourse attempted to transfer this fighter-pilot myth to the astronauts, with Americans embracing perhaps an unrealistic astronaut image of individual pilot control over technology at a time of a feared flagging masculinity.

As the 1990s historical field moved toward social movements, hidden narratives and individual agency, so too did the history of spaceflight.[48] In 2000, Roger Launius called for aerospace historians to continue researching aerospace history from different frameworks, lenses, disciplines and of course social movements to better see the multiple layers of spaceflight's impact at home and across the globe. Launius referred to this scholarship as the "New Aerospace History."[49] More recent scholarship has focused on the intersection of spaceflight and American culture, finding new angles to view the space race. Aerospace scholarship focused primarily on how spaceflight's public discourse drew upon a popular past of rugged explorers and pioneers conquering the American West. To help sell spaceflight, politicians fashioned the astronauts as the new frontier's explorers and pioneers.[50] This frontier narrative created a new proving ground for American democracy and American masculinity.

Launius's "Heroes in a Vacuum: The Apollo Astronaut as Cultural Icon" (2008) contextualized NASA within this reinvigorated masculine paradigm. Launius proposes that the media and NASA portrayed space fliers as both ordinary and extraordinary.[51] The men were to symbolize the "epitome" of masculinity. NASA looked for "real men" when choosing the first astronauts, the Mercury 7.[52] For the astronauts to symbolize American masculinity, NASA took great pains to control the public image of the astronauts. NASA's Officer for Public Affairs from 1958 to 1960, Walter T. Bonney, suppressed any news of the astronauts' wild parties or affairs with women. Launius maintains that Bonney turned the "hard-living, hard-drinking lot" into "God-fearing" family men who represented the American "everyman."[53] This everyman had to be in control of his spacecraft to make the ordinary man extraordinary.

As Americans constructed a discourse that emphasized—if not at times embellished—the astronaut's control over the spacecraft, the American press strove to depict the opposite in the Soviet cosmonaut. Soviet space historian Asif A. Siddiqi argues that the chief designer for the Soviet space program, Sergei Korolev, stressed the importance of automated capsule control over pilot control. Korolev suggested:

As has been repeatedly demonstrated in our automated flights […], our technology is such that we do not require, as the American Mercury

# INTRODUCTION 11

project does, that our early cosmonauts be highly skilled engineers. The American astronaut must help control the rocket systems at every stage of the flight.

Siddiqi maintains that Korolev's statement "was an indication of the depth to which automation was an intrinsic factor in the early Soviet piloted space program."[54] Unlike the Soviets, the Americans resisted the image of automation or what they viewed as feminine passivity.

Slava Gerovitch maintains that the early cosmonaut flights represented "ideological tensions in the Soviet discourse on the self."[55] The cosmonauts wanted to control the spacecraft. However, much like the American astronaut, the cosmonaut wavered between the illusion of the pilot's control and the reality of technological control. He defines this tension over the Soviet self as wavering between individual control and the cosmonaut as a cog in the spaceflight system. Cogs represented a lack of action or "discipline and subordination" or the Soviet "the domination of automata"—what famed jet test pilot Chuck Yeager referred to as "spam in a can."[56] Pilots—men—whether American or Soviet, desired action, not passivity. The moon landing epitomized pilot action and masculine technological control.

Matthew D. Tribbe's *No Requiem for the Space Age: The Apollo Moon Landings and American Culture* (2014) argues for two different perspectives of the moon landing. The dominant conventional narrative highlights American technological prowess and sees the moon landing as progress of man's ability to use science, technology and big government to create social change. On the other hand, Tribbe uncovers a narrative emblematic of President Jimmy Carter's "malaise" speech that looks at the loss of faith in these institutions.[57]

Likewise, Neil M. Maher's *Apollo in the Age of Aquarius* (2017) views the Apollo program in the context of social movements as civil rights activists and feminist warriors became harbingers of social change and looked to NASA to cure social ills.[58] Both books highlight the conventionally conservative spaceflight narrative at odds with a progressive social justice narrative. This idea of spaceflight technology as a symbol of progress goes back to Wernher von Braun's vision in Michael J. Neufeld's *Von Braun: Dreamer of Space, Engineer of War* (2007) that rocketry was a beacon of progress in the world and a demonstration of man's capabilities—despite that von Braun's *V-2* rockets were engineered with Third Reich money and constructed by enslaved concentration camp labor.[59]

Minorities and women were part of this narrative of progress and social change within spaceflight, albeit they remained hidden actors in the long civil rights movement. Richard Paul and Steven Moss's *We Could Not Fail: The First African Americans in the Space Program* (2015) details African American contributions to spaceflight before desegregation fully took place in the American South. Like Margot Lee Shetterly's *Hidden Figures: The American Dream and the Untold Story of the Black Women Mathematicians Who Helped Win the Space Race* (2016) Paul and Moss uncover the voices of Black Americans who were not part of the conventional civil rights movement but were instrumental in demonstrating the power of minority contributions at NASA. Paul, Moss and Shetterly highlight the theme of technology and race—one that *We Could Not Fail* argues is a cornerstone of American history going back to the 1793 cotton gin. Both books challenge historians to research more hidden figures in spaceflight but also NASA's role in the Jim Crow South.[60]

Brian C. Odom and Stephen P. Waring's collection of essays in the long overdue *NASA and the Long Civil Rights Movement* (2019) also focus on the importance of individual agency and uncovering hidden voices within spaceflight using Hall's "long civil rights movement" framework. The authors uncover women and minorities' fight to become part of spaceflight's democratic technology in what Odom calls NASA's "laboratory for social progress" in the 1960s. The essays highlight both progressive and conservative voices within NASA: those that viewed NASA as a vehicle for social change and those who did not think the space race should get involved with civil rights. Topics include civil rights movements to end segregation in Huntsville, Alabama, home to NASA Marshall Spaceflight Center, women's entrance into all-male engineering spaces, the importance of educational access, the lack of Black representation in the flight of Cuban cosmonaut Arnaldo Tamayo Méndez and the power of the Black caucus to demand the closure of NASA's Deep Space Instrumentation Facility-51 at Hartebeesthoek in apartheid South Africa. The collection of essays ends with historian Jonathan Coopersmith's call for the importance of the preservation of the past, specifically among those historically underrepresented in American spaceflight. The assumption that only the voices of those in power matter is a detriment to future generations' understanding of the historical past and the power of individual agency.[61]

Nathalia Holt's *The Rise of the Rocket Girls: The Women Who Propelled Us, from Missiles to the Moon to Mars* (2016) uncovers hidden voices from women working in rocketry, beginning with Frank Malina's 1930s "Suicide Squad" at the California Institute of Technology (Caltech) and those who worked for NASA's Jet Propulsion Laboratory (JPL). She uncovers women who aided the rocket teams since their inception. Despite the fact that these women pioneered rocket research, the Guggenheim Aeronautical Laboratory (later NASA JPL) classified the women as computers instead of the professional ranking of engineer. The women's work proved invaluable to rocket research, and NASA started to classify the women as engineers, mathematicians and

# INTRODUCTION

even in managerial positions at a time when private companies were reluctant to do so.[62]

Likewise, Jennifer M. Ross-Nazal's *Making Space for Women: Stories of Trailblazing Women from NASA's Johnson Space Center* (2022) uses twenty-two of her oral histories from women engineers, scientists, mathematicians, secretaries and managers to uncover the lives of women working in teams in a male-dominated space, especially before it was illegal to discriminate by sex in the workplace.[63] Ross-Nazal's oral histories of both men and women working for NASA are a phenomenal wealth of information for any researcher.

Other historians have focused on the impact of masculinity and man's performance with technology in the white, male space of spaceflight. David A. Mindell's *Digital Apollo: Human and Machine in Space Flight* (2008) contends that the relationship between the astronaut and the spacecraft forced NASA and the nation to come to terms with the relationship of people to machines in the expanding age of technology. Much like David Kauffman's *Selling Outer Space: Kennedy, the Media, and Funding for Project Apollo, 1961–1963* (1994), Mindell argues that to sell the billion-dollar Apollo program to the American people, the public discourse "drew upon American imagery of exploration, individualism, and geographical conquest" in which "the astronauts had to be in control. Frontiersmen could not be passengers." Finally, Mindell suggests, "Astronauts' accounts continually reaffirm that what it means to be a man is related to control and interpret threats to pilots' control as threats to their manhood." The astronauts wanted to master the craft and prove that they could fly. Sophisticated software and technology within Apollo questioned astronaut control over the craft. Mindell contends that the new Apollo Guidance Computer (AGC) "called the very nature of 'heroism'" into question. What did it mean to be in control? [...] Can it be "'manly' to control a machine by simply pushing buttons?"[64] Push-button masculinity offered a reimagined masculine control to one that shared control with technology and with teams at NASA. Teamwork and button-pushing were needed for "Whitey" to conquer the moon.[65]

Matthew H. Hersch's astronaut labor history *Inventing the American Astronaut* (2012) complicates the astronauts' daredevil subculture amid the pencil pushers and pocket protectors at NASA. Hersch argues that the astronauts were "not quite employees and not quite 'in charge,' astronauts walked a fine line between autonomy and subservience, their status ensured by their unique skills and celebrity." The astronauts faced being swallowed up by NASA engineering teams and spat out as William H. Whyte Jr.'s "organization men"—a man controlled by a bureaucracy or private corporations.[66]

*Gender and the Race for Space* conversely argues that the astronauts' self-determination was complicated by teams of scientists, technicians, engineers and flight controllers. Rather than turning the astronaut into an organization man, the American public discourse was forced to renegotiate the masculine astronaut image into that of sociologist Michael Kimmel's "democratic manhood"—a masculinity continually influx between the individualist and the team player.[67] Overall, the public discourse surrounding the astronaut image did the opposite of what it intended to prove. The astronaut demonstrated that gender was not fixed but rather that gender and gender roles were fluid or on a spectrum that could be negotiated and renegotiated.

The first chapter investigates Cold War gender roles and how workers at the National Advisory Committee for Aeronautics (NACA) Langley Research Laboratory both adhered to and railed against gender norms. Langley's female computers, mathematicians and engineers reflected both progressive and fixed gender roles, a contradiction that the NACA's successor NASA faced throughout the space race. While Langley women traversed fixed gender norms and demonstrated multiple feminine archetypes, the growing automation in aerospace platforms, such as the X-15, reflected the perceived Cold War masculinity crisis. Books, magazines, films, literature, academic works and political rhetoric feared a loss of rugged individualism and control through the rise of communism, conformity, feminism, homosexuality, bureaucracy, corporations, male consumerism, leisure, automation and the dreaded organization man.[68] Increased automation in aerospace technology reflected the transition from death-defying feats of lone-wolf pilots to the commercialization, routinization and domestication or feminization of flight technology. Within the context of the Cold War, the image of flight, of who flies and who controls flight, became refashioned around the individual-against-the-organization-man dichotomy, reflecting the perceived Cold War masculinity crisis. To regain the moxie that flying once had, pilots looked to space to regain individual control.

The second chapter explores the creation of the astronaut image from *Sputnik* to the Mercury 7 astronauts. This chapter establishes that the Project Mercury public discourse constructed the astronaut image as representing Cold War masculinity through the astronauts' ability to pilot their craft. Through his control, the astronaut performed and represented American masculinity in space. Women's roles during Mercury were important too, but as non-technological users. The astronaut wives wrote their own spaceflight stories, specifically as wives and mothers left behind while their husbands conquered space. The public discourse depicted astronaut wives as helpmates, paradigms of the role of the Cold War American wife—the epitome of femininity. They were women apart from spaceflight technology.

The third chapter follows women's fight for spaceflight equality through the FLATs. The FLATs demonstrated that women could control aviation

# INTRODUCTION

technology, thus once again cracking but not shattering fixed aviation gender roles. Men confronted their masculine technological control as women forced the conversation about sex and gender roles in spaceflight. NASA excluded women from spaceflight based on Cold War gender roles—specifically that the military barred women from flying military aircraft and because women had complicated bodies. Americans viewed femininity as lacking control, and a woman in the spacecraft would have symbolized such. The dialogue within the transcripts of the 1962 Subcommittee on the Selection of Astronauts is analyzed as arguments pertained to different roles for men and women's performance with Cold War technology. Two main concerns for the subcommittee were pilot control of a spacecraft and motherhood. The testimony was in line with the Cold War containment of women in the home. Blasting a woman into space would have contradicted spaceflight as symbolizing masculine control over a spacecraft. A woman in space would have represented passivity. In essence, women would have to wait for the domestication of spaceflight to fly.

Chapter 4 argues that the public discourse reinterpreted the past to continue the dialogue of masculine performance in space as NASA transitioned into Project Gemini. For instance, after the March 1965 launch of *Gemini 3*, *Life* proclaimed, "For the first time, rather than being nearly helpless riders aboard an intractable projectile, the Astronauts really [totally] controlled their craft."[69] Even as the Soviet Union performed an extra-vehicular activity (EVA or spacewalk) first, journalists and politicians touted the American astronaut's walk in the cosmos as being different from that of the Soviets. Americans argued that they were "first" with astronaut control of an EVA.[70] But self-determination and control became conflicted as computers onboard helped the astronaut with calculations, flying and reentry—ironically even if these were necessary to physically fly the craft. Further creating conflict, NASA accepted into the astronaut fraternity scientists who did not need to hold previous flight experience, even though NASA sent them to Air Force Undergraduate Jet Pilot School. This new hyphenated scientist-astronaut image had some suggesting that spaceflight was no longer dangerous but routine. NASA still dismissed women scientists with advanced degrees as potential scientist-astronauts. Women could not become scientist-astronauts anyway since military piloting was still off-limits to women. Women, automation and scientist-astronauts forced the public astronaut image to renegotiate masculinity once again. While the image of who could fly shifted, the importance of "firsts" continued.

Chapter 5 maintains that *Apollo* permanently shifted the astronaut public discourse to the need for teamwork both in space and in terms of curing social ills. The *Apollo 1* fire and subsequent deaths of three astronauts revealed a complete lack of control by astronauts, scientists, engineers and technicians. *Apollo 11* reinforced a continued need for pilot control and teamwork in space. *Apollo 13* highlighted the loss of individual astronaut control and stressed astronaut reliance on technology, teamwork and mission control. Finally, *Apollo 17*'s launch of the first scientist-astronaut demonstrated the ability of non-military men to enter the exclusive astronaut corps. The commissioning of the space shuttles as passenger vehicles further suggested—incorrectly—that spaceflight was safe.

Chapter 6 aims to complicate the idea of fixed Cold War gender roles even further as NASA accepted the first women and minorities as astronauts in 1978's astronaut Group 8. In the fall of 1972, NASA administrator James C. Fletcher suggested that a "plan be developed for our next selection of astronauts, with full consideration being given to minority groups and women."[71] The commissioning of scientist-astronauts and shuttles changed the narrative as space now appeared safe as scientific experiments replaced death-defying feats. Between 1973 and 1979, Skylab circled the Earth. On July 15, 1975, NASA launched the first *Apollo-Soyuz* mission from Cape Canaveral. By 1976, each of the United States' military branches had their first women pilot candidates, even as jet pilots. Cold War ideals of fixed gender roles were no longer necessary requirements to fly.

Americans cheered the entrance of women and minorities into the once-all-white male astronaut fraternity, but a cognitive dissonance in gender roles remained. The space shuttle's public discourse depicted images of women "Designing a Home in Space."[72] Average Americans with no flight or engineering experience eagerly awaited news of the Citizen Astronaut Program. As early as 1978, articles filled magazines and journals dedicated to spaceflight predicting who the first civilian flier would be and how much space fare would cost for a ride on the shuttle. Those who could not control masculine technology before the civil rights and women's liberation movements had waited until spaceflight was declared safe, routine or domesticated (feminized) for their chance to fly. However, the first American woman astronaut in space, Sally Ride, was not a flight attendant. She was a mission specialist. Even though spaceflight's domesticated narrative continued well into Ride's 1983 flight, the fact remained that she performed with spaceflight technology just as the male astronauts before her. The first women astronauts reflected not one femininity or masculinity—but rather gender on a spectrum. The first American women astronauts did not fill one feminine archetype other than the professionalism and skill of future women astronauts. The astronaut image began as a symbol of American masculinity, but with the introduction of push-button masculinity, teamwork, nerds in space, minorities and women,

# INTRODUCTION

the astronaut image demonstrated that technology and gender roles were not inherent or natural but socially constructed.

## Notes

1 "Jeff Bezos and Sir Richard Branson Not Astronauts Yet, US Says," *BBC News*, July 23, 2021, https://www.bbc.com/news/world-us-canada-57950149. See also, "FAA Ends Commercial Space Astronaut Wings Program, Will Recognize Individuals Reaching Space on Website," *Federal Aviation Administration*, accessed May 31, 2022, https://www.faa.gov/newsroom/faa-ends-commercial-space-astronaut-wings-program-will-recognize-individuals-reaching#:~:text=The%20Wings%20program%20was%20created,to%20carry%20humans%20into%20space.

2 Adam Gabbatt, "Wally Funk Fulfills Lifelong Dream to go to Space with Blue Origin Flight," *Guardian*, July 20, 2021, https://www.theguardian.com/science/2021/jul/20/wally-funk-space-blue-origin-flight.

3 Marisa Lati, "In 1962, She Lost her Chance to go to Space. Today, at 82, she finally got her Shot," *Washington Post*, July 20, 2021, https://www.washingtonpost.com/history/2021/07/20/wally-funk-astronaut-mercury-13/. See also, Alyssa Kraus, "Here's how Jeff Bezos's Spaceflight Unfolded this Morning," *CNN*, accessed July 20, 2021, https://www.cnn.com/business/live-news/jeff-bezos-space-flight-07-20-21/index.html.

4 Gabbatt, "Wally Funk Fulfills Lifelong Dream." At the time, Funk was the oldest person to fly into space. Her record was broken by William Shatner in October 2021 and then again by Ed Dwight in May 2024. All flights were aboard *Blue Origin's New Shepard*. See Daniel E. Slotnik, "At 90, William Shatner Becomes the Oldest Person to Reach 'the Final Frontier'," *New York Times*, October 13, 2021, accessed October 4, 2024, https://www.nytimes.com/2021/10/13/science/william-shatner-space.html and Amanda Holpuch, "63 Years Later, First Black Man Train as Astronaut Goes to Space," *New York Times*, May 19, 2024, accessed October 4, 2024, https://www.nytimes.com/2024/05/19/science/space/ed-dwight-black-astronaut-space-flight-blue-origin.html. The Kennedy administration was eager to diversify the astronaut corps. However, Chuck Yeager dragged his feet on Dwight integrating the astronaut corps because he viewed him as an average pilot. The integration of the corps ended with Kennedy's assassination according to the *New York Times*.

5 William Faulkner, *Requiem for a Nun* (New York: Vintage International, reprint 2011), 73.

6 Jaquelyn Dowd Hall, "How We Tell about the Civil Rights Movement and Why it Matters," in *NASA and the Long Civil Rights Movement*, ed. Brian C. Odom and Stephen P. Waring (Gainesville, FL: University of Florida Press, 2019), x. See also Jaquelyn Dowd Hall, "The Long Civil Rights Movement and the Political Uses of the Past," *The Journal of American History* 91, no. 4 (March 2005): 1233–1263.

7 The quotation is taken from Hugh Davis, a librarian and English teacher in Winston-Salem, North Carolina. Found in Dowd Hall's, "How We Tell about the Civil Rights Movement," xii–xiii.

8 Carrie Paechter, "Rethinking the Possibilities for Hegemonic Femininity: Exploring a Gramscian Framework," *Women's Studies International Forum* 68 (2018): 121–128,

# GENDER AND THE RACE FOR SPACE

122 and R. W. Connell and James W. Messerschmidt, "Hegemonic Masculinity: Rethinking the Concept," *Gender and Society* 19, no. 6 (2005): 829–859, 832–833.

9 Walter McDougall, *...The Heavens and the Earth: A Political History of Space Flight* (New York: Basic Books, 1985), 288

10 Sue Bridger, "The Cold War and the Cosmos: Valentina Tereshkova and the First Woman's Space Flight," in *Women in the Khrushchev Era*, ed. Melanie Ilic, Susan E. Reid, and Lynne Attwood (New York: Palgrave MacMillan, 2004), 226–227.

11 McDougall, *...The Heavens and the Earth*, 288. For Tereshkova's aeronautic training course, see James T. Andrews and Asif A. Siddiqi, eds., *Into the Cosmos: Space Exploration and Soviet Culture* (Pittsburgh: University of Pittsburgh Press, 2011); Asif A. Siddiqi, *Challenge to Apollo: The Soviet Union and the Space Race, 1945–1974* (Washington, DC: NASA SP-4408, 2000); and Asif A. Siddiqi, *Sputnik and the Soviet Space Challenge* (Gainesville: University Press of Florida, 2004).

12 Louise Sweeney, "Why Valentina and Not Our Gal?" *Berkshire Eagle* (Pittsfield, Massachusetts), June 21, 1962.

13 Margaret A. Weitekamp, *Right Stuff, Wrong Sex: America's First Women in Space Program* (Baltimore: Johns Hopkins University Press, 2005). While the secondary sources give the numbers of 19 women taking the tests, and 13 passing, hence the 1980s name, "The Mercury 13," within Cobb's own testimony at the July 1962 Subcommittee hearings, she suggests that "twenty-five women went through those tests, and from them 12 passed to form the group of which we speak." But she might not be including herself in this number; see Congress, House, Committee on Science and Astronautics, *Qualifications for Astronauts: Hearings before the Special Subcommittee on the Selection of Astronauts of the Committee on Science and Astronautics*, 87th Cong., 2d sess., July 17–18, 1962, 3. Hereafter cited as Congress, House, *Qualifications for Astronauts: Subcommittee Hearings*.

14 Weitekamp, *Right Stuff, Wrong Sex*, 184–186, and 121.

15 Amy Elizabeth Foster, *Integrating Women into the Astronaut Corps: Politics and Logistics, 1972–2004* (Baltimore: University of Johns Hopkins Press, 2011), 51 and Matthew H. Hersch, *Inventing the American Astronaut* (New York: Palgrave, 2012), 152.

16 John Lewis Gaddis, *Strategies of Containment: A Critical Appraisal of American National Security Policy During the Cold War*, Rev. ed. (New York: Oxford University Press, 2005).

17 Bettyann Holtzmann Kevles, *Almost Heaven: The Story of Women in Space* (Cambridge: The MIT Press, 2006), 1. See Robert A. Divine, *The Sputnik Challenge* (New York: Oxford University Press, 1994), for more on *Sputnik*.

18 For a discussion on Cold War gender and sex, see Elaine Tyler May's *Homeward Bound: American Families in the Cold War Era* (New York: Basic Books, 1988).

19 Johnnie R. Betson Jr., M.D. and Robert R. Secrest, M.D., "Prospective Women Astronauts Selection Program: Rationale and Comments," *American Journal of Obstetrics and Gynecology* 88 (February 1, 1964): 421–423. See also, Weitekamp, *Right Stuff, Wrong Sex*, 165–166.

20 Simone de Beauvoir, *The Second Sex*, ed. H. M. Parshley (New York: Vintage Books, 1989), 111.

21 Judith Butler, "Performative Acts and Gender Constitution: An Essay in Phenomenology and Feminist Theory," *Theater Journal* 40, no. 4 (1988): 519–531, 519, 521, 525.

# INTRODUCTION 19

22  Patricia Cooper, "Cigarmaking," in *Gender and Technology: A Reader*, eds. Nina Lerman, Arwen Mohun, and Ruth Oldenzial (Baltimore: The Johns Hopkins University Press, 2003), 209–210.

23  Molly Merryman, *Clipped Wings: The Rise and Fall of the Woman Airforce Service Pilots (WASPS) of World War II* (New York: New York University Press, 2001), 159.

24  Tom Wolfe, *The Right Stuff* (New York, Bantam Books, 1980), 22.

25  Cooper, "Cigarmaking," 210.

26  Ruth Schwartz Cowan, *More Work for Mother: The Ironies of Household Technologies from the Open Hearth to the Microwave* (New York: Basic Books, 1983).

27  Ruth Oldenziel, *Making Technology Masculine: Men, Women, and Modern Machines in America, 1870–1945* (Amsterdam: Amsterdam University Press, 1999). Judy Wajcman, "Feminist Theories of Technology," *Cambridge Journal of Economics* 34 (2010): 143–152, 149, 147, 149. See also Wiebe E. Bijker, Thomas P. Hughes, and Trevor Pinch, eds., "Foreword by Debbie Douglas," in *The Social Construction of Technological Systems: New Directions in the Sociology and History of Technology* (Cambridge, MA: The Massachusetts Institute of Technology Press, 2012).

28  Betty Friedan, *The Feminine Mystique* (fiftieth anniversary edition, New York: W.W. Norton & Company, 2013), 57, 77, 79–82. See also, Anne Fausto-Sterling, *Sexing the Body: Gender Politics and the Construction of Sexuality* (New York: Basic Books, 2000).

29  Judith Butler, *Gender Trouble: Feminism and the Subversion Identity* (New York: Routledge, 2000), 2.

30  Michael W. Hankins, *Flying Camelot: The F-15, the F-16, and the Weaponization of Fighter Pilot Nostalgia* (Ithaca, NY: Cornell University Press, 2021), 13.

31  Joan Wallach Scott, *Gender and the Politics of History* (revised edition, New York: Columbia University Press, 1999), 59.

32  See the papers presented at NASA's Symposium on the 50th Anniversary of Human Spaceflight. Space historians are turning more toward the cultural impact of space-flight. For information on NASA's Symposium, see NASA History Division, "Key Moments in Human Spaceflight, April 26–27, 2011," *The National Aeronautics and Space Administration*, accessed November 14, 2023, http://history.nasa.gov/1961-1981conf/index.html.

33  Joseph Corn, *The Winged Gospel: America's Romance with Aviation*, 2nd Printing (Baltimore: Johns Hopkins University Press, 2002).

34  Linda R. Robertson, *The Dream of Civilized Warfare: World War I Flying Aces and the American Imagination* (Minneapolis: University of Minnesota Press, 2003).

35  Hankins, *Flying* Camelot, 19.

36  Leslie Haynsworth and David Toomey, *Amelia Earhart's Daughters: The Wild and Glorious Story of American Women Aviators from World War II to the Dawn of the Space Age* (New York: Perennial, 1998), 10.

37  Haynesworth and Toomey, *Amelia Earhart's Daughters*, 11.

38  "A Round-The-World Flight Ends in the Pacific," *Life*, July 19, 1937, 21–25.

39  Bob Considine, "The Untold Story of Amelia's Tragedy," *The Minneapolis Journal*, August 8, 1937, 60.

40  Considine, "The Untold Story," 60.

41  Elizabeth Coates James, "Great Books in Brief: Review of *High, Wide and Frightened* by Louise Thaden," in *Arizona Republic* (Phoenix, Arizona) December 29, 1940. The Bendix Trophy is the most prestigious air race for pilots. It was formed in 1931.

Thaden became the first female winner in 1936. She flew from New York to Los Angeles in a C-17R.

42 Merryman, *Clipped Wings*, 175, 2–3, 82–92.

43 Michael Sherry, *The Rise of American Air Power: The Creation of Armageddon* (New Haven: Yale University Press, 1987), and Jennifer Van Vleck, *Empire of the Air: Aviation and the American Ascendancy* (Cambridge, MA: Harvard University Press, 2013).

44 Sarah Parry Myers, *Earning Their Wings: The WASPS of World War II and the Fight for Veteran Recognition* (Chapel Hill, NC: The University of North Carolina Press, 2023), 12–13, 7.

45 John Darrell Sherwood, *Officers in Flight Suits: The Story of American Air Force Fighter Pilots in the Korean War* (New York: New York University Press, 1996), 6.

46 Steve Fino, *Tiger Check: Automating the US Air Force Fighter Pilot in Air-to-Air Combat, 1950–1980* (Baltimore: Johns Hopkins University Press, 2017), 18–19, 8–12, 15.

47 Hankins, *Flying Camelot*, 3–5.

48 Margaret Weitekamp, "Space History Matures—and Reaches a Crossroads," in *NASA and the Long Civil Rights Movement*, eds. Brian C. Odom and Stephen P. Waring (Gainesville, FL: University of Florida Press, 2019), 11. See also, Eric Foner, ed. *The New American History* (Philadelphia: Temple University Press, 1990).

49 Weitekamp, "Space History Matures," 11. See also Roger D. Launius, "The Historical Dimension of Space Exploration: Reflections and Possibilities," *Space Policy* 16 (2000): 23–38 and Steven Dick and Roger D. Launius, eds. *Societal Impact of Spaceflight* (Washington, DC: NASA SP-4801, 2009).

50 Works that look at the frontier image of the astronaut are James L. Kauffman, *Selling Outer Space: Kennedy, the Media, and Funding for Project Apollo, 1961–1963* (Tuscaloosa, AL: The University of Alabama Press, 1994); Susan Landrum-Mangus, "Conestoga Wagons to the Moon: The Frontier, the American Space Program, and National Identity," PhD diss., (The Ohio State University, 1999); and Howard E. McCurdy, *Space and the American Imagination* (2nd edition, Baltimore: The Johns Hopkins University Press, 1997).

51 Roger D. Launius, "Heroes in a Vacuum: The Apollo Astronaut as Cultural Icon," *Florida Historical Quarterly: Special Issue Celebrating 50th Anniversary NASA in Florida (1958–2008)* 87, no. 2 (Fall 2008): 174–209.

52 Loyd, S. Swenson, Jr., James M. Grimwood, and Charles C. Alexander, *This New Ocean: A History of Project Mercury* (Washington, DC: NASA SP-4201, 1966), 163. See also, Launius, "Heroes in a Vacuum," 180.

53 Launius, "Heroes in a Vacuum," 175. Most NASA histories depict the astronauts as heroes, flawed at times, but still the narrative that this was important to Americans is dominant within the historiography. See Susan Faludi, *Stiffed: The Betrayal of the American Man* (New York: Harper Collins, 1999); Matthew H. Hersch, "Return of the Lost Spaceman: America's Astronauts in Popular Culture," *Journal of Popular Culture* 4, no. 1 (February 2011): 73–92, 78–79; Kauffman, *Selling Outer Space*; Launius, "Heroes in a Vacuum"; McCurdy, *Space and the American Imagination*, 92. See also, Linda T. Krug, *Presidential Perspectives on Space Exploration: Guiding Metaphors from Eisenhower to Bush* (New York: Praeger, 1991).

54 Siddiqi, *Challenge to Apollo*, 244.

55 Slava Gerovitch, "'New Soviet Man' Inside Machine: Human Engineering, Spacecraft Design, and the Construction of Communism," *OSIRIS* 22 (2007): 135–157, 138. See also Slava Gerovitch, "The Human Inside a Propaganda Machine: The

# INTRODUCTION 21

Public Image of and Professional Identity of Soviet Cosmonauts," in *Into the Cosmos: Space Exploration and Soviet Culture*, Andrews and Siddiqi, 77–106.

56 Gerovitch, "'New Soviet Man'," 138 and Wolfe, *The Right Stuff*, 64.

57 Matthew D. Tribbe, *No Requiem for the Space Age: The Apollo Moon Landings and American Culture* (New York: Oxford University Press, 2014), 227.

58 Neil M. Maher, *Apollo in the Age of Aquarius* (Cambridge, MA: Harvard University Press, 2017).

59 Michael J. Neufeld, *Von Braun: Dream of Space, Engineer of War* (New York: Vintage Books, 2008), 18.

60 Richard Paul and Steven Moss, *We Could Not Fail: The First African Americans in the Space Program* (Austin: University of Texas Press, 2015), 1–2. Margot Lee Shetterly, *Hidden Figures: The American Dream and the Untold Story of the Black Women Mathematicians Who Helped Win the Space Race* (New York: Harper Collins, 2016).

61 Brian C. Odom, "Introduction: Exploring NASA in the Long Civil Rights Movement," in *NASA and the Long Civil Rights Movement*, eds. Brian C. Odom and Stephen P. Waring (Gainesville, FL: University of Florida Press, 2019), 3, 1.

62 Nathalia Holt, *Rise of the Rocket Girls: The Women Who Propelled Us, from Missiles to the Moon and Mars* (New York: Little, Brown and Company, 2016).

63 Jennifer M. Ross-Nazzal, *Making Space for Women: Stories from Trailblazing Women of NASA's Johnson Space Center* (College Station, TX: Texas A&M University Press, 2022).

64 David A. Mindell, *Digital Apollo: Human and Machine in Spaceflight* (Cambridge, MA: The MIT Press, 2008), 12, 13 and 10. Machines in control as an affront to pilot masculinity was also argued by Wolfe in *The Right Stuff*, 60–64.

65 The term "Whitey" refers to Gil Scott-Heron's spoken word poem "Whitey on the Moon." See, Gil Scott-Heron, "Whitey on the Moon," Track 9 on *Small Talk at 125th and Lenox*, Flying Dutchman Records, 1970, record.

66 Hersch, *Inventing the American Astronaut*, 3, 1–2. See also, William H. Whyte Jr., *The Organization Man* (New York: Simon and Schuster, 1956), 3–4.

67 Michael Kimmel, *Manhood in America: A Cultural History* (New York: The Free Press, 1996), 333–335.

68 Erinn McComb, "Push-Button Masculinity: Democratic Manhood and Operation Paperclip's Transnational Transfer of German Aerospace Technology, 1946–1959," in *Yearbook of Transnational History, Volume 4*, eds. Thomas Adam, assisted by Austin E. Loignon (Madison, NJ: Farleigh Dickinson University Press, 2021), 201.

69 "Lift-Off to a New Era in Space," 35.

70 "Space: Closing the Gap," *Time*, June 11, 1965, 25, and "The Great Adventure Moves Ahead," *Newsweek*, June 14, 1965, 30.

71 George M. Low, NASA Deputy Administrator, memorandum for the record, on Center Directors' meeting, Peaks of Otter Lodge, September 11–12, 1972. See Joseph D. Atkinson Jr. and Jay M. Shafritz, *The Real Stuff: A History of NASA's Astronaut Recruitment Program* (New York: Praeger, 1985), 138.

72 *Space World*, June/July 1983, Front Cover.

# Chapter 1

# EARLY COLD WAR GENDER ROLES IN THE PUBLIC AND PRIVATE DISCOURSE

The Soviet Union successfully mounted the world's first artificial satellite, *Sputnik*, to an intercontinental ballistic missile and launched the pair into space on October 4, 1957. Americans watched with shock. The feat symbolized a masculinity crisis at home and abroad as anxiety grew over the satellite's capabilities. However, fear did not consume aerospace engineer Dorothy "Dottie" Lee. She was "thrilled" and understood that *Sputnik*'s launch meant more funding for the NACA. The NACA recruited Lee in 1948 to work as a mathematician at Langley Memorial Aeronautical Laboratory (later Langley Research Center) in Hampton, Virginia. Lee pored through physics books as a child, dreaming of one day landing on the moon.[1] While she did not go to the moon, Lee and hundreds of other women benefited from World War II and the Cold War's demand for computers—people who completed complex mathematical equations to allow engineers time to focus on research projects. The American cultural assumption was that women were better equipped for repetitive computing tasks as opposed to "creative thinking" with technology.[2]

Lee worked in Langley's Pilotless Aircraft Research Division or PARD. The division was headed by future spacecraft designers Dr. Robert Gilruth and Dr. Maxime Faget. Faget assumed that Lee had secretarial skills and asked her to work in his office while his secretary honeymooned. Lee was a self-professed poor typist. She took the job anyway for the opportunity to work with a brilliant aerospace designer. Lee spent her time in Faget's office solving complex equations for an engineer. An impressed Faget asked her to work for him full-time. She became an engineer—which was rare for women at Langley. At times, Lee worked until midnight with the "rush and thrill of trying to solve a problem."[3] Her friendship with Faget lasted a lifetime.

The following chapter details public discussions about proper Cold War gender roles and the women who privately fought against them. Lee's story of self-determination and her role in technology was unusual for women in early Cold War public discourse and reflected Jacquelyn Dowd Hall's "The

Long Civil Rights Movement." While World War II propelled women into skilled professional jobs on the national stage, the American public discourse encouraged women at the war's end to return home and seek individual fulfillment as wives and mothers. However, advanced Cold War technology demanded the continuation of skilled laborers. With this came social change. The NACA continued to hire women as computers for their mathematical skills not because there was a lack of men. Computer work increasingly became feminized as the administration hired more women. The NACA—later NASA—became a microcosm of American Cold War gender roles, publicly projecting masculinity and privately thwarting conventional gender roles through hiring women. But this progress was limited as the women were typically relegated to subservient roles. While historians argue that World War II proved to not be a watershed for women's rights as women returned to the home, many NACA and NASA women workers found themselves hidden pioneers for fluctuating feminine archetypes at a time when the public discourse focused on reformulating Cold War masculinity for the space race. The hidden work of women as computers and engineers demonstrated gender roles on a spectrum, but fixed gender role fanaticism outside the NACA and NASA created a perceived masculinity crisis at a time of great anxiety. This fear led women to remain invisible in spaceflight.

## Cold War Femininity

The government and public discourse implored women that it was their patriotic duty to leave the home and enter defense employment during World War II. Women took on conventional masculine roles, working in defense plants, on farms and joined the military. Women experienced greater pay, expanded opportunities and the freedom to explore their own identity outside the home.[4] Increased World War II technology demanded talent in engineering and mathematics. To fill these jobs, NACA centers across the country heavily recruited women. Women straight out of college had a phenomenal opportunity to work for the war effort in a professional skilled environment in which they would be calculating equations for the newest aviation platforms such as the PF-15 Mustang, B-26, B-29 bomber and X-series supersonic rocket planes.

Despite women's contributions to the war effort, Cold War anxiety led to a return to conventional gender roles. The Cold War heated up in the late 1940s with the Soviet Union acquiring nuclear technology, China falling to Communism, the Korean Conflict and with the creation of the North Atlantic Treaty Organization (NATO) and the Warsaw Pact. President Dwight Eisenhower's administration implemented the policy of massive retaliation, and science and technology research reached an all-time high, creating a marriage between universities, industry, the military and government. Weapons contracts expanded capitalism, but so too did the growth and power of technology and the federal government. Bert the Turtle happily sang to Americans to "Duck and Cover" in the event of a nuclear blast.[5] Americans retreated into their homes and purchased fall-out shelters. The home and conventional gender roles symbolized safety and security in a world of nuclear anxiety.[6] Early Cold War femininity defined "woman" as wife and mother—with little opportunity for choice and individuality.

The public discourse viewed the wife and mother feminine identity as necessary to beat communism and the unfettered growth of technological advancement—specifically as automation displaced men. For instance, giving the 1955 Smith College commencement address, former Democratic presidential hopeful, Adlai Stevenson, told the most brilliant female minds in the country that they could combat the new Cold War "crisis of the age"—the threat to Western man's individuality—"in the humble role of housewife." Technological advance created "specialization" that hindered Western man's individuality and led to a path of Western men becoming "wretched slaves" focused on the "group," "authoritarianism" or "totalitarianism." Women could fight men's shrinkage from individuality "with a baby on your lap or in the kitchen with a can opener in your hand." Marriage was not a "depressing future" but the key to creating "total human beings."[7] This future denied women the right to self-determination. Denying the Smith grads or any woman a public voice circled gender discussions back to the nineteenth century's Republican Motherhood.[8] The Democrat Stevenson's connecting wife and mother with the protection of men's individuality situated women in the home and the housewife as the beacon of American freedom.

The politics of conventional gender roles permeated both political parties when it came to new Cold War technology. Republican vice president Richard Nixon preferred to view increased technology and commodities as positive for the American male, demonstrating democracy through comfort, ease, choice and capitalism. Nixon traveled to Moscow for the American National Exhibition two years after *Sputnik* and engaged in the infamous "Kitchen Debate" with Soviet Premier Nikita Khrushchev. The exhibition focused on the connection between technology and American culture. The United States chose not to highlight military weaponry such as rockets and jets but rather they chose domesticated technology found within the quintessential American home. Khrushchev mocked the exhibit. Khrushchev asserted that the Soviets possessed superior rocket technology and "feel sorry" for the Americans.[9]

The Soviet Premier failed to understand that the United States chose domesticated household technology to entice countries around the world to embrace capitalism and democracy for the good life it promised. The technology did not represent hard power militarized masculinity but rather soft power techno-masculinity. The technology symbolized choice and individuality through the many companies, models, designs and colors of the newest kitchen devices. Nixon implored the Soviet Premier that "diversity, the right to choose [...] is the most important thing." The American kitchen represented the very best of American democracy. While historians equate the 1950s as an age of conformity, Nixon saw the American kitchen as helping capitalism by providing jobs and competition. Outfitting new kitchens with different countertops, stoves, ovens, appliances, tacky wallpaper and tawdry linoleum allowed Americans to express individuality and choice in the marketplace and differentiate themselves from their neighbors. Domesticated technology also "liberated" the American housewife by making "life easier."[10]

Advertisements within women's magazines touted the liberating effect of American household technology. Automated ovens, stoves, dishwashers, washing machines, dryers, household cleaners, automatic transmissions, feminine hygiene products and even Aunt Jemima completed work for women so they could go shopping, play bridge, ride horses or simply sit and read a magazine.[11] Whether or not the technology provided labor-saving time is debatable; however, Nixon's comments made an important connection between technology and American gender culture.[12] These pre-1960s women's rights movement advertisements demonstrated women as passive technological users and not as emancipated women controlling technology. The public discourse feared the rise of the emancipated woman, blaming women's independence outside and inside the home as a threat to American democracy and masculinity.

1940s and 1950s sociologists and psychiatrists held seminars, conferences and published essays and articles on the gender spectrum threat to American society. In *Look* magazine's "The Decline of the American Male" (1959), psychiatrist Dr. Clara Thompson viewed the threat to masculinity as "emancipated women." Single women who shunned housework emasculated their male suitors. If a career woman chose to get married, "she may threaten her husband's already-shaky sense of worth as a provider, master, man" or "crush him." The married career woman gained "equality" by taking away men's control over the "preferred position in society."[13] Dr. George Crane urged women not to take on male characteristics such as appearance, slang, whiskey drinking or smoking as this made them unattractive "Halfway creatures" trying to join "the strong or ruling class."[14] Both doctors acknowledged males as superior and women as inferior. Likewise, the 1957 Child Study Association of

# EARLY COLD WAR GENDER ROLES

America conference feared the end of "'modern civilization'" with the beginning of gender-fluid roles or what Dr. Irene Josselyn of Chicago's Institute of Psychoanalysis referred to as "he-women and she-men." But others argued that fixed male and female gender advocates should "simmer down" and that "each individual—regardless of sex—have instead the freedom to become his or her own best self."[15] The argument became which sex had the power of self-determination.

Betty Friedan's *The Feminine Mystique* (1963) blamed male writers for reinforcing women's limited roles in women's magazines. Men instructed women to negate intellectual curiosity and interest outside of marriage and motherhood. Writers dissuaded women from self-determination over their own identity, with Friedan arguing that "the Feminine mystique permits, even encourages, women to ignore the question of their identity." The public discourse instructed American women on the proper female image. "American woman no longer has a private image to tell her who she is or can be, or wants to be."[16] Despite Friedan's argument that legal barriers to sex equality had been lifted, women still fought gender culture barriers in opportunity, race, class, pay, reproductive rights, education and visibility. Within a public discourse that championed femininity as wife and mother, the NACA and NASA women pioneered their own path, creating their own feminine identities and became whole humans.

To meet the demand for skilled mathematicians, the NACA began recruiting women into flight research as early as 1935. Male computers balked at sharing space with women. The women proved themselves skilled mathematicians, and the men got used to the idea. The NACA rarely classified women as mathematicians; rather, the NACA hired women as "computers" because they worked in "computer programming, simulation techniques, trajectory computation, and analysis of tracking and communications data."[17]

Women's visibility within the NACA soared as World War II increased the demand for computers. NACA computer Virginia Tucker took affirmative action in recruiting women from local colleges and universities. Advertisements for women computers flooded newspapers and Langley's *Air Scoop*. Head of Langley personnel, Melvin Butler, wrote in Newport News' *Daily Press*: "Reduce your household duties! Women who are not afraid to roll up their sleeves and do jobs previously filled by men should call the Langley Memorial Aeronautical Laboratory." Recruiting efforts increased the number of computers to over three thousand by 1945.

The NACA hired the first Black women computers at Langley in 1943. This was on the heels of President Franklin Roosevelt's Executive Order 8802 that ended segregation in the defense industry and Executive Order 9346 that, in theory, led to the end of racial discrimination with The

Fair Employment Practices Committee. The NACA's Langley Memorial Aeronautical Laboratory (later Langley Research Center) operated under pre-*Brown v. Board of Education* (1954) state segregated Jim Crow laws. Langley's segregation lasted until the NACA's transition into NASA in 1958 with the white women computers at the East Campus and the Black women computers at the West Campus. Both groups of women defined femininity as self-determination apart from the public discourse's discussion of women's proper Cold War gender roles. They defied the suppression of women and demonstrated that they had a contribution to make to spaceflight. Sexism was a separate matter and the end of the war saw around two million of the three and a half million wartime working women return to the home or were fired. However, the NACA largely kept the computers because their skill was necessary as aviation transitioned into the jet and space age.[18]

As progressive as this was, the NACA had a pendulum swing between conventional and progressive gender roles. The coveted "mathematician" title came with the "professional designation" much like that of an engineer. The NACA designated "computers" as "subprofessionals" with less pay, with the SP-3 Junior Computer starting off at $1,440 a year. Men with the same bachelor's degree in mathematics often found themselves hired as "junior engineers," starting at $2,600 a year. Computers could climb as high as SP-8 Chief Computer, commanding a salary of $3,200 a year. This position often included supervising other women computers. The NACA offered excellent salaries for women in the 1940s and 1950s, especially for women of color.[19] For instance, Dorothy Vaughn left her job as a math teacher in Virginia to work for Langley in 1943. As a Black woman, she experienced greater pay compared to teaching, and unlike the state educational system, NACA salaries did not discriminate by race. Langley appointed Vaughn supervisor of the West Campus in 1949, making her the NACA's first Black female supervisor.[20]

A woman supervising other women was not unusual. While engineers outside the NACA and NASA viewed the increasingly "feminized" computer field as "rote" and "de-skilled," this did not appear to be the case at the NACA or NASA.[21] The engineers had a great deal of respect for the computers' work. For instance, Vaughn put close friend Katherine Goble (Johnson) into Langley's all-white and male Flight Research Division. Johnson was unsure how her colleagues would accept her as Black and as a woman. Overall, the men accepted her skill. Her computing was so good that astronaut John Glenn personally asked her to calculate the trajectory for his historic 1962 orbital flight. Johnson had to be tough in this new space for Black women. She refused to use "colored" restrooms and demanded women be allowed in the engineers' "editorial" meetings.

While the NACA/NASA forged a progressive path in hiring women regardless of race and marital status, the subprofessional designation ensured a lack of advancement in terms of pay or inroads into management, especially of men. Women's abilities to publish were hindered because the computers rarely knew which project went with their calculations.[22] Advancement was difficult without publications. Administrators, engineers and even astronauts respected women's work, but lack of promotion created women's lack of visibility in the aerospace industry.

The women pioneered different feminine paths in terms of career and skill-set, but also as wives and mothers. By 1966, Deputy Associate Administrator for Manned Space Flight, Dr. George E. Mueller, embraced the idea that three percent of women professionals at NASA "are successfully combining marriage with their careers in science."[23] Women found better pay at the NACA/NASA. Working as a computer with higher pay was necessary for Vaughn's fulfillment, but also for her family's financial and aspirational future. Vaughn's husband often worked out of state as a bellman, making her transition to a six-day work week at Langley, hundred miles from home, even more taxing. Vaughn's four children stayed in the care of relatives in Farmville, Virginia while Vaughn took the computer job. Vaughn eventually

**Figure 1.1** Katherine Johnson. *Source*: NASA. https://www.nytimes.com/2020/02/24/science/katherine-johnson-dead.html.

30    GENDER AND THE RACE FOR SPACE

moved her children to Hampton, Virginia. Katherine Goble became one of the first Black students to attend West Virginia University. While a stellar graduate student, she left to get married and start a family. Her love for mathematics eventually drove Katherine and her husband Jimmy Goble to Langley in 1953. Jimmy was a supportive husband and father, never complaining about Katherine's long hours, not coming home until after the children were asleep. Katherine became a single mother raising two children after Jimmy's death in 1956. She remarried Jim Johnson, another husband supportive of her career, in 1959.[24]

This family support network proved necessary for other computers and engineers. Eleanor Crockett Pressly was one of the highest-ranking women engineers at NASA through the 1950s and 1960s. She earned her master's degree in mathematics from Duke University in 1944. She worked as a teacher, a researcher at Harvard's Radio Research Laboratory and as an aeronautical research engineer at the United States Naval Research Library before NASA hired her as an aeronautical rocket research engineer. She calculated the wind's influence on rocket launches and trajectories. She supervised two dozen rocket launches for the Navy at White Sands.[25] Pressly became one of the few women visible within the aerospace public discourse. Newspapers took interest with headlines such as "Now Even Rocket Waits For Woman," suggesting, "A woman has quietly won another round in the battle of the sexes."[26]

Despite the fact that Pressly presided over a three-million-dollar budget, supervised male engineers and met with scientists from all over the world, public discourse focused on her attire. The *New York Times* described her as "out of place among a swarm of males" in her "sportshirt, bluejeans, bobbysocks, and red sneakers" at the rocket site.[27] *Sun Magazine* compared Pressly to "a pert housewife who looks as though she were about to demonstrate a cake on a tv commercial." She after all was a wife and mother of four boys. She and her successful medical doctor husband moved to Goddard where she became the supervisor of a team of thirty men as the lead engineer in the instrumentation branch of the Aeronomy and Meteorology Division.[28] Pressly's portrayal as a housewife demonstrates the public discourse's preference for viewing women as wives and mothers, continuing to marginalize Pressly, her accomplishments and even the NACA's progressive hiring tactics.

These NACA and NASA women renegotiated expectations of marriage and motherhood. For example, Langley hired South Florida farm girl Catherine Osgood as a computer, later aerospace engineer, when she was married with one child and another on the way. Luckily, Langley had not closed their daycare after World War II. Osgood published technical reports on wind effects for the Mercury Redstone rocket, radar election angles of orbiting vehicles and spacecraft trajectory reports. She hired a live-in nanny, and grandparents stayed at her house during winters and summers so that her children "always had plenty of people around."[29]

NACA and NASA women successfully managed their professions and home life. Dottie Lee had a similar situation and hired "full-time help," especially since she and her husband worked long hours at Johnson Space Center, with Lee not arriving home until after midnight.[30] Goddard hired the "pleasant, mild mannered" Melba Roy in 1959 after she graduated *summa cum laude* with a master's degree in mathematics. Through her time as a computer, she supervised twelve employees, plotted the course of the *Echo* satellite and published all while being married with three children.[31] Dr. Nancy Roman was not married with children but did bear the responsibility of caring for her mother. Roman had two jobs: NASA's Chief of Astronomy and taking care of her household. Her male colleagues had more time to research because they did not have to hurry home to do domestic chores. Despite this, she still managed to create the Hubble Telescope. Dr. Roman's assistant, Dr. Nancy W. Boggess, had children and Dr. Roman set her schedule around the children's care.[32]

**Figure 1.2** Melba Roy. Source: NASA. https://www.smithsonianmag.com/history/forgotten-black-women-mathematicians-who-helped-win-wars-and-send-astronauts-space-180960393/.

32  GENDER AND THE RACE FOR SPACE

Some NACA and NASA women anticipated continuing their careers after starting a family. After receiving her bachelor's degree from Northwestern University, twenty-six-year-old Barbara Lunde went to the Massachusetts Institute of Technology (MIT) to work as a research engineer on the Polaris missiles. NASA hired Lunde to work at Goddard as an aerospace engineer in the Spacecraft Systems and Projects Division, researching celestial sensors for orienting spacecraft. Her work also included the freeze valve used in the control of spacecraft and satellite projects. Lunde did not have any children when she completed these projects, but in a 1964 interview, she told reporters that she planned to become a mother and would not stop working for NASA.[33]

Other women at the NACA and NASA had fluid gender roles within the household. Mrs. Charles "Marjorie" Townshend became the first woman to graduate with a bachelor's in engineering from George Washington University. She became the lead engineer, supervising thirty-two male engineers, for the Instrumentation Branch for the Tiros and Nimbus meteorological satellite programs. Her work collecting and analyzing temperature distribution on earth, especially in clouds, through the creation of her "microminiature computer," was possible through teamwork and a housekeeper. She worked from 7:30 a.m. to 5:30 p.m. Her twelve-year-old son did the family shopping. Gender roles did not have boundaries in Mrs. Townshend's home, and she wished more women would not "steer clear in courses in engineering, to her mind; because it's not considered feminine or appropriate."[34] The NACA and NASA women challenged gender roles as they launched rockets, computed sonic booms, trajectory of jets, spacecrafts and satellites. Women published and fought for expanded opportunities in engineering and professional titles. As the NACA and NASA women chose self-determination apart from cultural expectations, men looked inward, analyzing women, conformity and automation as a threat to American masculinity.

## Cold War Masculinity

*Life* editor Henry Luce promised that if the "unhappy" and "nervous" Americans ended their "isolationist sterility" and "pitiful impotence" by using their "arsenal of democracy" to bring about "transformative powers," they could defeat World War II authoritarianism and make the twentieth century "Our Century."[35] World War II demanded more troops into the United States military, and women and people of color took on new roles as protectors and providers. These roles may have been temporary, but they challenged white masculine assumptions about military service, citizenship and talent.[36] Further challenges to white male as protector came with the gruesome reality on the battlefield. War correspondent Ernie Pyle, killed in

# EARLY COLD WAR GENDER ROLES

action at the Battle of Okinawa, uncovered the authenticity of frontline life. Literature such as Norman Mailer's *The Naked and the Dead* (1944) pinpointed men's horrors and fears during war.[37] Even military studies suggested men experienced anxiety while in combat.[38]

Works such as Philip Wylie's *Generation of Vipers* (1942), David Levy's *Maternal Overprotection* (1943) and Dr. Edward Strecker's *Their Mother's Sons* (1946) blamed maternal overprotection and homosexuality as cancers to American manhood.[39] During the infamous lavender scare, Wisconsin Republican Senator Joseph McCarthy accused gay men, especially those in the State Department, of being communist spies.[40] The homosexual panic continued as Americans were outraged that Indiana University's Dr. Alfred Kinsey's *Sexual Behavior in the Human Male* (1948) suggested that upward of thirty-eight percent of white American men engaged in some kind of homosexual sex act to the point of orgasm.[41] Americans attacked unconventional masculinity as subversive. Critics believed that collectivism and overprotective mothers created effeminate and gay masculinities.

To combat a perceived masculinity crisis, conservative Americans challenged men to reject collectivism and return to rugged, self-reliant individuality. Ayn Rand's works *The Fountainhead* (1943), *Atlas Shrugged* (1957) and *Anthem* (1961) portrayed the debate between the individual and the corporate organization that had emasculated men. For example, *The Fountainhead's* hero, modernist architect Howard Roark, struggled to invoke his architectural vision in his firm. In the 1949 movie, Roark railed against "soulless collectivism" while declaring that "Greatness comes from the independent work of independent minds."[42]

Harvard professor and Democratic Party supporter, Arthur M. Schlesinger Jr., preferred to view the individual versus the collective debate in terms of "hard" and "soft" personalities. He professed in *The Vital Center* (1949) that the "Western Man [*sic*] in the twentieth century is tense, uncertain, adrift. We look upon our epoch as a time of troubles, an age of anxiety." Capitalism, science and technology have led the charge in collectivism, detaching people from morals and individual self-fulfillment. Industrialization was responsible for the downfall of the individual. Schlesinger argued that as capitalism and corporations grew, "Man longs to escape the pressures beating down on his frail individuality; [...]. the surest means of escape seems to be to surrender that individuality to some massive, external authority." Schlesinger blamed human suffering on corrupt corporations and impersonality. This detachment forced people into communism. Communist states suppressed individuals and controlled people as if under a totalitarian dictatorship. Ironically for Schlesinger, the United States needed strong government leaders to free men from the group, bringing back his individuality and rugged self-reliance.[43]

Automated technology fell under attack as nineteenth-century pioneering tropes of individual self-reliance and self-determination formulated the antidote to the perceived masculinity crisis. Americans feared that automation or button-pushing took away that pioneer spirit and turned men passive and soft. Automation and passivity confused conventional gender roles and turned men's action with technology into a feminine performance. Intellectuals suggested that the Cold War man pushed buttons, while the nineteenth-century pioneer tamed and controlled the unsettled wilderness. Sociologist David Riesman supported the return to the nineteenth-century pioneer image. Riesman introduced American sociology and popular culture to the struggle between individual identity and conformity throughout American history in his work *The Lonely Crowd: A Study of the Changing American Character* (1950).

Riesman suggested that American character originally began with the *tradition-directed* man. This man's character held fast to familial and cultural traditions, leaving him with little autonomy to make decisions outside cultural norms. The industrial revolution in the mid-nineteenth century caused a shift toward the *inner-directed* man, whose individuality was highly developed through "personal choice" that allowed him to "master resource exploitation on all the fronts of which he is conscious."[44] The entrepreneur, machinist, pioneer, took risks and controlled and mastered their destiny, formulating a nineteenth-century *inner-directed* masculinity. Industrial revolution technology refashioned American culture and American masculine traits. Technology's advancement into automation led to the downfall of American mastery as the machine took control from the man and formulated Riesman's second shift in American culture.

Working with one's hands in agriculture and industries declined in the twentieth century, and the *other-directed* man emerged. Riesman observed that an education geared toward differences in cultures, services, leisure and the consumption of words and images from the new mass media, popular culture and peer groups gave rise to the new American character. He hypothesized that the *other-directed* "captains of Non-Industry, of Consumption, and Leisure" replaced the "*inner-directed* Captains of Industry." The *other-directed* man received direction from his contemporaries, whether that direction was from his family, friends, popular culture or from media outlets. These directions shifted depending on what "signals," "actions" and "wishes" he received from others. All peoples throughout time, at one point or another, "want to be liked," but the *other-directed* man makes it his primary goal. Emotion and feelings stifled American masculinity. Wanting acceptance from the group led to the downfall of individuality and control.

Riesman blamed women's economic emancipation for these shifts in society, suggesting that *traditional, inner* and *other-directedness* were transitions in masculinity.[45] David M. Potter argued in "American Women and the American Character" that since women traditionally have been dependent, they cultivated sensitivity to the mood and expectations of others. In their dependence, women quickly adapted to these moods and expectations. Women have always been *other-directed*.[46] Consequently, despite the women employed at the NACA and NASA, women could not have had an *inner-directed* character.

In 1951, sociologist C. Wright Mills followed Riesman's work on the *other-directed man*. Mills denigrated the new white middle-class man as conformist, not "their own men," who "failed to rise" and did not "threaten anyone." Blaming what he saw as the downfall of free entrepreneurship on male conformity, Mills stressed the "rise of the dependent employee" and the "decline of the independent individual."[47]

Five years later, William Whyte Jr. took the fears of this new Cold War conformist man and named him "the organization man." Whyte's organization men not only worked for the institution, but they belonged to it as well. Previously, the American character rested on independent, hard-working men like the nineteenth-century pioneer. The organization man lacked "self-reliance" and preferred "safety to adventure."[48] The solution to a besieged masculinity depended upon the creation of an invigorated Cold War masculinity focused on individualism, control and risk to become full humans. Cold War masculinity needed to be free from dependence on the group, employer, automation, women and fear. He needed to be his own man, independent and courageous.

Popular culture writers appeared to fear the organization man's safe society, preferring instead a society in which Cold War masculinity triumphed over conformity, passivity, safety and weakness. The year the Soviet Union launched *Sputnik*, journalist Richard Gehman lambasted the blurring of gender roles in "Toupees, Girdles, and Sun Lamps."[49] That same year, Norman Mailer's "The White Negro" warned of the "slow death [of the individual] by conformity with every creative and rebellious instinct stifled," especially "the courage to be [an] individual, to speak with one's own voice [...]."[50] In essence, white men became subservient Black men if they failed to exercise independence. Mailer's hipster rejected organized mainstream society in favor of escaping into the self. The hipster embodied the self-reliance of Whyte's Protestant Ethic and Strecker's self-preservation, as well as the individual man taking control back from the group.

As the American public discourse strove to define Cold War masculinity, the Soviets launched the doomed dog *Laika* (Barker) aboard *Sputnik II* on November 3, 1957.[51] A month later, the Americans failed to launch the *Vanguard* satellite, appropriately nicknamed "flopnick," after the rocket exploded.[52] The *Sputniks* did not specifically cause a masculinity crisis, but the satellites flew through a time of male self-reflection, leading *Look* magazine and Schlesinger to declare the early Cold War as *The Decline of the American Male* and "The Crisis of Masculinity."

Both *Look* and Schlesinger blamed the masculinity crisis on women's growing independence and the American male's increasing domestication. Schlesinger lamented that more men became a "substitute for wife and mother—changing diapers, washing dishes, cooking meals, and performing a whole series of what once were considered female duties."[53] The post–World War II man who defeated the Axis abroad now overworked himself at the office seeking economic prosperity or group approval. *Look* argued that young boys no longer had a masculine role model as their fathers became "a mother substitute" and boys spent most of their time with their teachers, mothers, nurses or girls who had become interested in sports or "science classes." The women in boys' lives "remained in control."[54] *Better Homes and Gardens* author Andre Fontaine blamed this maternal protection and automation for raising "a crop of sissies" who will never be "a he-man" or "independent."[55] Men became passive, feminized or the "neuter gender" as American technology and feminism advanced.[56] Cold War masculinity would fail in a society dominated by women and automation.

While American women were making the "big decisions" and "controlling men," the plight of the American male did not center on female aggression alone, but the "decay of masculinity" was also due to a shift to group mentality that led to the American male's "uncertainty about his identity in general. Nothing is harder in the whole human condition than to achieve a full sense of identity—than to know who you are, where you are going, and what you mean to live and die for."[57] *Look* echoed Schlesinger's sentiments, arguing that the American woman's political empowerment led to a passive American male who lost his individual identity, his ability "to say the word 'I'" because "teamwork and personnel relations reigned over all."[58] The women who subverted gender constructs at the NACA and NASA managed to work in teams and yet exercised the masculine trope of individuality apart from what the group expected. Their time was now.

Even with an American victory in World War II, gender roles led men to doubt their own identity, value and worth as they faced a perceived Cold War masculinity crisis. The decades after World War II ushered in male fears of complacency, complete with an expanding federal government, suburbs, shopping malls, consumer goods, teamwork, leisure, automation and air conditioning. While American men were expected to dominate and control, they were also expected to work well in teams, much like those in the growing aeronautical industry—leaving prevailing definitions of masculinity constantly shifting back and forth as if on a pendulum.

David Gilmore wrote that "manliness is a symbolic script" and "a cultural construct, endlessly variable [...]."[59] Rising government power over the military, industry and academic complex produced a behemoth technocracy in which individualists could not survive alone. The solution to combat the perceived masculinity crisis in an ever-increasing world of technocracy and systems engineering was through democratic manhood. Much like World War II's renegotiation of femininity, American definitions of masculinity could not be static; they had to be flexible if they were to survive on the Cold War stage. Cold War masculinity needed to be less about individuality and more about the ability to be an individual and a team player.

The Team players' identity led to successful spaceflight feats. The Americans were successful on January 31, 1958, with the launch of their own much smaller but more technologically capable satellite, *Explorer 1*. The following July, President Eisenhower and Congress created NASA.[60] For the next two years, the Soviets and Americans jockeyed back and forth, sending satellites into space. NASA's struggle to get off the ground created a misguided fear within the 1957 Gaither Report that a missile gap existed between the United States and the Soviet Union. Senator John F. Kennedy and Democrats pounced on the exaggerated report during Kennedy's senate and presidential races, exploiting the fear that the United States trailed the Soviets in missile production. Kennedy connected the perceived missile gap with the loss of individuality and growing complacency of American men.[61]

Kennedy used Whyte's demand for more danger and courage, drawing upon the nineteenth-century frontier and pioneer imagery to demonstrate American greatness while chastising "the steady replacement of men by machines."[62] The junior Senator lamented in 1960:

> We are, I am afraid, in danger of losing something solid at the core. We are losing that Pilgrim and pioneer spirit of initiative and independence—that old-fashioned Spartan devotion to "duty, honor, and country." We don't need that spirit now, we think. Now we have cars to drive and buttons to push and TV to watch—and pre-cooked meals and prefab houses. We stick to the orthodox, to the easy way and the organization man. We take for granted our security, our liberty, and our future—when we cannot take any of them for granted at all.[63]

Kennedy longed for a past in which Americans performed not only toughness but were doers; they welcomed a hard life of exploration, pioneering and independent living. Kennedy compared that past with a contemporary image;

he pointed to Whyte's organization man. The image presented there was a manifest softness, an American character lacking individuality and control as well as a can-do attitude. The organization man preferred passivity as he lived in a pre-arranged world of comfort and ease. Kennedy's use of Whyte infused the popular culture discourse into the dialogue of American politics, security and technology. The following summer, Kennedy drew upon the words of Thomas Jefferson and Teddy Roosevelt when he again rejected a safe society in *Life* magazine:

> Our national purpose consists of […] striving, risking, choosing, making decisions, engaging in a pursuit of happiness that is strenuous, heroic, exciting and exalted. When we do so as individuals, we make a nation that, in Jefferson's words, will always be "in the full tide of successful experiment."

Kennedy claimed the four goals of America's future were survival, competition, peace and prosperity. To reach these goals, the national purpose must be "The fulfillment of every individual's dignity and potential."[64] To Kennedy, the root of American purpose depended not just on individuality. The American purpose centered on what Kennedy laid out to an eager crowd at Rice University in September 1962. American exceptionalism, the American spirit focused on doing not what was "easy" but what was "hard."[65] But the question remained, did these attributes that made America so great apply to only men? Was it a woman's responsibility to focus on being a wife and motherhood to help her husband achieve masculinity?

While accepting the Democratic presidential nomination in 1960, Kennedy promised to bring "our Nation back to greatness." He demurred not only poverty and lack of human rights abroad and at home, but also "a revolution of automation finds machines replacing men in the mines and mills of America […]." To defeat the "famine of ideas" and the "slippage— in our intellectual and moral strength," Kennedy beckoned "new men" to come forward, "young men are coming to power—men who are not bound by the traditions of the past—men who are not blinded by the old fears and hates and rivalries—young men who can cast off the old slogans and delusions and suspicions." For these young men, Kennedy invoked the myth of the frontier—that space that made American manhood for centuries. Kennedy told the crowd, "For I stand tonight facing west on what was once the last frontier." Kennedy pointed to this new democratic manhood, a man who was both an individual and a team player, when he remarked:

> The pioneers of old gave up their safety, their comfort, and sometimes their own lives to build a new world here in the West [*sic*]. They were not

the captives of their own doubts, the prisoners of their own price tags. Their motto was not "every man for himself"—but "all for the common cause." They were determined to make the new world strong and free, to overcome its hazards and its hardships, to conquer the enemies that threaten from without and within.

Like men before him who looked across the ocean for a continued frontier to bring about the spreading of American democracy and greatness, Kennedy believed the frontier was still alive, if not always a physical space but also a mindset. The "New Frontier" provided a set of challenges for a reinvigorated "courageous" American to prove their "pioneer" greatness and not "shrink back from that frontier" to embrace "safe mediocrity." Kennedy called on Americans to remember that "normalcy" was the seed of "mediocrity" and that Americans must have "the nerve and the will" of "national greatness." Foreshadowing the race to the moon, Kennedy asked his audience to "Recall with me the words of Isaiah: 'They that wait upon the Lord shall renew their strength; they shall mount up with the wings as eagles; they shall run and not be weary.'"[66] Kennedy's challenge drew on imagery of both a real and imagined past of American pioneering—one that made American democracy great in the eyes of its citizens. His wings of eagles negating safety and security and normalcy for sacrifice foreshadowed the language of the space race and beckoned a masculinity rebirth once again focusing on environmental control. This time the remaking of American masculinity would take place on the frontier of space.

Dependence on automation stood in the way of this new pioneering venture. By the early 1960s, fears of automation were at an all-time high within the public discourse. Increased automation completed the work for men, leaving them passive and feminine. Men pushed buttons at work and created an identity through leisure and not hard work, grit or courage.[67] The displacement of men by machines and increased button-pushing masculinity found itself within the aviation and aerospace discourse as the scientist and engineer increasingly took over the role of the daredevil pilot.

## A Masculinity Crisis in Aviation

Former Nazi German sports medicine pioneer Dr. Bruno Balke entered the United States under Operation Paperclip, much like Dr. Wernher von Braun and other NASA employees. Balke spent his life's work in Germany and the United States trying to prove masculinity through superior physique. He conducted experimental testing on American airmen's endurance in the Rocky Mountains while creating the first American space capsule prototype at the

Air Force's School of Aviation Medicine (SAM) at Randolph Air Force Base in San Antonio, Texas. Much like his experiments on German mountain climbers in the Andes and Himalayas during World War II, Balke preferred to focus on spaceflight with the space flier performing "hard labor."[68] Balke lamented that "civilized life" and "automation" had "greatly reduced the need for physical exercise." These conclusions came after Balke tested five hundred airmen's endurance running and biking. Only eighteen percent had a "better or good work capacity," with the rest falling short as "fair" or "poor." Balke concluded that "power today rests in ideas, in motives, in organizations, and, above all, in technology." Man needed to learn skills to survive because "nations were destined to perish when a peak of civilization slowly softened the physical resistance of man against the forces of nature or against the onrush of a more vital enemy."[69] To Balke, physical strength trumped intellect and highly advanced button-pushing technology.

The end of World War II demonstrated that skill in warfare was moving away from physical combat to large push-button weapons that required the power of ideas, science and technology. Americans marveled at the advent of new radar, computers, missiles and rockets. The Americans gained a tremendous amount of research and ideas from the Manhattan Project, the Jet Propulsion Laboratory and Paperclip scientists. Beginning as early as 1945, the German missileers and rocketeers assembled at White Sands, New Mexico, and El Paso, Texas. Newspapers ran headlines, "Nazi V-2 Climbs Almost 75 Miles As 'Push-Button War' Tests Begin" and "Big V-2 Previews Push-Button War."[70] The American press commended the accuracy of the V-2, but this praise still echoed the push-button future. The *El Paso Times* explained, "The rocket is controlled by an internal control system which keeps it stable in flight. It reacts automatically to a pre-set program to maintain itself on the proper trajectory, hence the name 'guided missile.'"[71] This new push-button technology created by former Nazi engineers reflected the very authoritarianism and fascism Americans fought against—the totalitarian grasp of men by machines. Machines were historically "tropes to authenticated male authority in American society," but their button-pushing presented a *Frankenstein* fear that the technology emasculated men by taking control and individuality, making men another cog or component with the machine.[72]

Fears of a future push-button battlefield reverberated in the American press at the end of World War II. Even the Commander of the United States Army Air Force, Henry H. "Hap" Arnold, argued in 1945 that "Air Power should not be confined to manned vehicles. Controlled or directed robots will be of increasing importance, and although they probably will never preclude some form of human guidance [...] manual skills in pilotage will gradually decrease."[73] Similarly, the United States Navy was working on guided missiles to replace guns on ships and even a "pilotless, jet propelled aircraft with speeds up to several thousand miles per hour. Carrying an atomic-bomb that will be capable of 'sniffing out' targets with no help from human hands or brains."[74] Much like General Arnold, the *New York Times'* Hanson W. Baldwin predicted "'Drones' and 'Babes'—pilotless planes flown by remote control— will soon be a familiar sight in the skyways of the world as rehearsals begin for a 'push-button war' in the air."[75] Baldwin dreaded that the future of missile technology would be "all but human."[76]

Science writer David Dietz suspected in 1946 that conventional naval and aerial warfare would be "far too slow in the 'push-button' war of the future." Soldiers would not necessarily be drones but rather "fighting men in the push-button war of the future will be [...] highly skilled and highly trained scientists, technicians and engineers" who would operate far below the surface of the Earth to keep themselves and their installations safe from rocket and atomic weapons.[77] Military officials assured the public that "the G. I. with a bayonet will have to go in and take and hold the final objective."[78]

The *Alabama Journal's* Allen Rankin understood that man's "vanity" and his "pride" rested with his ability to be a good shot. And "as for war, what's marksman got to do with calculus, radar, and push-button rockets?"[79] Calculus, radar and pushing buttons had everything to do with successfully launching a guided missile into the new Cold War air and space battlefield. The Cold War arsenal needed teams of engineers and scientists. The *Berkshire Eagle's* Katherine H. Annin foresaw a United States that no longer revered or taught history lessons on talented individuals but "anonymous teams of scientists [...]. Who will be credited in future textbooks with the launchings of Sputniks and Explorers? [...] how can we belittle the influence of individuals on history?"[80]

Teams of scientists and engineers were necessary in systems engineering, but the romanticized physically strong soldier remained an important component of warfare. The Chief of Army and Navy Scientific Research, Dr. Vannevar Bush, dismissed the idea of a push-button war as "Buck Rogers [...] hooey," instead emphasizing that future wars would require "the same tough, slugging match that the last one was."[81] Bush's statement reinforced a masculinity focused on physicality in warfare, manly endurance and the strong male protector. Hanson Baldwin disagreed, lamenting that too much leisure and the good life led to the "softening of men [...]." Baldwin lay blame in the "Sedentarianism, push buttonitis, and indoorism have taken a heavy toll on fitness."[82] A renewed focus on the future of warfare created competing narratives of masculinity surrounding new Cold War aviation and aerospace technology. Man's individuality, technological control and physical strength remained paramount.

Control and physical strength as the epitome of American pilot masculinity was not a new aviation narrative. The *New York Times* argued American pilots in World War I lacked "a yellow streak" and "fear of danger" because the "wealth of manhood permitted us to select only the best [...]."[83] Piloting over war zones demonstrated "self-reliance and individualistic qualities."[84] As Robertson's *The Dream of Civilized Warfare*, Fino's *Tiger Check* and Hankins' *Flying Camelot* have already demonstrated, World War I through Vietnam created the military fighter-pilot image as symbolic of the heroism of medieval knights, risking their lives for their country while relying on only their individual skill and bravery. Hankins concludes that the fighter-pilot "culture was then passed down to subsequent generations for over a century, evolving over time but remained centered on the five elements of aggressiveness, independence, heroic imagery, technology, and community all coded with masculinity."[85]

Charles Lindbergh's 1927 historic solo flight across the Atlantic Ocean echoed these pilot qualities. Newspapers hailed that Lindbergh's "dominant American character" had opened a new "frontier" to be conquered by Americans. Lindbergh flew alone, and the great risks involved embodied masculine courage. *Outlook* magazine hailed the feat, "Charles Lindbergh is the heir of all that we like to think is best in America. He is the stuff out of which have been made the pioneers that opened up the wilderness, first on the Atlantic coast, and then in our great West. His are the qualities which we, as a people, must nourish." The *New York Times* wrote, "The fact that he flew alone made the strongest impression." The *National Geographic* pinpointed the solo flight symbolism and importance, "Courage, when it goes alone, has ever caught men's imagination."[86] This lone eagle narrative remained through World War II, but needed to be renegotiated as more automation and passengers entered aviation.

Pilots had to confront the reality that aviation's pushing the edge of the envelope required pushing buttons. The Washington DC Aero Club presented Charles Lindbergh with the Wright Brothers Memorial Trophy in 1949. In a speech that was broadcast throughout the country, the 47-year-old flier said that men became dependent on advanced aviation technology like the "self-starter" and "closed cockpit" that "hypnotize us into believing that simply by sitting in front of desks and drawing boards and instruments all day we are contributing to the character of man."[87] Pilot masculinity needed physicality and risk. The man needed to play a role.

The Society of Experimental Test Pilots (SETP) echoed these sentiments a decade later at the first annual banquet at the Beverly Hilton in Los

Angeles, California. The Assistant Secretary for Air Force Research and Development, Richard Horner, spoke of the need for pilot "SURVIVAL." As a former World War II test pilot and engineer, Horner understood that decades ago, helmets, parachutes, escape hatches and self-starters threatened pilot bravado. Today, increased automation threatened "the survival of the cockpit itself" and therefore, the survival of the pilot.[88] The individual pilot in control of his machine defined flying as a masculine performance, and advanced technology threatened this performance.

Unfortunately for the six hundred and fifty men at the SETP banquet, the post–World War II aviation era blossomed into a family-friendly atmosphere as comfort and ease took center stage.[89] New scientific and technical developments during World War II helped routinize private and commercial flying. World War II familiarized GIs with flight.[90] The 1950s economic boom brought in a new mode of transportation as well as a new relationship between Americans and the airplane. The emphasis on flying was no longer focused on individuality or death-defying stunts. In the late 1940s and 1950s, flying became a passive, if not domesticated, activity that could be done by men, women, children and the elderly. Manufacturers such as Stinson and Piper Cub equated private flying to driving a station wagon. Advertisers put images of women at the plane's control to demonstrate that flying was "that simple."[91]

Most Cold War "flyers" were not pilots, but rather, passengers. Flying equated "well-earned leisure."[92] At Curtiss-Wright, engineers made flying "more enjoyable for the passenger" and "simpler and more economical for the operator."[93] Commercial aviation still towed the line in terms of gender roles, with men as pilots and women as hostesses or stewardesses. Commercial airlines did not hire women as pilots because their role was wife and mother. Airlines only hired single women as stewardesses since married women and mothers' main jobs were in the home, not in the sky. Despite adhering to fixed gender constructs in the air, luxury, leisure and automation had taken the moxie out of commercial flight. Commercial aviation was becoming routine and domesticated.[94] To push the edge of the envelope as opposed to buttons, man would need to fly faster and higher.

Having the individual grit and courage to fly faster and higher meant a reinvigoration of military pilot masculinity for the Cold War. Charles "Chuck" Yeager epitomized the envelope-pusher. He captured American fascination and awe when he broke the sound barrier aboard the Bell X-1 Glamourous Glennis at Edwards Air Force Base on October 14, 1947. He did this all with broken ribs that he received from falling from a horse after a night of drinking.[95] His courage and skill captured the nation's attention.

However, not all the leading aviation/aerospace engineers in the private discourse agreed on man's future role within the cockpit. The October 1954 biannual meeting of the NACA Committee on Aerodynamics met to discuss formulating a plane for spaceflight. The majority view, led by Preston Bassett, president of the Sperry Corporation known for its automatic piloting instrumentation, was that man still had a role in the cockpit. The Navy and Air Force agreed. The dissenting minority voice came from the chief engineer at Lockheed, Clarence "Kelly" Johnson. Johnson oversaw designs on World War II's P-38 Lightning, the first American jet fighter (the P-80/F-80 Shooting Star), the F-104 Starfighter and U-2 spy plane. The F-104 Starfighter laid the foundation for the X-15. These were the best and most favored jets for pilots to fly. The room was shocked. Johnson reasoned that it would be quicker, cheaper and safer to design spaceflight without a man present. The engineers had automated technology to take over that role, plus, high-speed flights "have proven mainly the bravery of the test pilots' and not the success of the mission."[96]

The committee overruled Johnson, grasping the importance to American culture that a man be in the cockpit. The man must control the technology, specifically when the success of X-15 flights depended on government funding. The pilot needed to capture the American imagination even if the advanced technology "brought up the old chauffeur versus airmen dichotomy into the world of spaceflight and computerized control." The plane designed, the X-15, flew at Mach 6 upward to 354 feet (61 miles) in the air after being dropped from the belly of a B-52 bomber. For its short ten-minute flight, the pilot controlled the attitude as the X-15 arced into space, directed the flight path for reentry, pitched its nose up, maneuvered it to slow it down for a "'dead stick' (with no power) landing at Edwards." According to David Mindell's *Digital Apollo*, the combination of pilot and automatic control led to pilot oscillations, a struggle for control between man and machine. A solution to this danger was the introduction of X-15 simulators. This allowed pilots to study the systems and make improvements with engineers. Simulations would be essential for successful space missions. The introduction of the stability augmentation system or SAS was to stabilize oscillations, but the pilots often found the system unhelpful even though it was necessary to save their lives.[97]

Individuality and pilot control remained even as the outward appearance of pilots changed. The "short, wiry, and muscular" backcountry West Virginia Yeager presented himself as a man you did not make eye contact with for fear he would "put four more holes in your nose."[98] X-15 pilot Scott Crossfield looked more like a "banker," "family man" and "ordinary," as opposed to a "spaceman."[99] Despite his square appearance, the jet test pilot demonstrated bravery telling the press, "If you want to do big things, you must accept an element of risk." Crossfield welcomed risk as he viewed piloted crafts as necessary for space travel, thwarting that a machine-controlled craft

EARLY COLD WAR GENDER ROLES 45

was not "even one half as capable as the mind of man." The "man can make judgements" that machines could not.[100] After all, according to the *Detroit Free Press*, the X-15 landed "under Crossfield's control."[101]

Crossfield may have been independent and in control, but he understood the necessity of teamwork between engineers and pilots for pilot survival. Foreshadowing future spacecraft flights, not only could the X-15 fly itself, but mission success and safety depended on the pilot's constant communication with the "master control station at Edwards" during the entire flight. Mindell argues that the 1954 Committee on Aerodynamics meeting put pilots in hypersonic flight, especially the X-15, "on the defensive: from its origin the X-15 had to justify the manned presence in space."[102] X-series pilots, who were largely systems engineers themselves, fought a constant battle with technology and engineers over their role in the cockpit.

The public discourse viewed Crossfield and the other X-series pilots as heroes, and the NACA capitalized on this as the administration transitioned into NASA. NASA Langley Research Center opened its doors to the public for the first time in October 1959 to calm fears that the Soviets outstretched the Americans in spaceflight technology. Americans could view the rockets, satellites, Crossfield's X-15 and even mockups for the Mercury spaceflight missions. Astronaut John Glenn and his wife Annie toured the facilities, taking pictures in front of the *Mercury* spacecraft. The public's viewing of these important classified machines made Americans participants in this democratic race for space. It was a brilliant public relations move for the billions of taxpayer dollars needed for spaceflight. Something was missing as the men and their machines took center stage. NASA missed the opportunity to present American women with "a new image to help them find their identity" in this democratic race to space.[103] NASA's private discourse that women contributed to spaceflight bowed to the public discourse of projecting masculinity in spaceflight. The women computers and engineers were not visible at the open house. The visible women were Langley secretaries who acted as "hostesses" for the public and dignitaries.[104] Rather, the male engineers and pilots took center stage in the race to space, continuing the gendered assumption that men controlled technology and women were passive.

## Conclusion

World War II ushered in challenges to accepted American gender roles. Gender roles appeared fluid as women enlisted and took on masculine jobs. The public discourse took great pains to demonstrate that these roles were temporary, not upsetting American cultural gender differences. The NACA and later NASA continued to hire women for their skills; however, this progress fell short as women with the same education as men were put in sub-professional fields, while the men received professional grades. The women computers, mathematicians, astronomers, missileers and engineers at NASA defied separate Cold War gender roles as they carved out their own feminine identities in traditionally male jobs. Women subverted cultural assumptions about women's roles with technology, skill, and, of course, their roles as wives and mothers. As the NASA women pushed the edge of the gendered envelope, a masculinity crisis emerged within the public discourse. The crisis centered on the loss of the individual to the group or team—a loss of self-determination and control. American companies urged both men and women to consume. Corporations grew to create more consumer and military goods, and men donned gray flannel suits and marched from the battlefield to the corporate office. Intellectuals, pundits and sociologists explored the inner workings of both the American psyche and the American character. Machines displaced men's labor and intellect. Button-pushing freed men from hard work and led to leisure activity. Men turned soft. Anxiety took center stage as Americans feared communism, conformity, feminism, homosexuality, bureaucracy, male consumerism, leisure, automation and the dreaded corporate "organization man" as a threat to masculinity. Americans questioned what it meant to be masculine in the new nuclear age as gender roles appeared permeable. The American discourse suggested that Cold War masculinity meant a return to rugged individuality, both physically and mentally. Men wanted choice but this choice came into constant conflict with the corporate and technocratic team atmosphere. These elements of danger and bravery, coupled with pilot control and self-determination over machines, set the stage for the space race narrative and the epitome of American masculinity: the public astronaut image.

## Notes

1 Dorothy "Dottie" B. Lee, interview by Rebecca Wright, NASA Headquarters History Office, Johnson Space Center, November 10, 1999, 9, accessed April 20, 2023, https://historycollection.jsc.nasa.gov/JSCHistoryPortal/history/oral_histories/LeeDB/DBL_11-10-99.pdf. See also, Shetterly, *Hidden Figures*, 180.
2 Sheryll Goecke Powers, *Women in Flight Research at NASA Dryden Flight Research Center from 1946 to 1995* (Washington, DC: The National Aeronautics and Space Administration, 1997), 22.
3 Lee, interview, 2–4.
4 May, *Homeward Bound*, 87.
5 United States Federal Civil Defense Service, *Bert the Turtle Says Duck and Cover* (Washington, DC: Federal Civil Defense Administration, 1951).
6 May, *Homeward Bound*, 87.

# EARLY COLD WAR GENDER ROLES

7 Adlai Stevenson, "A Purpose for Modern Woman (1955)," W.W. Norton & Company, accessed October 17, 2023, https://wwnorton.com/college/history/archive/resources/documents/ch32_04.htm.

8 For a discussion on Republican Motherhood, see Linda Kerber, *Women of the Republic: Intellect and Ideology in Revolutionary America* (Chapel Hill, NC: The University of North Carolina Press, 1980).

9 For the Kitchen Debate transcripts see, "The Kitchen Debate Transcript," The Central Intelligence Agency, accessed June 6, 2023, https://www.cia.gov/reading-room/docs/1959-07-24.pdf., 2.

10 For the Kitchen Debate transcripts see, "The Kitchen Debate Transcript," 3, 1.

11 Aunt Jemima Easy-Mixes advertisement, "Spicy Oatmeal Bread Easy-Mix," *Ladies Home Journal*, September 1959, 95; "Cascade: Gives Spotless Results Never Before Possible in Your Dishwasher," *Ladies Home Journal*, March 1956; Hudson advertisement, "Wait! No Gear Shift Lever?" *Ladies Home Journal*, May 1937, 56; 1956 Kenmore Owner's Manual for their Automatic Dryer "Just Set the Dial and Relax a While," Automatic Ephemera, accessed October 15, 2023, http://www.auto-matice.org/cgi-bin/index.cgi?showdoc~520~kenmore~AX; "A Kitchen Packed with Performance," *Ladies Home Journal*, March 1956, 88–89. Magic Chef advertisement, "A Touch of Magic in Your Life with the New Magic Chef for 1960," *Ladies Home Journal*, August 1959, 31; "Now! A Better Fitting Napkin You Can Wear and Forget!" *Ladies Home Journal*, August 1959, 39; NuSoft Fabric Softener Rinse advertisement, "Cut Ironing Time with NuSoft," *Ladies Home Journal*, September 1959, 111; Tampax advertisement, "It's Great to Be Alive!" *Ladies Home Journal*, September 1959, 43; Tampax advertisement "Why Be Earthbound?" *Ladies Home Journal*, September 1966, 69; Windex advertisement, "I'm free from one housecleaning bugaboo," *Ladies Home Journal*, May 1937, 47.

12 Cowan, *More Work for Mother.*

13 Ward Cannel (NEA Staff Correspondent), "The American Male of 1958: Experts Wonder How He Survives Beset by Fear, Bereft of Strength," *Knoxville News-Sentinel*, July 27, 1959, 49.

14 Dr. George W. Crane, "Worry Clinic: Men Prefer Feminine Girls—Not Attracted By Masculine Characteristics," *Herald and Review* (Decatur, Illinois), August 27, 1951, 4.

15 Dorothy Barclay, "Trousered Mothers and Dishwashing Dads," *New York Times*, April 28, 1957, 25. Friedan echoes this sentiment that fixed gender roles created an identity crisis in Friedan, *The Feminine Mystique*, 75.

16 Friedan echoes this sentiment that fixed gender roles created an identity crisis in Friedan, *The Feminine Mystique*, 66, 70.

17 "Women in Space," NASA Historical Reference Collection, NASA Headquarters, Washington, DC.

18 Shetterly, *Hidden Figures*, 37–39, 51, 57, 5–7; Sarah McLennan and Mary Gainer, "When the Computer Wore a Skirt: Langley's Computers, 1935–1970," *News & Notes, NASA History Office*, 21, no. 1 (December 2017): 28, accessed October 17, 2023, https://history.nasa.gov/nltr29-1.pdf. See also, James R. Hansen, *Engineer In Charge: A History of Langley Aeronautical Laboratory, 1917–1958* (Washington, DC: The National Aeronautics and Space Administration, 1987), 206–207.

19 Shetterly, *Hidden Figures*, 5 and McLennan and Gainer, "When the Computer Wore," 28.

20 Shetterly, *Hidden Figures*, 92. See also, Margot Lee Shetterly, "Dorothy Vaughn Biography," National Aeronautics and Space Administration, accessed June 14, 2023, https://www.nasa.gov/content/dorothy-vaughan-biography.

21 Mar Hicks, Editor William Aspray, *Programmed Inequality: How Britain Discarded Women Technologists and Lost Its Edge in Computing* (Boston: The Massachusetts Institute of Technology Press, 2017).

22 Shetterly, *Hidden Figures*, 214–218, 25, 76, 122, 124, 179–182, 91–92 and Goecke Powers, *Women in Flight Research*, 18–19.

23 NASA History Program Office, "Address By Dr. George E. Mueller, Associate Administrator for Manned Space Flight, The National Aeronautics and Space Administration, at the Dedication of the Science Center Cedar Crest College, Allentown, Pennsylvania, October 19, 1966," The National Aeronautics and Space Administration, 2, accessed June 21, 2023, https://historydms.hq.nasa.gov/sites/default/files/DMS/e000040149.pdf.

24 Shetterly, *Hidden Figures*, 12, 22, 25, 76, 124, 179–182, 192.

25 Sara Azrara and Richard Stacks, "Women Behind the Spacemen and the Satellites," *Sun Magazine*, May 17, 1964, 19. "Women in Space," NASA Historical Reference Collection, NASA Headquarters, Washington, DC, and Val Gillispie, "Eleanor C. Pressly: A Duke Alumna at NASA," Duke University, accessed June 13, 2023, https://blogs.library.duke.edu/rubenstein/2019/07/12/pressly/.

26 Gladwin Hill, "Now Even Rocket Waits For Woman; A Slide-Rule Expert Decides if Weather is Right for Tests at White Sands," *New York Times*, April 14, 1957, 38.

27 Hill, "Now Even Rocket Waits," 38.

28 Azrara and Stacks, "Women Behind the Spacemen," 19.

29 Catherine T. Osgood, interview by Rebecca Wright, NASA Headquarters History Office, Johnson Space Center, November 15, 1999, 1–2, 10–12, accessed June 13, 2023, https://historycollection.jsc.nasa.gov/JSCHistoryPortal/history/oral_histories/OsgoodCT/CTO_11-15-99.pdf.

30 Lee, interview, 5.

31 Azrara and Stacks, "Women Behind the Spacemen," 18.

32 Nancy G. Roman, interview by Rebecca Wright, NASA Headquarters History Office, Johnson Space Center, September 15, 2000, 42–45, 31–2, accessed July 18, 2022, https://historycollection.jsc.nasa.gov/JSCHistoryPortal/history/oral_histories/NASA_HQ/Herstory/RomanNG/NGR_9-15-00.pdf.

33 Azrara and Stacks, "Women Behind the Spacemen," 19.

34 Azrara and Stacks, "Women Behind the Spacemen," 19.

35 Henry Luce, "The American Century," *Life*, February 17, 1941, 61–65, 61, 63, 65. See also, Faludi, *Stiffed*, 5, 7.

36 D'Ann Campbell, *Women at War with America: Private Lives in a Patriotic Era* (Boston: Harvard University Press, 1984); Lorry M. Fenner and Marie De Young, *Women in Combat: Civic Duty or Military Liability?* (Georgetown: Georgetown University Press, 2001), 52–55; Sally Hacker, *Pleasure, Power, and Technology: Some Tales of Gender, Engineering, and the Cooperative Workplace* (Boston: Unwin Hyman, 1989), 58–74; William C. Meadows, *The Comanche Code Talkers of World War II* (Austin, TX: University of Texas Press, 2002); Leisa D. Meyer, *Creating G.I. Jane: Sexuality and Power in the Women's Army Corps during World War II* (New York: Columbia University Press, 1998); Evelyn Monahan and Rosemary Neidel-Greenlee, *And if I Perish: Frontline U.S. Army Nurses in World War II* (New York: Anchor Books, 2003); and Doris A. Paul, *The*

*Navajo Code Talkers* (Philadelphia: Dorrance & Company, 1973). You have nothing on Blacks or Hispanics.

37 Ernie Pyle, *Brave Men* (1944; repr., Lincoln, NE: University of Nebraska Press, 2001); Ernie Pyle, *Here is Your War: The Story of G. I. Joe* (1944; repr., Lincoln, NE: University of Nebraska Press, 2001); Norman Mailer, *The Naked and the Dead* (New York: Holt, Rinehart, and Winston, 1948).

38 Raymond Sobel, "The Battalion Surgeons as Psychiatrist," in *Bulletin of the U.S. Army Medical Department* (Washington, DC: War Dept., Office of the Surgeon General, 1949), 38. As cited in Kimmel, *Manhood in America*, 225. See also, Bill Davidson, "Why Half Our Combat Soldiers Fail to Shoot," *Colliers*, November 8, 1952, 16–18.

39 Philip Wylie, *A Generation of Vipers* (New York: Farrar & Rinehart, 1942), 187–188; also cited in Kimmel, *Manhood in America*, 252–253, 255. David Levy, *Maternal Overprotection* (New York: Columbia University Press, 1943); Edward Strecker, M.D., *Their Mother's Sons* (Philadelphia: Lippincott, 1946).

40 David K. Johnson, *The Lavender Scare: The Cold War Persecution of Gays and Lesbians in the Federal Government* (Chicago: The University of Chicago Press, 2004).

41 Alfred C. Kinsey, *Sexual Behavior in the Human Male* (Philadelphia: W.B. Saunders & Company, 1948), 261, 6.

42 Ayn Rand, *The Fountainhead* (Indianapolis, IN: The Bobbs-Merrill Company, 1943); *The Fountainhead*, directed by King Vidor, Warner Bros., 1949; Kimmel, *Manhood in America*, 238–239.

43 Arthur Schlesinger Jr., *The Vital Center* (Boston: Houghton Mifflin Company, 1949), 3, 53, 1, 3, 4, 5, 9, 54, 56, 87, 36–38. See also, K. A. Cuordileone, "'Politics in an Age of Anxiety': Cold War Political Culture and the Crisis of American Masculinity, 1949–1960," *The Journal of American History* 87, no. 2 (September 2000): 515–545, 516.

44 David Riesman, Nathan Glazer, and Raul Denney, *The Lonely Crowd: A Study of the Changing American Character* (abr. edition New Haven: Yale University Press, 1974), 8, 15–18, 126, 209.

45 Riesman, *The Lonely Crowd*, 20–22, 209.

46 David M. Potter, "American Women and the American Character," in *American Character and Culture*, ed. John A. Hague (DeLand, FL: Everett Edwards Press, Inc., 1964), 74–75. See also James Gilbert, *Men in the Middle: Searching for Masculinity in the 1950s* (Chicago: University of Chicago Press, 2005), 46, 50–51.

47 C. Wright Mills, *White Collar: The American Middle Class* (New York: Oxford University Press, 1951), ix, xi, xii.

48 Whyte Jr., *The Organization Man*, 3, 4, 16, 18, 22.

49 Kimmel, *Manhood in America*, 242.

50 Norman Mailer, "The White Negro (Fall 1957)," *Dissent*, accessed October 17, 2023, https://www.dissentmagazine.org/online_articles/the-white-negro-fall-1957/. See also, Kimmel, *Manhood in America*, 242.

51 William L. Laurence, "Science in Review: Little Dog in Sputnik II May Show Animals Can Adjust to Weightlessness," *New York Times*, November 10, 1957, 215.

52 "What Flopnik! Britons Blare," *Chicago Tribune*, December 7, 1957, 4. Murray Brown, United Press International, "Satellite Flop May Force Ike to Attend Conference," *Yuma Daily Sun* (Yuma, Arizona), December 8, 1957, 1.

53 Arthur Schlesinger Jr., "The Crisis of American Masculinity," in *The Politics of Hope* (Boston: Houghton Mifflin Company, 1963), 237–238,

54 *Look Magazine, The Decline of the American Male* (New York: Random House, 1958), 4, 14.

55 Andre Fontaine, "Are We Staking Our Future on a Crop of Sissies?" *Better Homes and Gardens,* December 1950, 154, 156, 159. The article is also used in Kimmel, *Manhood in America,* 243 and May, *Homeward Bound,* 147.

56 Mary Hayworth, "Mary Hayworth's Mail: Much Neurotic Tension Today is Caused by Individuals Trying to Adhere to Ideals of King Arthur's Time," *Tampa Tribune,* February 11, 1952, 10.

57 Schlesinger Jr., "The Crisis of American Masculinity," 237–238, 242, 244.

58 *Look Magazine,* The Decline of the American Male, 25, 26, 29, 18, 19, 12.

59 David Gilmore, *Manhood in the Making: Cultural Concepts of Masculinity* (New Haven: Yale University Press, 1990), 202–206, 230.

60 Enid Curtis Bok Schoettle, "The Establishment of NASA," in *Knowledge and Power: Essays on Science and Government,* ed. Sanford A. Lakoff (New York: The Free Press, 1966).

61 For more on the missile gap, see Office of the Historian, "Report to the President by the Security Resources Panel of the ODM Science Advisory Committee On Deterrence and Survival in the Nuclear Age, NSC5724," The United States Department of State, accessed August 30, 2023, https://history.state.gov/historicaldocuments/frus1955-57v19/d158. See also, Divine, *The Sputnik Challenge*; Peter J. Roman, *Eisenhower and the Missile Gap* (Ithaca, NY: Cornell University Press, 1995); and David Snead, *The Gaither Committee, Eisenhower, and the Cold War* (Columbus, OH: The Ohio State University Press, 1998).

62 John F. Kennedy, "General Science: Candidates on Science—The Presidential Candidates Give their Views on Science and Technology," in *Freedom of Communications: Final Report of the Committee On Commerce, United States Senate, Part 3, The Joint Appearances of Senator John F. Kennedy and Vice President Richard M. Nixon and Other 1960 Campaign Presentations,* (Washington, DC: The United States Government Printing Office, 1961), 404–405, 405.

63 John F. Kennedy, *The Strategy of Peace,* ed. Allan Nevins (New York: Harper & Row, 1960), 201. See also Robert D. Dean, "Masculinity as Ideology: John F. Kennedy and the Domestic Politics of Foreign Policy," *Diplomatic History* 22, no. 1 (Winter 1998): 29–62, 29.

64 John F. Kennedy, "We Must Climb to the Hilltop," *Life,* August 22, 1960, 70B.

65 John F. Kennedy, "President John F. Kennedy Moon Speech—Rice Stadium, September 12, 1962," The National Aeronautics and Space Administration, Johnson Spaceflight Center, accessed June 14, 2022, https://er.jsc.nasa.gov/seh/ricetalk.htm#:~:text=We%20choose%20to%20go%20to%20the%20moon%20in%20this%20decade,to%20postpone%2C%20and%20one%20which.

66 John F. Kennedy, "Acceptance of Democratic Nomination for President, July 15, 1960," The John F. Kennedy Presidential Library and Museum, accessed June 7, 2022, https://www.jfklibrary.org/learn/about-jfk/historic-speeches/acceptance-of-democratic-nomination-for-president.

67 Ernest Havemann, "The Emptiness of Too Much Leisure, Part 1," *Life,* February 14, 1964, 76–90, 76; "The Point of No Return for Everybody," *Life,* July 19, 1963, 68A–68B; Havemann, "The Task Ahead: How to Take Life Easy," *Life,* February 21, 1964, 84–94, 91, 92, and Keith Wheeler, "Big Labor Hunts for the Hard Answers," *Life,* July 19, 1963, 73–88, 81.

68 North American News Alliance, "Air Force Tests Seek 'Superman': Experiments Seek to Prove Hard Labor Can Be Done 3 Miles Above Sea Level," *New York Times*, October 18, 1959, 131.

69 Bruno Balke and Ray W. Ware, "The Present Status of Physical Fitness in the Air Force," School of Aviation Medicine, ASF, Randolph Air Force Base, Defense Technical Information Center, May 1959, 1, 9, 8, accessed October 20, 2023, https://apps.dtic.mil/sti/pdfs/ADA036235.pdf.

70 Hanson W. Baldwin, "Nazi V-2 Climbs Almost 75 Miles as 'Push-Button War' Tests Begin," *New York Times*, May 11, 1946, 1, 40.

71 Bill Lathan, "V-2 Rocket Sets Altitude Record of 72 Miles in White Sands Test," *El Paso Times*, May 11, 1946, 1.

72 Oldenzial, *Making Technology Masculine*, 31. See also, Mary Shelley, *Frankenstein* (New York: Penguin Books, 1985; first published in London, 1818).

73 Henry H. Arnold, "Text of Final Section of Arnold's Report Blueprinting Needs for Maintaining Air Power," *New York Times*, November 12, 1945, 14.

74 International News Service (INS), "No Flight of Fancy; Tourists Are Assured Jet Travel to Moon By 'Guided Missiles'," *Atlanta Constitution*, August 12, 1946, 1.

75 Hanson W. Baldwin, "The "Drone": Portent of Push-Button War; Recent Operations Point to the Pilotless Plane as a Formidable Weapon in War's New Armory," *New York Times*, August 25, 1946, 10, 120.

76 Hanson W. Baldwin, "Missiles in Push-Button War; Frightening Import of these Weapons is Heightened by Varieties Made Possible by a Fusing of Principles," *New York Times*, July 8, 1946, 5.

77 David Dietz, "ADVENTURES IN SPACE: The Story of Radar; No. 8: Push-Button Warfare," *Mount Carmel Item* (Mount Carmel, Pennsylvania), April 9, 1946, 7.

78 "War and Economics of the Push Button Variety," *Montana Standard* (Butte, Montana), November 29, 1946, 4.

79 Allen Rankin, "Gun Vanity, 'A Lost Voter,' and Plain English," *Alabama Journal* (Montgomery, AL), January 12, 1950, 8.

80 Katherine H. Annin, "Let Us Now Praise Famous Men," *Berkshire Eagle* (Pittsfield, Massachusetts), February 18, 1958, 15.

81 "Push-Button, War Talk Draws Blast," *Salt Lake Tribune*, January 9, 1947, 1.

82 Hanson Baldwin, "Our Fighting Men Have Gone Soft," *Saturday Evening Post*, August 8, 1959, 13, 15, 82–84. See also, Steven Watts, *JFK and the Masculine Mystique: Sex and Power on the New Frontier* (New York: St. Martin's Press, 2016), 21, 24, 32.

83 Lieutenant Colonel Henry Horn, "Acid Test of the Airman; Seventy-five Monitors at Issoudon Selected on Practical Grounds Met All the Theoretical Medical Requirements," *New York Times Magazine*, April 20, 1919, 90.

84 H. Brock, "The Flying Man is Etched in Court," *New York Times Magazine*, December 6, 1925, 9, 12.

85 Hankins, *Flying Camelot*, 13.

86 John W. Ward, "The Meaning of Lindbergh's Flight," *American Quarterly* 10, no. 1 (Spring 1958): 3–16, 10, 6, 9–10, 8, 9.

87 "Lindbergh Says Man Must Balance Science with Morality to Survive; LINDBERGH LINKS SCIENCE WITH MORALITY," *New York Times*, December 18, 1949, 1, 53.

88 Richard Horner, "Banquet Address before the First Annual Awards Banquet of the Society of Experimental Test Pilots," *SETP Quarterly Review* 2, no. 1 (Fall 1957): 1–10, 1, 3–4. See also Mindell, *Digital Apollo*, 17–18.

89 Corn, *The Winged Gospel.*

90 David T. Courtwright, "The Routine Stuff: How Flying became a Form of Mass Transportation," in *Reconsidering a Century of Flight*, ed. Roger D. Launius and Janet R. Daly Bednarek (Chapel Hill, NC: The University of North Carolina Press, 2003), 214.

91 Piper Cub, advertisement, *Life*, August 13, 1945, 14; Stinson, advertisement, *Life*, November 17, 1947, 155; Piper, advertisement, *Time*, March 26, 1965, 84.

92 American Airlines, "The Scheduled Airlines of the United States," advertisement, *Colliers*, November 1, 1947, 79.

93 Curtiss-Wright, advertisement, *New York Times*, January 2, 1947, 43.

94 For the routinization of commercial and private aviation see, American Airlines, advertisement, *Life,* July 8, 1946, 93; American Airlines, advertisement, *Colliers*, November 1, 1947, 79; Douglas Super DC-3, advertisement, *Saturday Evening Post*, July 23, 1949, 74; American Airlines, advertisement, *Colliers*, November 15, 1947, 83; TWA, advertisement, *Colliers,* November 22, 1947, 59; Martine Aircraft, advertisement, *Colliers*, and Pilot Dan Cooney, System Administrator, TWAPilot.Org., "Grandma Leads a Fast Life and <u>Loves</u> It!" TWAPILOT.Org., accessed June 6, 2023, http://www.twapilot.org/images/Grandma%20Leads%20a%20fast%20life%20and%20loves%20it.jpg.

95 Wolfe, *The Right Stuff*, 43–46.

96 Mindell, *Digital Apollo*, 43–46,

97 Mindell, *Digital Apollo*, 43–46, 48–51.

98 Wolfe, *The Right Stuff*, 37.

99 Herbert D. Wilhoit, Associated Press, "Test Pilot: He May Fly 4,000 m.p.h.," *Corpus Christi Times*, April 26, 1957, 13 and Stewart Alsop, "Crossfield Aims for the Stars!" *Tennessean* (Nashville, Tennessee), December 29, 1957, 11.

100 Aslop, "Crossfield Aims for the Stars!," 11.

101 Joseph N. Bell, "Scott Crossfield's Story: X-15—Past and Future," *Detroit Free Press*, December 24, 1960, 11.

102 Mindell, *Digital Apollo*, 46, 48.

103 Friedan, *The Feminine Mystique*, 71.

104 James R. Hansen, *Spaceflight Revolution: NASA Langley Research Center from Sputnik to Apollo* (Washington, DC: The National Aeronautics and Space Administration, 1995), 27–32.

# Chapter 2

# LIGHT THIS CANDLE: PROJECT MERCURY AND COLD WAR MASCULINITY

On May 5, 1961, NASA launched the first American astronaut into space aboard the Mercury craft *Freedom 7*. The feat came less than a month after the Soviets blasted cosmonaut Yuri Gagarin into orbit on April 12, 1961. Aboard his capsule, *Vostok I*, Gagarin spent a total of one hundred eighty minutes in space. He orbited the Earth once. Shepard's flight lasted around fifteen minutes, about five of which were in space. He did not orbit the Earth but rather completed a suborbital flight. However, the American public discourse lauded Shepard's feat as more impressive than Gagarin's because Shepard exercised control over his craft. Even Shepard recalled in his memoir that while shifting his capsule he shouted out, "We're doing something in space on our own. We're first with it! Manual control of a spaceship. Dyn-o-mite!"[1]

Shepard's emphasis on being first with manual control acted as a metaphor for a reinvigorated masculinity as the Americans trailed the Soviets into space. Jet test pilot-controlled spacecraft defined the American astronaut image. The spacecraft and its technology in relation to the astronaut's body created a cultural narrative of spaceflight that brought hope for the future. This astronaut-controlled spacecraft railed in the face of a perceived flagging American vigor. The first astronauts reinvigorated masculinity as they performed death-defying feats while mastering technology. They were men who performed masculinity through Michael W. Hankins' fighter-pilot characteristics of aggressiveness, independence, heroic imagery, technology and community that depicted astronauts as metaphorical medieval space knights.[2] But the first astronauts were also men who were reliant on automation, button-pushing and teams of engineers for successful spaceflights on the New Frontier. However, the astronaut image that won out during Mercury was the public discourse's astronaut who continuously wrestled control from a faulty machine to save the mission—a self-reliant, heroic, lone wolf. The following looks at why and how a jet test-pilot astronaut was chosen for the first

54 GENDER AND THE RACE FOR SPACE

American astronaut image and how that image created a masculine astronaut corps that focused on fixed gendered roles.

After the first satellite launches, the most difficult question before NASA was who would fly into space. In 1952, Dr. Wernher von Braun suggested in *Colliers*, "Here is how we shall go to the moon. The pioneer expedition, fifty scientists and technicians, will take off from the space station's orbit in three clumsy-looking but highly efficient rocket ships."[3] Former World War II general, pilot and hero of the Pacific, Dr. James Doolittle, echoed von Braun's scheme on a smaller scale. During the 1958 NASA Act senatorial debates, Doolittle suggested that the ideal space traveler would be a scientist.[4] Both men were dismissed by NASA's Space Task Group (STG)—the head of manned spaceflight programs.

On November 3, 1958, an aeromedical team consisting of Drs. Stanley C. White, William S. Augerson, Dr. Robert "Bob" Gilruth and industrial psychologist naval Lieutenant Dr. Robert Voas discussed the attributes they wanted in an astronaut. The team concluded the following five points: the astronaut needed to survive, perform, serve as a backup for the automatic controls and instrumentation, and finally, act as a competent scientific observer and engineer.[5] Voas asked if they should consider different ethnicities, foreign pilots and even women. STG director Gilruth directed the men to consider that their focus was on engineering and a person to operate the vehicle as opposed to what might be best suited for public relations.[6]

The assumption of the operator's gender is evident from the first job announcement for NASA Project A on December 22, 1958:

> Although the entire satellite operation will be possible, in the early phases, without the presence of man, the astronaut will play an important role during the flight. He will contribute by monitoring the cabin environment and by making necessary adjustments. He will have continuous display of his position and altitude and other instrument readings and will have the capability of operating the reaction controls, and of initiating the descent from orbit. He will contribute to the operation of the communications system. In addition, the astronaut will make research observations that cannot be made by instruments; these include physiological, astronomical, and meteorological observations.[7]

The use of the word *he* suggests NASA assumed the astronauts to be men. STG originally envisioned jet pilots, combat veterans, submariners, parachutists, and even sky divers, mountain climbers and explorers as potential astronauts. The STG focused on men with physical strength and endurance—not button-pushing. They wanted men with physical moxie and courage who personified the new Cold War explorer and pioneer. NASA nixed the idea for endurance junkies as they faced an accelerated timeline to get a man into space. The agency could not afford to waste time on civilian kooks, cracks or those with inflated egos.

The STG's Gilruth, Brigadier General Donald "Flick" Flickinger of the Air Force's Research and Development branch on bioastronautics and President Eisenhower met in December 1958 to discuss the use of military jet test pilots as astronauts. Jet test pilots had backgrounds in flight systems and experience with G-forces. As military personnel, they possessed secret security clearance, were used to taking orders and were readily at the government's disposal.[8] NASA could also skirt the tedious civilian hiring process. A jet test-pilot astronaut also assumed pilot control over the craft.

The potential for the American astronaut to fly the craft was important. Chief of Manned Spaceflight, George Low, surmised that "the success of the mission may well depend upon the actions of the pilot, either in his performance of primary functions or backup functions. A qualified jet test pilot appeared to be best suited for this task."[9] Of course, one could not

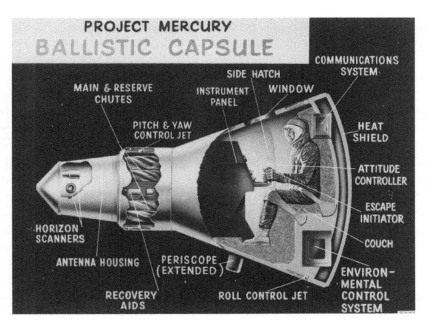

**Figure 2.1** Project Mercury ballistic capsule. Source: https://www.space.com/14498-photos-nasa-mercury-space-capsule-spaceflights.html.

deny the presence of former pilots within NASA.[10] These men championed the idea of pilot control over the craft. Aeronautical engineer Gilruth reminisced:

> Being an old aviation person myself, I thought there was nothing quite like test pilots who were used to flying a vehicle with wings instead of behind a rocket. They are used to altitude, the need for oxygen, bends and accelerations. They are used to high discipline and to taking risks, so I always felt that we should draw from professional aviators. The test pilots would be best because they also had the technical knowledge to understand the ins and outs of the space capsule and the rockets and navigation.[11]

The STG also understood that learning new engineering systems was paramount to the astronaut's knowledge, and NASA settled on the requirement of a college degree. NASA finalized the military and educational requirements in January 1959, leaving out some of the best pilots in the country. The revered Chuck Yeager did not have a college degree. X-plane pilots Scott Crossfield and Joseph A. Walker were civilian pilots working on the Man in Space Soonest (MISS) Air Force X Series program.[12] These pilots did not mind being passed over as they wanted pilot control over their craft and envisioned the astronaut as "Spam in a can."[13] Yeager and other X-plane pilots saw the astronaut pilot as an afterthought in a great cog of new aerospace systems engineering, a capsule that could literally fly itself. These qualifications limited the pool of NASA astronaut candidates down to around five hundred candidates.[14]

The decision to use military pilots proved extremely important in the creation of a white masculine astronaut—whether the conscious intention or not—and the continuation of patriarchal control over flight. NASA closed the door for women astronaut candidates since the military barred women from pilot training. NASA and military brass met on January 5, 1959, to begin pulling astronaut candidates from the Navy, Air Force and Marines. With the military's long history of segregation and discrimination, after almost a decade of integration, neither test-pilot schools of Edwards Air Force Base in California nor the Naval Air Station at Patuxent River, Maryland, had graduated a person of color. Thus, this requirement of fifteen-hundred hours of test piloting and a qualified jet test pilot "ensured [...] a racial and gender homogeneity of the astronaut corps [...]." The requirements created an all-white male public visibility of test pilots and astronauts, creating a space in which women and people of color were apart. Other requirements included that astronaut candidates could not be older than forty years of age, with a maximum height of five feet, eleven inches, weighing no more than one hundred eighty pounds. The military would give "astronaut detail" to the candidates as "3-year detached duty status," in which they were "responsible to NASA, and not to the military services," especially since their salaries were paid by NASA.[15] The annual pay for the American astronaut fell at the GS-12 to GS-15 level, allowing a salary of $8,330 to $12,770.[16]

NASA named the first spaceflight program Mercury after the Roman messenger god—sending a message of American democratic technological superiority to the world. The project's objective was to orbit a manned spacecraft around Earth, investigate man's ability to function in space and recover both man and spacecraft safely. Mercury was to assure American "confidence" in space, specifically, that a craft could be made to safely take a man into space, but also that the man "was a necessary component of the system"—with the ability to use his own "judgement and skills"—as if the man and machine were a team in space.[17]

NASA appointed the STG's Voas as the astronauts' trainer to ensure the astronauts remained calm, cool and collected.[18] This calm mental state under pressure represented masculine control and self-determination. However, Voas was not exactly the astronauts' therapist. Voas had an engineering background. During World War II, he joined the Navy Electronics Laboratory, working on ergonomics or human factors in defense engineering issues.[19] Noticeably, the astronauts' initial training took place "at a medical and mental-health clinic not an airstrip."[20]

However, Voas' role as astronaut trainer was not quite that simple. Voas previously worked in the Aviation Psychology Laboratory at the Navy Flight Medical School in Pensacola, Florida. The group developed tests to choose naval aviators. Later, the Navy transferred Voas to Bethesda, Maryland, to work on Project Strata—a high-altitude flight study focused on balloon ascents. Voas had ample experience working on the human factors—life sciences—of engineering and the physiological effects of high-altitude flight—the necessary research to choose an astronaut for spaceflight. Coupled with his previous background, NASA chose Voas—who had worked with von Braun at White Sands—to work on the "pilot's compartment, the controls and the displays and general provisions for what would become the astronaut."[21]

NASA tasked the military and STG with recruiting the astronauts. STG needed jet test pilots who had engineering knowledge. They also knew they had to emphasize that the pilot would fly the spacecraft since "no self-respecting pilot, particularly a test pilot would be likely to get in this man-in-a-can situation."[22] Voas also worked as one of NASA's manned spaceflight designers and recognized the astronauts' need for pilot control. He compiled a list of major tasks that highlighted astronaut control. Voas first identified sequence monitoring. Here, the astronaut monitored the stages of the mission, such as the staging of the boosters, the separation of the escape tower, the firing of the retro-rockets and the deployment of the parachute. The astronauts also held responsibility for systems management. The astronaut monitored all the onboard systems for any machine failures. The astronaut controlled the craft's attitude, or its orientation to the Earth in space. Finally, the astronaut researched and evaluated the craft during flight conditions.[23]

The astronaut's job was not unlike that of a pilot as engineers introduced more automation into the cockpit. The astronaut would be a systems engineer. Much like with piloting an X-plane, future astronaut Michael Collins related that flying in space required classroom lectures, testing, test data, and of course reports, charts and graphs.[24] Test pilots and astronauts were the engineers of the skies and space, but with added daring and moxie to withstand upward to nine G-forces and horrific dangers.[25] Spaceflight's dangers meant NASA needed to find mentally and physically fit astronaut candidates for the rigors of spaceflight.

In February 1959, NASA sent one hundred ten astronaut candidates to Washington, DC to be interviewed. Eighty percent volunteered for spaceflight. NASA narrowed the pool down to thirty-two candidates after consultations and interviews.[26] NASA sent the men in groups for a week's worth of further testing at Dr. William Randolph "Randy" Lovelace's clinic in Albuquerque, New Mexico. Here, they endured examinations that brought their bodies to their maximum capacity for physical and mental stress. Tests included studies of their blood, circulation, nerves, heart, tissue, eye, ear, nose, throat, X-rays and a host of enemas.[27]

NASA then sent the men for psychological and stress tests under the watchful eye of military personnel at Wright Air Development Center and Aeromedical Laboratories, Wright-Patterson Air Force Base, Dayton, Ohio. The psychiatrists conducting the tests made it clear in their research that they were looking to see which candidates could handle stressful situations while "reading instruments and recording observations."[28] The men faced tests relating to "personality evaluation, stress, fatigue, acceleration, high noise level, thermal stress, equilibrium and vibration." Each candidate underwent a Rorschach (ink blot) test. The astronauts answered over five hundred questions including, "Who am I?"[29] While it became clear that the astronauts were treated as "lab rats" for experimental testing as opposed to "righteous pilots," what was important was their ability to endure the physical and mental examinations—to test their bodies beyond their natural limits and endure the pain—both physical and mental.[30] Even Voas argued that the Mercury men were chosen for their "personalities" but makes no mention of their flying abilities.[31] The men submitted to six days and three evenings of tests to which astronaut Gordo Cooper argued that the psychiatrists' main goal was

LIGHT THIS CANDLE
59

to "separate the tigers from the pussycats."[32] The slang "tiger" meant an aggressive pilot.

After the series of examinations, STG met at NASA Space Flight Activity, Langley Field, to narrow the group down to seven men. Seven were chosen so that each astronaut would have a chance to participate in the list of Mercury missions. NASA's first press release emphasized the individuality of each astronaut: "The seven ultimately selected were chosen as a result of physical, psychological [sic] and stress tolerance abilities and because of the particular scientific disciple, or specialty, each represents."[33] However, while the press focused on the astronauts' individuality, physical prowess and courage, the psychiatrists at Wright-Patterson Air Force Base focused more on the future of human systems engineering—that of democratic manhood. The psychiatrists envisioned that "candidates should not be over-dependent on others for the satisfaction of their needs. At the same time, they must be able to accept dependence on others when required for the success of the mission. They must be able to tolerate either close associations or extreme isolation."[34]

The psychiatrists who helped choose the first astronauts may have found men who were "direct, action-oriented individuals," but they also wanted men who exhibited the traits of democratic manhood. The astronaut embodied differing masculinities: that of the individual and that of the team player. Masculinity itself was not fixed but rather fluid. To go even further into this masculine spectrum, the psychiatrists noted that of the thirty-two finalists, "pronounced identifications with one parent were about equally divided between fathers and mothers, although mothers with whom such identifications were present were strong, not infrequently masculine figures."[35] For instance, astronaut Wally Schirra's mother did acrobatics on the wings of flying planes—thus Schirra's mother engaged in gender roles not typically fitting for the female sex.[36] The psychiatrists emphasized that the pilots' masculine mothers did not emasculate their sons. The psychiatrists preferred men with confidence but not inflated egos. Lovelace psychologists George Ruff and Ed Leavy noted that the candidates exhibited "strong needs for achievement and mastery."[37] In this control and mastery, the objective was not simply about getting the job done—beating the Soviets. The goal was getting the job done right. Astronaut mastery and achievement through pilot control echoed the Cold War masculinity crisis narrative of the ideal American male.

NASA's first press conference with the Mercury 7 on April 9, 1959, focused on the human element of flying the spacecraft. When eager reporters asked whether NASA believed the Soviets would put a man in space first, Flickinger reiterated what was becoming the dominant narrative. He would not be surprised if the Soviets launched a man on the moon first. But, he proposed, "I maintain that given cards and spades that the quality of our human component will be far superior to theirs, and we will learn more from our manned flights than they will from theirs."[38] The American astronauts' skill as pilots mattered to the mission's success. The pilots viewed flying as a "way for good men to show what they can do."[39] The *New York Times* ran the headline: "Pilots Get Some Good News; Group is Assured Machines Won't Supplant Humans on Probes into Space," calming fears of automated space capsules.[40] One NASA official put it eloquently to the press, "The Mercury capsule is a job for a pilot, not a berth for a passenger."[41] The astronauts would be active pilots and not passive passengers.

At this first televised press conference in April 1959, the world was introduced to the United States' first astronauts. The media literally crawled over each other trying to get a glimpse of what they imagined to be supermen—men who were willing to risk life and limb by sitting atop an American rocket—rockets that sometimes blew up. The men looked like average American white males with athletic builds and crew cuts. White American men literally could see themselves as astronauts. Seeing themselves in the astronaut image meant they could become astronauts—the best of the best of American masculinity.

The men's backgrounds and boyhoods were quintessentially American. Of the original seven NASA astronauts: Navy Lieutenant Malcolm Scott Carpenter (35), Air Force Captain Leroy Gordon "Gordo" Cooper (32), Marine Corps. Lieutenant Colonel John Herschell Glenn Jr. (37), Air Force Captain Virgil "Gus" Ivan Grissom (33), Navy Lieutenant Commander Walter "Wally" Marty Schirra Jr. (36), Navy Lieutenant Commander Alan Bartlett Shepard Jr. (35) and Air Force Captain Donald "Deke" Kent Slayton (35), all grew up during the Great Depression. Their parents raised them in small towns like Shawnee, Oklahoma; Hackensack, New Jersey; Cambridge, Ohio; Mitchell, Indiana; East Derry, New Hampshire; Boulder, Colorado; and Sparta, Wisconsin. Some served during World War II, and all fought in Korea. Astronauts Shepard and Schirra were blue bloods of "the service aristocracy."[42] Their fathers were career military, retiring as high-ranking officers. Shepard and Schirra both attended the Naval Academy. Similarly, Cooper's father also spent most of his career in the military, received his law degree and retired as a colonel.[43] Carpenter lost his mother at a young age and was raised primarily by his grandfather, a well-to-do newspaper owner from Colorado. Grissom and Glenn came from working-class factory families. Slayton grew up on a Wisconsin farm. These men attended public universities or military academies, not private or Ivy League institutions. Their climb from average American to college-educated heroic military fighter pilots represented American rugged individualism, making their stories uniquely part of the American character that Kennedy romanticized.

**Figure 2.2** The Mercury. 7 Source: NASA. https://www.smithsonianmag.com/air-space-magazine/the-seven-122709304/.

Combat experience was an important part of the romanticized astronaut masculinity. Schirra was a World War II and Korea combat veteran. He, next to Glenn, had the most experience flying, serving in combat and testing planes for the Navy at Pax River.[44] Slayton flew in World War II and had tested jet fighters at Edwards. Slayton was the only astronaut who was a member of the SETP. Shepard served on an aircraft carrier in the Pacific during World War II and Korea. In 1946, the Navy almost dropped Shepard from basic flight training in Corpus Christi, Texas. Shepard took private flying lessons to become a better pilot. Shepard passed advanced training at the Naval Air Station in Pensacola, Florida. After serving in the Pacific, he tested planes at Pax River, Virginia.[45]

John Glenn was a Marine combat veteran who received a host of distinguished flying medals and crosses for his fifty-nine World War II combat missions and sixty-three ground-support missions in Korea—along with an additional twenty-seven missions with the Air Force in an F-86 Saber jet. He shot down three MiGs. He graduated from the U.S. Naval Test Pilot School and flew a transcontinental supersonic flight in 1957.[46] Gus Grissom also flew in Korea and received the Distinguished Flying Cross and air medals. Like Slayton, Grissom and Cooper graduated from the USAF Test Pilot School at Edwards Air Base. Cooper stood out as the engineer of the group—and was severely mocked for it.[47] Carpenter flew the multiengine platform, the Lockheed P-2 Neptune with Patrol Squadron 6. He spent most of his pre-NASA career in intelligence and navigation and was self-conscious about his lack of test piloting and jet piloting experience.[48]

The romanticized pilot astronaut image was the idealized American Cold War male. The astronauts were both extraordinary and ordinary. They were family men with houses in the suburbs, televisions and barbeques. The domesticated individualist family man who left his wife and children behind to engage in a great battle for freedom reflected the parameters of what von Braun described as the "Pride of American manhood."[49]

This perfect manhood rested on the astronauts being "individualists all."[50] Each man had a unique story to tell. Time-Life, Inc. bought the rights to the astronauts' stories on August 5, 1959, for half a million dollars. NASA approved and encouraged the contract to sell spaceflight.[51] The astronauts became celebrities. They purchased sports cars with $1 per year leases and nice homes, if they chose, something not possible on their government salaries. Sports cars represented individualism and danger, and *Life* would do the same in telling the astronauts' stories through "daring and courageous" narratives.

The astronauts were "physically strong of course," encountering "greater stresses than most pilots had ever encountered, even in combat." The astronauts possessed nerves of steel. They would have to be devoid of emotional flaws that could rattle them or destroy their efficiency when they found themselves in a crisis. The public discourse depicted even the hobbies of the astronauts as reflecting their individuality. Riding, hunting, fishing, boating, archery, skin diving and guns made the list of astronaut hobbies. They preferred rugged individualism to team sports—although Alan Shepard did enjoy golfing with his wife Louise. *Time* wrote that the astronauts were seven men with similar backgrounds, education, size and shape; they were not "seven peas in a pod" but "a team of seven distinctly original personalities [...]." The men were "seven highly motivated individuals, each of whom had found his way into the group under his own power [...]. They were individualistic even when it came to keeping in shape." Not only did the media write glowing stories of the men's individualism and courage, but reporters sold their "self-sufficient" personality.[52] *Life* depicted the astronauts as "pioneers" and space as their "frontier."[53] The astronauts were the antidote to the Cold War organization man.

However, the vacillation between an idealized individualist masculinity and democratic manhood was clear from the beginning. In 1962, *Life* magazine's John Dille wrote that the man in the spacecraft cockpit needed to be "daring and courageous" as well as "masters of their own destiny," in essence, "part pilot, part engineer, part explorer, part scientist, part guinea pig—and part hero." They were the jack of all trades. This masculine image wanted Cold War men to be everything. They were "ordinary supermen" on the Cold War stage—but as astronaut Glenn pointed out—there was nothing "superhuman" about the astronauts or piloting, but rather the men were "the

LIGHT THIS CANDLE

product of normal human skill and technical proficiency [...]. and human cogs that had to be inserted into the system at the proper time."[54]

As pilots, the astronauts focused on the thrill of building and testing the newest flying platforms. Their input was necessary, if not at times balked at by NASA engineers. The astronauts were successful in getting McDonnell Aircraft to change the design of the escape hatch, the instrument panel, a single stick rudder for pitch, yaw, and attitude, and even a window in the capsule representative of a respectable pilot. The astronauts understood their role as engineer "slide rule pilots" who could not possibly "*master* (emphasis in original) everything" working in a vast organization that required individuality in a team player atmosphere. Schirra reiterated the importance of democratic manhood; a pilot "knows that even a mountain climber cannot go it alone. He needs a team of other experienced climbers to back him up. So do we."[55] The astronauts laid out what they viewed as the reality of their work. They were pilots and systems engineers who, in a team of thousands of people, had the final responsibility of testing this craft. They had to be able to control the systems and guide the craft safely back to Earth with all the world watching. They were the craft's protectors and problem solvers, ensuring the craft's safety and the reputation of American aerospace engineering and American masculinity.

However, some pilots questioned the astronauts' ability to fly their own crafts. Yeager's "Spam in a can" reference to the astronaut became the paradox of the Mercury 7.[56] The rigorous astronaut training that the original seven engaged in included lectures on space topics, astronomy, rockets and physics. The seven flew a lot, but as passengers flying to private companies, NASA contractors and subcontractors.[57] The astronaut could not even direct his own flight path aboard the spacecraft. Ballistic missile trajectory fixed the flight path when the craft was in orbit. But the astronaut could control the spacecraft attitude, its position within orbit—but not its flight path. Even *Life* referred to the astronaut as a "passenger."[58] *Time* referred to astronaut control "as passive as floating down a river on an oarless raft."[59] This lack of control and fear of failure of the autopilot was referred to by Grissom as the "hairiest part of the mission." As part of Team Mercury, the autopilot was Grissom's area of expertise. Grissom described the autopilot as controlling the

> pitch, roll and yaw of the capsule as it plunges about 100 miles downward. Every time it takes the slightest deviation from a normal path, the auto-pilot corrects this by signaling for the firing of small jets of hydrogen peroxide on the outside of the capsule. But if the auto-pilot doesn't work, the pilot is going to have to bring the capsule down himself [...].[60]

Grissom appeared uneasy in the possible role of passenger.[61] Questions about the astronaut's ability to control his craft became a microcosm of the perceived masculinity crisis. The American discourse hoped to move away from this narrative and ensure a democratic individual control narrative to demonstrate superiority over Soviet technology.

Astronaut masculinity took another blow in the fight against automation as NASA shot the first chimpanzee—affectionately known as Ham (Holloman Aero Medical)—into space on January 31, 1961.[62] Ham's flight demonstrated that all systems were working properly and could support a man. Mission control monitored Ham's blood pressure, oxygen levels, ability to withstand G-forces and weightlessness, and conducted a test run of the heat shield, landing, deployment of the hatch, as well as the search and rescue of the craft and chimp.

Ham's flight took about eighteen minutes, and he flew some four hundred and twenty miles above the Caribbean at a speed of roughly five thousand miles per hour.[63] The chimp's job was to pull a series of levers as banana-flavored treats were dispensed. If he failed the sequence, he was given a "mild electric shock through his foot."[64] Ham and other chimps proved that one of the astronauts could have handled the flight—or even a non-astronaut.[65] Six chimps in total were trained as "astronauts," leaving the question that if the chimp could do it, what was the purpose of a jet test pilot?[66] In winged test flights, the pilots would have control—but this was a non-winged flight, a flight controlled by new engineering systems in a capsule that technically did not need a man—or woman—or chimp—present. To NASA and the astronauts, it made good engineering sense to have a man present to correct the technology. But Ham questioned the need for a pilot at all. If Ham could be the hero of the story of spaceflight, anyone could.

Despite Ham's success, the Soviets struck first the following April with a man in space. On April 12, 1961, Yuri Gagarin completed the world's first orbital flight. The public discourse referred to him as "the Soviet conqueror of the Cosmos."[67] The Associated Press went so far as to suggest that "the conquest of space by a man" represented "another feat of communist superiority."[68] *Life* magazine lamented that at this point, even if the Americans did get one of the Mercury Astronauts into space, "the achievement will seem pallid."[69] The *New York Times* blamed President Kennedy's failed "vigorous" bravado for allowing the "Conquering Wave" of communism in space.[70] President Kennedy fought back, underscoring American masculinity when he warned: "The Complacent, the self indulgent, the soft societies are about to be swept away with the debris of history. Only the strong, only the industrious, only the determined, only the courageous [...] can possibly survive."[71]

The American public discourse focused on whether the cosmonaut was a passenger or a pilot in control of his machine. The *New York Times* wrote

LIGHT THIS CANDLE 65

that while Gagarin's craft was equipped with an automatic computer, there appears to have been "opportunity for action by the passenger if he wished."[72] "Emphasizing he was no mere passenger," Gagarin stated, "I was entirely concentrated on carrying out the flight's program [...]. There was a lot of work. The entire flight meant work."[73] However, the *Chicago Tribune* reported, "There were ground controled automatic devices aboard to guide and operate the spaceship and 'take care of the man himself.'" The Associated Press reported that Gagarin did not even fire the retro-rockets to take him back to Earth.[74] The *Times* (London) speculated "Judging by accounts, Gagarin rode almost as a passenger."[75] The *Atlanta Constitution* reported that of the known details of the flight, "The spaceship was under control of scientists on the ground."[76]

After Gagarin's flight, NASA director James E. Webb snapped, "The first American manned flight will demand greater participation by the pilot than apparently was involved in the Russian flight."[77] The American press pounced on this language, with Pennsylvania's *Tyrone Daily Herald* declaring: "U.S. Astronaut Will Have Partial Control of Capsule."[78] The American flight would be much shorter than Gagarin's. However, the article pointed out, "America's astronaut will be given limited navigational control," while Gagarin's flight "was under control from the ground."[79] Thus, the Americans could still be first in space with pilot control of a spacecraft. The Americans might not actually be trailing but leading through their individuality and mastery over the spacecraft.

Most Americans assumed Glenn would be chosen first to master the spacecraft because he "portrayed the most consciously thought-out image of what an 'Astronaut' should be and how he should behave—both in public and in private—of any of his colleagues." NASA chose Shepard, the trickster, leader, womanizer and mediator as the first American into space. Shepard possessed "the urge to pioneer and to accept a challenge and then try to meet it."[80] The *New York Times* ran the headline: "U.S. Hurls Man 115 Miles into Space; Shepard Works Controls in Capsule, Reports by Radio in 15-Minute Flight." The paper stated that Shepard's flight was much slower than Gagarin's—and even Ham's. However, Shepard's flight completed a world first as "Commander Shepard maneuvered his craft in space—something the Russians have not claimed for Major Gagarin."[81] The article included the mission transcript in which Shepard reported to mission control that he switched from automatic to manual pitch, yaw, and roll during his short flight. Similarly, the *Chicago Tribune* argued that Shepard became America's first man in space "in the world's first pilot controled [*sic*] space ship."[82] The Associated Press followed suit with "Separd's [*sic*] attempt to control his space capsule—even though it was backed up by automatic systems that insured against error—seemed somewhat more than Gagarin's."[83] The *Washington Post* took a different route and suggested that Shepard's suborbital flight could not be compared to the great achievement of the Soviets' orbital flight. However, Shepard's flight proved man could have manual control of a spacecraft in a weightless environment.[84]

Congressman Phil Weaver (R-NE) (Appropriations Committee) commented on Shepard's flight; he took great pains to show the critical issue of control. "Shepard," according to Weaver, "was able to control his capsule from an interior instrument panel whereas the Soviet 'cosmonaut' [*sic*] flight was completely controlled from the ground."[85] Famed aviatrix Jackie Cochran told the press, "He's [Shepard] not just lying there like a banana, there's a lot more control than I ever thought this first one would have."[86] NASA reported to the Associated Press that Shepard "is working like a test pilot reporting facts and procedures. This was something new in space flight. No other human being had ever done it."[87] In his own memoir, Shepard highlighted the fact that the Soviets equipped Gagarin's capsule with manual controls but did not want to risk jeopardizing the mission by allowing Gagarin to use them.[88]

The May 12, 1961, edition of *Life* also accentuated Shepard's control over the capsule. The article stated, "He did not fly as far, fast or high as Russia's Yuri Gagarin. However, he controlled the flight of his capsule—which Gagarin did not—and carried out his fantastic mission under the relentless pressure of television and worldwide publicity." The article continued to argue, "Whereas Cosmonaut Gagarin was apparently a passive passenger in an automatically controlled craft, Shepard's more sophisticated instrument panel with its imposing array of 165 dials, switches, levers, buttons, and colored lights, gave him a degree of protection and control *not* [emphasized in original] provided by Gagarin's."[89]

The article described emphatically Shepard's control over his craft. Not only did the article profess that Shepard controlled the flight, but it also suggested that if the automatic controls failed "*he* [emphasis added] could have readjusted the temperature and oxygen supply inside the cabin—and inside his space suit." The article labored the point that Shepard was in full control of his craft:

> He could have separated the capsule from the rocket and jettisoned the escape tower. He could have fired the retro-rockets and thrown off the leftover rocket pack. He could have opened the drag parachute as well as the main parachute which lowered the capsule gently into the sea— and if that hadn't worked there was a reserve parachute *he* could have sprung. He could and did take over personal control of the pitch, yaw,

and roll of the capsule through the peak of its flight, and could turn it downward for re-entry.[90]

Shepard told his *Life* audience that when the capsule left the atmosphere and entered space, he wanted to see if he could control the craft. At that point, the craft was traveling at around four thousand five hundred miles an hour and was free and weightless in space. "Now using my three-axis control stick, I switched over to manual control, one axis at a time." The most interesting part of his story of controlling the craft is that he managed to do it all within his short fifteen-minute flight. He ended by feminizing Gagarin's flight when he remarked: "Major Gagarin may have had a fine long ride but, as far as we can tell, he was a passenger all the way."[91]

Shepard's control over his emotions was just as important to creating astronaut masculinity as his physical control over the craft. On May 6, 1961, the *Albuquerque Journal* wrote that Shepard found the eleven G-forces "no sweat at all."[92] The *New York Times* proclaimed that during Shepard's flight, "He was probably the most unperturbed member of the crew." Even Shepard's own mother said, "Alan has never feared anything."[93] In *Life*, Shepard stated that as his launch date approached, he "began to feel some small effects of the tension that was growing everywhere around me." Shepard refused to call this "tension" fear. Instead, he maintained, "They aren't real fears; if they were, you'd quit altogether. They are normal apprehensions anyone might have before a big event."[94]

*Life* argued that the "nation caught Shepard's spirit of confidence."[95] No other statement on this confidence was clearer than President Kennedy's bold declaration before Congress and the world a month after the failed Bay of Pigs invasion. Kennedy would not be happy with just one "first." He wanted to go bigger and bolder. On May 25, 1961, before a joint session of Congress, Kennedy openly challenged the Soviets and the American people. In promoting "the freedom doctrine," Kennedy militarized and thus masculinized the American space mission when he argued that the "great battlefield for the defense and expansion of freedom today" was not only Southeast Asia but also in space. He said that in space, "our eagerness to share its meaning is not governed by the efforts of others." The United States must assert its own individuality, its own control, or in other words, masculinity. He boldly stated: "I believe that this nation should commit itself to achieving the goal, before this decade is out, of landing a man on the moon and returning him safely to the earth." He acknowledged that it would be costly but justified such an expensive mission was that:

> If we are to only go halfway, or reduce our sights in the face of difficulty, in my judgment it would be better not to go at all. Now this is a choice

68 GENDER AND THE RACE FOR SPACE

which this country must make [...]. it is a heavy burden, and there is no sense in agreeing or desiring that the United States take an affirmative position in outer space, unless we are prepared to do the work and bear the burdens to make it successful.

Kennedy called upon scientists and engineers to fulfill their duty not just as citizens of the United States but as individuals with the "technical and scientific manpower" to complete the job.[96] Kennedy laid down the challenge. The Americans controlled their own destiny in space. Kennedy asked the astronauts how he could support them. Shepard responded, "Just let us go! We are being protected too much with equipment." The astronauts desired "to be free to explore space with less protection and more initiative and daring."[97]

The theme of astronaut control continued into the less-than-stellar suborbital flight by Gus Grissom. The pilot image remained center stage as the *New York Times* reported of Grissom's feat, "Senators hail flier."[98] As anticipation lingered for the flight, the *New York Times*'s John W. Finney wrote that, "Like Commander Shepard, the astronaut will 'fly' the capsule with manual controls, but he will not be required to perform as many flight maneuvers." Finney grasped the importance of individual astronaut control and explained that in the new manual control system "the astronaut's hand motions are translated into electrical signals."[99] The astronauts pushed buttons to fly. The once disparaged push-button masculinity transferred into self-reliant masculinity with astronauts behind the buttons.

Despite praise for Grissom's piloting abilities, Gus and his wife Betty did not receive the red-carpet Washington DC ticker tape parade that the Shepards enjoyed. NASA held the Grissoms' "low rent" reception on a hot tarmac at Patrick Air Force Base in the Cocoa Beach, Florida summer heat.[100] Grissom received the Distinguished Service Medal from NASA Administrator James Webb, not President Kennedy. Perhaps the pathetic ceremony was due to the blown *Liberty Bell 7 (Mercury-Redstone 4)* hatch that led to the craft sinking in the Indian Ocean. Before the sinking, Grissom blasted the retro-rockets to bring *Liberty Bell* back to Earth. The suborbital flight lasted fifteen minutes and thirty-seven seconds.

The USS *Randolph* deployed a Marine helicopter to pick up Grissom and *Liberty Bell*. The helicopter needed to pull up Grissom's craft in a horse-collar and hook the craft to the chopper. To do this successfully, "the helicopter crewman had to snip off a long recovery radio antenna that had deployed from the cylindrical nose section of the capsule." As the crewman bent down to perform this task, the craft hatch "suddenly blew off." Water rushed into the craft and, thankfully, Grissom mustered the strength to climb out. The water weighed down the craft and became too heavy for the helicopter. The crewman watched the craft sink but did not notice the drowning astronaut. The third chopper, flown by Marine pilot Lieutenant George Cox—the pilot who picked up Shepard and Ham—had the presence of mind to rescue the struggling Grissom. Grissom was livid at the helicopter crew, who appeared to care more for the craft than the man. He was adamant that he did not blow the capsule hatch. The only evidence that Grissom had not blown the hatch was that he lacked bruising from triggering the hatch. More than likely static electricity running through the craft caused by rotor wash blew the hatch seal.[101]

American spaceflight enthusiasm proved short-lived once again with the August 6, 1961, Soviet launch of *Vostok 2*. Major Gherman S. Titov orbited the Earth seventeen times in twenty-five hours. It took Titov approximately eighty-eight minutes to circle the Earth. The craft orbited over four hundred and thirty-five miles, the estimated distance to go to the moon and back. The Soviets claimed that Titov exercised "manual control" but not "to alter his course through space. They (the controls) merely made it possible to change the attitude of the craft—to pitch it up or down, roll it one way or the other, or yaw the nose right or left."[102] These were the same controls used by the astronauts. Cosmonaut Gagarin reiterated pilot control as he flew to congratulate his fellow cosmonaut, "Titov had complete control of his craft and 'could land it anywhere.'"[103] Russian planetarium scientist V. Lutsky insisted, "The importance of this flight lies, among other things, in the fact that Major Titov's flight is a piloted one. This is the first time that a man-controlled flight in space has ever been made."[104] Titov himself exclaimed that he "felt like a real pilot" because while "my space ship was a very smart machine and it was very easy to guide. I could turn it any way I wished. I could steer it any direction needed and I could land it wherever I wanted."[105] Titov announced in *Life*: "I felt myself the complete master of the ship."[106] Cosmonauts wanted the same masculine pilot control as the astronauts despite Soviet propaganda of superior socialist technology that completed work for the man—or woman.

The world praised the technological achievements of the Soviets and expressed concern for the American space program. The director of London's Jodrell Bank radio-astronomy station lamented that the Soviet achievement did not shock him because "In comparison with the Americans, you can guess which country appears to be struggling, and it is certainly not Russia." *Vostok 2* demonstrated "the high state of Soviet science and technology." Similarly, the president of the French Astronautic Society mourned, "I fear the lag can never be made up."[107]

The Pentagon dismissed Titov's flight as: "There is nothing new to this flight from a military standpoint and […] it doesn't add to their military capability."[108] The Soviets, especially the cosmonauts, shot back at the Americans. In an October 1961 speech to the 22nd Congress of the Soviet Union (CPSU),

Titov suggested that the American astronaut goal in space was "a real bour-geois-exploiter," while the cosmonauts were "transformers of nature, dream-ers, and romantics who volunteer to go into space for the sake of its conquest and the good of mankind."[109] Titov essentially compared the astronauts to gluttonous organization men and suggested a lack of pioneering spirit, if not integrity and honor. Undeterred, the American public discourse continued on the path to prove that the United States was the first to have pilot control of a spacecraft.

Lieutenant Colonel John H. Glenn Jr. was the perfect choice for the first American to orbit the Earth. Glenn epitomized the ideal American hero. He was a Marine and had been a national hero since World War II. He exercised masculinity through his combat experience and personified the male protec-tor as a devoted husband and father. He was likable, attractive, a rare breed of pilot who would rather stay at home with his wife and kids than drink and race cars. He drove an NSU Prinz—a small, modest car. He even invoked God and country during the first Mercury 7 press conference. Americans treated him like a saint. He was America personified, or as the *New York Times* wrote, "Courage, modesty, and quiet patriotism, love of family and religious faith are not exactly the predominant themes of our novels, plays, TV shows, movies, or newspapers these days. Yet, Glenn dramatized them all coast to coast and around the world." Americans did not want to lose the man who brought "humanity" and "civilization" to a dangerous spaceflight mission.[110]

After ten nail-biting canceled mission launches, Glenn orbited the Earth aboard *Friendship 7* (*Mercury-Atlas 6*) on February 20, 1962.[111] Glenn flew at approximately seventeen thousand miles an hour for almost four hours and fifty-six minutes. The flight "closed the gap" between the Soviets and Americans. The *Times* ran a cartoon depicting Soviet Premier Nikita Khrushchev's posterior being ramrodded by *Friendship 7*.[112] Man's triumph over technology is emphasized when the automatic control system failed dur-ing the first of three orbits. *Freedom 7* controlled its position by shooting out hydrogen peroxide. The system that performed this function crashed, leaving the craft unable to deorbit automatically.[113] The public discourse emphasized that Glenn felt healthy after four hours in a weightless condition while Titov "experienced disorientation and nausea on his flight."[114] The American pilot won the day, but Soviet Premier Khrushchev shot back, reminding, "The plain people of America" that "the road to the cosmos was paved by Soviet people [...]."[115]

The masculinity pendulum started to swing between both individualism and teamwork, creating an early archetype of Apollo's democratic manhood to describe Glenn's flight. The *New York Times* beamed of the "teamwork" between the seven Mercury astronauts.[116] *Life* reported, "No man at any

# LIGHT THIS CANDLE 71

instant in human history was ever less alone," but rather the orbital flight "was born out of a vast panorama of human and technical effort, of the patience and the skills of tens of thousands [...]."[117] *Time* wrote of the tens of thousands involved in his flight, from scientists and technicians to average Joe factory workers. The numbers needed to send one man into space spoke volumes to the prowess of individual initiative in a team setting, coupled with democratic capitalism.[118]

The astronaut also needed to engage in teamwork with the technology. The editors at *Life* suggested of the sophisticated machine, "It could steer itself, cool itself, land itself, release dye to attract attention to itself. It was a machine designed to operate, ideally, without the intercession of man [...]." However, while the adeptness of the machine is explained, the necessity of man to control the machine, specifically that of democratic manhood, is also adamant in the article: "The singular fact of Friendship 7's three-orbit voyage is that it would have been impossible without the intervention of the man in the capsule and the men on the ground."[119] Glenn acted as part of a team, even with the machine, on which the success of the mission depended.

From *Friendship 7's* automatic control debacle, NASA scientists and engineers learned that even under weightlessness and pressure, the human mind can act skillfully while the machine performs poorly. Glenn expressed his feelings of man versus machine by suggesting, "Now we can get rid of some of that automatic equipment and let man take over."[120] The *New York Times* reported that "Project Mercury officials are now convinced that man should no longer be viewed as primarily a passenger in an automated vehicle, but rather should and can be used as an active pilot in controlling and navigating the spacecraft." Removing some of the automated systems from the capsule would lighten the craft and be more efficient for longer spaceflights that required more fuel.[121]

NASA engineers wrote of Glenn's reaction to the faulty automatic stabilization and control system: "Glenn realized that he would have to live with the problem and become a full time pilot responsible for his own well-being [...]" because of the faulty technology.[122] He would have to act as *Newsweek* described, "an authentic individualist."[123] The Associated Press mocked the failed technology: "But unlike the fragile scientific hardware [...] Glenn is a rugged customer who never faltered once physically or psychologically."[124] Glenn never appeared "unruffled" and exercised "cool courage" as he calmly answered questions from reporters.[125] Carleton J. King (R-NY) asked to insert in the House of Representatives *Daily Record* the "Tribute to a Hero" by P.C.C. Becker. Becker wrote of the flight: "Colonel Glenn personifies the best in American manhood."[126] Glenn himself was humbled, saying, "There is nothing superhuman, however, about being an astronaut."[127] The American astronaut demonstrated masculinity in his humble character, courage, piloting skill over faulty hardware and his teamwork ability.

A perfected body was also needed with courageous piloting skills and teamwork. Despite the fact that Deke Slayton flew fifty-six combat missions during World War II in B-25 bombers, he missed his chance to go into space during Project Mercury.[128] In July 1962, flight surgeons deemed him unable to fly after they discovered he had an "erratic heart rate."[129] Slayton went on to have a brilliant career as the head of the astronaut office—exercising masculine individuality in deciding which astronauts flew missions.

NASA replaced Slayton with Scott Carpenter. Carpenter was a Navy Test Pilot School graduate, but he was the most "introspective" and most "self-conscious" about his flying. He only had three hundred hours flying jets because he spent most of his career in Hawaii flying multiengine, P2V patrol planes.[130] The reality that Carpenter was not the Tom Wolfe "right stuff" jet test pilot made no matter to the American public, if they knew or cared at all. He possessed masculinity simply by putting on the astronaut suit.

The public discourse depicted Carpenter's flight with the same independent, self-reliant man narrative. On May 24, 1962, Carpenter flew in *Aurora 7* (*Mercury-Atlas 7*) aboard the Atlas rocket. Before his flight, *Life* presented Carpenter to the public as a wanderlust pioneer, hunting, climbing and exploring. The article depicted Carpenter as very much an individual, left alone for most of his childhood because of his mother's illness. Other than his grandfather, his only companion was a horse named "lady."[131] The article's use of the words "independence" and "freedom" situated Carpenter's isolated childhood alongside both the self-reliant pioneer and Mercury astronauts left alone to control their flights.

Carpenter's memoir in *Life* carefully constructed his control over the spacecraft. Carpenter reminisced, "I turned the capsule around so that the blunt end would be headed along the right track I would follow. On this maneuver I used the manual control system and it worked perfectly. I then checked out the system thoroughly and found that the capsule responded beautifully to my movements on the stick." He emphasized his control over the automated systems. Carpenter praised the pioneering mission of Glenn before him, which he argued "showed that a man can handle the machine under very difficult conditions [...]."[132]

Several of Carpenter's automatic control systems failed during his flight, and his craft used up all its maneuvering fuel. This was partly due to his stabilization system not holding the correct pitch, yaw and attitude. Carpenter was also at fault. Carpenter acted as an individualist in space, not following the flight sequence and thus made an error in the flight. He demonstrated—what engineers knew all along—that man could be a liability. Carpenter rushed

LIGHT THIS CANDLE

to go back to the flight sequence after his daydreaming left both the fly-by-wire control mode and manual system running simultaneously. He used too much fuel for about ten minutes and lost contact with mission control.[133] The Associated Press reported, "Carpenter's craft, struck dumb at the 12:30 p.m. reentry, never again regained its voice."[134]

Carpenter took over the controls. He wrote in *Life*, "If we started the re-entry at the wrong angle and the fuel was exhausted, I would be unable to control the craft during the descent. The chances that I would survive such an uncontrolled re-entry were not good."[135] The situation continued to get worse as he had not aligned the spacecraft correctly for retrofire. Due to a glitch in the control system, Carpenter manually pushed the button to fire his solid-fuel retro-rockets that were strapped to his heat shield. Because Carpenter's craft was not at the correct attitude, he overshot the landing. However, officials at NASA suggested that even if he had allowed the computer to fire the retro-rockets, the craft would have overshot its landing even further.[136] Pilot control was key to his survival.

Carpenter's autonomous actions aboard his flight enraged flight director, Christopher Columbus Kraft Jr. The flight director scolded Carpenter for not following the flight plan and the directions of the ground crew. This raised questions of who really controlled the flight: Carpenter or Kraft. Back on the ground, the two men's disagreement infuriated Voas. Carpenter's flight supported the need for human control and acted as a great "public relations feature that the man had performed and brought back a damaged craft, or a partially nonfunctioning spacecraft."[137] Voas understood the assignment of creating a new Cold War warrior in space and that this warrior needed independence and grit.

The tension between spaceflight control, astronauts and mission controllers played out within the press. Some within the Associated Press took Kraft's side and warned, "There is no individual effort of darting men off on their own and taking chances in a competitive spirit. The conquest of space must remain a piece of teamwork under rigid control."[138] The *New York Times* praised Carpenter. However, one article emphasized the control of Kraft, the "slightly built Virginian [...] calls the plays." Even though Kraft is of "slight build" and "reticent off the job," he is a "take-charge guy" who "can crack the whip when he has to."[139] The realities of necessary teamwork behind masculine control offered the public a different masculine archetype of democratic manhood, a masculine image exercised by any man no matter the size. The image offered masculinity not as fixed but on a spectrum.

While Americans struggled with defining masculinity, the Soviets followed Carpenter on August 11, 1962, with the launch of Major Andrian G. Nikolayev aboard *Vostok 3*. Nikolayev orbited the Earth seventeen times in twenty-five hours and eighteen minutes at a speed of eighteen thousand miles per hour. He broke the previously held record by Titov. The purpose of the flight was to test cosmonaut "communications, control, and landing." The cosmonaut slept for a total of seven hours while "instruments on board his spaceship was [sic] carried out automatically."[140] The Associated Press reported that the television image transmitted from his capsule showed "his hands moved to work the controls."[141] The Soviet news agency, TASS, underscored the "Iron Endurance" of Nikolayev.[142] The *Times* lamented that Glenn and Carpenter only completed three orbits of the Earth.

The Soviets struck again. On August 12, 1962, the Soviets launched cosmonaut Lieutenant Colonel Pavel Popovich aboard *Vostok 4* to orbit the Earth. Both craft weighed about eight and a half tons, about six tons more than the American craft.[143] The *Times* wrote that Popovich operated his craft "manually."[144] TASS reported that the cosmonauts "flew" the craft and "controlled the ships manually and effected the necessary measurements, recording the results in their flight logs."[145] Through the porthole of his craft, Nikolayev said he could see his fellow cosmonaut in orbit.[146]

The public discourse refused to let reports of cosmonaut control stifle American pilot control over a spacecraft. Wally Schirra—the "unrelenting competitor"—flew next. Schirra grasped that systems engineering was the future of piloting. He embraced these new machines but never lost the confidence and the end goal that the pilot and systems engineer was "to master this thing."[147] NASA shot Schirra into space on October 3, 1962 aboard *Sigma 7* (*Mercury-Atlas 8*). Headlines hailed his flight as "Proving Pilots' Space Role."[148] His flight lasted just over nine hours, completing six orbits. Schirra said he turned off the automated sequence ten minutes and thirty seconds after liftoff and "the capsule was all mine now."[149] The *Chicago Tribune* claimed Schirra demonstrated "precision control of the orbital flight." Schirra himself even boldly declared that nobody had "flown a capsule before, much less under pilot control." He reminisced on his days as a test pilot as he argued, "My instincts as a test pilot told me that *Sigma 7* would not fail—not unless somebody, including me, goofed."[150]

Schirra daringly cut off the automatic sequences of the ground stations to control his retrofire and bring him down. He insisted that he had "full pilot control."[151] Schirra claimed that "the controls worked beautifully." He continued, "The control system was so sweet that it responded perfectly with just a few light touches on either axis. I could point it at anything I wanted to, and I could have parked it on a dime if I had to. We have to control technique; that's for sure."[152]

*Life*'s article on Schirra once again presented this image of the astronaut as free from fear, suggesting that before the flight, Schirra did not have any

LIGHT THIS CANDLE

butterflies in his stomach. Schirra, the article proposed, hoped to perfect the machine (the craft) to make it safer for the astronauts who followed in his footsteps. Therefore, he approached flying in space as a "professional test pilot." And yet, paradoxically, the article argued that it was the "marvelously" named Christopher Columbus Kraft Jr. who "controls the destiny of astronaut flights from the moment of lift-off to impact in the landing area."[153] Unlike Schirra's story of a lone individual in space controlling his machine, *Life*'s article argued that Kraft ultimately controlled Schirra.

On May 15, 1963, Major Gordon Cooper flew for thirty-four hours aboard *Faith 7 (Mercury-Atlas 9)*. His flight was the last for the Mercury Program. The *Life* article on the spaceman's feat, "He Brings it in Right on the Old Bazoo," implied that, "In the beginning machinery stole the show."[154] *Newsweek* described Cooper's 1963 flight: "Once more, the ancient drama of the solitary individual against the elements was re-enacted."[155] The *New York Times* headlines hailed "Cooper Maneuvers to a Bullseye Landing with Manual Control as Automatic Fails." During his twenty-two orbits of the Earth, on the nineteenth circuit, his automatic system that lined up the capsule to fire the retro-rockets upon reentry failed. After the failure, Cooper performed this task of the automatic controls by himself.

Cooper experienced firsthand man's mastery over technology. The *New York Times'* Richard Witkin wrote that "the astronaut guided himself to safety by manually controlling his capsule when his automatic controls failed."[156] Cooper remembered that after his twenty-first orbit he was certain that the automatic power system would not come back on and that "the positioning of the spacecraft for retro-fire and running the whole rough ride back from space was going to be up to me." While he envisioned ground control sweating bullets, Cooper insisted that "all of us in the Mercury program have felt that pilots are capable of flying the spacecraft through the complete re-entry sequence."[157] After six hundred thousand miles and thirty-four hours "Gordo Cooper made it—on his own." Situated as the astronaut capsule communicator or (Capcom), Glenn radioed asking for his attitude. "Right on the old bazoo," roared Cooper, as he "steered his capsule through the critical re-entry."[158]

Teamwork once again entered the narrative. When Cooper's .05G panel light came on, the pilot did not take over but rather engineers at Cape Canaveral alerted the astronaut to his next moves. Flight director Kraft ordered Cooper to turn on his automatic controls. Ground control soon discovered that "Cooper would have to steer his ship manually."[159] The craft's inverters that supplied AC electrical support for entry also did not work. This meant that Cooper did not have the aid of the automated systems during reentry. The article reported, "He would have to pilot his spacecraft back from orbit by human skill alone—and keep it from tumbling and burning up."[160]

The operations director for Project Mercury, Walter C. Williams, summed up the importance of Cooper's flight when he said, "It demonstrated more than ever the importance of man in space-flight as a pilot, not as a passenger."[161] Famed physicist and astronomer, Sir Bernard Lovell, argued that machinery could not demonstrate the capabilities of man. In effect, "the machines cannot make on-the-spot judgments; neither can it discriminate and select from alternatives which cannot be anticipated by its designers. *The ability to adapt to the unexpected situation or discovery is a vital factor in exploration.*" [italics in original][162] According to NASA engineers, the most important lesson that the agency learned from Project Mercury "was that man was still invaluable to the machine. Mercury saw the evolution of the astronaut from little more than a passenger in a fully automatic system to an integral and fully integrated element in the entire space flight organism."[163]

Astronaut Carpenter remained optimistic about the pilot's role. In April 1963, before a Dallas crowd at the AIAA Manned Space Flight meeting, Carpenter stressed that man would continue to play an important role in the future of spaceflight. "Although we will be aided and backed by the same flight operations team that has made our Mercury flights so successful," Carpenter professed, "pilot decision is going to play a large part in the spaceflight missions of the future."[164]

Despite the continued American narrative of pilot control, the Soviet Union constantly ridiculed American machinery and control during public media events. On April 12, 1963, Cosmonaut Nikolayev announced that after viewing Schirra's capsule,

> To be frank [...] I would not like to have been in his place. You have no idea how cramped and uncomfortable his capsule looks in comparison with the cabins of our remarkable cosmic ships [...]. One looks at this unreliable American contraption and one is again forced to feel proud of our country and our people, who have created such powerful and perfect cosmic ships.

Cosmonaut Valery Bykovsky followed Nikolayev, brazenly mocking what was once the pride of American ingenuity. When an audience member asked Bykovsky if the American cosmonauts could have "left their couches while in orbit," he teased: "They would have liked to do so but their cabins were not large enough. They are all strong and courageous fellows, but they are not to be envied. There is no question of comfort in their cabins [...]." During a radio show that same day, Cosmonaut Titov told his audience that he was once asked who was braver, the American or Soviet cosmonauts. Titov and his fellow cosmonauts replied "that the Americans were braver because they had to fly in a rocket that goes one time and blows up another."[165] The cosmonauts acknowledged the supremacy of Soviet technology or at least that the technology over the man remained the state-mandated important factor. Titov's colleagues expressed the same sentiment of the technology over the man.

Soviet Major General Kamanin told an East German crowd that an interviewer once asked if the cosmonauts would fly in an American spacecraft. The cosmonauts all answered: "Why should we change from our miracle ships, the *Vostoks*, to such small, primitive, and unreliable capsules?"[166] Despite foreign and at times domestic mockery, Americans celebrated the fact that as space machinery faltered, the American astronaut exercised masculinity as he took over the controls and tamed the technology. Exercising individuality and control became an essential element to the astronaut gender and American space race narrative.

## Conclusion

Americans touted the individuality of the X-Plane series. But the reality behind these great X-planes was that they were not enough for an adventure story that would carry Americans into the far reaches of space. The X-15 timeline lagged behind what the Soviets were doing in space with rocketry, satellites, dogs and humans. To catch up, Americans needed more systems engineering and automatic controls to traverse the vast two hundred and thirty thousand miles to the moon and back. Sharing control with automatic systems and button-pushing was at odds with masculinity, but that did not need to be the public narrative that captured the hearts and minds of Americans as the price for space climbed. Despite spaceflight segueing to a civilian organization run by teams of scientists, engineers and technicians, Americans reimagined spaceflight as a beacon of astronaut control over the craft.

The public discourse surrounding the six Mercury flights represented the importance of the Cold War masculine astronaut image. It can be argued whether the astronauts controlled their craft. However, in the public discourse surrounding the flights, the purpose of spaceflight was clear. Human control, and being "first" with it, was clearly important to the domestic and international image of NASA. Thus, who could fly was of central importance. The flier could not be just anyone. He had to be someone who exemplified the best virtues of technological control and protection in the dangerous battle for space. Men possessed individuality, control and protection. In emphasizing the individualism and control of the space flier, Americans gendered manned spaceflight as a masculine sphere. Americans continued the spaceflight control dialogue into Projects Gemini and Apollo. As Americans basked in the glow of the astronaut as a symbol of American superiority, questions pertaining to the role of women in space thrived in the press. Beginning in 1959, women challenged NASA, suggesting that they too were fit for spaceflight. Women tested not only the boundaries of gender and power, citizenship and military service, but also the astronaut image.

## Notes

1 Alan Barlett Shepard Jr. and Deke Slayton, with Jay Barbree and Howard Benedict, *Moon Shot: The Inside Story of America's Race to the Moon* (New York: Turner Publishing, 1994), 118.
2 Hankins, *Flying Camelot*, 3–6.
3 Wernher von Braun, "Man on the Moon: The Journey," *Colliers*, October 18, 1952, 52. See also David J. Shayler and Colin Burgess, *NASA's Scientist-Astronauts* (New York: Springer-Praxis, 2006), 1.
4 U.S. Congress, Senate, *Hearings before the Special Committee on Space and Astronautics*, H.R. 1181, 85th Cong., 2d sess., 1958, 13.
5 Atkinson Jr., and Shafritz, *The Real Stuff*, 31.
6 Dr. Robert B. Voas interview by Summer Chick Bergen, NASA Headquarters History Office, Johnson Space Center, May 19, 2002, 14, accessed October 21, 2023, https://historycollection.jsc.nasa.gov/JSCHistoryPortal/history/oral_histories/VoasRB/VoasRB_5-19-02.pdf.
7 Swenson, Jr., Grimwood, and Alexander, *This New Ocean*, 130.
8 Hersch, *Inventing the American Astronaut*, 13–15.
9 Swenson, Jr., Grimwood, and Alexander, *This New Ocean*, 131. Atkinson Jr., and Shafritz, *The Real Stuff*, 35.
10 Weitekamp, *Right Stuff, Wrong Sex*, 3, 121.
11 Atkinson Jr., and Shafritz, *The Real Stuff*, 35–36. In an oral interview conducted by Atkinson and Shafritz of Dr. T. Keith Glennan, the authors suggest that Eisenhower wished for the first group of astronauts to be picked from military test pilots. They quote Eisenhower as saying, "Of course you should use service test pilots. They are in the service to do as the service requires of them at various times. They ought to have a chance to volunteer if they wish."
12 Since both Crossfield and Walker flew into space in the X-15, they were astronauts.
13 Wolfe, *The Right Stuff*, 63–64.
14 Atkinson Jr., and Shafritz, *The Real Stuff*, 39–40 and Hersch, *Inventing the American Astronaut*, 19.
15 Hersch, *Inventing the American Astronaut*, 15–16. See also George M. Low, "Memorandum to T. Keith Glennan Re: Pilot Selection for Project Mercury," April 23, 1959, Folder 16404, NASA Historical Reference Collection, NASA Headquarters, Washington, DC.
16 Atkinson, Jr., and Shafritz, *The Real Stuff*, 35. See also Shayler and Burgess, *NASA's Scientist-Astronauts*, 12. To note, the first group of Soviet astronauts was picked on February 20, 1960. It should be noted that in regard to qualifications to become an

# LIGHT THIS CANDLE

astronaut, the Soviets' requirements were lower than those of the United States. The Soviet program did not require that this flying time be in a jet aircraft. After medical testing disqualified candidates, the Soviets relaxed the requirement of weight (70 kg), height (170 cm) and age, less than 30 years old, due to a significant lack of candidates. While this brought older, more experienced pilots into the Soviets' first class of cosmonauts, the candidates still lacked the jet test qualifications of the American astronauts. David J. Shayler and Colin Burgess argue that the lack of qualified jet pilots in the Soviet Union was due to their proclivity toward "automated systems" of rocketry. Not only were the Americans able to have higher standards, but this American idea of the individual man controlling technology can be seen as compared to the human machine, the automated systems and the Soviet Union.

17 M. Scott Carpenter et al., *We Seven* (New York: Simon and Schuster, 1962; January 2010 edition), 25–26.

18 Wolfe, *The Right Stuff*, 158.

19 Voas, interview, 2–3.

20 Faludi, *Stiffed*, 455.

21 Voas, interview, 3, 8.

22 Voas, interview, 12.

23 Atkinson Jr. and Jay Shafritz, *The Real Stuff*, 29.

24 Michael Collins, *Carrying the Fire: An Astronaut's Journeys* with a foreword by Charles A. Lindbergh (New York: Farrar, Straus, and Giroux, 1975, 4th edition 2009), 14. See also, Hersch, *Inventing the American Astronaut*, 11.

25 Jerome B. Hammock, et. al., "NASA Project Mercury Working Paper No. 192: Postlaunch Report for Mercury-Redston-3 (MR-3), June 16, 1961," NASA Johnson Space Center Historical Collection, 5, accessed June 20, 2023, https://historycollection.jsc.nasa.gov/JSCHistoryPortal/history/mission_trans/MR03_TEC.PDF.

26 Atkinson Jr., and Shafritz, *The Real Stuff*, 39–40 and Hersch, *Inventing the American Astronaut*, 19.

27 "NASA Release No. 59–113: Mercury Astronaut Selection Factsheet, April 9, 1959," The Ohio State University, 1–4, accessed October 22, 2023, https://library.osu.edu/site/friendship7/files/2017/06/SelectionFactSheet.pdf. See also, Wolfe, *The Right Stuff*, 75–76. For an in-depth look at the experiments, see Ch. 4 "The Lab Rats," 65 through 89. See also Hersch, *Inventing the American Astronaut*, 22.

28 George E. Ruff and Edwin Z. Levy, "Psychiatric Evaluation of Candidates for Space Flight," *American Journal of Psychiatry* 116 (1959): 385–391, 385.

29 "NASA Press Release No. 59–113," 4, 8.

30 Wolfe, *The Right Stuff*, 78, 87.

31 Voas, interview, 24.

32 Carpenter et al., *We Seven*, 54.

33 "NASA Press Release No. 59–113," 4.

34 Ruff and Levy, "Psychiatric Evaluation of Candidates for Space Flight," 385.

35 Ruff and Levy, "Psychiatric Evaluation of Candidates for Space Flight," 385, 389.

36 Carpenter et al., *We Seven*, 58.

37 Ruff and Levy, "Psychiatric Evaluation of Candidates for Space Flight," 385, and Hersch, *Inventing the American Astronaut*, 22.

38 "Press Conference, Mercury Astronaut Team, April 9, 1959," NASA Historical Reference Collection, 1–34, 23, accessed October 22, 2023, https://history.nasa.gov/40thmerc7/presscon.pdf.

80 GENDER AND THE RACE FOR SPACE

39 Ruff and Levy, "Psychiatric Evaluation of Candidates for Space Flight," 389.

40 Gladwin Hill, "Test Pilots Get Some Good News; Group is Assured Machines Won't Supplant Humans on Probes in Space," *New York Times*, October 9, 1959, 12. See also, Mindell, *Digital Apollo*, 80–81.

41 "How Seven Were Chosen," *Newsweek*, April 20, 1959, 64. See also, Faludi, *Stiffed*, 454.

42 Wolfe, *The Right Stuff*, 124–125. It should also be noted that Schirra and Shepard spent a year preparing their studies before entrance into the Naval Academy. Schirra spent a year at the Newark College of Engineering, and Shepard studied at Admiral Farragut Academy in New Jersey. See Carpenter, et al., *We Seven*, 59, 64.

43 Colin Burgess, *Selecting the Mercury Seven: The Search for America's First Astronauts* (New York: Springer-Praxis, 2011), 337.

44 Carpenter et al., *We Seven*, 58–61.

45 Neal Thompson, *Light This Candle: The Life and Times of Alan Shepard, America's First Spaceman* (New York: Crown Publishers, 2004), 84–87. See also, Wolfe, *The Right Stuff*, 100.

46 Carpenter et al., *We Seven*, 31–32, 103.

47 Collins, *Carrying the Fire*, 25.

48 Carpenter et al., *We Seven*, 44.

49 Everett B. Irwin, "Reds Can Beat Us To The Moon," *Hopewell News* (Hopewell, Virginia), April 13, 1959, 4.

50 "Rendezvous with Destiny," *Time*, April 20, 1959, 17.

51 Swenson Jr., Grimwood, and Alexander, *This New* Ocean, 235.

52 Carpenter et al., *We Seven*, 6–7, 26–43, 10, 18–20.

53 "The Astronauts—Ready to Make History," *Life*, September 14, 1959, 26.

54 "The Astronauts—Ready to Make History," 6–7, 27, 102.

55 The Astronauts—Ready to Make History," 69–72, 77, 90–91, 80, 89, 91, 93.

56 Wolfe, *The Right Stuff*, 64 and Swenson Jr., Grimwood, and Alexander, *This New Ocean*, 131.

57 Wolfe, *The Right Stuff*, 125–127.

58 "The Astronauts—Ready to Make History," 33, 26.

59 Kauffman, *Selling Outer Space*, 62.

60 "The Astronauts—Ready to Make History," 39.

61 Carpenter et al., *We Seven*, 76.

62 Voas, interview, 5, 10, 11, 19, 43. Pigs were used first because their skin closely resembled that of human skin, and NASA strapped pigs into the Mercury craft and dropped from the sky to test the damage to their skin. See, Voas, interview, 9 and Gerard De Groot, *Dark Side of the Moon: The Magnificent Madness of the American Lunar Quest* (London: Vintage Books, 2007), 130.

63 Richard Witkin, "Space Chimpanzee is Safe After Soaring 420 Miles," *New York Times*, February 1, 1961, 1, 17; "Chimp Ready to Blaze Trail in Space for U.S. Astronauts; Hope of Manned Flight this Year Tied to Test," *Spokesman Review* (Spokane, Washington), January 28, 1961, 5; "Chimp Boosted 550 Miles Aloft In Test for Man-in-Space Try; Capsule Spotted on Bahama Isle After Fifteen Minutes," *Santa Maria Times* (Santa Maria, California) January 31, 1961, 1.

64 "Chimp Ready to Blaze Trail," 5.

65 "Chimp Found ok After Space Hop," *Los Angeles Mirror*, February 3, 1961, 5. See also, De Groot, *Dark Side of the Moon*, 131–132.

## LIGHT THIS CANDLE

81

66 "May Launch One Tuesday; Six Chimps Undergoing Last Tests Before Blazing Trail Into Space," *Journal and Courier* (Lafayette, Indiana) January 28, 1961, 1.

67 The Associated Press, "Pioneer's Story of Space!" *Chicago Tribune*, April 13, 1961, 1, 2.

68 The Associated Press, "Soviet Lands Man After Orbit of World; K [Khrushchev] Challenges West to Duplicate Feat," *Washington Post*, April 13, 1961, 2.

69 Hugh Sidey, "How the News Hit Washington—With Some Reactions Overseas," *Life*, April 21, 1961, 27.

70 Harry Schwartz, "Moscow: Flight is Taken as Another Sign that Communism is the Conquering Wave," *New York Times*, April 16, 1961, 171. See also, De Groot, *Dark Side of the Moon*, 133.

71 President John F. Kennedy, "Address Before the American Society of Newspaper Editors, April 20, 1961," John F. Kennedy Library, accessed August 17, 2021, https://www.jfklibrary.org/archives/other-resources/john-f-kennedy-speeches/american-society-of-newspaper-editors-19610420.

72 Osgood Carruthers, "Pilot Could Fire Braking Rockets," *New York Times*, April 13, 1961, 14.

73 The Associated Press, "Red Describes Eerie Space Flight," *Hammond Times* (Hammond, Indiana), April 13, 1961, 1.

74 The Associated Press, "Pioneer's Story of Space!" 2.

75 "America Puts on a Brave Face: President's Congratulations on 'Outstanding' Feat," *Times* (London, United Kingdom), April 13, 1961, 12.

76 Henry Shapiro, "Russia Cheers Its Cosmonaut," *Atlanta Constitution*, April 13, 1961, 8.

77 Phillip Dodd, "Behind in Space Race: Kennedy Denies Weakness in Struggle on Ideology," *Chicago Tribune*, April 13, 1961, 3.

78 Alvin Webb, Jr., "U.S. Astronaut Will Have Partial Control of Capsule," *Tyrone Daily Herald* (Tyrone, Pennsylvania), May 1, 1961, 1.

79 Dodd, "Behind in Space Race," 3.

80 Carpenter et al., *We Seven*, 13–14, 66.

81 Richard Witkin, "U.S. Hurls Man 115 Miles into Space; Shepard Works Controls in Capsule, Reports By Radio in 15-Minute Flight; In Fine Condition Astronaut Drops into the Sea Four Miles from Carrier; Astronaut Sends Data from Craft; Shepard's Condition is Fine After 15-Minute Trip from Cape Canaveral," *New York Times*, May 6, 1961, 1.

82 Phillip Dodd, "To Space—And Back!" *Chicago Tribune*, May 6, 1961, 1.

83 The Associated Press, "Hero's Welcome Awaits Astronaut Shepard as U.S. Charts Plans to Put Spaceman in Orbit," *Reno Gazette Journal*, May 6, 1961, 1.

84 John G. Norris, "Flight Proves Man Can Control Space Ship Outside Gravity Pull," *Washington Post*, May 6, 1961, 1.

85 Congressman Phil Weaver, May 14, 1961, "White House Central Files-Subject Files," Box 652, Folder 84, "Outer space, January 18, 1961–January 25, 1962," John F. Kennedy Presidential Library and Museum, Boston, MA.

86 Joy Reese Shaw, "Even Newspaperman Weeps as Redstone Takes To Air," *Miami Herald*, May 6, 1961, 82.

87 The Associated Press, "Shepard Pilot's Capsule on Sky Flight; U.S. Astronaut Reaches Height of 115 Miles; Spaceman Termed in Good Condition After Historic Hop," *Albuquerque Journal*, May 6, 1961, 1A, 7A.

88 Shepard Jr. and Slayton, with Barbree and Benedict, *Moon Shot*, 119.

89 "Emotions of the Nation Ride in Astronaut's Capsule, So … Shepard and U.S.A. Feel 'AOK'," *Life*, May 12, 1961, 19, 22.

90 "Emotions of the Nation Ride in Astronaut's Capsule," 22–23.

91 Alan Shepard Jr., "The Astronaut's Story of the Thrust into Space: Personal Account: 'Butterflies, a Feeling of Go, They're Yelling for Me'," *Life*, May 19, 1961, 28. The article found it prudent to write that Shepard fulfilled his mission without a breakfast containing "coffee or other stimulant."

92 The Associated Press, "Nation Lauds Courage of Spaceman Shepard," *Albuquerque Journal*, May 6, 1961, 7A.

93 Richard Witkin, "Shepard had Periscope: 'What a Beautiful View'; 'What a Beautiful View,' Shepard Exclaims from Capsule at 115 Miles in Space; Astronaut Calm During his Flight; Reports Data Methodically to Center at Canaveral—Ground Crews Cheer," *New York Times*, May 6, 1961, 10.

94 Shepard Jr., "The Astronaut's Story," 26. See also Shepard Jr., Slayton, Barbree and Benedict, *Moonshot*, 103.

95 "Emotions of the Nation Ride in Astronaut's Capsule," *Life*, 19–20.

96 President John F. Kennedy, "Special Message to the Congress on Urgent National Needs, May 25, 1961," The John F. Kennedy Presidential Library and Museum, accessed October 24, 2023, https://www.jfklibrary.org/archives/other-resources/john-f-kennedy-speeches/united-states-congress-special-message-19610525.

97 Kennedy, "Special Message to the Congress."

98 "Capital Calls Flight a Good Omen," *New York Times*, July 22, 1961, 9.

99 John W. Finney, "2 Astronauts Put on Diet for Flight; Grissom Believed Choice for Space Shot this Week," *New York Times*, July 16, 1961, 36.

100 Wolfe, *The Right Stuff*, 246.

101 Michael Neufeld, "The Sinking of *Liberty Bell 7:* Gus Grissom's Near Fatal Mission," The National Air and Space Museum, July 21, 2021, accessed October 25, 2023, https://airandspace.si.edu/stories/editorial/sinking-liberty-bell-7-gus-grissoms-near-fatal-mission. See also, Carpenter et al., *We Seven*, 227.

102 Seymour Topping, "Soviet Astronaut Down Safely After Orbiting Earth 17 Times; Exercised, Ate, and Slept Aloft," *New York Times*, August 7, 1961, 1; See also, Preston Grover, "Soviet Astronaut Still Up; Khrushchev Says Quite a Number of Orbits Slated," *Lake Charles American Press* (Lake Charles, Louisiana), August 12, 1962, 1 and Theodore Shabad, "Russians Acclaim Astronaut After Flight of 435,000 Miles," *New York Times*, August 8, 1961, 1, 12, 6. Shabad suggests on page 12 that Titov took over the controls twice.

103 The United Press International, "Gagarin Flies Home to Moscow After Learning of Soviet Shot," *New York Times*, August 6, 1961, 6.

104 The Associated Press, "White House in a Message to Soviet Union Expresses Hope for a Space Accord; Soviet Shot Viewed by World As a Big Advance in Space Race," *New York Times*, August 7, 1961, 6.

105 Theodore Shabad, "Titov Describes His Space Flight," *New York Times*, August 9, 1961, 5.

106 "Titov's Triumph in 17 Orbits," *Life*, August 18, 1961, 42.

107 The Associated Press, "White House in a Message to Soviet Union," 6.

108 John W. Finney, "Pentagon Shrugs at Titov's Flight," *New York Times*, August 8, 1961, 1.

# LIGHT THIS CANDLE

109 United States, Senate, Committee on Aeronautical and Space Sciences, *Soviet Space Programs, 1962–1965; Goals and Purposes, Achievements, Plans, and International Implications*, 89th Cong., 2d sess., 1966 (Washington, DC: U.S. Government Printing Office, 1966), 48.

110 James Reston, "Cape Canaveral; Is the Moon Really Worth John Glenn?" *New York Times*, February 25, 1962, 127.

111 Amy Shira Teitel, *Fighting for Space: Two Pilots and their Historic Battle for Female Spaceflight* (New York: Grand Central Publishing, 2020), 279–280.

112 "Opinion of the Week: At Home and Abroad; Major Topics: The John Glenn Flight," *New York Times*, February 25, 1962, 128.

113 Paul Mandel, "The Ominous Failures that Haunted Friendship's Flight," *Life*, March 2, 1962, 39.

114 John W. Finney, "Glenn's Condition Good," *New York Times*, February 22, 1962, 1, 12.

115 "Pravda Hails Glenn for 'Great Courage,'" *New York Times*, February 23, 1962, 12.

116 "Premier Mission Pilot Prepares," *New York Times*, December 10, 1961, 156, 326.

117 "He Hit the Keyhole in the Sky," *Life*, March 2, 1962, 20–27, 20, 21.

118 "Five Key Groundlings," *Time*, March 2, 1962, 15.

119 Mandel, "The Ominous Failures," 39.

120 Mandel, "The Ominous Failures," 39.

121 John W. Finney, "Glenn feels Pilot Can Replace Much of Spaceship Automation; Glenn Enhances Astronaut Role," *New York Times*, February 23, 1962, 12.

122 Swenson Jr., Grimwood, and Alexander, *This New Ocean*, 429. See also, Mindell, *Digital Apollo*, 81.

123 "Spaceman Ordeal," *Newsweek*, February 5, 1962, 18; See also, Kauffman, *Selling Outer Space*, 57.

124 The Associated Press, "John Glenn Tried to Keep Himself, Family in Background of Mission," *Danville Register* (Danville, Virginia), February 22, 1962, 3.

125 Ben Price, "'Moment of Doubt' Reported by Glenn," *Abilene Reporter-News*, February 24, 1962, 1.

126 Charleton J. King, House of Representatives, April 16, 1962, 87th Cong., 2d sess., *Cong. Rec.* 108, pt15: 6118.

127 Carpenter et al. *We Seven*, 27.

128 Carpenter et al. *We Seven*, 68.

129 Swenson Jr., Grimwood, and Alexander, *This New Ocean*, 440–442. See also, The Associated Press, "Deke Won't Be Making Solo Flight," *Tucson Daily Citizen*, July 12, 1962, 36.

130 Carpenter et al., *We Seven*, 44.

131 Loudon Wainwright, "From a Mountain Boyhood Full of Roaming and Recklessness Comes a Quiet Man to Ride Aurora 7," *Life*, May 18, 1962, 30, 32, 33.

132 Wainwright, "From a Mountain Boyhood," 32–33.

133 Swenson Jr., Grimwood, and Alexander, *This New Ocean*, 453.

134 The Associated Press, "The Carpenter Drama: 3 Orbits, Overshoot, Disappearance Reveal New Dangers, Solutions, Vistas," *Fitchburg Sentinel* (Fitchburg, Massachusetts), May 25, 1962, 1.

135 Scott Carpenter, "A Sensitive Man's Exhilaration on a Rugged Ride: 'I Got Let in On the Great Secret'," *Life*, June 8, 1962, 30.

136 Swenson Jr., Grimwood, and Alexander, *This New Ocean*, 454.

137 Mindell, *Digital Apollo*, 81.

138 The Associated Press, "Another Chapter Written," *Kingsport Times-News* (Kingsport, Tennessee), 27 May 1962, 1, 4B. See also Richard Witkin, "Error by Carpenter Made Craft Use too Much Fuel; He Used Two Systems During Last Phase of Flight—Officials are Considering Seven Orbits for Next Astronaut," *New York Times*, May 27, 1962, 1, 44.

139 The Associated Press, "Mercury Flight Chief, Christopher Columbus Kraft Jr.," *New York Times*, May 26, 1962, 8.

140 Seymour Topping, "Third Russian Orbiting the Earth in Flight Expected to Set Record; Soviet Watches Him on TV Screen; He Sleeps 7 Hours; 'Feel Fine,' Astronaut Informs Khrushchev in Talk by Radio; Third Soviet Astronaut is Launched into Orbital Flight Expected to Outlasts Titov; Fliers TV Report Says He is Well; Khrushchev Praises Pilot as They Chat by Radio on 4th Trip Around Earth," *New York Times*, August 12, 1962, 1, 24.

141 Preston Grover, The Associated Press, "Russ Orbit Spaceman No. 3, 'Might Stay Up for a Week'; K. Airs Shot, Asks: No A-Test Please," *Salt Lake Tribune*, August 13, 1962, 1, 11, 11.

142 Topping, "Third Russian Orbiting," 24; See also, "Astronaut is Former Lumberjack," *New York Times*, August 12, 1962, 24.

143 The Associated Press, "Soviets Hail Space Hero," *Logansport Press* (Logansport, Indiana), August 16, 1962, 1.

144 Seymour Topping, "Soviet Pilots Spin On in Orbit; One has Flown Million Miles; He is Tired but Still Efficient; Astronauts Busy; They Work and Chat-Time of Landing is Still Undisclosed," *New York Times*, August 14, 1962, 1, 14, 14.

145 Topping, "Soviet Pilots Spin," 14, and The United Press International, "Soviets Drop Back To Earth; Spacemen End 4-Day Spectacle; Both Men Said to be Healthy," *Bakersfield Californian*, August 15, 1962, 1–2.

146 Seymour Topping, "Two Soviet Space Craft Circling Earth in Adjacent Orbits After New Launching; Pilots Keep in Touch by Sight and Radio; Astronauts on TV; Both Report All is Well; Nikolayev Breaks Titov's Record," *New York Times*, August 13, 1962, 1, 10, 1.

147 Carpenter et al., *We Seven*, 18, 60.

148 Richard Witkin, "Flight by Schirra Viewed as Proving Pilots' Space Role," *New York Times*, October 5, 1962, 1.

149 Wally Schirra, "A Real Breakthrough—The Capsule Was All Mine," *Life*, October 26, 1962, 39–43, 39. See also, Mindell, *Digital Apollo*, 82.

150 "Six Perfect Orbits; Safe," *Chicago Tribune*, October 4, 1962, 1.

151 "Six Perfect Orbits," 1.

152 Schirra, "A Real Breakthrough," 39–43; see also Mindell, *Digital Apollo*, 82.

153 John Dille, "At the End of a Great Flight, Big Bull's-Eye," *Life*, October 12, 1962, 50.

154 "He Brings it in 'Right on the Old Bazoo,'" *Life*, May 24, 1963, 28–33.

155 "On the Bazoo," *Newsweek*, May 27, 1963, 61; See also, Kauffman, *Selling Outer Space*, 57.

156 Richard Witkin, "Cooper Maneuvers to a Bullseye Landing with Manual Control as Automatic Fails; 'I'm In Fine Shape,' He Says After 22 Orbits; Dramatic Return, Astronaut was Aloft Over 34 Hours—Aided By Glenn," *New York Times*, May 17, 1963, 1; See also, Kauffman, *Selling Outer Space*, 57.

157 Gordon Cooper, "Everyone Was in a Sweat, I was Secretly Pleased," *Life*, June 7, 1963, 31.

# LIGHT THIS CANDLE

158 "On the Bazoo," 61.

159 "On the Bazoo," 62–63. A .05G panel normally tells the astronaut that his capsule is knifing into the top of the atmosphere during reentry and is starting to slow down. At this point, the astronaut returns from his weightless condition in space and begins to feel deceleration, or G, forces. Since Cooper knew he was still weightless and still on his charted path, that is, not reentering the atmosphere, he knew something was wrong.

160 To note, without his "indicators," Cooper had no way of knowing if he was lined up properly for reentry and landing. The *New York Times* indicates a similar circumstance here, suggesting Cooper had to do the job usually "entrusted to an automatic computerized system." See Witkin, "Cooper Maneuvers to a Bullseye," 1.

161 Witkin, "Cooper Maneuvers to a Bullseye," 18.

162 "World Will be Ruled from Skies Above," *Life*, 17 May 1963, 4.

163 Swenson Jr., Grimwood, and Alexander, *This New Ocean*, 509.

164 Lt. Commander M. Scott Carpenter, "AIAA Manned Space Flight meeting in Dallas, April 22, 1963," Impact Files, "Space Quotes Folder 15767," NASA Historical Reference Collection, NASA Headquarters, Washington, DC.

165 U.S. Congress, Senate, Committee, Aeronautical and Space Sciences, 48.

166 U.S. Congress, Senate, Committee, Aeronautical and Space Sciences, 48.

# Chapter 3

# THE FIRST LADY ASTRONAUT TRAINEES (FLATS)

Dr. Wernher von Braun asked a crowded November 1962 Mississippi State College auditorium why the Soviets continued ahead of the Americans in space. He reasoned that Americans had become too "soft" with a "life of comfort, ease, and pleasure." He challenged the students to embrace new technologies and sciences and to "vigorously" explore space. However, when it came to physically flying a spacecraft, one of the most popular questions reporters asked was when a woman would fly into space. The audience need not worry. Von Braun and Bob Gilruth were "reserving 110 pounds of payload for recreational equipment."[1] Von Braun's joke about women space fliers, his fears of "soft" living and his plea to move "vigorously" in space mirrored the masculinity crisis in the public discourse. His speech created spaceflight as a masculine space where women belonged as a novelty and not in the serious business of spaceflight.

Women proved themselves to be contributors and active participants in aviation, beginning with the Wright Brothers' sister, Katherine, who was instrumental in selling flight.[2] Despite sex and racial discrimination, women eagerly earned their pilots' licenses while corporate airline owners used women as stewardesses to publicly sell the safety of flight. Women pilots accentuated femininity on a spectrum, such as the more conventional femininity of pilot Jackie Cochran, or the more masculine appearance of Amelia Earhart, Florence Lowe "Poncho" Barnes, and the first Black licensed woman pilot, Bessie Coleman. Whatever version of femininity they presented, these women in early aviation danced atop planes, created clubs, flew in air derbies, across oceans and even tested and ferried airplanes during World War II.[3]

American culture shifted back to the more conventional after World War II, and the American public discourse wanted women to return to their limited roles as wives and mothers. There was no need for women pilots in the military or in commercial aviation with male pilots returning from war. Gender roles became important to security and safety as the Cold War heated up.[4] Vice President Nixon and the American public implored the female sex to return to the kitchen, where their liberation came from their choices in appliances, wallpaper and tawdry linoleum. Freedom came with technology that completed women's labor so that women could spend their time with their children or in leisure activity.[5]

This renewed limited role for women came at a time when Americans viewed the space race as a militarized battle, one in which the safety and containment of Soviet technology could only be won by the combat astronaut who possessed the ability to control both communism and technology. Femininity insinuated a lack of control. A woman in a spacecraft symbolized passivity. The American media mocked Soviet cosmonauts for their lack of masculine control over spaceflight technology. Blasting a woman into space would have contradicted the American spaceflight public narrative. Sending an American woman into space would have questioned the need for an astronaut jet test pilot if women could fly. The astronaut jet test pilot requirement and the military's ban on women pilots helped craft the space race along gendered lines.

The domestication of women was of the utmost importance in selling spaceflight and American culture to the country and the world. Sarah Parry Myers argues in *Earning Their Wings* that the media depicted women's World War II jobs outside the home as "self-sacrificing, serving to support men rather than pursue career goals," insinuating the war's upset of gender roles to be temporary.[6] NASA and the public discourse did the same with the astronauts' wives, depicting them as doting wives and mothers, temporarily taking on masculine and feminine roles while they awaited their husbands' return from the dangers of spaceflight. Since women belonged in the domestic sphere, women would have to wait for the domestication and routinization of space to fly. In essence, women would have to wait until spaceflight was safe.

The following chapter looks at how women challenged their exclusion in aviation and spaceflight from the end of World War II through the early space race. Women infiltrated the space race narrative controlled by white heterosexual men and forced the public conversation about gender discrimination in spaceflight. The subversive nature of the FLATs to redefine the astronaut image and enter the spacecraft reflected a burgeoning women's rights movement within American aerospace history on the eve of legal and societal challenges to conventional gender roles. Whether one agreed or disagreed with these women, Americans consumed new public images of women as pilots and engineers. The consumption of differing feminine images led to conversations apart from conventional notions of women's identities as confined to wife and mother. Similarly, to the women computers, engineers and scientists before them, women pilots acted as subversive actors—defying the roles thrust upon them by society, navigating their own identities, making their own choices and demonstrating that gender roles were a cultural construct that oppressed rather than liberated. Ultimately, women were left out of the spaceflight for the same reason Congress failed to militarize the WASPs: women astronauts were unnecessary, and women's roles were that of wife and mother and not that of combat hero.

While women served in limited numbers in the Army Signal Corps during World War I, World War II led to the first public discussion about American women in military aviation.[7] Women's roles expanded in commercial and transport flights as male pilots were drafted into the military. The demand for test pilots and pilot instructors grew as the military increasingly looked to women to fill these roles. First Lady Eleanor Roosevelt viewed the weaponization of women pilots as essential to victory. On September 1, 1942, Roosevelt wrote in her column "My Day": "We are in a war and need to fight it with our ability and every weapon possible, Women pilots, in this particular case, are a weapon waiting to be used."[8] Historians attribute the decision to use women pilots to the relentless insistence of famed female flier Cochran and Chief of the Air Corps, General Arnold. In September 1942, celebrated female flier Nancy Harkness Love beat Cochran and Arnold to the punch and founded the Women's Auxiliary Flying Squadron (WAFS) or Women's Auxiliary Ferrying Squadron (WAFS). Never wanting to be outshined, the "smart and pretty" Cochran did not want to see herself or her organization play second fiddle to what she saw as a bunch of heiress pilots in the WAFS.[9] She wanted real pilots to take center stage, not an elitist spectacle of glamour girls. In the summer of 1943, at the behest of Cochran and Arnold, the Army joined both Cochran's and Love's organizations into the Women's Army Service Pilots (WASPs).

Molly Merryman argues in *Clipped Wings* that the Congressional Ramspeck Committee Report claimed military pilot standards were lowered for women—although incorrectly—and that women pilots both during and after the war were not necessary.[10] Myers argues in *Earning Their Wings*, that the military did not see women pilots as "weapons" but rather as "experimental substitutes whose presence in the male-dominated military was a threat in need of regulation."[11] To not upset the military's masculine space and conventional notions of adventure, heroism, combat, protection and citizenship, the military created the WASPs as a civilian organization. Conversely, women in the Women's Army Corps (WACs), Women Accepted for Volunteer Emergency Services (WAVES), United States Coast Guard Women's Reserve (SPARS), and women Marines were militarized. Women in these branches worked in both conventionally feminine and masculine jobs; however, they were not supposed to be in dangerous combat roles, although sometimes these women faced deadly situations such as bombing or strafing.[12]

The WASPs did not serve in combat, but testing and flying military aircraft was also dangerous. To prevent an upset in the masculine role of combat, Congress did not militarize the WASPs, and they did not receive military recognition or benefits even though they flew and ferried military planes out of Avenger Field in Sweetwater, Texas as well as other bases around the country.[13] Women flying during the war—and of course their service in the Army, Navy, Coast Guard and Marines—elicited fears of women's public participation in the military as over four-hundred-thousand women eagerly enlisted. The government allowed none of these women to fight in combat and take over the masculine role of protector, but women still found themselves in harm's way. Between 1942 and 1944, over one thousand WASPs ferried planes from factories to bases throughout the United States and Canada. The WASPs tested and piloted the same aircraft as their male counterparts. The women flew sixty million miles, and thirty-eight lost their lives.[14]

Even Curtis Wright's "cadettes" engaged in an advanced aviation engineering program in which they wrote the pilot manuals for the P-40 Warhawk

**Figure 3.1** Jackie Cochran and Brigadier General Ralph Stearley inspects the WASPS of the Target-Towing Squadron at Camp Davis, North Carolina, 1943. Source: Getty Images. https://www.dailymail.co.uk/news/article-8230655/Remembering-unsung-heroes-WWII-Womens-Airforce-Service-Pilots.html.

# FIRST LADY ASTRONAUT TRAINEES

and SB2 Helldiver.[15] Some six hundred women were needed at seven participating Curtiss Cadette university programs across the country to free up men for military service. Journalist Lela Cole Kitson described the cadettes' advanced aerospace engineering courses "as arduous as military training and demanding an equal singleness of purpose and effort."[16] NACA Muroc Test Unit (Edwards Air Force Base) hired the cadettes in a work-study program as computers that plotted trajectory by hand. Muroc hired other women mathematicians as computers who worked closely with male engineers on technical reports that were co-authored by the women.[17] Charles Planck, author of *Women with Wings* (1942), predicted that with women's entrance into masculine aviation, "It is not hard to imagine a winged-swarm of pretty girl-pilots descending upon Congress, when the time is ripe, to raise again the demand that often has resounded throughout Washington, equal rights for women."[18]

Americans celebrated women in masculine fields as national patriots during World War II but often viewed their contributions as helpmates rather than equal contributors. Myers argues that "Women pilots' military aviation acumen and courage were trivialized as a novelty, which masked their dangerous roles and undermined their place as professionals [...]."[19] Despite their dangerous jobs, the public discourse often focused on the attractiveness of these "girls"—ensuring their feminization and infantilization. For instance, The *Democrat and Chronicle* (Rochester, New York) explained that a local "Girl Holding Down One Man's Job Seeks Another—as Army Pilot."[20] *Life* magazine featured these "Girl Pilots" on the front cover of their July 1943 issue. The article maintained that the "girls" fly with "skill, precision, and zest, their hearts set on piloting with an unfeminine purpose that might well be a threat to Hitler."[21] Cochran took great pains to ensure to the American public that these girls or young women would remain feminine to "ease the American public's fears about the sexuality and morality of women in such a masculine environment."[22]

*Life* grasped the reality of the situation that women exercising an "unfeminine purpose" meant gender roles were flexible, even when it came to controlling technology. The women would not be trained in gunnery or flying formation, but the "girls are very serious about their chance to fly for the Army at Avenger Field, even when it means giving up nail polish, beauty parlors, and dates for a regimented 22½ weeks."[23] Journalist Elmo Scott Watson congratulated the achievements of the WASPs aiding the Red Army's assault on the Nazis—pushing them back to the West. To Watson, the "girls'" work "wasn't glamorous" but rather "hard-working," and able to take on the "physical excursion" of "ferrying the deadly, Airacobra" the one thousand, eight hundred miles from Niagara Falls, New York to Great Falls, Montana.[24] Flying World War II military aircraft took "physical strength, acumen, and specialized training to fly" at a time in which "women's bodies" have often been used to "exclude them from specific military roles or combat."[25] The planes were then shipped to the Soviet Union. Despite congratulating women's participation, it was still clear that the women would not take on the role of masculine protector, or as famed World War I Naval test pilot, Major Alfred Joseph Williams quipped, "Quit kidding yourselves. I may be a bit old-fashioned, but I don't believe we as a nation are ready to send our women into combat."[26] Major Williams was correct.

Cochran took a risk with the success of the WASPs and asked Congress to introduce a bill that would militarize women pilots after the war. Each branch had bills before Congress, and the WASPs were the last. House Bill 4219, the Costello Bill, failed. Cochran blamed herself for what she viewed as a premature move on her part.[27] Myers argues that with the failed bill the women pilots' "heroism was masked."[28] Thus, as Merryman has argued in *Clipped Wings*, leaving women out of combat allowed for the continuation of artificial gender constructs with masculinity focused on "domination, self-control, violence, physical expression, and conquest—are rewarded in men," and "denied" for women.[29] The military disbanded the WASPs in 1944. It would not be until 1977 that these women were fully recognized for their military service.[30] The WASPs did not receive the recognition they deserved, but at the behest of military brass, the Congressional Armed Services Committee passed the Women's Armed Services Integration Act (1948), giving women a permanent role in the military. Despite arguments that as citizens women should "actively participate in its protection and defense," Congress allowed women to serve on a limited base.[31] The message to women was clear. Even though the WASPs had flown over sixty million miles and were certified on sixty-eight different platforms, including four-engine bombers, they were no longer needed as military pilots. Women would not be accepted on a regular basis into military culture if there was no national security need—an argument that resurfaced during spaceflight.

The WASPs' disbanding became a missed opportunity for women to gain an identity outside of wife and mother. The end of World War II led to very little public change in gender roles. Women could not serve in combat—including in flight—with Lt. Col. Geraldine May (Director of the New Women's Air Force Unit) citing, "No pilots for the moment."[32] Unlike the more progressive actions at NASA, the Navy further reinforced women's gendered roles by only recruiting unmarried women.[33] During the height of the Korean Conflict, General George C. Marshall put his weight behind the Defense Advisory Committee on Women in the Services (DACOWITS) to expand women's roles in the military but also to "assure the public that those [women] it needed were conforming to American conventions of feminine respectability."[34] Despite women's past success in wartime roles, the United States was reluctant to disrupt gender roles by letting women take on the male role of protector, possibly in order "to preserve male privilege."[35] As Debbie Douglas argues in *U.S. Women in Aviation, 1940-1985* (2004), after the war, the debate shifted from "Can women fly?" to "Should women fly?"[36]

Women were to return to the home, or as social activist Agnes E. Meyer argued in the *Atlantic Monthly*, women should not bear "the burden of an individual identity." Women's main "vocation" was that of "motherhood," which was necessary "to restore security in our insecure world." After all, "no job is more exacting, more necessary, or more rewarding than that of housewife and mother. Then they will feel free to become once more the moral force of society through the stabilization of the home."[37] A 1951 *Seventeen Magazine* article entitled "How to Be a Woman," instructed young girls to be "a partner of man [...] not his rival, his enemy, or his plaything."[38] Not rivaling men sent messages to young women of their inferiority, subjugation or at the very least, equality as undesirable.

The Mercury 7 wives personified the male partner image publicly as NASA molded the astronaut wives into the modern American woman. As young brides, the astronaut wives took jobs as operators, clerks, typists and movie theater ushers as they put their husbands through college or supported the home financially while their husbands went through undergraduate pilot training. NASA tried to control the astronaut wives' narrative right down to airbrushing out red lipstick as they appeared on the cover of *Life* in September 1959. The astronauts left their wives behind as they battled in space. The astronaut wives became feminine heroines in the press. Eager reporters saw the women's identity as wives and mothers, writing extensively about their religion, patriotism, recipes, hair, makeup, fashion and time spent at the Parent-Teacher Association (PTA). The wives reflected the lack of women's individual identity and choices in Betty Friedan's *The Feminine Mystique*. However, they were hardly the *Stepford Wives*. The women took over both masculine and feminine roles while their husbands were away and exercised a great deal of control over media access to their homes—including Annie Glenn's refusal to host Vice President Lyndon Johnson. When NASA instructed Glenn to tell Annie to invite the vice president inside her home, Glenn and the other astronauts refused the request—demonstrating not only a united front but also that the wives had a private role in determining their part in the space race narrative.[39]

The astronaut wives, as heroines of the American household, in many ways mirrored women's roles in flight. Commercial airlines and private companies continued to use women to sell the safety of flight after the war. Alan Meyer's *Weekend Pilots: Technology, Masculinity, and Private Aviation in Postwar America*

94 GENDER AND THE RACE FOR SPACE

(2013) argues that the performance of private flight was gendered, with the husbands controlling technology and the wives taking on the dual "role that combined the duties of housewife with those of an unofficial, and definitely unequal, copilot."[40] Women represented fewer than three percent of licensed pilots in the United States by 1959.[41]

Spaceflight followed similar lines with the public discourse viewing women's roles as that of passengers and not pilots. In September 1958, the *Los Angeles Times* reported that at the American Psychological Association meeting in Washington, D.C., psychologists and space scientists joked that "feminine companionship" might make interplanetary flight "less rigorous." While the University of Florida's Dr. Wilse B. Webb—much like Dr. Von Braun— suggested that the addition of the female space traveler would "cure boredom," the idea was not perfect. "Imagine," advised Dr. Webb, "hurtling tens of millions of miles accompanied by a nagging back-seat rocket pilot. It would be enough to make the spaceman hit the liquor lever too hard and make the wrong turn as he approached Saturn."[42]

Some acknowledged women's contributions to the future of spaceflight beyond their roles as hostesses and novelties. The following summer, a research firm nominated a married Beverly Hills stewardess, Pamela Jayson, as the first stewardess aboard a manned spaceflight. Jayson viewed women as "equally intelligent, if not more so than men" and "emotionally and psychologically superior." Jayson hoped women would petition Congress for equality into the astronaut corps.[43]

In 1959, eccentric television producer Ivan Tors posed that women's size and weight would be ideal for space travel. He told readers that the loss of such talent and contribution to spaceflight fell on the fault that "Americans pamper their women." Tors hoped "Russia will force us into mobilizing our womenpower as they do. [...] we can't pass up 52% of our possible space personnel out of a false sense of gallantry." Tors viewed women's bodies, especially their relationship to pregnancy, as assets because women's bodies were used to trauma and had extra fat layers to shield them from the cold. However, he still believed the ideal woman astronaut would be an astronaut's wife.[44]

Most Americans disagreed, seeing women's contribution in the role of helpers and not active participants.[45] NASA and most of the mainstream media portrayed women's roles as equally important to the individualist male astronaut, but within the role as wife and mother left behind while their husbands conquered space. Publicly, the astronaut wives were intelligent, brave, efficient caretakers of the home and children and above all, they eagerly awaited their husbands' return from the dangers of space.[46]

Some aerospace researchers also saw women's smaller size as advantageous to spaceflight but still restricted their roles to wives. In 1959, Brigadier

# FIRST LADY ASTRONAUT TRAINEES

General of the Air Research and Development Command (ARDC), Donald Flickinger, proposed Project "Women in Space Earliest" (WISE) to research women's bodies for spaceflight. Flickinger worked with Randy Lovelace in the 1950s on the Central Intelligence Agency's secret U2 spy planes. Flickinger anticipated both sexes living and working in space. The ARDC assessed famed female aviator, 58-year-old Ruth Nichols, to see if she could pass the astronaut tests. Nichols made the important aeronautical point to the press that it was not simply "chivalry" to blame for women's lack of inclusion but rather that researchers did not have data on the effects of flight on women's bodies.[47]

Nichols was one of the oldest licensed women pilots, receiving her license in 1919. She was from a well-to-do family, attended Wellesley College and was one of the original founders of the all-female flying organization, the Ninety-Nines. Nichols crushed Charles Lindbergh's cross-country flight time. Nichols believed women would be better space fliers—ironically—because "women are passive. Submissive. Patient by birthright. We could stand up under any long and arduous space journey. [...]. I think it is significant that every live animal sent up so far has been female—the Russian dog—our two monkeys."[48] Nichols suffered from depression and died a year later of a barbiturate overdose.[49] Indiana women's columnist Mrs. Walter Ferguson argued that Nichols' want for women space fliers was "overdone" and "Feminine Independence shouldn't be carried too far."[50] Ferguson's comment followed along the lines of women's gender roles as limited and not equal to those of men.

In the same year, 1959, *Look* magazine gained permission to use NASA facilities to put famed flier Betty Skelton through astronaut tests. *Look* conducted the tests to sell magazines, not champion women's right to spaceflight. A year before Skelton's tests, *Look* had published their multi-essay work blaming liberated women for destroying American manhood. *Look* took the opportunity to criticize women's bodies and reinforce restrictive gender roles in spaceflight by suggesting, "Our first girl in space will probably be a flat-chested lightweight under 35 years of age and married [...]. Her first chance in space may be as the scientist-wife of a pilot-engineer."[51] The assumption again confined women to the role of wife aboard a spacecraft.

Even when research suggested benefits of women in spaceflight, the public discourse turned again to female gender stereotypes. The Director of the Air Force Aeronautical Laboratory at Wright Field told the Associated Press in January 1959 that the woman's performance within the isolation chamber overshadowed that of the male subjects. The men's performances showed that, unlike the women, the men "start worrying about their families and become aggressive and irrational too soon to stand a long and confining interplanetary trip." However, the director explained, the drawback to women alone in space is that "the gregariousness of the sex is well known. Name one famous woman hermit. Name one who prefers solitaire (except on the ring finger) to a kaffe klatsch." The Associated Press continued mocking the dangers of female solitude. The editorial suggested that the "old pioneer spirit [would] evaporate" when "all chance of seeing the boy-friend for an indefinite time" became reality. Strikingly, when Colonel John Stapp, director of the laboratory, expressed his opinion that women could not go into space because spaceflight equipment was designed for male bodies, the Associated Press responded with a progressive view that the Colonel's answer was a "picayune obstacle."[52] The argument that women's bodies were too complicated for spaceflight persisted into NASA's shuttle program.[53]

The Associated Press article hit papers across the country. The Air Force feared "adverse publicity," and the ARDC canceled WISE before it even got started. An article in *Look* acknowledged "many believe that women's biggest obstacle to being first is our cultural bias against exposing them to hazardous situations." Margaret A. Weitekamp suggests that scientists feared that if men and women went into space together, they would engage in sexual relations. However, a married female astronaut implied stability.[54] Married stability implied control and the domestication of spaceflight. Married couples going into space represented colonization—but space needed to be conquered first.

*Look* and the ARDC were not the only programs open to public debate. As early as August 1960, the public knew about Lovelace's testing women pilots using the same tests as the Mercury astronauts. Lovelace and Flickinger met Jerrie Cobb, a "tomboy" from Oklahoma, and her boss Tom Harris while visiting Miami Beach. At the time, Cobb was an Aero Commander sales pilot. Cobb found employment as a pilot difficult as she was often told by potential employers that "this is a man's industry."[55] Cobb had sixteen years of flight experience when she met Lovelace and Flickinger, and her knowledge of Russian aircraft and her speed and altitude records piqued their interest. At dinner, they discussed the Russian tests on women space fliers. Lovelace told Flickinger and Cobb to put together a list of potential women pilots for American spaceflight tests.

The ARDC previously turned down testing women pilots as they feared "negative publicity."[56] Therefore, the women pilots would be tested at Lovelace's clinic as his own research project—without government backing.[57] Lovelace's good friend Cochran and her wealthy husband, Floyd Odlum, largely funded the program and the women pilots' travel expenses. Beginning in 1960, the women visited the Lovelace Albuquerque clinic at different times, some taking the tests alone. Lovelace and his clinic tested some twenty women pilots—all with at least one thousand flying hours—putting them through the same physical and psychological tests as the male astronauts. The women who passed included (in alphabetical order): Myrtle Cagle, twin sisters Jane and Marion Dietrich, Wally Funk, Sarah Gorelick, Jane "Janey" Briggs Hart, Jean Hixson, Rhea Woltman, Gene Nora Stumbough, Irene Leverton, Jerri Sloan (Truhill) and Bearnice Steadman.

Cobb and Lovelace referred to the women pilots as "the First Lady Astronaut Trainees" or FLATs. *Life* argued that the FLATs proved a "very important astronautical point: women are as capable as men of enduring the rigors of space flight." The same article accentuated Cobb's aeronautical achievements. Participating in a "tough masculine trade" as an experienced pilot, Cobb completed over seven thousand five hundred hours flying numerous planes from crop dusters to B-17s. After passing the seventy-five astronaut tests—which included running on a treadmill and cycling to the point of exhaustion, needles the size of matchsticks shoved into one's hands, eighteen needles thrust in one's head, ice water injected into the ear, swallowing three feet of rubber hoses and of course the enemas—Cobb "complained less than the Mercury men had […]." Lovelace proposed that women were better equipped for space travel because they ate and drank less, had a lower

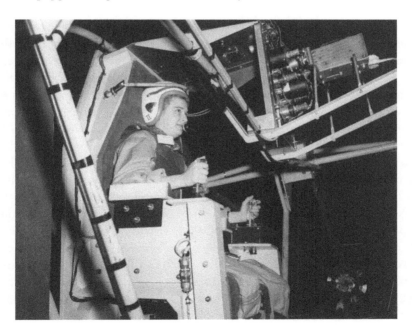

**Figure 3.2** Jerrie Cobb was tested in the gimbal rig in the Altitude Wind Tunnel in 1960. Source: The National Air and Space Museum. https://airandspace.si.edu/stories/editorial/remembering-geraldyn-jerrie-cobb-pioneering-woman-aviator.

body mass, used less oxygen and therefore might be able to fly in lighter craft or stay in space longer than men while using the same equipment. Lovelace suggested that women's "less exposed reproductive system should also give them a higher radiation tolerance." Spaceflight, the article concluded, would be "coeducational" in the future.[58]

The press jumped at these findings. Cobb's face graced papers and magazines across the country in the summer of 1960. Cobb flew to New York City to do a press conference and was asked questions about her fears, what women could contribute to spaceflight, and "Can you cook?" "What do you cook?" and "Why do you want to beat a man into space?"[59] More questions and photos arrived with *Life's* August 29, 1960, edition featuring "A Lady Proves She's Fit For Space Flight."[60] Letters from eager young women and adoring fans poured into Cobb's place of employment. Women wanted to go to space and sought encouragement. They appreciated having visible examples of what women could achieve, showing that gender roles should not limit opportunities. In the summer of 1961, NASA Administrator James Webb announced Cobb as a consultant for NASA. The administration swore her in that summer.[61] In her home state of Oklahoma, the *Daily Oklahoman* called Jerrie Cobb a "Space Suffragette."[62]

Despite Cobb's "consultant" status, in the public discourse, NASA denied any current or future women astronaut program but assumed women would someday "ride spacecraft."[63] The term "ride" implied that women would be passengers and not pilots. The *New York Times* reiterated this after twelve additional women passed the tests, telling their readers, "The prime purpose is to determine to what extent women may be used in space-flight research, rather than to select space women."[64] Women were not on the spaceflight radar other than as future passenger wives for research purposes. Lovelace received a letter from the director of NASA's Life Science Programs, Clark T. Randt, in which the employee and friend admitted, "Perhaps I am just one of the old school who favors keeping them barefoot and pregnant!"[65] *Space World's* Donald Cox wrote sarcastically that if NASA allowed psychiatrists to run the astronaut program, they would bypass the "normal American male" as space travelers in favor of "schizophrenics, extreme introverts, Eskimos, aborigines [...] and even women!" Cox suggested that there was a "cultural bias of American men against exposing their women to the hazards of spaceflight."[66] Lovelace conducted the FLAT experiments for space travel research, but as the media picked up the story, the narrative increasingly followed along the lines of confining women's public roles.

Testing the FLATs as pilots in military aircraft ultimately halted the Lovelace program. In September 1961, Lovelace sent a request to the

Pentagon asking for permission to use the Naval School of Aviation Medicine in Pensacola, Florida. He wished to continue testing the FLATs to find differences between men and women in high-speed flight. The request read, "Request authority for civilian Miss Jerrie Cobb to fly in Naval aircraft for the purpose of base-line studies to determine the fundamental differences between male and female astronauts." The Chief of Naval Operations replied to the request, "If you don't know the differences already, we refuse to put money into the project."[67]

Sarcasm aside, the Deputy Chief of Naval Operations (Air), Vice Admiral Robert B. Pirie, had already been conversing with the powerful Cochran on the matter since the previous August. Cochran implored Pirie that a women astronaut program should not be put together haphazardly and that it should not interfere with the present Mercury program. Jackie wanted caution and the right moment to train women astronauts. After her unsuccessful attempt to integrate the WASPs into the military, Cochran emphasized the stereotypical feminine virtue of patience. She played into the male belief that women wait their turn. Privately, she conducted jet test flights at Edwards.[68] The only other woman to fly a military jet before Cochran was WASP Ann B. Carl, who flew experimental jet fighters at Wright-Patterson Air Force Base during World War II.[69] Money, connections and a friendship with Chuck Yeager could get Jackie into the cockpit of a military jet. She even broke the sound barrier in a Canadair F-86 Sabre jet in 1953. Cochran may have catered to male views on women's virtues and safety, but this did not prevent her from training as a potential astronaut.

Pirie was aware of Lovelace's plans to use the Pensacola base for jet test exercises. He contacted NASA to see if the organization had a specific request to use the base for training women astronauts. NASA responded that they had not. Without the backing of federal funds from NASA, Pirie was not about to use his men and planes for the exercises or, worse, kill a woman in a jet crash.[70]

Cobb was livid and eagerly wrote letters to NASA and congressional leaders protesting the cancellation. She argued before the First Women's Space Symposium in Los Angeles, California, that American competition in space should remain with the Russians and not a "battle of the sexes" with American women.[71] The persistence of the Lovelace women had officials saying, "don't call us, we'll call you."[72] NASA fumed at Cobb's notoriety and the media's insistence on calling her "America's first women astronaut trainee."[73] Vice President Johnson agreed to meet with both Cobb and fellow FLAT Janey Hart, the wife of Democratic Senator (MI) Phillip Hart. Two days before Johnson met with the FLATs, NASA Deputy Administrator Hugh Dryden sent a memo to the vice president that read:

Orbital Flight is not yet a routine operation and still a matter of too great a hazard to give anyone who has not yet had 1) high speed military test flying, and 2) engineering background, so they could take over the controls in the event it became necessary. *If there was a woman with this background, we should consider her as orbital flight becomes more routine we can relax these rules.* (Italics added)[74]

Even if a woman was a jet test pilot and an engineer, Dryden believed women should wait for spaceflight because it was too dangerous for women.

In March 1962, just before a major shift in thinking about women's public roles, Johnson's office was flooded with letters from women and some men advocating for women astronauts. Johnson's office replied that the astronaut requirements were not "based on 'sex, color, creed or other extraneous factors'" but rather on the need to fly a high-powered aircraft.[75] Women could not possibly apply for the astronaut corps in a culture that limited women's roles to wife and mother. The United States still viewed engineering and test piloting as masculine pursuits. An affirmative action plan did not exist to encourage women or even minorities to enter the white heterosexual male-dominated space of military piloting or engineering.

The space race depended on congressional funding. NASA did not need negative publicity even if the Democratic Party had been supporting women's rights through the Commission on the Status of Women and the 1963 Equal Pay Act. On March 15, 1962, Johnson instructed Webb, "I'm sure you agree that sex should not be a reason for disqualifying a candidate for orbital flight." Privately, Johnson handwrote a note on the letter instructing Webb: "Let's stop this now!" As Johnson understood the NASA qualifications, the candidate had to have piloted a high-speed military jet and earned an engineering degree, which gave the astronaut the ability to control the craft. Johnson ended the letter with, "I know we both are grateful for the desire to serve on the part of these women and look forward to the time when they can."[76]

Johnson then met with Cobb and Hart on March 17, 1962. He understood their passion and persistence. He might even have understood their argument that women had a scientific contribution to make to spaceflight. But, above all, Johnson knew that if women were allowed into the astronaut corps, "every man on the street would argue they too were fit for spaceflight. The qualifications were put in place by highly informed professionals for the astronauts' and the program's safety."[77] His response suggested that Americans might see women astronauts as representing a more passive or domestic role in spaceflight. It implied that if a woman could handle the challenges of space travel, it would make spaceflight seem more accessible to anyone. Famed aviatrix Louise Thaden believed, "Nothing impresses the safety of aviation on the public quite so much as to see a woman flying an airplane."[78] The American space race public discourse was not ready to project an image of astronaut passivity and safety.

Cochran wrote to Cobb a few days later. She sent the letter to Lovelace, the FLATs, the upper brass of NASA and the Navy. In the letter, Jackie acknowledged that in aviation, women found themselves as competent as men. But she argued women needed to be patient, telling Cobb a separate women's astronaut program would be "terribly expensive" when "There is no real present national urgency about putting a woman into space. To attempt to do so in the near future might indeed interfere with the space program now underway which is urgent from a national standpoint." Cochran did not share Cobb's belief that a woman astronaut would be a victory for women but rather a situation that could "backfire." Cochran preferred not to engage in a battle of the sexes and let men do the work since there was "no need" for women in this "urgent project from the standpoint of national defense."[79] Cochran strikingly used the same language of a lack of need for women in spaceflight as the pernicious Ramspeck Congressional Report used not to militarize her WASPs. Cochran whole-heartedly disagreed with the Ramspeck Report and even issued an official War Department response to the report. But she had learned the power of gender culture from the report—a culture she spent her entire life subverting. She knew Americans were not ready to blast a woman into space, and she used masculine language of combat to prevent what she viewed as a careless women's astronaut corps that would fail. Cochran's use of "national defense" depicted the space race as it had been since 1957—a battle in which men go off to war and women wait behind to help serve.

Most importantly, if NASA used a crash program to send a woman to space before the Soviets, it might question why the Mercury 7 needed three years of hard training, "if a woman can do the same thing without a long background of experience followed by careful special training." Sending up a woman without training would suggest anyone could be an astronaut. Cochran reiterated that she did not think there was a difference between men and women when it came to flying, but that since the astronauts had extensive training, they should be allowed to go first. Cochran did not want a haphazard crash program for "propaganda reasons." Cochran failed to see the space race and landing a man on the moon as propaganda to reinforce American prestige, advanced military weaponry, courage, physical prowess and teamwork.

Cochran, Johnson, Webb, Dryden and even critics of a woman's space program overlooked the fact that landing a man on the moon was driven as much by American technological and cultural pride as by the desire to contain communism. Sending a woman into space would have demonstrated

America's commitment to equal rights and enhanced its prestige. However, Cold War Americans did not see equality in terms of equal opportunity or inclusion. Equality followed along limited gender roles, where women's equality rested in their rights to be wives and mothers. In fact, Cochran argued that women's second-place status was natural in flight, "Women for one reason or another have always come into each phase of aviation a little behind their brothers. They should, I believe, accept this delay and not get into the hair of the public authorities about it."[80] In other words, women should remain passive—adhere to their natural feminine gender—for their chance at spaceflight.

Cobb was determined not to let men define the roles of astronauts and gender expectations. While in Washington, Cobb met with George P. Miller (D-CA), the new head of the House Space Committee. Miller not only wanted to further women's rights but viewed a moon landing as secondary to the technological and scientific research needed to cure problems on Earth.[81] Miller's committee put together a special Subcommittee of the House Committee on Science and Astronautics that convened on July 17, 1962, with "standing room only" to investigate alleged discrimination in NASA employment.[82] Victor Anfuso (D-NY) chaired the eleven-member special subcommittee. Jessica McCullough Weis (R-NY) and Corinne Boyd Riley (D-SC) were the two women on the committee.[83] Women had forced the conversation about their right to spaceflight, which the public discourse framed as "their latest battle for equality with men."[84]

Representative Anfuso's opening remarks during the subcommittee hearing suggested a paradox of women's roles in spaceflight. Anfuso made it clear that the space race should be open to both men and women, utilizing "all human resources" available, but he celebrated Hart as not only a "famed pilot" but an "outstanding wife and mother." Nobody on the subcommittee congratulated expert witness astronauts Scott Carpenter and John Glenn in their roles as husbands and fathers. Instead, the subcommittee simply referred to the men as "Americans of heroic stature, of whom nothing further need be said."[85]

Cobb was the first to make the argument for women astronauts before the subcommittee. She wrote a note to herself before her testimony that read, "Never apologize, no timidity, in control."[86] Cobb told the committee that she did not want to enter a "battle of the sexes" but desired "a place in our Nation's (*sic*) space future without discrimination." Cobb explained that "as citizens of this nation," the women wanted "to be allowed to participate with seriousness and sincerity in the making of history now, as women have in the past." Cobb suggested that being the "first" woman into space would "bring glory to our Nation [...]."[87] Sending a woman would demonstrate the prowess of American technology and democracy.

Hart spoke next and represented a more vocal feminist voice, especially her desire that NASA not "be restricted to men only, like some sort of stag club." Unlike the self-made Cobb and Cochran, Hart was of the upper class, and granted a little more latitude with her sharp wit. Hart was a gold star mother of nine children who subverted gender constructs. Hart argued that women should be admitted into the astronaut corps because they "have a real contribution to make." For some, argued Hart, the "PTA just isn't enough." NASA knew women possessed skills since they continued to employ women when there was not a manpower shortage. Hart used this to her advantage, applauding men: "There have always been men, men like the members of this committee, who have helped women succeed in roles that they were previously thought incapable of handling."[88]

Hart used women's wartime participation to illustrate her point. She suggested that utilizing women as nurses in war hospitals one hundred years ago would have been unthinkable because of societal beliefs about women's "frail and emotional structure." Hart continued, "It seems to me a basic error in American thought that the only time women are allowed to make a full contribution to a better nation is when there is a manpower shortage [...]." She asked the committee: "Why must we handicap ourselves with the idea that every woman's place is in the kitchen despite what her talents and capabilities might be?" Hart believed women should be given the opportunity to choose whether being a housewife was enough, or whether their talents would be useful elsewhere. Women, like men, should have control over their own identity to become a full individual. Taking Hart's testimony out of context, Representative Anfuso asked: "Would you go so far, Mrs. Hart, that anything man can do, woman can do better?" Hart replied, "No, sir, I would not."[89] Cobb and Hart wanted to demonstrate women's contributions and empowerment over individual identity, but a battle of the sexes rhetoric commenced.

Aiming to avoid a battle of the sexes, Cobb implored that women deserved to be proactive actors in space exploration as opposed to passive actors. She proposed that, scientifically, women might be better equipped for spaceflight. Cobb indicated that scientific evidence existed showing that women weighed less and consumed less than men, thereby making it cheaper for women to go into space. She also suggested that women were less prone to heart attacks and radiation. Lovelace argued previously that women were less susceptible to radiation because their reproductive organs were inside the body. She proposed that women suffered from heat, cold, monotony, loneliness and pain less than men. When questioned whether or not she was aware that NASA required women to be jet test pilots, Cobb answered: "Some of us have worked as test pilots, but it is impossible for a woman in this country to be a jet test pilot because there are no women pilots in the military services and the test pilot schools are operated solely by the military services."[90] The military—led by men—defined gender roles for spaceflight.

Cobb pointed out that despite their lack of military service, the FLATs had twice the flying hours as the male astronauts. To this, Representative Joseph E. Karth (D-MN) asked Cobb: "There is a considerable difference between straight flying—commercial or private—and test piloting; isn't there?" Cobb responded that what was needed to fly in a spacecraft was "flawless judgment, fast reaction, and the ability to transmit that to proper control of the craft." Cobb added that some of the women "have 8,000 to 10,000 [flying] hours— have flown a million miles in all types of airplanes—this is the hard way to acquire that experience [...]."[91] Astronaut Carpenter, for instance, only had "2,800 hours of any kind of flying, and only 300 of this was jet time."[92]

Turning the hearing into a battle of the sexes, Representative James G. Fulton (R-PA) fished for Cobb to answer if women were "as competent or are they better than the men?"[93] When the women suggested they were as capable as men, some of the men on the committee read that to mean the women viewed themselves as superior to men. This cognitive dissonance suggested that women succeeding in culturally defined masculine spaces challenged definitions of masculinity and perhaps threatened masculine identities.

Cobb refused to engage in the battle of the sexes and reiterated that women could not be jet test pilots in the United States military. To this, Fulton asked: "Given the same planes that are generally available and the same number of hours, how does the safety record of woman pilots compare with that of the men?" Cobb responded that she was not sure if any study had ever been conducted. However, safety did not depend on whether you were male or female; it depended on whether you were a safe pilot. Hart responded that every year for the past seventeen years, there is a transcontinental air race of more than one hundred female participants. No fatalities had occurred in the past seventeen years. Fulton interjected. He advised that The National Safety Council had statistics suggesting women were safer pilots and automobile drivers. Anfuso asked: "Do you believe that the recognized hazards in such a feat and the possible worldwide repercussions to our prestige are worth the risk and expense for us to achieve that objective of trying to put the first woman in space?" Cobb gave the affirmative: "I very definitely do—very strongly do." Representative J. Edward Roush (D-IN) did not appear convinced. He brought the hearing back to the topic of women as the weaker sex. The public discourse applauded the astronauts' emotional control. Roush alleged that Cobb lacked the emotional control needed to be an astronaut when he overheard her telling Anfuso that she was "scared to death." Cobb replied that spaceflight could not possibly be "as frightening as sitting here."[94] Her response incited laughter from the panel.

After discussing the cancellation of the Pensacola tests, Fulton asked if it was because "the men [NASA] thought the women were too successful?" Subcommittee members and the audience laughed again. When asked if she thought she personally was qualified to go into space, Cobb answered that while she had passed astronaut testing, she had yet to endure astronaut training. The panel inquired if she wanted to incorporate women into the existing astronaut program or start a separate program. Cobb responded that the women should enter the same astronaut training program since they had passed all the astronaut tests.[95]

The next day, Cochran fielded questions from the committee. The press assumed that the "godmother" of the project would advocate for women to be admitted into the astronaut corps.[96] However, to Cobb and Hart, it appeared that Cochran turned against the FLATs. Cochran was a self-made woman from the Florida panhandle's picking fields and textile mills. She left home at the age of twelve, started her own cosmetics business and eventually made a fortune. Cochran challenged gender roles throughout her life and followed her own path. A generation older than Cobb, Cochran understood better than most women pilots how to handle and address the sexist attitudes of men to enter male-dominated spaces. Cochran always made sure to apply her best lipstick while flying; she was no man; but like Cobb, Cochran offered a different feminine identity apart from the societal notions of what a woman should be.[97]

However, Cochran's testimony reinforced male attitudes and suggested women belonged in the roles of wife and mother. Women should be patient for their chance for spaceflight. Cochran denied sex discrimination within the astronaut program. Much like Cobb and Hart, Cochran also used the rhetoric of national security to make her case. She argued that with the space race's national urgency, expense and risk, astronauts should be selected from "male pilots who had already proven by aircraft testing and high-speed precision flying that they were experience [sic], competent, and qualified to meet possible emergencies in a new environment." Cochran did not think that the sex of a candidate should be the determining factor for spaceflight. She was more concerned with whether the integration of women into the program would "speed up, slow down, make more expensive, or complicate" the present program that had enough male candidates for spaceflight missions.[98]

Anfuso asked her to expand upon her comment that it would be too expensive to train women. Cochran replied that she drew her knowledge from her experiences with the WASPs. She responded that roughly forty percent of the

106 GENDER AND THE RACE FOR SPACE

WASPs left the program for marriage. Cochran acknowledged that women flew every type of military aircraft and with fewer accidents than the men. However, she brought her testimony back to wifely duties and motherhood, suggesting that in her fourteen years as director of an airline, she could confidently say that the reason women were not even civilian airline pilots was because it cost around fifty thousand dollars "to check a pilot out on a 707 or Convair 880. That is expensive if you lose them through marriage." She emphasized the importance of strict gender roles as she played into the male cognitive dissonance: "I think first and foremost no one is successful unless they are first a woman and first a man and have all of the instincts and desires of the two sexes."[99] Marriage and motherhood were essential to female identity.

Anfuso asked if women should be trained as jet test pilots. Cochran responded that it would be too expensive. She alleged that in 1956, it cost $144,000 to train a B-47 pilot. Cochran warned that it would be a waste of money if a female candidate left for marriage and motherhood. Anfuso asked if NASA should start training women as crewmembers. Cochran replied in the affirmative. Not one of the members on the subcommittee asked, nor did Cochran offer, how much it cost the government to train a crewmember.[100] At the time, about half the male candidates in military flight schools dropped out or "crashed," also costing the military money.[101] NASA did not want to pause their breakneck speed to get to the moon by incorporating more space missions to test women in spaceflight. Webb did not want another seven-to-twelve-million-dollar space mission.[102] Cost-effectiveness was vital for a bureaucracy dependent on government funding.

Representative Roush pointed out that most of the Lovelace women were well past their twenties and not focused on starting families. Cochran retorted smartly: "A very good friend of mine, age 42, just had triplets—so I don't know."[103] The United Press International took her words to suggest that astronaut women were "handicapped by extra curricular [sic] complications, such as motherhood." A United Press International reporter was "inclined to favor Miss Cochran's suggestion that women be trained as space crew members, rather than as pilots."[104] The *Miami News* reported that 36-year-old FLAT Myrtle Cagle "has temporarily put aside dreams of fitting on a spacesuit—she's shopping for maternity clothes instead."[105] A South Carolina paper implored that women remain in the roles of wives and mothers, asking what parent or spouse would condone their daughters or wives to pursue the "dangers" of spaceflight as opposed to the "normal one of raising and caring for a family." A woman's family came before her individual choices, wants and needs. The editorial failed to see women as astronauts as presenting "equality" but rather "sameness" in a society that did not welcome "identical" sexes.[106] Equality of the sexes did not mean equal opportunity to pursue one's individual identity. Conservative advocates viewed equality as the right to adhere to the gender role assigned at birth by sex and cultural norms.

Representative James C. Corman (D-CA) asked Cochran if marriage prevented women from having careers. Cochran stated no. However, to her, flying was different. If a woman left for a year to get married or have a baby, "you lose a whole year, as fast as we move, your [sic] practically have to start over." While Cochran said that you "cannot compare that to a normal job," she advised that jobs in technical fields would also be hindered by a woman leaving for a year or so as she would be way behind in technological advancement when she returned.[107] Cochran believed NASA did not discriminate against women, simply those without jet test piloting or an engineering degree.[108]

Representative Ken Hechler (D-WV) pointed out that three of the twelve women who passed the Lovelace tests were married and their marriages did not seem to affect their training. Cochran replied, "No, I didn't say it did, but if you initiate a program I say you are going to lose, if the WASP program is any criteria—that is all I have to go by—a great many through marriage, who are pretty soon producing their families." Cochran did not offer the evidence that the WASPs were typically much younger than the FLATs. Cochran did not want to seem anti-woman and added, "I think that I have proved that I am interested in women having a chance at this, but I think it should be done, and can't overstress it, in a very careful and well-planned fashion across the board."[109] Cochran assumed women who became wives and mothers would not want to continue their careers.

Representative Fulton pressed Cochran, "I hope you will not take marriage as a disqualification for space." Cochran replied, "I would not." Fulton said he certainly hoped not, especially since presently all the astronauts were married. Fulton asked, "So either marriage or children would seem to be an asset for space rather than a defect; wouldn't it?" Cochran did not think so: "It would not be an asset while you were having the babies. They didn't have them, you know."[110] Cochran wanted research to be completed on women pilots; she wanted patience and a well-organized women's astronaut program when the time was right, but Jackie would easily have said yes to a spaceflight herself.

Cochran stuck to the arguments her generation was used to making when it came to integrating or allowing women into an all-male space. She played into men's sentiments on how women should behave, act and look as not to upset the masculine sex. Cobb was of a new generation of women, those willing to stand up and make an argument for why women should be allowed in a male space, one that did not give way to male sensitivities. Hart found a middle ground, calming male fears of being emasculated by unconventional women and suggested women had societal contributions to make apart from marriage and motherhood. The country was not quite ready for Cobb's outspokenness. On the eve of women challenging gender roles legally and culturally, most Americans were not ready for what they viewed as radical changes to gender roles. To prevent what she viewed as a rush to send women into space, Cochran used the argument that resonated with most Americans. Cochran argued spaceflight would interfere with motherhood, thus, using motherhood as a tool to prevent change in women's opportunities—constricting their very identities to wife and mother.

Fulton asked if Cochran believed women should be used on Gemini and Apollo's multi-crew projects as "assistants." Cochran replied that she was not against women being in the program or going into space; they could even be "assistant pilots." She offered no information on whether marriage would hinder a possible assistant pilot program. Congressman Fulton told her that her testimony did not suggest she was against women in space. He then continued with a list of women who contributed to the founding of America: Queen Isabella, Queen Elizabeth, Pocahontas, Molly Pitcher, Sacajawea and the women who crossed the west in covered wagons along with their husbands. Cochran agreed, but again emphasized that she did not want to see women as astronauts "in a haphazard manner." Fulton concluded that instead of men "talking about keeping you out of space. We should be helping you. Women have come to the fore and taken over and performed a magnificent job when men failed." Cochran concluded her testimony by agreeing that "women can fly as well as men," however, "we are in a new environment. We are in a new era. Even if we are second in getting a woman into the new environment, it's better than to take a chance on having women fall flat on their faces."[111]

On July 18, George Low's testimony focused on the jet test pilot requirement and the intelligent use of government funds to land Americans on the moon first. Low explained that NASA had chosen the qualification of jet test pilot because "all jet test pilots are selected and trained to make rapid decisions and take immediate action based upon their own evaluation of the situation in the presence of high personal risk." He told the committee that picking only jet test pilots limited the applicant pool, making it easier to pick from a small number of candidates. However, advised Low, "These qualifications are not static but will be reviewed from time to time and are subject to modifications as our space flight experience increases."[112]

Low believed a women astronaut program would detract from the accelerated timetable to land on the moon. NASA was already planning and seeking funding for Apollo well before Mercury was over. The ability to take a spacecraft out of Earth's orbit and into the moon's orbit and back required deft piloting skills. These skills took center stage for astronaut qualifications

# FIRST LADY ASTRONAUT TRAINEES

as NASA poured money into Apollo.[113] The military pilot image presented a safety precaution to counter spaceflight risk that was dependent on tax dollar funding. Since the military barred women from military piloting, it would not have made sense to derail attention from Apollo by sending women into space. NASA, the military and the government were more fixated on the prestigious moon landing than on depicting equal opportunity within the spacecraft.

John Glenn's testimony focused on the need for pilot control and combat experience to fly a spacecraft. The astronauts laid out the importance of the pilot as an in-control systems engineer in their autobiography. In *We Seven*, Glenn argued that experience as a combat pilot and jet test pilot gave him "the ability to work with large, high powered engines and new control techniques and to react quickly and coolly in a different situation—are also basic requirements for a space pilot." Glenn's time ditching and rolling at fifteen thousand feet in the midst of enemy fire, escaping aircraft gunners, shooting down MiGs in his F-86, and landing his own damaged F9F were all possible because of his military "training and instinct."[114] The jet test pilots brought these skills with them to the astronaut corps. Glenn viewed the astronaut as "an integral part of this system, not just a passenger who goes along for the ride, as a biological specimen. He is an integral working part of it."

Much like media reports of the Mercury flights, Glenn imparted an idea of astronaut control over the craft while thwarting any talk of the feminized term "passenger." "A lot of the things we had in the past to protect human life in the early missions, will be given over to the control of the astronaut," explained Glenn, "where his function will not be backed up by automatic systems [...]. The astronauts' function is actually then to take over full control [...]."[115] The necessary skills and the platforms and combat situations necessary to gain these skills could not be possessed by women since women were not allowed to enter military pilot training nor engage in combat. In crafting the narrative of spaceflight, and this need for jet test-pilot control, women were left out of the masculine place of space. Glenn was emphatic that combat experience

> instill[ed] confidence in us that we could handle ourselves and our equipment in a crisis. You go out into an unknown every time you fly in combat, and you often face stress situations that are far more exacting than the mere physical strain of pulling Gs. [...] combat pilots build up the experience required for quick reaction which they can rely on, almost without thinking, whenever they get into trouble.[116]

Cobb had some eight thousand flying hours, including ferrying the T-6 in dangerous mechanical situations, but she failed to have combat experience.[117]

When Representative Anfuso asked Glenn if the "psychological adjustment of a test pilot to hazardous flight" was necessary to become an astronaut, Glenn responded, "It certainly is the same type of thing." Low reiterated Glenn's statements on manual control over the spaceship. He told the subcommittee, "We all know that in John's flight, he had trouble with his automatic control system. He had to assess the difficulties then calmly go on the manual system and use it, and use it effectively, under trying conditions." If the field was so dangerous and mentally taxing as the testimony purports, Representative Anfuso asked the men why one would want to be a test pilot. Carpenter responded, "I think part of it is curiosity, part of it is a need to do something on your own, something new." Glenn answered, "I think we all aspire to the top of the heap in our particular professions because it gives us the most control over the future."[118] The House Subcommittee also solicited advice from an unknown "space committee aide" who viewed women in space as only causing more "problems" such as "the engineering of space suits with the proper contours and capsules with the necessities of feminine life."[119] The theme in the testimony was that only men were interested in exploring new individual paths and women's bodies were both abnormal and in need of male protection. The testimony infuriated Cobb.

The two most important questions the subcommittee asked the astronauts concerned the qualifications of jet test piloting and the requirement of an engineering degree. Representative Jessica A. McCullough Weise (R-NY) stated that even though Low testified that all jet test piloting was closed to women, she believed a "roadblock" existed. Glenn replied with an answer that normalized men as pilots and engineers: "The men go off to fight the wars and fly the airplanes and come back and help design and build and test them. The fact that women are not in this field is a fact of our social order." NASA and the military did not discriminate; both institutions adhered to gender roles as man as the protector and woman as the protected. However, while the NASA requirements on jet test piloting precluded the women, NASA waived the requirement of an engineering degree for the men. Fulton refused to see NASA's astronaut "requirements as rigid" since Glenn and Carpenter did not have bachelor's degrees.[120]

Fulton questioned Glenn's testimony as patriarchal and discriminatory. He told Glenn, "It is the same old thing cropping up, where men want to protect women and keep them out of the field so that it is kept for men."[121] Fulton was so passionate about women's inclusion in spaceflight that Representative Anfuso interrupted "at one point and inform[ed] the ladies that Representative Fulton was a bachelor, and undoubtedly was quite sincere in wanting to 'see women out there in space—way out of this world.'"[122] Glenn's response to Fulton "brought down the house" when he suggested: "If we can find any women that demonstrate that they have better qualifications for going into a program than we have going into that program, we would welcome them with open arms."[123] The use of the term "better" highlighted a battle of the sexes argument that the FLATs were not interested in engaging.

Glenn's testimony ended with the same economic argument as Cochran's. He warned, "Now, to spend many millions of dollars to additionally qualify other people whom we don't particularly need, regardless of sex, creed, or color, doesn't seem right, when we already have these qualified people."[124] Fulton was not satisfied and preferred the creation of a women's astronaut program that did not interfere with the men's program. While the astronauts' testimony did provide ample evidence that there were enough men to complete the current Mercury spaceflight missions, they missed the importance of women's visibility and potential contributions to spaceflight. Visibility would make a tremendous impact on the future of women and minority voices and the knowledge that they also had the freedom to create their own path and determine their own future. NASA had a moment to create a culture of belonging and instead chose to focus on the prestige of a moon landing.

In his final words, Anfuso directed the NASA officials to "go back and talk to Mr. Webb [...] and come up with some kind of a program so that you can continue to have the bipartisan support which you have always seen."[125] On July 15, 1962, Anfuso sent a telegram to President Kennedy urging a woman-in-space program. As for sex discrimination within NASA, the subcommittee found nothing of substance. The subcommittee's final report in October 1962 was:

> After hearing witnesses, both Government and non-Government, including Astronauts Glenn and Carpenter, the Subcommittee concluded that NASA's astronaut selection program was basically sound and properly directed, that the highest possible standards should continue to be maintained [...].

The subcommittee did add the caveat: "Some time in the future consideration should be given to inaugurating a program of research to determine the advantages to be gained by utilizing women as astronauts."[126] The fact that NASA needed a study to determine the value of using women in spaceflight spoke volumes to society's inability to see women as equal contributors. For now, the only flight women pilots would be taking was aboard Bissell's new "Flight" Speedmaster Cleaner.[127]

The FLATs may not have won the day, "but they won the hearts of the audience."[128] Media reports of the hearing pinned two femininities against one another: equality now or exercise patience.[129] In the *Chicago Tribune's*

"Give Us Space Role, Women Pilots Urge," author Joseph Hearst pitted these two feminine identities against each other. He commented that "two women pilots today urged that women be given an opportunity to become astronauts, but a third urged a go-slow approach."[130] The *Akron Beacon Journal* ran the headline "Women Fail to Qualify For Space."[131] A South Carolina newspaper argued that Cochran's approach was correct in the face of Cobb's "demands," suggesting, "this is where some females go off the deep end. [...] It is doubtful if there can be happiness without a difference in the roles for the sexes."[132] The *Chicago Daily News Service* took a less indignant approach but stayed along the lines of women as passive actors within the cockpit until "physical standards can be lowered and when it will not be necessary for everyone to be a test pilot."[133] Women's contributions outside that of wife and mother were seen as secondary to the prestige of the space race. A science teacher attending a University of South Florida aerospace conference lamented that while he encouraged his female students to enter the science field "society does not" and "a lot of brain power in women is wasted. [...] a girl who makes straight A's usually comes to a halt by only getting a secretary's job and getting married."[134]

The Ninety-Nines, the oldest women's pilot organization in the country, grasped spaceflight's discrimination the best. They understood that it was the jet test pilot requirement that sealed women's exclusion. The women acknowledged that they could not be jet test pilots because "the equipment hasn't been made available to them." The *St. Louis Post-Dispatch*'s Clarissa Start did not see herself as a "women's rights" or "equality with men" crusader when she interviewed the Ninety-Nines, but she was still a woman who empathized with the FLATs' plight. It was not that Start wanted to fly into space. Her frustration stemmed from dismissing women with statements like "tut-tut, little girl, don't bother your pretty head about such things," which was common in the public discourse on women's rights and opportunities.[135] The Soviet Union capitalized on the United States' missed opportunity to project female liberation.

The Soviets launched Tereshkova into space almost a year later to symbolize spaceflight safety, peace and future colonization. According to the head of cosmonaut training, General Nikolai Kamin, Tereshkova's flight was not supposed to represent gender equality in the Soviet Union.[136] The Russian "Heroine" was the perfect candidate to depict Soviet communism in space. She came from a working-class background. Her tractor-driving father lost his life in World War II. Like her mother before her, she started working at tire and cotton textile factories at the age of seventeen. Her brother and sister also followed in their parents' footsteps. Tereshkova was one of the youngest members of the Communist Party.[137] She was a poster girl for Soviet advancement and the new Soviet woman, but not necessarily equality. She was a blue-collar worker who went to night school. She went to the Zhukovsky Air Force Academy and became an engineer. She flew a Mig-15UTI—which did not even make the papers or news reports.

The focus in the Soviet and American press remained on physical appearance and femininity.[138] The Soviet paper, *Izvestia*, described that Tereshkova had a "weakness for spiked heels" and "beautiful light brown hair, blue eyes, and an oval face with dimples."[139] One Moscow office worker said of the cosmonette, "What a beautiful smile. She sure knows how to smile."[140] Yuri Gagarin described Tereshkova as "a quiet, attractive girl with kind eyes and a good-natured smile."[141]

*Izvestia* paid close attention to her possible engagement to bachelor cosmonaut Andrian Nikolayev, and her "chic" fashion sense.[142] In interviews, Valya "wore a blue woolen suit described as 'very fashionable' and white shoes with spiked heels [...]."[143] When dressed for space, the "bulky" space suit "was not alien to her beauty" but "seemed to flatter her."[144] She topped off her spacesuit with "make-up on her historic mission." One Soviet interviewer commented, "Her voice is pleasant and deep and unforgettable."[145] The Associated Press's George Syversten lamented that the space suit hid Vayla's "feminine curves."[146] Her "eyes like cornflowers" made up for not being able to view her feminine figure.[147] The United Press International emphasized marriage and motherhood, suggesting that soon the requirement for jet test pilots would be dropped, making it normal for women to become astronauts as "mothers of generations borne en route to explore and perhaps colonize distant planets."[148] The article failed to mention that Tereshkova graduated from jet test-pilot training.[149]

Some within the American press criticized Tereshkova's body and flight as unfeminine. Alvin B. Webb described the flight as "'the dog days' for the American scientific male" due to the "invasion of space by the lipstick-and-powder set in the plumpish form of one Valentina Tereshkova." Of course, her flight added insult to injury for male scientists because it occurred on "Father's Day—On a Day when the American male was supposed to reign supreme, a Russian female was getting all the attention."[150] One unnamed NASA employee told the press "the thought of women in space 'makes me sick to my stomach,'" with another quipping, "Well, there is an allowance for 125 pounds for recreation equipment aboard the Apollo (moon) spacecraft."[151] Racine, Wisconsin's Tex Reynolds mocked that the Husbands' Advancement and Protective Assn. (HAAPA) issued the following statement:

> The female Russian cosmonaut is single and we do not have the slightest interest in what women do before they're married. We are dedicated to keeping wives in their proper place and maintaining family discipline.

If this Valentina had left a husband and children, and a home without the dishes done, beds made, lawn mowed, garden cultivated, and car washed, it would be a different matter.[152]

American reactions were "mixed" depending on "whether viewed from a male or distaff perspective." Americans joked about "women drivers" and "publicity stunts," with Senator Maurine Neuberger (D-OR) citing that Tereshkova's flight was a "show" that the Americans should not attempt.[153] The Associated Press emphasized that Tereshkova was "lacking in piloting skills" and "not a pilot," which might have accounted for her inability to "perform a complicated link-up maneuver" with *Vostok 5*.[154] Questions remained if the Soviets were planning a "moon colony" since "Miss Tereshkova is not a pilot."[155] Using an "untrained [...] pilot" would make it more difficult for NASA's "'male only' sign at Cape Canaveral."[156] Some within the American press ridiculed Tereshkova as a pilot, referring to her as "Russia's Meteor Maid."[157]

*Life* noted in "She Orbits over the Sex Barrier" that 26-year-old Tereshkova did not even have the flight experience of the thirteen American women who had passed Lovelace's physical tests. The article explained, "By American standards her selection might seem a fantastic gamble" if it were not for the Soviet craft's automated systems. Tereshkova's *Vostok 6* was to link up with fellow cosmonaut Lt. Colonel Valery Belkovsky's *Vostok 5* in space. Both crafts flew at the same time, but the link-up between the two did not take place. Tereshkova logged forty-eight orbits around the Earth at a speed of seventeen thousand five hundred miles an hour, orbiting the Earth every eighty-five minutes. She completed more orbits in space than all the American astronauts put together.

Like the argument to not militarize the WASPs, *Life* stereotyped that if a woman could fly in a cosmonaut space capsule, it must have meant a cosmonaut did not need to possess piloting skills. The article claimed that NASA's "outstanding lack of enthusiasm" meant that an American woman had never been seriously considered as an astronaut.[158] NASA did not perform stunts. Despite the breakneck pace to get to the moon, the public discourse reported the institution as "far removed from the pressures of politics and publicity" and that astronauts "will continue to be chosen on the basis of technical qualifications, not sex."[159] The public discourse questioned the American emphasis on test-pilot training for astronauts, as it suggested, "The Russian woman, far from being a test pilot, is said never to have flown an aircraft. Yet she was able to complete more than twice as many orbits as any American has done." This might be because of "automatic guidance control" or perhaps that "the Russians have learned that test pilot skills are not necessary" to fly into space.[160] For the Americans, "skill" will be the determining factor in whether to send a woman into space.[161]

# FIRST LADY ASTRONAUT TRAINEES

To add insult to the Americans, Jerri Cobb spoke with Tereshkova at the 1963 International Aeronautical Federation, in which Tereshkova told Cobb that "she controlled the space vehicle." To Cobb, this disproved the need for jet test-pilot American astronauts, even though the Soviets were training women as jet pilots.[162] However, the United Press International reported that neither Tereshkova nor Byovksy "attempt[ed] to take manual control and 'fly by wire' for a 'cosmic boy-meets-girl act.'"[163] The *Philadelphia Inquirer* ran the headline "U.S. Gals Green at Red Feat."[164] Mrs. Phillip A. Hart "hit the ceiling" after learning of Tereshkova's flight. Hart once again accused NASA and the United States of wasting the "resources" of "American womanhood" by hinging the requirements to be an astronaut on the discriminatory jet test pilot requirement.[165] This ensured that NASA would not send a woman into space. Hart told the press she was so annoyed at American male ignorance that "I'm tempted to go out to the barn and tell the whole story to my horse and listen to him laugh."[166] Not everyone agreed. Playwright Lillian Hellman thought the flight was "nice" but asked, "But it probably doesn't prove anything, does it?"[167] George Miller—the representative who pulled the Subcommittee hearing together for Cobb—told reporters, "I don't want to downgrade their achievement, but it doesn't mean we have to follow suit."[168] The press dismissed Tereshkova's skill and argued that the first American woman in space would have to "earn" her place.[169]

Meanwhile, the Soviet Union celebrated but failed to truly embrace gender equality. Nikita Khrushchev boasted after her orbit, "Now you see what women are capable of [...]."[170] The Soviet press was not shy to point out, "Tereshkova alone remained in space longer than all the American cosmonauts taken together."[171] Viewing Tereshkova's launch from a Western perspective as the British Parliament battled women's lack of economic emancipation and the Profumo Affair, the *London Daily Express* called Tereshkova "a soaring symbol of female emancipation."[172] Tereshkova wished to remain in the Soviet space program and further her career in engineering and space science. Unfortunately, the Soviet government forced her to go into public service because of her "dependability and confidence when speaking in public"—ironically the same traits that made her a preferred candidate for spaceflight.[173] Soviet women were allowed to fly in space, but the Soviets did not free Tereshkova from conventional feminine standards.

Equal rights supporters viewed Tereshkova's feat through their own lens. In June 1963, writer, philanthropist, former Connecticut Republican representative, and ambassador to Italy, Clare Boothe Luce wrote, "But Some People Simply Never Get the Message." The *Life* article chastised politicians and NASA officials for suggesting that Tereshkova's flight was a publicity stunt and failing to look at women's contributions and skills. Luce balked at Glenn's notion that the "qualifications we were looking for [...] were best taken care of by men." Luce quoted *New York Times* reporter Harold M. Schmeck Jr. as trying to lighten the mood by suggesting, "there appears to be no hard evidence that female physiology or psychology would confer any special advantages on a woman space traveler."[174] To Schmeck, women needed to prove themselves better equipped than men for spaceflight. People assumed men had a contribution to make for spaceflight. Women had to prove their value and worth. Luce did not believe that any of these men came to the right answer as to why the Russians sent Tereshkova into space.

Luce considered the astronauts to be the most popular heroes of a nation. Americans adored and respected the astronaut because he possessed "high technical skills and even higher virtues of intelligence, endurance, resourcefulness, discipline, courage, and the capacity to make life-and-death decisions." Not only did he possess these superhuman attributes but, as Kennedy would have advocated, "he [the astronaut] is the symbol of the way of life of his nation." The question remained: Could an American woman possess these attributes? In entrusting a 26-year-old woman with a cosmonaut mission, "the Soviet Union has given its women unmistakable proof that it believes them to possess these same virtues." Luce believed that Tereshkova was "symbolic of the emancipation of the Communist woman. Her flight symbolizes to Russian women that they actively share (not passively bask, like American women) in the glory of conquering space."[175]

The idea that Tereshkova's flight represented the equality of the sexes in the Soviet Union was misguided; however, Luce echoed the arguments that the astronauts represented the epitome of American masculinity. Within this image, women were not necessary. Luce saw women as having a real contribution to make and asked men to stop treating them like they are "paper dolls. They don't like it. They don't need it."[176] This myth of the male astronaut helped create NASA as a masculine sphere. In the United States, the thought of sending Jerrie Cobb into space became a battle between the sexes. The unspoken secret was that Tereshkova had "'panicked'" or so said the "Soviet cosmonauts" as they "privately reassured their worried American rivals [...]."[177]

The unspoken secret that Tereshkova panicked reinforced gender constructs in dangerous situations as breakdowns, meltdowns, pre-menstrual syndrome and menstruation were reasons to stop women from piloting a spacecraft. Publicly, women lacked control. Not only did the United States government not want to risk the lives of women in this war for space, but the very doctors who administered the tests on the women at the Lovelace Foundation turned against them. While the successful launch of Shepard into space rendered women's lower weight and smaller size irrelevant, doctors suggested that they found scientific "evidence" for the exclusion of women astronauts. Two Lovelace Foundation doctors, Johnnie R. Betson Jr. and Robert R. Secrest, argued that women's menstrual cycles compromised their ability to go to space. Their reasoning for this was that "mental illness is higher, crime rate increases, and there are more attempted and successful suicides just prior to and during the menstrual flow."[178] Similarly, NASA aerospace medicine researcher, Dr. Joseph Connor, suggested that menstrual pain might prevent women from flying into space because they might lose "efficiency."[179] The Americans viewed women's bodies as too complicated for spaceflight. Women's bodies would impede the race to the moon.[180]

In February 1964, NASA training officer Robert Voas, delivered a speech on women astronauts to the New York City YMCA. He noted that NASA employed five hundred and eighty women at the Manned Spacecraft Center in Houston, Texas. These women worked as nurses, physiologists, calculators and artists who painted the spacecraft. Two women even worked as senior NASA astronomy scientists. However, Voas stated that he was "rather unimpressed with the technical importance of putting women into space." He insisted that women's ability to withstand isolation better than men no longer mattered because men had discovered just how exciting space travel was. Voas joked that if a woman were to fly into space, she would have to leave her purse behind to lower the weight. He mocked that overweight women should be sent into space so they could go on a diet. He told the crowd at the YMCA that there was no benefit in sending a woman, only risks from launching someone unqualified. He ended his speech by saying, "I think we all look forward to the time when women will be part of our space flight team for when this time arrives, it will mean that man will really have found a home in space—for the woman is the personification of the home." [181] Women would wait until spaceflight was safe to fly as colonizing wives and mothers.

## Conclusion

The arguments made to keep women out of spaceflight in the 1960s are more important than the question of whether NASA should have chosen women astronauts. It was sensible to use jet test pilots for their skill and ability to take orders. The narrative that women lacked contribution, had unpredictable bodies and emotions that needed to be protected by men, situated early Cold War gender roles with technology in a cultural context. The United States left the dangerous duty of blasting into space to the male jet test pilots. The mission of the American space race was clear. The race was to demonstrate American engineering superiority, but within the public discourse, the race

## GENDER AND THE RACE FOR SPACE

also symbolized a superior masculinity through pilot control over the space-craft. Women performed femininity by awaiting the astronauts' return.

## Notes

1 Dr. Wernher von Braun, "Speech to Mississippi State College, November 19, 1962," Special Collections, John Stennis Collection, Series 46, Box. 88, Folder #11/19, Congressional and Political Research Center, University Archives, Mitchell Memorial Library, Mississippi State University.

2 Ian Mackersey, *The Wright Brothers: The Remarkable Story of the Aviation Pioneers Who Changed the World* (London: Little, Brown, 2003).

3 Corn, *The Winged Gospel*, 76. Kathleen Morgan Barry, *Femininity and Flight: A History of Flight Attendants* (Durham, NC: Duke University Press, 2007), 1–59. See also, Myers, *Earning Their Wings*, 19.

4 May, *Homeward Bound*.

5 "The Kitchen Debate Transcript," 1, and Lizbeth Cohen, *A Consumer's Republic: The Politics of Mass Consumption in Postwar America* (New York: Vintage Books, 2003).

6 Myers, *Earning Their Wings*, 10.

7 Elizabeth Cobb, *The Hello Girls: America's First Women Soldiers* (Boston: Harvard University Press, 2017).

8 Myers, *Earning Their Wings*, 5. Myers argues that the Army Air Force had already commenced the program that would become the WASPs before Roosevelt's column was published.

9 "Bayard Girl Departs for Avenger Field; Miss Lois Bristol Will Train in Texas for Ferry Command," *Bayard Transcript* (Bayard, Nebraska), September 30, 1943, 1.

10 Merryman, *Clipped Wings*, 83, 85.

11 Myers, *Earning Their Wings*, 5.

12 Leisa D. Meyer, *Creating GI Jane: Sexuality and Power in the Women's Army Corps During World War II* (New York: Columbia University Press, 1996).

13 Myers, *Earning Their Wings*, 5–16. See also, Byrd H. Granger, *On Final Approach: The Women Air Force Service Pilots of World War II* (Kingwood, TX: Falcon Publishing Company, 1991), 70–120. See also, Jean Hascall Cole, *Women Pilots of World War II* (Salt Lake City: University of Utah Press, 1992); Merryman, *Clipped Wings*, 5; and Marianne Verges, *On Silver Wings: The Women Airforce Service Pilots of World War II* (New York: Ballantine Books, 1991).

14 Shira Teitel, *Fighting for Space*, 93.

15 "Cadettes Guests of R.P.I. Head," *Troy Record* (Troy, New York), September 1, 1943, 5; "Chosen as Curtis-Wright Cadette," *Milan Standard* (Milan, Missouri), March 4, 1943, 8; "State Coach on War Jobs," *Pittsburgh-Sun Telegraph* (Pittsburgh, Pennsylvania), July 16, 1943. The 7 universities that hosted the Curtis-Wright Cadettes include Cornell, Iowa State University, University of Minnesota, Purdue University, Penn State University, Rensselaer University, and the University of Texas.

16 Lela Cole Kitson, "El Paso Girl Prepares for Arduous War Work; Mary Leola Freeman Soon to Complete Training as Cadette," *El Paso Herald-Post*, September 22, 1943, 6.

17 Powers, *Women in Flight Research*, 16, 19–20.

## FIRST LADY ASTRONAUT TRAINEES 119

18 "3000 Girls Want Air: Pilots are Grounded by Men Only Rule," *Buffalo Evening News* (Buffalo, New York), April 4, 1942, 23. The newspaper cites from Charles Planck, *Women with Wings* (New York: Harper & Brothers, 1942).

19 Myers, *Earning Their Wings*, 6.

20 "Girl Holding Down One Man's Job Seeks Another—As Army Pilot," *Democrat and Chronicle* (Rochester, New York), April 19, 1944, 16.

21 "Girl Pilots: Air Force Trains Them at Avenger Field, Texas," *Life*, July 19, 1943, 73, 75.

22 Myers, *Earning Their Wings*, 11.

23 Myers, *Earning Their Wings*, 11.

24 Elmo Scott Watson, Western Newspaper Union, "American Women Pilots Helped Deliver Planes Which Enabled Red Armies to Launch Offensive that may have been Turning Point of the War," *Midland Journal* (Rising Sun, Maryland), January 5, 1945, 7.

25 Myers, *Earning Their Wings*, 2–3.

26 "3000 Girls Want Air: Pilots Are Grounded by Men Only Rule," 23.

27 Shira Teitel, *Fight for Space*, 90–93. California Representative John Costello sponsored House Bill 4219. See also, Merryman, *Clipped Wings*, 75, 92–100.

28 Myers, *Earning Their Wings*, 8.

29 Merryman, *Clipped Wings*, 168.

30 Leslie Haynsworth and David Toomey, *Amelia Earhart's Daughters: The Wild and Glorious Story of American Women Aviators from World War Two to the Dawn of the Space Age* (New York: Perennial, 1998), 146–147.

31 United States Capitol Visitor Center, "The Women's Armed Services Integration Act: Letter from Edith L. Stallings to the Chairman of the House Armed Forces Services Committee, March 11, 1948," United States Capitol Visitor Center, accessed July 25, 2022, https://www.visitthecapitol.gov/exhibitions/artifact/letter -edith-l-stallings-chairman-house-armed-forces-service-committee-march.

32 "Women Forces Seek Recruits: Four Distaff Military Services Open Drive For New Enlistees," *Arizona Daily Star* (Tucson, Arizona), June 17, 1948, 15.

33 "Marines Seek Exes Only, Army and Air Force in Market For Fem Recruits," *San Angelo Evening Standard* (San Angelo, Texas) August 13, 1948, 7; See also, "Regular Navy to Enlist 6,000 Women by '50," *Brooklyn Daily Eagle* (Brooklyn, New York), July 31, 1948, 3.

34 Foster, *Integrating Women into the Astronaut Corps*, 11. Quoted from Cynthia Enloe, "The Politics of Constructing the American Woman Soldier as a Professionalized 'First Class Citizen,' Some Lessons from the Gulf War," *Minerva* 10, no. 1 (31 March 1992): 14.

35 Linda Bird Francke, *Ground Zero: The Gender Wars in the Military* (New York: Simon & Schuster, 1997), 26. D'Ann Campbell, "Women in Combat: The World War II Experience in the United States, Great Britain, Germany, and the Soviet Union," *The Journal of Military History* 57 (April 1993): 302. The disdain for female service members is well documented in both Meyer, *Creating G.I. Jane*, and Treadwell, *The Women's Army Corps*, Vol. 8, *The United States Army in World War II, Special Studies* (Washington, DC: United States Government Printing Office, 1954).

36 Deborah G. Douglas, *American Women and Flight Since 1940* (Lexington, KY: University of Kentucky Press, 2004).

37 Agnes E. Meyer, "Women Aren't Men," *Atlantic Monthly* 186 (1950): 32–33. Agnes E. Meyer wrote the article in conjunction with the National Citizens Commission for

120           GENDER AND THE RACE FOR SPACE

the Public Schools, the President's Commission on Higher Education, and the Mid-Century White House Child Conference.

38 Alice Thompson, "How to Be a Woman," *Seventeen*, July 1951, 106.

39 The first astronaut wives were introduced by *Life* magazine on September 21, 1959. The women appeared on the front cover under the headline "Astronauts' Wives; Their Inner Thoughts, Worries." See Annie Glenn et al., "Seven Brave Women Behind the Astronauts; Spacemen's Wives Tell of their Inner Thoughts and Worries," *Life*, September 21, 1959, 142–163. For an excellent look at the astronaut wives, see Lily Koppal, *The Astronaut Wives' Club: A True Story* (New York: Grand Central Publishing, 2013), xvi, 31, 20, xv.

40 Alan Meyer, *Weekend Pilots: Technology, Masculinity, and Private Aviation in Postwar America* (Baltimore: The Johns Hopkins University Press, 2013), 2.

41 Meyer, *Weekend Pilots*, 3.

42 "A Mrs. in the Missile?" *Los Angeles Times*, September 7, 1958, 12, Impact Series, "Women in Space II: Early 1960s File," NASA HQ.

43 Lee Belser, "Blond Would Go into Orbit," *Los Angeles Mirror*, May 22, 1959, 18

44 "Women Best Suited For Space Travel, According To Ivan Tors, TV Producer," *Times-Mail* (Bedford, Indiana), December 22, 1959, 10.

45 "Astronauts' Aide?" *Washington Post*, April 30, 1959, Impact Series, "Women in Space," Folder: 008998," NASA HQ.

46 For an excellent account of the reality behind the astronaut wife as the "modern woman," see Koppal, *The Astronaut Wives Club*, xvi.

47 The United Press International, "Ruth Nichols Says: Women Ideal Astronauts," *Akron Beacon Journal* (Akron, Ohio), November 19, 1959, 38.

48 The United Press International, "Ruth Nichols Says," 38.

49 Gay Pauley, United Press International, Women's Editor, "Famous Aviatrix Ruth Nichols Dies Before Completion of Dream," *San Bernardino County Sun* (San Bernardino, California), October 6, 1960, 61.

50 Mrs. Walter Ferguson, "Gallantry Overdone," *Evansville Press* (Evansville, Indiana), December 10, 1959, 18.

51 Weitekamp, *Right Stuff, Wrong Sex*, 67. See original, Ben Kocivar, "The Lady Wants to Orbit," *Look*, February 2, 1960, 113.

52 The Associated Press, "Woman Space Pioneer," *Philadelphia Inquirer*, January 15, 1959, 24. See also, Impact Series, "Women: Mercury Astronauts file," NASA HQ.

53 Foster, *Integrating Women into the Astronaut Corps*, 106 and Weitekamp, *Right Stuff, Wrong Sex*, 76.

54 Weitekamp, *Right Stuff, Wrong Sex*, 75, 73, 63–69. See also, Kocivar, "The Lady Wants to Orbit," 113.

55 Teitel, *Fighting for Space*, 187–188, 178. See also Jerrie Cobb and Jane Rieker, *Woman into Space: The Jerrie Cobb Story* (Englewood Cliffs, NJ: Prentice-Hall International, Inc., 1963), 154–155, 164. I use the term "tomboy" in the historical context as it suggests natural and fixed gender roles. Cobb took on masculine traits and "tomboy" would have been a phrase used at the time to describe Cobb.

56 Teitel, *Fighting for Space*, 187–191.

57 Cobb and Riecker, *Woman into Space*, 164–168.

58 "A Lady Proves She's Fit For Space Flight," *Life*, August 29, 1960, 73. and "Still Struggling to Get a Chance at Space," *Kansas City Star*, September 28, 1962, 39. See also, Weitekamp, *Right Stuff, Wrong Sex*, 76–77. Marion and Jan Dietrich told reporters

## FIRST LADY ASTRONAUT TRAINEES

they had passed 110 tests, see, "Sisters Tell Why They Want to Be Astronauts," *Medford Mail Tribune* (Medford, Oregon), July 20, 1962, 5.

59 Teitel, *Fighting for Space*, 203–206.

60 "A Lady Proves She's Fit For Space Flight," 73–74.

61 Weitekamp, *Right Stuff, Wrong Sex*, 165.

62 "Space Suffragette," *Daily Oklahoman* (Oklahoma City), July 17, 1962, Impact Series, "Women: Mercury Astronauts file," NASA HQ.

63 Donald Cox, "NASA Refutes Space Girl Story," *New York World Telegram*, September 29, 1960, "Women: Mercury Astronauts file," NASA HQ.

64 "12 Women To Take Astronaut Tests," *New York Times*, January 26, 1961, 9.

65 Teitel, *Fighting for Space*, 207. See original, Letter, Clark T. Randt to Randy Lovelace. September 23, 1960, Impact Series, Women/Mercury Astronauts Folder, NASA HQ.

66 Donald Cox, "Woman Astronauts: Dubbed 'Astranettes,' A Team of Women Pilots is Now in Training for Space Flight," *Space World* 1, no. 10 (1961): 37, 58–60.

67 "Vive la difference!" *Popular Mechanics*, October 1963, 24. The quote can also be found in Weitekamp, *Right Stuff, Wrong Sex*, 111.

68 Teitel, *Fighting for Space*, 265, 269.

69 See Ann Carl, *A WASP Among Eagles: A Woman Military Test Pilot in World War II* (Washington, DC: Smithsonian Books, 2010). See also Myers, *Earning Their Wings*, 133.

70 Weitekamp, *Right Stuff, Wrong Sex*, 126–127. See also, Teitel, *Fighting for Space*, 273.

71 Teitel, *Fighting for Space*, 281–282. The First Women's Space Symposium was on February 22, 1962. See also Helen Waterhouse, "They're Irked: Gals Want a Shot at Space Ride," *Akron Beacon Journal* (Akron, Ohio), April 22, 1962, 97. "Women Astronaut Trainee," *Calgary Albertan*, February 27, 1962, 7.

72 Waterhouse, "They're Irked," 97.

73 "Women Astronaut Trainee," 7.

74 Teitel, *Fighting for Space*, 294.

75 Teitel, *Fighting for Space*, 289.

76 Copy of a series of memos to Vice President Johnson on a request to meet with him from Mrs. Philip A. Hart and Miss Jerrie Cobb. Copied by James Osberg at the Lyndon Baines Johnson Library, to Roger Launius and Margaret A. Weitekamp. Found in the Impact Series, "Women: Mercury Astronauts file," NASA HQ. See also, Weitekamp, *Right Stuff, Wrong Sex*, 90, 136–137, and Teitel, *Fighting for Space*, 295, 297.

77 Teitel, *Fighting for Space*, 299.

78 Corn, *The Winged Gospel*, 75 and Foster, *Integrating Women into the Astronaut Corps*, 10.

79 Teitel, *Fighting for Space*, 302–303. There is a photocopy of the letter from the Eisenhower Library in Shira Teitel's appendix.

80 Teitel, *Fighting for Space*, 302–303.

81 Teitel, *Fighting for Space*, 310–311 and *New York Times News Service*, "The Moon Comes Second: George Paul Miller," *Chattanooga Times*, March 23, 1962, 2.

82 Neal Stanford, "Women as Astronauts," *Star Phoenix* (Saskatoon, Saskatchewan, Canada), July 28, 1962, 15.

83 Martha Ackmann, *The Mercury 13: The True Story of Thirteen Women and the Dream of Space Flight* (New York: Random House Trade Paperbacks, 2003), 150. For an entire list of the Committee on Science and Astronautics and its Subcommittee on the Selection of Astronauts, see: Congress, House, *Qualifications for Astronauts: Subcommittee*

# 122 GENDER AND THE RACE FOR SPACE

*Hearings*, II. Ackmann writes that Riley began serving in Congress three months prior to the subcommittee hearing and had little knowledge of the space program.

84 The Associated Press, "Lady Astronauts: 3 Blondes Ask Equality-In Space," *Corpus Christi Times*, July 17, 1962, 1. This article suggests sex discrimination at NASA based on the jet test pilot requirement.

85 Congress, House, *Qualifications for Astronauts: Subcommittee Hearings*, 1, 39.

86 Weitekamp, *Right Stuff, Wrong Sex*, 155.

87 Congress, House, *Qualifications for Astronauts: Subcommittee Hearings*, 5.

88 Congress, House, *Qualifications for Astronauts: Subcommittee Hearings*, 7–8.

89 Congress, House, *Qualifications for Astronauts: Subcommittee Hearings*, 7–8, 10.

90 Congress, House, *Qualifications for Astronauts: Subcommittee Hearings*, 5, 12. See also, Cobb and Rieker, *Woman into Space*, 215–216 and Weitekamp, *Right Stuff, Wrong Sex*, 147.

91 Congress, House, *Qualifications for Astronauts: Subcommittee Hearings*, 13.

92 Carpenter et al. *We Seven*, 44.

93 Congress, House, *Qualifications for Astronauts: Subcommittee Hearings*, 15.

94 Congress, House, *Qualifications for Astronauts: Subcommittee Hearings*, 14–16, 18.

95 Congress, House, *Qualifications for Astronauts: Subcommittee Hearings*, 20.

96 Lou Hiner, Jr., The Washington Bureau, "14 Women Pass Astronaut Test," *Indianapolis News*, July 18, 1962, 29.

97 For a look into Cochran's early life, see Teitel, *Fighting for Space*, 1–41.

98 Congress, House, *Qualifications for Astronauts: Subcommittee Hearings*, 23–24.

99 Congress, House, *Qualifications for Astronauts: Subcommittee Hearings*, 27, 35, 28.

100 Congress, House, *Qualifications for Astronauts: Subcommittee Hearings*, 28–29.

101 Voas, interview, 3.

102 Richard Witkin, "Mercury Flight Debate: Question of Another One-Man Trip Poses Technical and Cost Problems," *New York Times*, March 25, 1963, 7.

103 Congress, House, *Qualifications for Astronauts: Subcommittee Hearing*, 32.

104 Dick West, United Press International (Washington), "The Lighter Side: House Space Committee Ponders Problems of Pregnant Astronauts," *News-Review* (Roseburg, Oregon), July 18, 1962, 4.

105 "Time For Baby Before Space," *Miami News* (Miami, Florida), July 26, 1963, 12A.

106 "Women Astronauts?" *Times and Democrat* (Orangeburg, South Carolina), August 20, 1962, 4.

107 Congress, House, *Qualifications for Astronauts: Subcommittee Hearings*, 34.

108 Jacqueline Cochran and Maryann Bucknum Brinley, *Jackie Cochran: An Autobiography* (New York: Bantam Books, 1987), 318.

109 Congress, House, *Qualifications for Astronauts: Subcommittee Hearings*, 34.

110 Congress, House, *Qualifications for Astronauts: Subcommittee Hearings*, 35–37.

111 Congress, House, *Qualifications for Astronauts: Subcommittee Hearings*, 35–37.

112 Congress, House, *Qualifications for Astronauts: Subcommittee Hearings*, 45–46.

113 Teitel, *Fighting for Space*, 276–277.

114 Carpenter et al., *We Seven*, 32–33.

115 Congress, House, *Qualifications for Astronauts: Subcommittee Hearings*, 48–49.

116 Carpenter et al., *We Seven*, 34–35.

117 Teitel, *Fighting for Space*, 134–137.

118 Congress, House, *Qualifications for Astronauts: Subcommittee Hearings*, 49, 54, 51.

# FIRST LADY ASTRONAUT TRAINEES

119 The United Press International, "Women Cry "Unfair!"—Ask Congress For Equal Rights In Space," *Memphis Press-Scimitar*, July 17, 1962, 13.

120 Congress, House, *Qualifications for Astronauts: Subcommittee Hearings*, 66–67, 55. See also, Weitekamp, *Right Stuff, Wrong Sex*, 151.

121 Congress, House, *Qualifications for Astronauts: Subcommittee Hearings*, 57. See also, Weitekamp, *Right Stuff, Wrong Sex*, 151.

122 Stanford, "Women as Astronauts," 15.

123 Congress, House, *Qualifications for Astronauts: Subcommittee Hearings*, 58.

124 Congress, House, *Qualifications for Astronauts: Subcommittee Hearings*, 74.

125 Congress, House, *Qualifications for Astronauts: Subcommittee Hearings*, 74.

126 Ackmann, *The Mercury 13*, 171.

127 "Speed Master Cleaner," advertisement, *Life*, September 21, 1959, 148.

128 Stanford, "Women as Astronauts," 15.

129 Marie Lathers, "'No Official Requirement': Women, History, Time, and the U.S. Space Program," *Feminist Studies* 35, no. 1 (Spring 2009): 14–40, 16, 17, 15, 30.

130 Joseph Hearst, "Give Us Space Role, Women Pilots Urge," *Chicago Tribune*, July 18, 1962, 8.

131 "Women Fail To Qualify For Space Journeys, House Committee Told," *Akron Beacon Journal* (Akron, Ohio), July 18, 1962, 3.

132 "Women Astronauts?" 4.

133 *Chicago Daily News Service*, "New Astronaut Unit to be Vets of Jets: High-Speed Test Pilots are Regarded as Ideal For Perils of Space," *Record* (Hackensack, New Jersey), March 15, 1962, 41.

134 Virginia Davis, "Need Encouragement in Science: Women Astronauts? Maybe," *Tampa Times*, July 18, 1962, 14.

135 Clarissa Start, "Why Just Tut-Tut Girl Astronauts?" *St. Louis Post-Dispatch*, October 2, 1962, 36.

136 Bridger, "The Cold War and the Cosmos," 227.

137 The Associated Press, "Valentina Has A Good Background," 3. See also, Bridger, "The Cold War and the Cosmos," 226.

138 "Cosmonette's a Cutie," *El Paso Herald-Post*, June 17, 1963, 14.

139 The United Press International, "Her Weakness: Spiked Heels and Beethoven; New Soviet Heroine," *San Francisco Examiner*, June 17, 1963, 9.

140 "Cosmonaut May Land Tonight," *Knoxville News-Sentinel*, June 17, 1963, 2.

141 Jeremy Wolfenden, "Russia's Woman Pioneer In Space; Valentina a day late for rendezvous; Second Man May Go Up Today," *Daily Telegraph* (London, Greater London, England), June 17, 1963, 1.

142 The United Press International, "Her Weakness," 9.

143 "Cosmonettes a Cutie," 14. See also, The Associated Press, "Valentina Meets Soviet Reporters," *Philadelphia Inquirer*, June 17, 1963, 3.

144 The United Press International, "Valentina Goes for Spike Heels, Long-Haired Music," *Tampa Tribune*, June 17, 1963, 5.

145 The United Press International, "Her Weakness," 9.

146 George Syversten, The Associated Press, "One of the 'Boys': Woman Cosmonaut is Athlete," *Decatur Daily Review* (Decatur, Illinois), June 17, 1963, 1.

147 The Associated Press, "Val, Valery Land Safely; His 82 Orbits; Hers 49; Both Feeling Well; Moscow Radio Blares," *Dayton Daily News*, June 19, 1963, 3.

148 The United Press International, "Skill to Decide U.S. Astronauts," *Macon News* (Macon, Georgia), July 17, 1963, 1.

149 Rex D. Hall, Shayler David, and Bert Vis, *Russia's Cosmonauts: Inside the Yuri Gagarin Training Center* (Chichester, U.K.: Springer, 2007), 129–135.

150 Alvin B. Webb, The United Press International, "Women Irked, too: 'Cosmonette' Puts U.S. Men On Spot," *Daily Press* (Newport News, Virginia), June 17, 1963, 1.

151 Combined News Services, "U.S. Reaction?: It's All a Matter of Sex," *Newsday* (Nassau edition, Hempstead, New York), June 17, 1963, 67.

152 Tex Reynolds, "Between the Lines: A Woman in Orbit; HAAPA Statement; Bid for Air Rights," *Journal Times* (Racine, Wisconsin), June 17, 1963, 1.

153 The United Press International, "America Reacts to Space Feat with Woman Driver Wheezes," *Macon News* (Macon, Georgia), July 17, 1963, 1.

154 The Associated Press, "Cosmonette Lacking in Piloting Skills; Attempt to Launch Third Flier Rumored," *Lubbock-Avalanche Journal*, June 17, 1963, 1, 10.

155 The United Press International, "Valentina Pioneer for Moon Colony?" *Dayton Daily News* (Dayton, Ohio), June 19, 1963, 3.

156 "Feminine First," *York Dispatch* (York, Pennsylvania), June 21, 1963, 4.

157 The Associated Press Wire Photo, *Journal Times* (Racine, Wisconsin), June 17, 1963, 1.

158 "She Orbits Over the Sex Barrier," *Life*, June 28, 1963, 28.

159 John L. Myler, "No US Space Woman Planned—Yet," *San Francisco Examiner*, June 17, 1963, 9.

160 "Space Pilot Training," *Greenwood Commonwealth* (Greenwood, Mississippi), June 24, 1963, 6.

161 The United Press International, "Skill to Decide," 1. The quote is from NASA's Dr. Joseph Connor in aerospace medicine.

162 NASA Says No to American Woman in Orbit," *Sault Star* (Sault St. Marie, Ontario, Canada) October 21, 1963, 14. "5th Russian Orbit; Girl May Be Next; Space Influence In Long Flight Under Study," *Chicago Tribune*, June 15, 1963, 2.

163 The United Press International, "Soviets Apparently Will Not Attempt Space Ship Link-Up; Moscow Rumor Reports Third Shot Planned," *Macon News* (Macon, Georgia), June 17, 1963, 1.

164 The Associated Press New, "U.S. Gals Green at Red Feat," *Philadelphia Inquirer*, June 17, 1963, 3.

165 Harry Golden Jr., "Jane Hart Seethes: 'Why No US Space Girl?'" *Detroit Free Press*, June 17, 1963, 3

166 The Associated Press, "Lady 'Astro' Hopefuls Blast NASA Brushoff; Red Girls Success Doesn't Shift U.S. Policy Despite 'Equal Rights'," *Pittsburgh-Post Gazette*, June 17, 1963, 4.

167 New York (HTNS), "What the Women Say," *Tampa Tribune*, June 17, 1963.

168 The Associated Press, "Soviet Union's Latest Space Feat Evokes Little Concern in Washington," *Record Searchlight* (Redding, California), June 17, 1963, 1.

169 The Associated Press, "U.S. Cosmonette Will Have to Earn her Place in Space: Myths of Superiority of Physical Endurance Hit By Scientists," *Record* (Hackensack, New Jersey), June 17, 1963, 5.

170 The Associated Press, "U.S. Cosmonette will have to Earn her Place," 5.

171 U.S. Congress, Senate, Committee, Aeronautical and Space Sciences, "Soviet Space Programs, 1962–1965," 49.

# FIRST LADY ASTRONAUT TRAINEES 125

172 The United Press International, "Cosmonette—The Gal's Delight," *Record* (Hackensack, New Jersey), June 17, 1963, 5.
173 Bridger, "The Cold War and the Cosmos," 236.
174 Clare Boothe Luce, "But Some People Simply Never Get The Message," *Life*, June 28, 1963, 31.
175 Luce, "But Some People," 31.
176 New York (HTNS), "What Women Say," 1.
177 Lawrence Wright (*Texas Monthly*), "Tribulations and elations of a woman astronaut," *Charlotte News* (Charlotte, North Carolina), August 31, 1981, 15.
178 Betson Jr., M.D. and Secrest, M.D., "Prospective Women Astronauts Selection Program," 421–423. See also Weitekamp, *Right Stuff, Wrong Sex*, 165–166.
179 The Associated Press, "U.S. Cosmonette, 5.
180 Weitekamp, *Right Stuff, Wrong Sex*, 166.
181 Weitekamp, *Right Stuff, Wrong Sex*, 166, 158.

# Chapter 4

# REFRESHINGLY HUMAN AND WINNING: PILOT CONTROL AND PROJECT GEMINI

NASA released the first job announcement for their new hyphenated scientist-astronauts in 1964.[1] The space administration wanted candidates who possessed a minimum of a bachelor's degree in natural sciences, medicine or engineering but preferred a doctorate degree. The applicants had to be born on or after August 1, 1930, be United States citizens, no taller than six feet and be able to pass the Class I Military Flight Status Physical.[2] With no flying experience required, the scientist-astronauts did not have to be jet test pilots. The goal was to have an astronaut trained to conduct scientific research in space as opposed to relying on a pilot astronaut to conduct experiments.

Up until this point, Dr. Jocelyn Gill taught the astronauts space science. Gill received her bachelor's degree from Wellesley College in 1938, going on to earn a master's from the University of Chicago in astronomy and astrophysics and finally her doctorate from Yale University.[3] Gill started working at NASA in 1961 after serving as a professor at Wellesley and Smith Colleges. She had also previously been a research scientist for MIT. Gill developed close relationships with the astronauts and gave them science debriefings before each launch. At the age of 47 she was too old to be a scientist-astronaut despite that her "petite and attractive figure" would easily fit into the spacecraft.[4] The talent of Gill and her women colleagues had reporters wondering, "With women soaring so high in the space program, what's to keep them from making future voyages to planets?"[5]

It appeared that the new scientist-astronaut offered an entering wedge for women's integration into the astronaut corps. As the Mercury Program segued into Gemini, the immediate answer to reporters' question of why a woman was not in the astronaut corps despite women's "calm mastery" over science and engineering would be the focus on human and machine interaction in spaceflight—not scientific experiments.[6] The scientist-astronauts did not need to be jet test pilots, but NASA put the candidates through fifty-five weeks of Air Force Undergraduate Jet Pilot Training, a military program still off-limits to women.

With women left out of the gendered astronaut image, the astronauts continued to reinforce pilot control of the spacecraft. Ironically, as engineers introduced more technology into the spacecraft, the astronauts gained greater pilot control. For instance, astronauts Gus Grissom and Alan Shepard pled their case to the 1962 SETP East Coast Section meeting that the astronauts exercised pilot control over the spacecraft. Going against the public discourse, Grissom claimed the Mercury astronauts were "self-experimenting guinea pigs" in their spacecraft and engineers designed Gemini to be "the first true pilot's spacecraft." The astronaut would no longer be the "spam in a can" that the jet test pilots mocked him to be. Grissom asserted that in Gemini, "the test pilot will have stepped into his proper role—the explorer of space."[7] Grissom used the more masculine "explorer" as opposed to the word "pioneer"—who could be a man or a woman.

Despite the Mercury public discourse of astronauts wrestling control from faulty hardware, Gemini was to be the first spacecraft in which designers envisioned a human component. The following chapter argues that the public discourse refashioned the Gemini astronaut image to a true test pilot in control of his craft.[8] Much like in Mercury, the Gemini technology failed during each flight, forcing the astronauts to wrestle the controls. However, the Gemini astronauts did not fly alone, and the advanced technology of automated computers—known as the "third astronaut"—forced more teamwork in the craft and with mission control.[9]

NASA and the public discourse hailed the individualist astronaut's control over technology and the team player image, once again positioning Cold War masculinity as embodying both self-determination and democratic manhood. This need for a renewed emphasis on individual control and teamwork at NASA was situated within the context of growing civil rights and feminist movements that brought challenges to white heterosexual masculinity at home and abroad. The chapter concludes with the new hyphenated scientist-astronaut adding a layer to the gendered astronaut image that demonstrated masculinity on a spectrum. However, the military ban on women pilots and the public discourse's continuation of astronaut pilot control into Gemini continued the marginalization of women in spaceflight, leaving the astronaut gender as strictly masculine.

On December 7, 1961, NASA approved the two-man team Project Gemini flights. Between 1965 and 1966, NASA flew ten manned Gemini missions. NASA named the project after the twin Greek gods Castor and Pollux. *Gemini 1* and *Gemini 2* were unmanned spaceflights, demonstrating that the craft could fly with automated technology. Project Gemini's objectives were to prepare astronauts for longer duration missions and to perfect rendezvous, docking, reentry and landing a spacecraft for future Apollo missions. Longer flights meant more teamwork with mission control.

Before NASA launched the first manned Gemini missions, on October 12, 1964, the Soviet Union sent a three-man team into orbit aboard *Voskhod 1* (*Sunrise*) for two days. Aboard the craft were pilot and flight commander Colonel Vladimir M. Komarov and two non-military pilots, the engineer-scientist Konstantin Feoktistov and medical doctor Boris Borisovich Yegorov.[10] *Voskhod 1* represented the ability of non-pilots to go into space, but in a subordinated role. The Soviets envisioned the engineer and doctor as passengers, not pilots.[11] A week after the Soviets launched *Voskhod 1*, American scientists wanted their turn and pressured NASA to recruit scientist-astronauts to keep up with the Soviets. Unlike the First Lady Astronaut Trainees (FLATs), the scientists won their argument.[12]

While Martin Luther King Jr. and hundreds of unarmed protestors were savagely beaten by Alabama State Troopers in three attempts to march peacefully across the Edmund Pettis Bridge from Selma to Montgomery, Alabama, to exercise their right to vote, "Gloom descended over the Cape [Kennedy]. The sound of disappointment ranged from profanity to polite and frustrated Pollyanity," wrote *Time*.[13] The Soviets had struck again. On March 18, 1965, cosmonaut and Soviet fighter pilot Alexei Leonov, performed the world's first extra-vehicular activity (EVA or spacewalk) aboard *Voskhod 2*. Leonov "walked" in space, and Pavel Belyayev piloted the craft. Leonov's proximity to *Voskhod 2* was about fifteen feet when he was outside the craft. In approximately twelve minutes, he completed four somersaults, a headstand and filmed his surroundings.[14]

To make matters more embarrassing for American masculinity, engineers estimated that the rocket carrying the Soviets contained about 1.43 million pounds of thrust, about three times that of *Gemini*'s *Titan* rocket. The capsule reached three hundred and seven miles of altitude, the highest of any previous Soviet or American spacecraft. Unlike previous Soviet spacecraft that demanded the cosmonaut parachute out of the craft after the return from space, *Voskhod* came equipped with a solid-fuel braking rocket that allowed the Soviets to land the craft on the ground as opposed to parachuting out.[15] Similarly to the American automated systems, *Life* reported on the faulty Soviet automatic control system. Belyayev was forced to manually land his craft. However, he did overshoot his mark by hundreds of miles. International scientists believed that the scientific information taken from the EVA, "put the Soviet Union even more months ahead of the United States in the race for a manned moon landing."[16] TASS reported that "the target before us now is the moon, and we hope to reach it in no distant future."[17]

Americans speculated about the cosmonauts' work and control over their craft. *Time* doubted Leonov controlled his EVA, viewing his somersaults as unintentional. While the Soviet press insisted that Leonov "inspected the outside of Voskhod II and did useful work," *Newsweek* maintained that Leonov failed to work outside the capsule. The popular print magazine reported that the video footage of Leonov's flight "did not show all these actions" and the cosmonaut's "work" was "slight."[18] Jim Webb attempted to calm American defeatism, maintaining the superiority of American flights since they were "not based primarily on propaganda."[19] Deputy Center Director of Houston's Manned Spaceflight Center, Dr. George Low, insisted that NASA's manned spaceflight program was operating at its maximum capacity. George P. Miller (D-CA), chairman of the House Space Committee, remarked that the Soviets did not do anything the United States was not expecting. Nevertheless, since the Soviets had "gotten ahead of us," it was time for Americans to "tighten our belts and get going."[20] Miller's fears were not alone. Space pundits and congressmen believed that with the Soviet's EVA, the Americans might need another year to "match the Russians feat."[21]

The Americans continued to perform their own firsts openly to the world— both in spaceflight and domestic strife. Two days before Dr. King Jr. declared on the steps of the Alabama State Capitol, "Our aim must never be to defeat or humiliate the white man, but to win his friendship and understanding," white masculinity left Earth aboard Gemini.[22] On March 23, 1965, NASA launched Gus Grissom and John Young aboard *Gemini 3*. The craft was nicknamed the "Molly Brown," a fitting tribute to Grissom's lost *Liberty Bell* and *Titanic* survivor, Molly Brown.

*Newsweek* proclaimed that the astronauts controlled the craft "like jet pilots."[23] The Associated Press reported that "Grissom and Young scored a world 'first' by actually maneuvering their Molly Brown through three orbital changes."[24] The United Press International stated that *Gemini 3* completed a "first" as officials reported "it was the first-spaceship to be steered in flight by either U.S. or Russian pilots."[25]

*Life* refashioned their own Mercury astronaut control narrative by arguing that "For the first time, rather than being nearly helpless riders aboard an intractable projectile, the Astronauts really controlled their craft." Grissom reoriented the craft three times. Grissom's movements included reducing the oval-shaped orbit into a near-precise circle, changing the vehicle's yaw around the Earth into a new course, and finally lowering the orbit of the craft. Grissom argued, "No Astronaut from anywhere had ever performed these maneuvers." The astronauts were more interested in flying than in the scientific experiments they performed. Grissom explained, mocking the Soviet cosmonauts, "As test pilots John and I were not quite as fascinated by sea

## REFRESHINGLY HUMAN AND WINNING

urchins and sandwiches as we were by the chance to carry out some real 'firsts' in space flight [*sic*]."[26] The *Washington Post's* Charles Stafford heralded the new spaceflight era as Gemini became the "first true flying machine to enter the space race."[27] A *Post* editorial boasted, "The Russians have shown that homo sapiens can 'walk' in space; Astronauts Virgil Grissom and John Young have confirmed mankind's ability to 'fly' in space."[28]

Not only did journalists proclaim that the Gemini pilots controlled their craft, but they also mentioned the ability to steer during landing. After his flight, Grissom declared that the automated computer informed him and Young that they would land just short of their mark, the aircraft carrier, the USS *Intrepid*. Therefore, Grissom took over the controls and flew his own craft. He remarked that the craft maneuvered almost like an "airplane," and that he alone "was able to reduce the error considerably."[29] Pilot control succeeding where technology failed remained paramount in the public discourse. Even veteran space journalist John W. Finney, wrote that the difference between Mercury and Gemini was that the Gemini would be "under the control of the astronauts rather than automatic instruments. In effect, the astronauts will be flying the capsule."[30]

However, with Gemini, the astronaut image experienced a shift from the autonomous explorer to a two-man exploration "team."[31] President Johnson viewed the flight as "an impressive testament to the teamwork of our fine talents […] who have worked together so successful on Project Mercury and now on this important first step of Project Gemini."[32] The individualistic astronaut in space was slowly becoming a team member—a reality needed for the dangers of spaceflight.

In a statement before the Congressional Committee on Science and Astronautics, NASA Deputy Administrator Hugh Dryden said that when the Wright brothers created the first powered flight, "it was possible for any individual to learn and know all there was to know about aeronautics and airplane design" but in spaceflight "no member of the team has complete knowledge of the final product in all its detail." Dryden's speech suggested adding additional layers of masculinity—one of a team player—to the gendered astronaut image. Dryden argued, "The building of modern airplanes, boosters, and spacecraft require[d] a highly developed concept of team activity and functional coordination."[33] Individualist astronauts and mission control teams continued with purposeful firsts in space as self-reliant, individualist masculinity embraced democratic manhood.

The United States performed its first spacewalk on June 3, 1965. After *Gemini 4*'s fourth orbit, Lieutenant Colonel Edward "Ed" Higgins White Jr. left the capsule. White walked in space for twenty minutes at a speed of Seventeen thousand five hundred miles per hour. He reported to mission

132    GENDER AND THE RACE FOR SPACE

control, "This is fun."[34] His distance from people on Earth was a mere one hundred twenty miles.

*Life* claimed that White's walk was not a "mere stunt" but rather "a deliberate and methodical test of the techniques which future astronauts may have to use in docking maneuvers and making extraterrestrial emergency repairs."[35] The public discourse viewed the Soviet space program as propaganda with no real technological or scientific purpose. This aligns with the insistence that Valentina Tereshkova's flight was a mere publicity stunt, a woman in space had no value to technology or scientific advancement.

The public discourse reinforced the Soviet lack of spaceflight purpose with the claim that cosmonaut Leonov did not control his spacewalk. Rather, he was "slowly somersaulting and floating as though in a vast midnight swimming pool," connected to the craft only by a cord.[36] Conversely, White controlled his direction during his spacewalk with a "jet gun."[37] The *Chicago Daily News* stated, "In some respects, notably his use of a 'space gun' for individual propulsion, he surpassed the Russian achievement [...]." Opinions within the *New York Times* followed suit, arguing that White's spacewalk "shattered" notions that the Americans lagged behind the Soviets.[38] *Time* concluded that the "daring flyer" and "superb pilot and first-class engineer" White controlled his spacewalk while Leonov became "dizzy" with his lack of "maneuverability."[39] *Newsweek* went so far as to proclaim White's walk as "the most dazzling human achievement yet in the space age."[40]

The Western world commended White's individual control as a symbol of democratic prowess over the communist system. Stockholm's *Svenska Dagbladet* rejoiced that the American feat proved what an open system can do compared to the Soviet closed society. The Swedish paper wrote, "The fact that the U.S. dares to expose even its shortcomings, dares to give advance notice, dares to speak the whole truth, is a sign of strength and confidence. But above all, it is so refreshingly human and winning." Buenos Aires' conservative *La Nacion*, and their independent *Clarin*, both "declared flatly that White's performance had clearly surpassed the similar feat of the Soviet Cosmonaut Leonov."[41] London's *Daily Express* reported that while Russia performed the first spacewalk, Major White walked in space with his own means of propulsion.[42]

After White and McDivitt secured themselves back onto the capsule's couch, they completed sixty-two orbits of the Earth in three and a half days. *Gemini 4*'s reentry system broke down, forcing McDivitt to manually fire the retro rockets and land the craft.[43] They landed fifty-six miles short of their recovery vessel stationed in the Atlantic, the carrier the USS *Wasp*. Despite the much-anticipated first American spacewalk, the mission did have one setback. The astronauts and mission control hoped that *Gemini 4* would be able to test a rendezvous with a rocket booster in space. Unfortunately, a large

**Figure 4.1** Astronaut Ed White's June 3, 1965, Spacewalk. Source: NASA. https://www.nasa.gov/image-article/flashback-americas-first-spacewalk/.

amount of *Gemini 4's* fuel burned up during maneuvering, and the astronauts were unable to attempt such a feat.[44]

In sharing their stories with *Life*, the public discourse of astronaut control was familiar, but the astronauts admitted that they were not always in control. The complexity of spaceflight demanded computerized systems. McDivitt told Americans that he was not scared or fearful for his "personal safety," but when it came to rocket boosters, "You don't have any control over the booster at launch; you're really at its mercy."[45] The astronauts emphasized the need for traits such as "keen eyes, stable hands, and cool heads" to rendezvous with the booster. Computers and solving equations were also necessary. The astronauts needed the minds of engineers and mathematicians. To aid the astronauts in space, IBM created a powerful new computer that calculated trajectories, attitude, velocity, and the astronaut responded. David Mindell argues, "Heroic action now involved not only controlling the spacecraft but also loading code into a digital machine."[46] Masculinity required the heroics of strapping oneself to a rocket that the astronaut could not control, piloting and engineering skills, coupled with teamwork with mission control. Individuality, teamwork, bravery and superior intellect crafted a Cold War masculinity that was continually renegotiated.

On August 19, 1965, NASA's Martin *Titan II* rocket failed on the Cape Canaveral launchpad. Engineers and technicians repaired the rocket. Two days later, the rocket launched perfectly at a speed of almost eighteen thousand miles per hour, making *Gemini 5* the fastest American craft. The August 21 to August 29, 1965 *Gemini 5* mission of command pilot Gordon Cooper and pilot Charles "Pete" Conrad Jr. had two goals. First, to test to see if an astronaut could work eight days in space, and second, to test space equipment for possible linkage between crafts in space. However, it did not go unnoticed in the press that Cooper and Conrad "were out to break the 119-hour and 6-minute flight record of Soviet Lieut. Col. Valery F. Bykovsky, who flew for five days in a *Vostok* capsule in 1963."[47] *Gemini 5* was not without its electrical system setbacks. Mission controllers and astronauts worked together to fix the problem. The plan could not go off as expected if it were not for the astronauts in the craft turning off electrical devices to conserve power. Mission control debated what to do next. Flight Director Chris Kraft pressed on. The astronauts aboard suffered from a lack of sleep. The astronauts' doctors demanded that the men get some rest. Conrad growled, "I try to, but you guys keep giving us something to do."[48] After the flight, TASS accused the United States government of forcing NASA "to carry out a crash program," a claim which mission control officer John Hodges denied.[49]

The fascination with the astronauts' use of the cockpit controls and individuality continued to attract media attention. Conrad learned the art of "diplomacy"—teamwork—while contributing to the instrument panel and cockpit "design." From this, the astronaut concluded, "Being pilots and individualists, astronauts are notorious for not agreeing on what they like to see on the instrument panel." The *New York Times* claimed that the reason Cooper flew the last Mercury flight was because he was such a "maverick" that it "irritated space officials and may have caused them to hold back his flight."[50] Conrad admitted that he signed up for the astronaut corps from a "pilot's point of view" and he doubted if he would feel the same excitement of the "constant changes in G-forces" from jet piloting. Conrad was wrong and argued that the astronauts "demonstrated the value of a pilot in a spacecraft, and I look forward to some of the presently automatic functions becoming pilot functions. I hope one day to see Astronauts ignite and control the lift-off of their boosters just as they do jet takeoffs."[51]

The *Gemini 5* astronauts completed rendezvous maneuvers that would be necessary to go to the moon. The objective of the mission was to test the space equipment for linkups in space. Conrad and Cooper were pleased that during

# REFRESHINGLY HUMAN AND WINNING

the flight they performed the first rendezvous with an invisible rocket. The astronauts came within fifteen nautical miles of the phantom rocket, a point in space intended to mimic the position of the later *Agena* upper stage rendezvous vehicle. The success of the task took the skill of the pilot astronaut using the computer and radar to "shift and set the capsule." [52] But piloting skill to maneuver the craft was not the sole reason for the success. Doctors worried that the astronauts might suffer from a lack of sleep. Allowing ground control to take over the craft and plot the *Agena's* coordinates while Cooper and Conrad slept added to the mission's achievement. As astronauts spent more and more time in space, cooperative teamwork took over the rugged individual astronaut of the Mercury Program. The onboard computer also aided the American space victory. The astronaut became less of an individualist in space as spaceflight technology progressed.

*Gemini 6A* and *Gemini 7* performed the fourth and fifth manned spaceflights for Project Gemini. Between 4 December and December 18, 1965, command pilot Frank Borman Jr. and pilot James "Jim" A. Lovell Jr. flew *Gemini 7*. The mission was to rendezvous with *Gemini 6A*. Leaving the launchpad on December 15, 1965, *Gemini 6A* carried both command pilot Wally Schirra and pilot Thomas Stafford. The two crafts met in space within inches of each other. The *New York Times* presented a story of human and machine cooperation in space. The machines calculated the trajectories, the distance to the landing zone, and even fired retro-rockets. However, the craft would not have worked without the astronauts' ability to "guide" it through space and even prevent the capsule from "tumbling" by incorrectly firing its thruster rockets.[53] Schirra preferred to illustrate that he was in control. He said:

> Using what I called my "eyeball ranging system," I did an in-plane fly around of *Gemini 7*, like a crew chief inspecting an aircraft [...] I was amazed at my ability to maneuver, controlling attitude with my right hand and translating in every direction by igniting the big thrusters with my left hand mechanism.[54]

Command pilot Neil Armstrong and pilot David "Dave" Scott further presented astronaut control with *Gemini 8*. The mission was to become the world's first space vehicle to dock with another space vehicle. On March 16, 1966, NASA launched *Gemini 8* to dock with the *Agena* rocket that had been in orbit for the past five months. *Gemini 8* could use the *Agena's* power to navigate through space.[55] *Life* magazine depicted the flight as man's triumph over the machine. The astronauts reported that "Neil made the closing maneuvers and Dave handled the computer calculations which told us the exact amount and direction of thrust needed."[56] When Armstrong docked with the *Agena*, both vehicles spun violently around. Scott radioed mission control, "We have a serious problem here. We're—we're tumbling end over end up here. We're disengaged from the Agena." The astronauts began "regaining control of the spacecraft" by 7:18:45 and lost sight of the *Agena*.[57]

The spinning knocked out the astronauts' control of the yaw and roll systems, with only the yaw control returning during the rest of the flight. Reports suggested that the astronauts remained calm during the unrehearsed spinning that cut the three-day trip down to one day as the "pilots" had to make an emergency landing.[58] *Life* argued that even at the mission's scariest moments, Armstrong's voice remained "laconic" and his control of the situation never wavered.[59] While Armstrong and Scott's calm demeanor was extremely necessary for regaining craft control, they also needed the engineering teams and their backup astronauts on the ground to aid them in regaining this control. Democratic manhood was necessary for the success of the "first emergency landing" in space.[60] Armstrong and Scott narrowly escaped with their lives as the astronauts could have lost consciousness or the spinning *Agena* could have ripped the spacecraft in two.[61] Luckily for the mission, Armstrong was considered one of the physically strongest and best test-pilot astronauts.[62]

Reporters also emphasized the engineers but never wavered from the in-control pilot astronaut image. *Time* depicted the scene at Houston as "controllers huddled over their consoles" trying to pinpoint the trouble. But it was the astronaut who ultimately prevailed. Armstrong regained control by activating the thrusters that were used to stabilize the capsule during reentry. He was a pilot in control. Armstrong radioed back to Houston, "We are regaining control of the spacecraft slowly."[63] After stabilizing the craft, "the plucky spacemen [...] managed to regain control of the ship by employing a last-resort measure—and thus not only escaped becoming the first martyrs of the space age but wound up steering their craft to an unprecedented bullseye landing [...]."[64]

The rescue pilots described the astronauts as "cool" and "eating sandwiches" when they found them.[65] The press jumped on this, writing several articles focused on the astronauts as "icy nerved," "vocally calm, cool" and "extremely ho-hum" as they regained "control" of the craft.[66] The press fixated on the pilots' heartbeats and voices on the transcript tapes. NASA hesitated to release the tapes. The astronauts' heart rates were elevated upward to one hundred and fifty beats for Armstrong and one hundred thirty-five for Scott. But that was simply normal adrenaline needed to get the job done, according to NASA physician Dr. Charles Berry.[67] While NASA officials told the press they had not determined what caused *Gemini 8*'s rolling and bucking, the one thing they were sure about was that "there was not a trace of panic in the Gemini 8 capsule."[68] Armstrong stated that as a "test pilot" he

## REFRESHINGLY HUMAN AND WINNING

was trained in "identifying problems and getting the answers. We never once doubted we would find an answer."[69]

Papers lauded the flying careers of Armstrong and Scott—especially their jet test-pilot experience. Armstrong had a pilot's license before he even had a driver's license. He completed seventy-eight combat missions in Korea and flew the X-15 seven times into space, reaching forty miles into the atmosphere at lightning speed. The command pilot admitted that "he gave Mercury too little credit" now that he found himself at the controls of a spacecraft.[70] Air Force Major David Scott flew fighter-interceptor aircraft before being chosen for NASA's Astronaut Group 3.[71]

Papers depicted the astronauts as "playing cat and mouse with the target ship (the *Agena*) during a one hundred five thousand mile chase, flying formation with it." The public discourse reported that Armstrong and Scott controlled their craft by pushing buttons, leading the *Philadelphia Inquirer* to conclude that "there was no question about the flying skill and the mathematical computing of both Armstrong and Scott."[72]

Flying a jet still proved extremely dangerous as the astronauts established themselves as prime pilots who controlled faulty technology, making spaceflight appear routine. Tragedy struck less than a month before *Gemini 8*'s flight. On February 28, 1966, the slated crew for *Gemini 9*, Astronaut Group 2's Elliot See and Group 3's Charles Bassett, were killed when their T-38 crashed into McDonnell Aircraft Building 101 in St. Louis, Missouri. See piloted the T-38 and Bassett was in the backseat. Accompanying them in a second T-38 were backup crew Group 3's Eugene 'Gene' Andrew Cernan and Thomas Stafford. The astronauts were headed to the McDonnell plant for space simulator training. Poor weather forced See to rely on instrumentation, and his jet overshot its landing. See and Bassett died on impact.[73]

Their deaths came two years after Group 3 astronaut, Air Force Captain Theodore Freeman, was killed when his T-38 struck a goose while landing at Ellington Air Force Base in Houston. Freeman attempted to land short, avoiding crashing the plane into military housing. The plane tilted downward, and he ejected almost horizontally. His parachute failed to deploy at the short distance of around three hundred and fifty feet from the ground. Freeman was killed when he struck the ground. He became the first American astronaut to die. He was returning from simulation training at McDonnell.[74]

It was a tragedy all too familiar with jet piloting. See understood the strong relationship between piloting and engineering skills to fly. In an interview before his death, See told reporters, "To be a good test pilot requires a basic interest in extending the known engineering capabilities."[75] See broke down the exploration spirit to its core; to explore new technologies and new spaces was at the very heart of what it meant to be human. The ability to explore

138 GENDER AND THE RACE FOR SPACE

and then pioneer or control new technologies despite the risks involved demonstrated masculinity of the highest order.

NASA launched Gemini missions every two months as journalists continued to emphasize astronaut control over imperfect technology. Command pilot Thomas Patten Stafford and pilot Gene Cernan experienced firsthand the faulty technology as they waited atop their *Titan 2* for NASA controllers to launch *Gemini 9A* for a four-day mission in space.[76] The third try worked. On June 3, 1966, *Gemini 9A* launched from Cape Canaveral. Unfortunately, as the astronauts attempted a docking maneuver in space, the "protective shroud" of the *Agena*, malfunctioned, leaving the docking target looking like an "angry alligator."[77]

Astronaut control persisted through faulty *Agena* technology. The rocket's guidance system may have launched *Gemini 9A* into space, but Stafford "fired the thrusters for a minute to make the first adjustment in the craft's orbit [...]." As the craft reached the target vehicle, the astronauts were able to "steer their craft to their rendezvous with the target vehicle," but Kranz "ordered the astronauts to 'leave it alone.'"[78] The United Press International hailed the feat, perhaps incorrectly suggesting that the astronauts had "mastered" the rendezvous procedure.[79] Cernan then went for a spacewalk, but fogging inside his helmet forced the "cool-nerved" astronaut to cut his walk short.[80] With Cernan strapped back onto the couch, Stafford proceeded home, "steering Gemini to a slightly lower orbit."[81] Reporters hailed that the "astronauts steered their spacecraft" to its "Near Perfect Landing" in the Atlantic Ocean.[82] Once again, another American "Troubled Flight Ends in Success" as man took over the machine.[83] President Johnson praised the astronauts' "coolness and courage under pressure."[84]

On July 18, 1966, NASA launched command pilot John Young and pilot Michael Collins aboard *Gemini 10*, less than two months after *Gemini 9A*. Papers hailed the countdown as the "smoothest" and "cleanest" of any spaceflight. Project Gemini was making space travel appear routine. The mission was to perform a successful docking with the *Agena*. *Gemini 10* broke the former altitude record held by the Soviets' *Voskhod 2* at three hundred and seven miles. The link-up between *Gemini 10* and the *Agena* reached an altitude of four hundred and seventy-four miles.[85] The script of astronaut control appeared routine with reports that "Young controlled the Gemini."[86] While Young was "at the controls," the "imperturbable" Collins braved a spacewalk twice, maneuvering himself and becoming the first spaceman to "work" with another space vehicle, the *Agena*.[87] After the "physically bold" Collins retrieved a micrometeorite detection box from the rocket, "Young steered the spacecraft into a new orbit to be ready for splashdown [...]."[88] Both men's eyes experienced a burning sensation during the mission from the new anti-fogging helmet spray. Young told the press he did not alert mission control "because I figured I'd just be a sissy."[89] Astronaut emotions remained remarkably "calm" during a dangerous landing that heated up their craft to "3,000 degrees, blackening it on all sides."[90]

The *New York Times'* official space race box score had the United States commanding the lead. By July 1966, the Americans had tripled their amount of time in space compared to the Soviets. The United States had seven successful rendezvous in space, while the Soviets completed zero. The United States had two space linkups, and the Soviets had none. The Americans had eight maneuverable spacecrafts, while the Soviets failed to create pilot-controlled spacecrafts.[91] Astronauts controlled spaceflight while the cosmonaut relinquished his masculinity to the technology. According to *Time*, the perfection of the American flights made spaceflight appear "almost routine."[92]

Flying from September 12 to September 15, 1966, *Gemini 11*, piloted by command pilot Pete Conrad and pilot Richard Francis Dick Gordon Jr., smashed the previous altitude record as they soared to a new altitude of eight hundred and fifty miles.[93] The team completed the world's first-ever successful rendezvous during a spacecraft's first orbit.[94] But, the public discourse shifted. As *Gemini 11* splashed into the Atlantic, the *New York Times* and the Associated Press underscored not pilot control but rather, computer control. John Noble Wilford wrote that the "Gemini 11 astronauts let their computer take over today to steer them automatically to a safe and accurate splashdown [...]."[95] The Associated Press hailed the technology, celebrating that "Gemini 11 guided its proud pilots to a breathtaking bull's eye landing [...]."[96] The United Press International reveled in the "batch" of new "space records" that Gemini accomplished, especially its "automated Atlantic landing [...]."[97] The *Syracuse Post-Standard* reported that "Glinting in the tropical sun, their spaceship automatically guided the thrilled spacemen to a breathtaking, bull's-eye landing [...]."[98] Astronaut masculinity did not falter as the pilots let the technology control the landing.

Reporters once again celebrated the computer landing with *Gemini 12*. The *New York Times* stated that "for their return to earth, the Gemini 12 pilots let an onboard computer the size of a hat box take over both the guidance and firing of the maneuvering rockets. Gemini 12 made the first [*sic*] such automatic controlled landing [...]."[99] But again, it was command pilot Jim Lovell and pilot Edwin "Buzz" Aldrin who allowed the automated system to land the craft. The *Washington Post* continued to emphasize astronaut maneuverability while arguing that there is no "indication that the cosmonauts can actually maneuver their craft."[100]

Despite the continued script of astronaut control, *Gemini 12*'s mission left famed *Life* NASA reporter Loudon Wainwright underwhelmed. In fact, the space reporter forgot the date when the craft would return to Earth. It was not that Wainwright was falling short of his exemplary reporting. "Truthfully," Wainwright writes, Americans were suffering from "total ignorance" of the spaceflights. In his article "All systems are Ho-Hum," Wainwright asked a group of six people for information on the flight's landing. No one in the group had any idea when the astronauts were expected to land, or if they did land and if the landing was successful.[101]

Spaceflight was becoming more routine; the extraordinary became ordinary. Wainwright reminisced over the Mercury astronauts. He remembered how "each flight was packed with drama and suspense—fuel running low, automatic controls not working, flaming re-entries, temporarily lost pilots, last minute rescues" followed by parades, crowds, presidential welcomes and congressional hearings. The hysteria was so great that five years ago during John Glenn's New York parade, the crowd broke through the barricades and crushed the fender of Glenn's car. The Gemini technology was more sophisticated and—ironically—pilot and automatic control were greater. Jim Lovell spent over three times as much time in space as Glenn, but the average American was more likely to recognize Glenn. Too many astronauts made the feats less special. NASA had fifty astronauts whereas Charles Lindbergh flew alone. If Lindbergh had flown as a two-man team, "a second man in that cockpit would have lessened his glory." Independent self-reliance gave way to teams.

The team element, for the moment took away the daring, and the technological "soundness" destroyed the Americans' anticipation of "half expecting the whole thing to blow up." The astronauts were no longer rugged individuals controlling faulty machinery in space. They were skilled pilots and engineers who worked as a team both with man and technology. Astronaut Scott Carpenter told Wainwright that the lackluster public attention to the flights did not bother NASA. The pilots still performed their job. Carpenter prophetically suggested that future trips to the moon will "seem a bit ho-hum," but "one day Grandmothers will be making the flight [...] and will be impatient when they don't get their baggage on time."[102]

*Life* magazine, the only media outlet with the rights to the astronauts' stories, dedicated only two pages to the last *Gemini* flight. They implied the routinization of spaceflight with a playful picture taken by Lovell and Aldrin. The flight was so smooth that "where previous space-walkers had encountered some scary difficulties, Aldrin had none." On the bright side,

> the success of Gemini, has established beyond doubt man's capacity for controlling space. No longer is he a "captive" of a womblike capsule but its master, able to maneuver it, to hook up with another vehicle and harness that vehicle's power, or to step out in space and act as a celestial mechanic with undue sweat, as Aldrin proved so well.

## REFRESHINGLY HUMAN AND WINNING

The article deemed it hard to imagine that just a short twenty months ago "the astronauts were essentially passengers rather than pilots."[103] The astronauts controlled the once faulty technology so well that they now mastered and commanded the technology, demonstrating a combination of rugged individual masculinity and democratic manhood.

Who controlled the spacecraft shifted as the technologically sophisticated and efficient Gemini craft strengthened the United States' lead in the space race. The astronaut, the symbol of Cold War masculinity during a time of a perceived masculinity crisis, was changing. On November 21, 1966, after a tour of the growing quagmire in Vietnam, President Johnson congratulated American efforts in space, specifically praising the efforts of the individuals involved to come together in such a highly technical and dangerous project. He said:

> Today's flight was the culmination of a great team effort, stretching back to 1961, and directly involving more than 25,000 people in the National Aeronautics and Space Administration, the Department of Defense, and other Government agencies; in the universities and other research centers; and in American industry.[104]

The rugged individual astronaut image was at odds with spaceflight as a team effort. Johnson recognized the dangers of these complex systems within the spacecraft. He predicted that "the Apollo program which follows is much more complicated. [...] The months ahead will not be easy, as we reach toward the moon."[105] In the press, the need for teamwork and computers reimagined the astronaut image as rugged individuals engaged in democratic teamwork both at home and abroad in space. The scientist-astronaut symbolized these fluctuating masculine tropes, even though piloting the craft remained paramount to spaceflight success and the astronaut image.

### Scientist-Astronauts

In 1958, President Eisenhower had instructed the Space Task Group to choose jet test pilots for their ability to pilot, take orders and face the risk of death. Eisenhower also wanted NASA to ensure the peaceful exploration of space. The manned spaceflight program was missing the space science element as it moved into the 1960s. Jet test pilots conducted scientific experiments aboard the craft, but the National Academy of Sciences (NAS) wanted a professional scientist aboard for future moon landings. President Kennedy could not care less about space science. He preferred the brawn and daring "thrust" of a moon landing. But scientists had clout and political power during the Cold

142  GENDER AND THE RACE FOR SPACE

War. NASA's well-respected associate administrator, renowned aerospace and missile engineer Dr. Robert C. Seamans, Jr., respectfully requested the president not "emasculate" the pursuit of space science.[106]

In the summer of 1963, the NAS sponsored the Space Science Summer Study. The group compiled the *Review of Space Research* for administrator Webb. The men concluded that space exploration was scientific and urged NASA to include "trained scientist-observers" on Gemini or Apollo as scientist-astronauts, scientist-passengers, astronaut-observers and ground scientists. The scientists suggested that those with backgrounds in meteorology, geology, astronomy and biology be selected for space missions.[107] Within NASA, Gemini director George Muller and the Office of Space Science and Applications, Dr. Homer Newell, pushed for the new scientist-astronaut.[108]

This new hyphenated astronaut raised questions about the masculine pilot astronaut image depicted in the public discourse. Early on, it was clear that NASA did not want scientist-astronauts for fear that they were not physically capable of facing the dangers and rigors of controlling spaceflight technology. Consequently, men who lacked courage and control over spaceflight technology were considered passive or feminized. Despite NASA's misgivings, scientists won the battle for the recruitment of scientist-astronauts.[109] The scientists did not win the war. The scientist-astronauts would not be part of the first moon landing. The pilot astronauts needed to demonstrate "the safety of the trip to the moon" first.[110]

William A. Lee, Director of Systems Studies at NASA Headquarters, wrote to Dr. Joseph E. Shea, Deputy Director of Systems Engineering, suggesting that in recruiting scientist-astronauts "we would have to relax our present stringent requirements for jet test pilot experience; thereby gaining training experience with non-test pilots."[111] The "relaxing" of the requirements for the scientist-astronauts insinuated an inferior masculinity. Finding men of science who could pass "stiff astronaut physicals" led NASA to be "disappointed that more men didn't qualify."[112] Lowering standards questioned if a man needed to be physically tough to control spaceflight technology, to face G-forces, untamable rockets, pressure and failed technology all while pushing buttons. The astronaut image faced its own crisis of masculinity. Spaceflight control once displayed by the astronaut pilot shifted. The rugged individual astronaut was becoming less and less alone and more of a team player within the cockpit. The democratic manhood presented in the new public astronaut image might follow a direct path to domestication, passivity or the feminized astronaut image.

By the application deadline of December 31, 1964, NASA received over one thousand three hundred applicants. In February 1965, NASA and NAS officials narrowed the applicants to four hundred. Four of them were women, thus commencing a renewed discussion about women's place in spaceflight. Engineers and scientists believed that the rigors of spaceflight had become less physically demanding as NASA lowered the scientist-astronaut requirements. NASA discontinued the stress tests that the first three astronaut groups endured—no more weeks of rigorous enemas. Unlike the military astronaut candidates, medical testing on the scientists found that some of the candidates possessed varicose veins, inguinal hernias, nasal polyps and myopia. The fact that they had more medical abnormalities implied a physically weaker group than the jet test-pilot astronauts. This presented a democratization of space technology, however, only regarding masculinity. None of the women who applied to be scientist-astronauts made the shortlist of potential candidates.[113] NASA had plenty of women employees with advanced degrees in the sciences and engineering. Despite the burgeoning women's rights movement and the passage of the 1963 Equal Pay Act and the 1964 Civil Rights Act, NASA did not create an affirmative action program to recruit women inside or outside the space agency.

NASA officials provided multiple reasons for not choosing a woman scientist-astronaut. Other than the FLATs, there was a lack of studies on women's bodies, specifically in relation to G-forces. Former chief of the medical division for the Air Force School of Aerospace Medicine in San Antonio, Dr. Lawrence E. Lamb, participated in the 1962 FLATs testing. He believed sending a woman into space was a stunt that held "no useful purpose." He viewed women as potential astronauts handicapped by a lack of physical strength and their menstrual cycles. The latter might be "taken care of by the pill."[114]

Despite House Representative Victor Anfuso's request at the end of the 1962 Subcommittee Hearings that NASA "come up with some kind of a program so that you can continue to have the bipartisan support which you have always seen," no program to include women on spaceflights existed in the pipeline.[115] NASA did not create technology suited for women's bodies, including a spacesuit. Scientist-astronaut applicant Mrs. Emily G. Kozakoff scoffed at NASA's excuse that women's spacesuits had yet to be designed. The University of Maryland research programmer said, "I'm hard pressed to believe that NASA can send a rocket to the moon but doesn't know what to do about the problem of feminine hygiene." After NASA turned down seventeen women scientist-astronaut applications, journalist Jack Anderson wrote that if the space agency and NAS deny "discrimination," how come they have not "lifted a pencil to begin research on space suits and other trappings a woman would need in space."[116] Finally, NASA required the scientist-astronauts to complete Air Force Undergraduate Jet Piloting Training, a requirement still off-limits to women. NASA insisted they did not discriminate and welcomed applications from both sexes despite the military requirement.

Women as potential scientists-astronauts came at an important time in discussions about sex equality both at the federal and administrative levels. Tereshkova's 1963 flight brought mixed reactions from the American public in terms of the need or want for women astronauts. While many supported the idea of women's right to spaceflight, there did not seem to be enough public demand to warrant risking necessary federal funding. The primary goal was the moon landing and not "accommodating a social agenda that seemed to be a serious concern to only a small minority of people."[117]

NASA officials told reporters they would not reject an applicant because of sex, but astronaut Cooper felt otherwise. He told reporters that even the scientist-astronauts "must be able to take his turn flying the lunar spacecraft." He admitted this "may not sound very gentlemanly, but he just would not trust them (women) with the prime responsibility of the spacecraft."[118] Papers reported that former NASA Deputy Administrator, Dryden, "didn't trust women with the responsibility for the space craft or the mission."[119]

NASA officials failed to grasp that the space race was a social statement that showcased the United States' capability to act as a unified nation and highlighted the superiority of its democratic spaceflight technology— a technology that left half the population out. As civil rights movements and violence continued across the country, Congress passed Title VII of the Civil Rights Act (1965), which made discrimination in employment based on race and sex illegal. Congress funded the Equal Employment Opportunity Commission (EEOC) out of President Kennedy's Equal Pay Act (1963) a year later. Aileen Hernandez, the only woman on the five-member EEOC, recalled that the commission was more focused on combating race discrimination as opposed to the complaints by women that numbered around one-third.[120]

Administrator Webb made clear his intention to follow the wave of gender change when he issued Policy Directive NPD 3713.3, creating NASA's equal employment opportunity for women statement on March 31, 1966. Webb instructed management to follow the policy of finding the best candidates "without discrimination on the basis of sex" and created an equal opportunity officer at NASA to ensure the administration followed suit.[121] But, Webb did not create an affirmative action program to find qualified women.

A year later, President Lyndon Johnson added "sex" to the protected categories of his Executive Order 11246, which banned discrimination based on "race, creed, color, or national origin" in the workplace. Foster is correct in her argument that Webb was "forward-thinking" and "showed remarkable open-mindedness," but "Societal change at NASA would happen 'gradually.'"[122] For instance, the astronaut corps may have been immune from Webb's directive, but the corps did not do its due diligence in finding a woman qualified to be a scientist-astronaut. Nor was it even clear that the military would allow a woman scientist-astronaut candidate to fly a T-38.

On June 29, 1965, NASA introduced the first scientist-astronauts. They included: Owen Kay Garriott, PhD (electrical engineer); Edward George Gibson, PhD (physicist); Duane Edgar Graveline, MD (flight surgeon); Joseph Peter Kerwin, MD (flight surgeon); Frank Curtis Michael, PhD (space sciences); and Harrison Hagan "Jack" Schmitt, PhD (geologist). At the time of their service, all were civilians except for Kerwin, who was in the Navy.[123] All the men had flying experience but one. However, their flying experience differed greatly. Kerwin and Michael had jet experience and did not have to take the qualification Air Force training. The others went through the Air Force Undergraduate Pilot Training Program. As a flight surgeon for the Air Force, Graveline flew both single and dual-seat T-birds. However, NASA believed Graveline would not be able to transition into the T-38 without further training. Before NASA, Gibson held a private pilot's license. Garriott flew small tail-dragger airplanes. The astronauts, especially Shepard and Slayton, mocked the scientist-astronauts for their lack of flying. Jack Schmitt held absolutely no piloting experience.[124] Even if these men had flown as

**Figure 4.2** The first hyphenated scientists-astronauts. Source: NASA. https://en.wikipedia.org/wiki/NASA_Astronaut_Group_4#/media/File:PORTRAIT_-_SCIENTIST-ASTRONAUT_GROUP.jpg.

pilots, to the astronauts, the scientist-astronauts had never experienced any real flying and certainly not combat.

The press asked NASA officials why they had not chosen a woman scientist-astronaut, especially since they might have "'scientific value.'" Director of Operations at the Manned Spaceflight Center, astronaut Deke Slayton, responded, "We seek the best qualified persons [...]. Male or female, it makes no difference." New scientist-astronaut Kerwin responded to the same question, "I can't think of any valid scientific experiment to include or exclude women."[125] The reaction from the public appeared mixed. Some felt it a "shame" to dismiss women, and one person asked, "Why should some darn fool woman want to shoot herself at the moon." Others expressed a need to "protect" women until they "can contribute, but space flights should be left up to the men for the time being."[126] Americans were not ready to see women in the dangerous role of astronaut and failed to see women as equal contributors.

While women were to patiently wait for their turn for spaceflight, the public discourse focused on the lack of scientist-astronaut piloting skills. The *Tucson Daily Citizen* declared that even though two of the chosen were qualified jet pilots, of the other scientist-astronauts, "three of the scientists had never flown jets and two had not flown at all."[127] While busy with their jet training, recruit Gibson lamented, "we feel too isolated from the other astronauts and from the space program, especially the scientific aspect of it."[128] The scientist-astronauts attempted to demonstrate that they could control the spacecraft through conducting scientific experiments rather than piloting. They too wanted to show that they could not be replaced by automation and their skill presented a real contribution to spaceflight. When interviewed at the Manned Spacecraft Center near Houston, the scientist-astronauts suggested their role was "to fill the gaps left by instruments." Michael suggested that "without human involvement instruments limit you in scope." Gibson reiterated his new teammate's assessment replying, "You need much theoretical background so you can make on the spot decisions instruments can't make."[129] Chairman of the NAS Selection Board, Dr. Harry Hess, backed up the new astronauts with "Man can differentiate between a thousand possibilities while instruments cannot."[130]

By the end of the training of the "scientific-six," NASA faced paradoxical messages regarding its future and funding but continued to hire more astronauts. On the one hand, NASA envisioned the next fifteen years of *Apollo* flights, lunar landings and space stations. At the same time, NASA feared cutbacks as rumors of budget cuts and loss of interest grew. Amid American disinterest in space, NASA envisioned multiple *Apollo* landings and an onslaught in the need for scientists in space. In May 1966, despite the opposition of Slayton, NASA picked another nineteen pilot astronauts as part of Group 5.

On September 26, NASA called for a second group of scientist-astronauts. Much to the chagrin of the jet test-pilot astronauts, NASA further eased the physical requirements to become an astronaut. With the growing number of astronauts and scientist-astronauts, it seemed as if everyone could qualify for the right stuff. In the NASA press release, Gene Shoemaker, chair of the NAS committee, wrote of the new role of scientist-astronaut: "While such missions call for daring and courage of a rare kind, for the scientist they will also represent a unique adventure of the mind, requiring maturity and judgment of a higher order."[131] The public image of astronaut masculinity shifted from a physical, tough masculinity to one that prided brains over brawn.

On August 4, 1967, NASA announced eleven new scientist-astronauts. Headlines read: "Female Astronauts Lose Again."[132] NASA and the NAS chose three astronomers, two physicists, one chemist, a geophysicist and an electrical engineer. One was an MD/physicist and two were MD-PhD physiologists. None of the men had flying experience. All eleven spent fifty-three weeks in the Air Force's jet pilot course.[133] With the arrival of Group 6, NASA had fifty-six astronauts. Twenty-three astronauts were civilians.[134] Slayton told those in Group 6 that if they had any fantasies that they would be flying on the shrinking Apollo program, they should leave. No one did. The second group of scientist-astronauts nicknamed themselves "the XS-11."[135]

Astronauts publicly expressed their dissatisfaction over the new direction of the astronaut corps. The press dubbed the scientist-astronauts as a "new breed" demonstrating a renegotiated astronaut masculinity. Engineers and scientists now had Tom Wolfe's "right stuff." Originally, NASA chose "the toughest, most experienced test pilots they could find, men with combat under their belts." Whether or not the first astronauts were the best test pilots is debatable, but they were certainly willing to risk their lives. NASA now wanted intellectuals, with chief astronaut Slayton suggesting the best astronauts had a combination of flying and advanced science degrees. The test pilots turned astronauts, specifically those since Group 2, had advanced degrees. Nineteen held doctorate degrees, such as Aldrin, who earned his in astronautics from MIT. This led to anger in the corps that NASA and the NAS did not have faith that pilot astronauts could conduct experiments during missions. In this case, the pilot astronauts did not have the right stuff. Schirra viewed the geology courses the astronauts took at NASA to be sufficient for the Apollo flights. McDivitt argued that test pilots are essentially scientists because of advancing technology in the cockpit. Borman backed this up with, "You've got to have a darn good scientific education, a very well-rounded flying background and something a little bit more" to be a test pilot. He felt that sending up those without test-pilot backgrounds would have to wait until space transportation became "more routine."

148  GENDER AND THE RACE FOR SPACE

Dr. Joseph P. Kerwin disagreed that scientist-astronauts were less competent than the "pilot" astronauts. He disliked that the astronauts were separated into two groups because it harmed camaraderie and "we don't have the luxury of twiddling our thumbs on a flight, as the title implies. We'll be part of the crew."[136] It is no wonder that Kerwin hated the hyphenated scientist-astronaut title. He was a former Navy captain with four thousand five hundred logged hours flying as a flight surgeon. The astronaut image shifted to differing images of masculinity, from that of a test pilot to scientists with both groups jockeying for the right to the astronaut title; to the right to share masculinity. Both astronauts and scientist-astronauts argued that they were not passengers but rather trained together as a team. One thing remained that kept the astronauts and scientist-astronauts in two groups. The scientist-astronauts could never command a mission. Command, being in charge in such dangerous situations, was left to the pilot astronauts, thus denigrating the scientist-astronauts' masculinity.[137]

It is difficult to imagine women entering the corps at a time when the scientist-astronaut felt unwanted. Jack Anderson wrote in 1967 that "As long as men dominate the space program, an American woman may not make it into space until she can book a seat as a passenger on a commercial spaceship." The seventeen women who applied for astronaut Group 6 had advanced degrees, were published, and yet failed to have the right stuff. Little is known of the women applicants, but they were smart and accomplished and depicted themselves as having a love of "adventure" and the "pioneering spirit." NASA preferred to see women "marry, have kids, and stay home," according to Mrs. Janet Trubach, a gravitational theory researcher.[138]

Of the women rejected, Dr. Lina L. Robinson Painter, 27, had a doctorate in radiation physics and a fellowship with the Atomic Energy Commission. Dr. Linda Maria Hunter, 27, became the first woman to graduate from Florida State University with a doctorate in chemistry. She had been working on a post-doctorate at the University of Notre Dame's radiation laboratory. Dr. Marjorie "Charlie" Haynes was a veterinarian and former model who fought her way into Camp Lejeune's U.S. Marines scuba diving class, a class that only allowed male Marines. Abigail Butler held a bachelor's degree in physics from Radcliffe College and three master's degrees. She had professional experience working on guided missiles and was an associate space research physicist at the University of Michigan. She was also divorced with three children and "wants to believe it is the lack of a PhD and not prejudice that kept her out of a space capsule."[139] Dr. Gladys Philpott's research on oxygen levels and telemetry for bio-adhesives would have complemented the spacecraft environment.

# REFRESHINGLY HUMAN AND WINNING 149

Finally, Elizabeth Cuadro provides an interesting American dream realized and shattered. Cuadro held a master's degree in fluid mechanics and acoustics and argued that growing up on a Kansas tenant farm that did not have "sex roles so sharply drawn" led her to believe she "could do anything."[140] Cuadro had eleven published papers to her name while working for Wyle Laboratory. NASA consulted her published papers on equations for shock and sound waves.[141] In her spare time, Cuadro flew in the 1953 Powder Puff Derby and climbed mountains. Despite their degrees and publications, NASA told the press they chose those with the best qualifications, those with "proven research abilities." However, of the men chosen for Group 6, "four were in their 20's and four got their doctorates only this year," leading Anderson to speculate that NASA and the NAS must have selected these scientists because of their future "promise" not their "accomplishment."[142] For the time being, the only woman going into space was Mattel's Rocket Scientist Barbie.[143]

## Conclusion

Regardless of the first page headlines that declared astronauts controlling the Mercury spacecraft, the public discourse paradoxically asserted that Gemini was the first craft to be piloted by an astronaut, demonstrating the continued importance of astronaut control. However, the acceptance of the first scientist-astronauts into the astronaut corps forever shifted the gendered astronaut image. The future of spaceflight assumed scientists without any previous jet training could become astronauts. Spaceflight was becoming so routine that even NASA was entrusting scientist-astronauts to fly. The once superior rugged individual masculine astronaut image was tested. The scientist-astronauts changed how astronauts controlled spaceflight technology. Furthermore, advanced technology and automation in the spacecraft questioned the pilot astronaut's self-determination. Charles Lindbergh argued that advancing technology took away man's individuality to the point that technology "reduce[s] man's awareness." To the famed pilot, technology had the power to both shrink and expand human knowledge, of which he asked the ominous questions: "Can we harmonize the two? What does the future hold for man?"[144] While Lindbergh addressed concerns of ever-growing technology and man's control over that technology—democratic manhood, scientist-astronauts and women threatened Cold War masculinity and fixed gendered roles. As NASA headed into Apollo, there was an ongoing debate about whether the use of technology in a collaborative team environment challenged conventional masculinity.

## Notes

1 "World Reaction to Gemini IV Space Flight. Research and Reference Service, United States Information Agency, June 11, 1965," Impact Series, Folder 15767, NASA Historical Reference Collection, NASA History Division, NASA Headquarters, Washington, DC.

2 *Chicago Tribune Press Service*, "Scientist-Astronaut Crewman Are Sought," *Spokesman-Review* (Spokane, Washington), November 29, 1964, 51 and Shayler and Burgess, *NASA's Scientist-Astronauts*, 31–40.

3 Wellesley College, "1970 Alumni Achievement Awards: Dr. Jocelyn R. Gill," accessed July 13, 2023, https://www.wellesley.edu/alumnae/awards/achievementawards/allrecipients/jocelyn_r._gill_38.

4 The Associated Press, "Woman in "Space": She Star Gazes With the Astronauts," *Columbia Record* (Columbia, South Carolina), December 14, 1964, 9.

5 The Associated Press, "Displaying Calm Mastery: Women are Finding Place In Sun In Space Program," *Columbia Record* (Columbia, South Carolina), December 14, 1964, 9.

6 The Associated Press, "Displaying Calm Mastery," 9 and Mindell, *Digital Apollo*, 83.

7 Mindell, *Digital Apollo*, 83. For the full speech, see, "Talk Delivered by Major Virgil Grissom at an SETP East Coast Section Meeting, November 9, 1962," *SETP Newsletter* (November-December 1962), 5–12.

8 Barton C. Hacker and James M. Grimwood, *On the Shoulders of Titans: A History of Project Gemini* (Washington, DC: NASA, SP-4203, 1977), 383.

9 Phil Hand, "IBM Computer to Be the 'Third Man' on Gemini Flight," *Press and Sun-Bulletin* (Binghamton, New York), March 22, 1965, 3.

10 Henry Shapiro, (United Press International), "Soviet Craft Carrying Three Launched into Earth Orbit," *Anniston* (Alabama) *Star*, October 12, 1964, 1 and Henry Tanner, "Soviet Spaceship is Landed Safely After 16 Circuits; 3 Astronauts Stay in Cabin During Descent—Use of Braking Rockets Hinted 437,000 MILES Covered Crew Wanted to Remain Aloft for 24 More Hours, but Plea Was Refused Soviet Spaceship IS Landed Safely After 16 Circuits of the Earth in 24 Hours Crew in Capsule as it Hits Ground; 3 Men Look Tired as They Leave Cabin on Farm—Interior is Described," *New York Times*, October 14, 1964, 1.

11 Andrews and Siddiqi, eds., *Into the Cosmos*, 225–233.

12 The Associated Press, "Astronaut Recruiting Plan Slated; Soviet Gains Spur NASA?," *Spokesman-Review* (Spokane, Washington), October 20, 1964, 1.

13 "Space: Adventure into Emptiness," *Time*, March 26, 1965, 86.

14 Wire Services, "Historic Space Step Taken by Cosmonaut: Feat Puts Russia Months Ahead of U.S. in Moon Race," *Independent* (Pasadena, California), March 19, 1965, 1. See also, "Space: Adventure into Emptiness," 85 and "Take a Giant Step—Into Space," *Newsweek*, March 29, 1965, 52–57.

15 The United Press International, "Soviet Ship Returns Safely," *Athens Messenger* (Athens, Ohio), March 19, 1965, 1. See also, "In Moscow, a Welcome to the Space Walker," *Life*, August 2, 1965, 42B and "Take a Giant Step," 53.

16 The United Press International, Moscow, "Soviet Ship Returns Safely," 1.

17 Fred Coleman, "Soviet Capsule Spins On, On After Russ 'Swims' in Space: Red Millions Witness Moon-Stride on TV," *Salt Lake Tribune*, March 19, 1965, 1.

18 "Space: Adventure into Emptiness," 85A.

# REFRESHINGLY HUMAN AND WINNING 151

19  The Associated Press, "Space Chiefs Claim U.S. Program Still Superior," *Independent* (Pasadena, C.A.), March 19, 1965, 4.

20  Nate Haseltine, "Russian is First Man to Leave Craft in Orbit," *Washington Post*, March 19, 1965, 1.

21  Hacker and Grimwood, *On the Shoulders of Titans*, 240. *Newsweek* makes the same claim in "Take a Giant Step," 54.

22  Dr. Martin Luther King, Jr., "Our God is Marching On," Speech delivered in Montgomery, Alabama on 25 March 1965, The Martin Luther King, Jr. Research and Education Institute, Stanford University, accessed September 19, 2023, https://kinginstitute.stanford.edu/our-god-marching.

23  "Gemini: 'It Didn't Last Long Enough'," *Newsweek*, April 5, 1965, 49.

24  The Associated Press, "The Gemini Success," *Lawrence Daily Journal-World* (Lawrence, Kansas), March 24, 1965, 4.

25  The United Press International, "Grissom and Young Undergo Tests After Successful Gemini Journey," *Coshocton Tribune* (Coshocton, Ohio), March 24, 1965, 9.

26  Gus Grissom and John Young, "Lift-Off to a New Era in Space," *Life*, April 2, 1965, 35, 42.

27  Charles Stafford, "Gemini's Maneuvers Start Era of History," *Washington Post*, March 24, 1965, A14.

28  Editorial, "Gemini Confirmed Mankind's Ability to Fly in Space," *Washington Post*, March 24, 1965.

29  Grissom and Young, "Lift-Off to a New Era," 42.

30  John W. Finney, "Pilots will Control Gemini Spacecraft," *New York Times*, October 15, 1962, A1, A5. See also, Kauffman, *Selling Outer Space*, 62; and Mindell, *Digital Apollo*, 84.

31  The Associated Press, "Gemini: Space Pilots' Blood Tests Appear Fine; Astronauts Begin Telling Experts of 3-Orbit Journey," *Emporia Gazette* (Emporia, Kansas), March 24, 1965, 1.

32  Caroll Kilpatrick, "Johnson Phones His 'Well Done' to Gemini Pair," *Washington Post*, March 24, 1965, 13. See also, The United Press International, "Invited to Whitehouse; Two Astronauts Hear Johnson 'Well Done,'" *Albuquerque Journal*, March 24, 1965.

33  Dr. Hugh L. Dryden, "Space Accomplishments are Product of a Team," Statement Before Committee on Science and Astronautics, House of Representatives, March 1965, Impact Series, "Space Quotes, Folder 15767," NASA Historical Reference Collection, NASA Headquarters, Washington, D.C.

34  Al Rossiter, United Press International, "Gemini Space Twin takes Laughing Stroll into History: Medic Says Pair Doing 'Real Great'," *Independent* (Long Beach, California), June 4, 1965, 1.

35  "The Glorious Walk in the Cosmos," *Life*, June 16, 1965, 26.

36  Coleman, "Soviet Capsule Spins On," 1.

37  Walter Sullivan, "Jokes in the Void; Talk of Two Astronauts is Heard by Millions on Radio and TV," *New York Times*, June 4, 1965, 1.

38  *Chicago Daily News*, Impact Series, "Space Quotes" Folder 15767," NASA Historical Reference Collection, NASA Headquarters, Washington, DC. The *Times* quote appears within the *Chicago Daily News*.

39  "Space: Closing the Gap," 25.

40  "The Great Adventure Moves Ahead," 30.

41 "World Reaction to Gemini IV Space Flight," Impact Series, "Space Quotes, File 15767," NASA Historical Reference Collection, NASA Headquarters, Washington, DC.

42 "British Press Hails Whites Space Feat," *New York Times*, June 4, 1965, 14.

43 Sullivan, "Jokes in the Void," 39–40A.

44 Robert C. Toth, "U.S. Took a Gamble in Planning Rendezvous of Spacecraft, Booster," *Los Angeles Times*, June 4, 1965, 1, 18.

45 James A. McDivitt, "The Astronauts' Own Stories about Gemini 4," *Life*, June 25, 1965, 25.

46 Mindell, *Digital Apollo*, 86–87.

47 Harold M. Schmeck Jr., "Gemini 5 Orbited but a Power Loss Threatens Duration of Planned 8-Day Mission Uncertain; 2 Astronauts Strive to Continue," *New York Times*, August 22, 1965, 72, and Howard Simmons, "Failure of Oxygen Warmer Appears to be Cause of Trouble on Gemini 5," *Washington Post*, August 22, 1965, 1, A35.

48 Evert Clark, "Gemini Cleared for 32 Circuits; It may go 8 days; Power Restored; Astronauts return to Original Flight Plan—New Tests Set," *New York Times*, August 23, 1965, 1.

49 The Associated Press, "TASS Accuses U.S. of Risking Gemini 5 to Outstrip Soviet," *New York Times*, August 23, 1965, 16.

50 "The Loquacious Astronaut and the Taciturn One," *New York Times*, August 23, 1965, 16.

51 Pete Conrad, "'Astronauts' Personal Stories about Their Gemini 5 Flight," *Life*, September 24, 1965, 84C.

52 Harold M. Schmeck, Jr., "Pilots Maneuver to Meet 'Rocket': Gemini Tests Rendezvous Technique with Computer," *New York Times*, August 24, 1965, 16.

53 John Noble Wilford, "Gemini 7's Pilot Return From Record 14 Day Trip; Both Reported Healthy; Land on Target," *New York Times*, December 19, 1965, 68.

54 Wally Schirra and Richard N. Billings, *Schirra's Space* (Annapolis, MD: Naval Institute Press, 1995), 164; also quoted in Mindell, *Digital Apollo*, 84–85.

55 John Barbour, "Spacemen Head for Okinawa in Good Condition," *Philadelphia Inquirer*, March 17, 1963, 1, 3.

56 "A Case of 'Constructive Alarm'," *Life*, April 8, 1966, 87–90.

57 "Gemini VIII Voice Communications (Air-To-Ground, Ground-To-Air, and On-Board Transcription), MAC Control No. C-115471," History Collection, Mission Transcripts, Johnson Spaceflight Center, 75–76, accessed September 7, 2022, https://historycollection.jsc.nasa.gov/JSCHistoryPortal/history/mission _trans/GT08_TEC.PDF.

58 "Gemini VIII Voice Communications," 88 and "Moment of the First Docking in Space," *Life*, April 1, 1966, 91.

59 "High Tension Over the Astronauts," *Life* March 25, 1966, 34.

60 "Gemini-8 Tumble Mystery Probed; Astronauts Safe on Rescue Ship; Capsule Recovered; Headed to Okinawa," *Knoxville News-Sentinel*, March 17, 1963, 1.

61 Andrew Chaikin, *A Man on the Moon: The Voyages of the Apollo Astronauts* (New York: Penguin Books, 1998), 168–169.

62 Barbour, "Spacemen Head For Okinawa," 3.

63 "Space: Gemini's Wild Ride," *Time*, March 25, 1966, 38.

## REFRESHINGLY HUMAN AND WINNING 153

64 John Troan, Scripps-Howard Science Writer, "Space Race Pace Hinges on 'Trouble'; Finding Cause of Tumbling Is Key to Schedule," *Knoxville-News Sentinel*, March 17, 1966, 1.

65 "Gemini-8 Tumble Mystery Probed," 1.

66 The Associated Press, "Their Men Landed Safely; Astronauts' Families are Sad but Glad," *Knoxville News-Sentinel*, March 17, 1966, 8; United Press International, "Irony from African Tracking Station: Armstrong Vocally Calm, Cool," *Morning Call* (Paterson, New Jersey), March 17, 1966, 14; The Associated Press, "We Got Serious Problems," *Democrat and Chronicle*, (Rochester, New York), March 18, 1966, 1, 4.

67 The United Press International, "Heartbeats Double During Crisis in Space," *Tampa Bay Times*, March 18, 1966, 4.

68 *Time* Wire Service, "Recordings Provide No Clue: Astronauts Head for Home; Mishap Remains a Mystery," *Tampa Bay Times*, March 18, 1966, 1A, 4, 4.

69 "A Case of 'Constructive Alarm'," 88.

70 "Scott and Armstrong Extend Horizons Of Colorful Flying Careers," *Philadelphia Inquirer*, March 17, 1966, 3.

71 "Scott and Armstrong Extend," 3.

72 Barbour, "Spacemen Head For Okinawa," 3.

73 The Associated Press, "Gemini 9 Astronauts Die as Jet Hits Building Housing Capsule; Elliot See and Charles Bassett Are Killed at St. Louis; Stafford and Cernan to Fill In," *Rutland Daily Herald* (Rutland, Vermont), March 1, 1961, 1, 2, 1.

74 The Associated Press, "Ted Freeman, Astronaut Dies in Plane Crash," *Miami Herald*, November 1, 1964, 3A; The Associated Press, "Paper Reports Goose Hits Astronaut's Plane," *Tampa Tribune*, November 8, 1964, 14A; and The Associated Press, "Veteran Pilot Victim in Landing Accident," *Indianapolis Star*, November 1, 1964, 1.

75 Ronald Thompson, The Associated Press, "Crew Dedicated Lives to Flying," *Rutland Daily Herald* (Rutland, Vermont), March 1, 1966, 1, 3.

76 John Noble Wilford, "Gemini 9 Delayed Until Tomorrow," *New York Times*, June 2, 1966, 1.

77 John Noble Wilford, "Loose Shield Blocks Gemini Docking; Mission Continuing—Astronaut Floats in Space Today Loose Shield Blocks Gemini Docking but Flight is to Continue for Scheduled 3 Days ASTRONAUTS GAIN ORBIT ON 3D TRY are to Practice rendezvous—2 Hour Sojourn in Space Set for Today Problem is Studied Jagged Edges a Danger Makes First Adjustment," *New York Times*, June 4, 1966, 1, 10, 1.

78 Wilford, "Loose Shield Blocks Gemini," 10.

79 The United Press International, "Rendezvous Key in Moon Plans," *Kingsport News* (Kingsport, Tennessee), June 4, 1966, 1.

80 Howard Simmons, "Astronauts Relax after 3d Rendezvous, Reschedule Space Walk this Morning; Docking Maneuver is Dropped; Space Pilots Told Not to Attempt Release of Shroud," *Washington Post*, June 5, 1966, 1 and John Noble Wilford, "Gemini Postpones a 'Walk' in Space; Docking Canceled," *New York Times*, June 5, 1966, 1.

81 Howard Simmons, "Cernan Walks in Space for Two Hours; Fogged-Up Visor Cuts Activity Short; Splashdown of Gemini 9 Set Today; Pilots Maneuver Craft Into Orbit for Re-Entry," *Washington Post*, June 6, 1966, 1.

82 John Barbour, The Associated Press, "Jubilant Astros Back Home after Near-Perfect Landing; 'Jinxed' Gemini Ends in Success," *Salt Lake Tribune*, June 7, 1966, 1, 2.

83 John Noble Wilford, "Gemini 9 Lands Safely Near Bullseye; Astronauts Flow to Cape For Debriefing on Mission," *New York* Times, June 7, 1966, 1, 34.

84 John D. Prompet, "President Hails Crew's Coolness," *New York Times*, June 7, 1966, 34.

85 John Noble Wilford, "Gemini Docks With Agena and Then Joined Vehicles Rocket into Higher Orbit," *New York Times*, July 19, 1966, 1 and J. V. Reistrup, "Astronauts Enter Orbit After Target; Outlook for Dual Rendezvous is Good; Gemini X Liftoff Hailed as 3-Day Space Mission Starts in Perfect Timing," *Washington Post*, July 19, 1966, 1, A8.

86 Alvin B. Webb Jr., United Press International, "Fuel Shortage Cuts Collins' Stroll in Space," *Billings Gazette* (Billings, Montana), July 21, 1966, 1.

87 "Collins Very Quiet but Pukish, When Schoolboy at St. Albans," *Washington Post*, July 21, 1966, A3, and John Noble Wilford, "Maj. Collins 'Walks' to Nearby Agena And Retrieves a Space Dust Detector," *New York Times*, July 21, 1966, 1.

88 "Quiet Man in Space; Michael Collins," *New York Times*, July 21, 1966, 16, and David Bird, "A Hand-Held Gun is Used to Maneuver in Space," *New York Times*, July 21, 1966, K16.

89 "Closing in on the Moon," *Newsweek*, August 1, 1966, 52–54. The eye inflammation was probably caused by lithium hydroxide in the anti-fogging spray.

90 Ronald Thompson, "Spacemen Make Perfect Landing in Sight of Ship; Call Flight of 3 Days Lots of Fun; Spacemen Make Perfect Landing," *Atlanta Constitution*, July 22, 1966, A11; and Webb Jr., "Fuel Shortage," 1.

91 "U.S.-Soviet Box Score On Astronauts' Flights," *New York Times*, July 22, 1966, 14.

92 "Fattening the Record Book," *Time*, July 29, 1966, 28.

93 John Noble Wilford, "Astronauts Soar 850 Miles, Spin Tethered With Agena; Gemini 11 reaches 850-Mile Altitude," *New York Times*, September 15, 1966, 1.

94 John Noble Wilford, "Gemini, in Its First Orbit, Docks with Agena Target in a 94-Minute Maneuver; Link-Up is on Time Main Object Of 3-Day Mission is Achieved with Seeming Ease Gemini, in First Orbit, Docks with Agena Target Satellite in 94-Minute Maneuver Link-Up is Made without Mishap Object of the 3-Day Mission is Achieved on Schedule and with Seeming Ease," *New York Times*, September 13, 1966, 1.

95 John Noble Wilford, "Astronauts' Capsule Hits the Atlantic in Full View of Recovery Ship; Computer Guides Gemini's Re-entry and Splashdown; Automatic Landing is First for U.S.—Astronauts Go Aboard Carrier Guam; 3-Day Mission Saw the First Single-Orbit Rendezvous and Tethered Flight; Computer Guides Gemini Re-Entry and Splashdown Near Carrier Guam in Atlantic; Copter Picks Up Two Astronauts; 3-Day Mission Saw the First Single-Orbit Rendezvous and tethered Flight," *New York Times*, September 16, 1966, 1.

96 The Associated Press, "Astronauts Healthy; Gemini Hits Ocean Safely On Target," *Wisconsin State Journal* (Madison, Wisconsin), September 16, 1966, 1.

97 The United Press International, "The Best One Ever; Gemini Astronauts Return Triumphantly to Earth; Bring Back Batch [*sic*] New Space Records," *Aiken Standard and Review* (Aiken, South Carolina), September 16, 1966, 1.

98 The Associated Press, "Sun-Splashed Return for Gemini; Spacemen Even Kept Feet Dry," *Post-Standard* (Syracuse, New York), September 16, 1966, 1.

## REFRESHINGLY HUMAN AND WINNING 155

99  John Noble Wilford, "Gemini Program Ends in Success," *New York Times*, November 16, 1966, 30.

100  Thomas O'Toole, "Gemini Drops Almost on Target," *Washington Post*, November 16, 1966, A7.

101  Loudon Wainwright, "All Systems are Ho-Hum," *Life*, December 2, 1966, 30.

102  O'Toole, "Gemini Drops Almost on Target," A7.

103  Ronald Bailey, "Gemini's Last Mission is a Lulu—Now On to the Moon," *Life*, December 2, 1966, 41.

104  Hacker and Grimwood, *On the Shoulders of Titans*, 381.

105  Hacker and Grimwood, *On the Shoulders of Titans*, 382.

106  Presidential Recordings Program, "John F. Kennedy, Tape 63A: 'Fly Me to the Moon,'" Courtesy of the John F. Kennedy Library and Museum, University of Virginia, Miller Center, accessed November 10, 2023, https://millercenter.org/the -presidency/educational-resources/fly-me-to-the-moon.

107  Shayler and Burgess, *NASA's Scientist-Astronauts*, 29–30.

108  William David Compton, *Where No Man has Gone Before: A History of Apollo Lunar Exploration Missions* (Washington, DC: The National Aeronautics and Space Administration, 1989), 68.

109  Atkinson Jr., and Shafritz, *The Real Stuff*, 69, 71.

110  The Associated Press, "Scientist-Astronaut Sees Moon as 'Unclimbed Mountain,'" *Orlando Sentinel*, June 28, 1965, 4.

111  Atkinson Jr., and Shafritz, *The Real Stuff*, 69, 71.

112  Donald Drake, "NASA Strains to Find Scientist-Astronauts," *Newsday* (Nassau Edition, Hudson, New York), June 30, 1965, 15.

113  Atkinson, Jr., and Shafritz, *The Real Stuff*, 81 and Shayler and Burgess, *NASA's Scientist-Astronauts*, 37–39.

114  Anne V. Thompson, World Book Science Service, "Why No Women Astronauts? Equality of Sexes Ends Where Outer Space Begins," *Tribune* (Coshocton, Ohio), October 8, 1967, 10.

115  Congress, House, *Qualifications for Astronauts: Subcommittee Hearings*, 74

116  Jack Anderson, "Would-be Astronauts: Legions of Angry Women," *Boston Globe*, November 19, 1967, 262–264, 262.

117  Foster, *Integrating Women into the Astronaut Corps*, 62.

118  William McGaffin, News World Service, "NASA Needs Scientists, Women Eligible for Moon Trip," *Charlotte News* (Charlotte, North Carolina), May 4, 1964, 21.

119  Thompson, "Why No Women Astronauts?," 10.

120  Foster, *Integrating Women into the Astronaut Corps*, 70–71.

121  Foster, *Integrating Women into the Astronaut Corps*, 71.

122  Foster, *Integrating Women into the Astronaut Corps*, 70–71, 62–63.

123  Harold M. Schmeck, "The Scientist to Play Vital Role on Lunar Flight," *New York Times*, July 4, 1966, E8.

124  Atkinson Jr. and Shrafritz, *The Real Stuff*, 82; Shayler and Burgess, *NASA's Scientist-Astronauts*, 57, 93–94. It should be noted that NASA asked for Duane E. Graveline's resignation when his wife filed for divorce citing his "violent and ungovernable outbursts of temper […]." See The Associated Press, "Wife of Astronaut Sues for Divorce, Charging Cruelty," *New York Times*, July 22, 1965, 17.

125  The Associated Press, "Space Chiefs Brush Aside Female Issue," *Waco-News Tribune* (Waco, Texas), June 30, 1965, 12B.

# GENDER AND THE RACE FOR SPACE

126 The Associated Press, "Reaction is Mixed: Four Women Rejected as Scientist-Astronauts," *Belleville News-Democrat* (Belleville, Illinois), April 27, 1965, 2.

127 William J. Cromie, World Book Encyclopedia Science Services, "Look forward to Flights; Scientist Astronauts Near End of First Year in Space Training," *Tucson Daily Citizen*, July 4, 1965, 24. See also, William J. Cromie, World Book Encyclopedia Science Services, "Early Training is Over; Moon Explorers Anxious for Mission," *Daily Times News* (Burlington, North Carolina), December 19, 1966, 38.

128 Cromie, "Look forward to Flights," 24.

129 The Associated Press, "Six Scientist-Astronauts Declare: Instruments Leave Space Gaps Only Man Can Fill," *Independent*, (Long Beach, California), June 30, 1965, B-5.

130 The Associated Press, "The New Six: Scientist-Spacemen View their Jobs," *San Antonio Express*, June 30, 1965, 13A.

131 Donald Beattie, *Taking Science to the Moon: Lunar Experiments and the Apollo Program* (Baltimore: Johns Hopkins University Press, 2001), 175. See also, Compton, *Where No Man Has Gone Before*, 66, and Shayler and Burgess, *NASA's Scientist-Astronauts*, 117–118.

132 The United Press International, "Female Astronauts Lose Again," *Fresno Bee* (Fresno, California), March 31, 1967, 17.

133 The United Press International, "NASA Selects 11 to be Astronauts; Civilian Spacemen Include Two Naturalized Citizens," *New York Times*, August 5, 1967, 7.

134 The Associated Press, "11 Scientists Join Team of Astronauts," *Spokane-Review*, August 5, 1967, 10.

135 Shayler and Burgess, *NASA's Scientist-Astronauts*, 122.

136 Ronald Thompson, The Associated Press Aerospace Writer, "The New Breed," *Cincinnati Enquirer*, September 24, 1967, 62.

137 Compton, *Where No Man Has Gone Before*, 72.

138 Anderson, "Would-be Astronauts," 262–263.

139 Anderson, "Would-be Astronauts," 264.

140 Anderson, "Would-be Astronauts," 263–267.

141 D. M. Lister, "Digital Computation of Downstream Modes Generated by the Interaction of a Shock Wave with an Upstream Containing the Three Disturbance Modes," Wyle Laboratories—Research Staff, Technical Memorandum 69-1, Work Performed Under Contract No. NAS8-21100, accessed August 3, 2023, https://ntrs.nasa.gov/api/citations/19690026452/downloads/19690026452.pdf. Dr. Cuadro's papers include "Flow Perturbations Generated by a Shock Wave Interacting with an Entropy Wave" and "Flow Perturbations Intensities and Noise Levels Downstream of a Shock Wave Interacting with a Random Upstream Field Containing Turbulence, Entropy Fluctuations, and Sound Waves."

142 Anderson, "Would-be Astronauts," 263–264.

143 Jenna Bertschi, "Barbie: An Astronaut for the Ages," The National Air and Space Museum, July 18, 2023, https://airandspace.si.edu/stories/editorial/barbie-astronaut-ages.

144 Collins, *Carrying the Fire*, xi–xii.

# Chapter 5

# IT'S HIP TO BE SQUARE: DEMOCRATIC MANHOOD AND THE APOLLO PROGRAM[1]

It was only supposed to be a test. But for the families of command pilot Gus Grissom, senior pilot Ed White and rookie astronaut pilot Roger B. Chaffee, January 27, 1967, was a nightmare. At approximately 6:31 p.m., after spending five hours atop a non-fueled *Saturn B* rocket at Cape Kennedy, an *Apollo 1's* astronaut's voice radioed to the Saturn blockhouse in a "casual tone[s], Fire [...] I smell fire."[2] A couple of moments later, White cried out, "Fire in the cockpit." A "hysterical shout, 'There's a bad fire in the spacecraft!'" Eleven seconds of silence passed and the "shrill voice" of Chaffee cried out again, "We're on fire—get us out of here!"[3]

The engineers and astronauts at the blockhouse heard cries of excruciating pain as flames engulfed the craft. The only escape route, the hatch door, was sealed shut. Veteran space reporter, John Noble Wilford, described the *Apollo 1* astronauts' last moments as "scrambling, clawing, and pounding to open the sealed hatch [...]. There was no automatic release button"—one of the very few automatic components North American Aviation (later North American Rockwell) engineers failed to design. NASA made the decision to bolt both the outer and inner hatch doors during the test. The combination of scorching heat, malfunctioning gas masks, toxic smoke and fears of an explosion left the ground crew helpless to intervene. The only way for the astronauts to open the hatch was to use the ratchet that was secured directly above the astronauts' heads. It would have taken the astronauts ninety seconds to open the hatch with the tool. The astronauts did not have ninety seconds as the hatch heated up to over two thousand degrees Fahrenheit within a few seconds. While inspecting the craft after the fire, technicians found the skin of the astronauts' melted fingertips on the hatch door.[4] The *Apollo 1* astronauts were the first to die aboard a spacecraft.[5]

An electrical wiring spark ignited the craft's pure oxygen environment into a fireball. All three astronauts perished from carbon monoxide asphyxiation, and their bodies burned in the fire. Accounts of the accident flooded

**Figure 5.1** An investigator looks at the burned *Apollo 1* command module that killed astronauts Gus Grissom, Ed White and Roger Chaffee. Source: AP. https://www.nbc-news.com/slideshow/nasa-s-first-tragedy-50-years-apollo-1-fire-n713416.

the media. The United States mourned their deaths, and the world grieved with their families.[6] *Life* reported that these astronauts may have had "square and almost sissy names" but "they were always willing to force themselves past the point of danger and deep fatigue to perfect their understanding of the machines they flew."[7] They were athletes, Eagle Scouts, family men and jet test pilots. They exercised masculinity through their individuality and bravery, but the fire represented a loss of individual masculine control over technology.

*Apollo 1* displayed American impotency in bureaucratic management, communication, and above all, teamwork. The fire led Flight Control Director Gene Kranz to reiterate NASA's core mission values of "toughness and competence"—and yet, Kranz "*knew*" *Apollo 1* was not ready. "And yet, I continued on." The entire mission control team knew this, and yet "nobody stood up and assumed the accountability and said, 'We're not ready. It's time to regroup.'" Kranz understood that moving into the future meant, "From now on, we are forever accountable for what we do or what we fail to do. It is up to us! It is up to every individual within this program to make things right."[8] As a former F-86 Sabre pilot during the Korean Conflict, Kranz understood the importance of communication and teamwork for successful missions. *Apollo*'s success depended not only on astronauts' and engineers' individuality but for all the individuals to demonstrate democratic manhood as they worked and communicated in teams.

Mercury and Gemini astronauts represented American Cold War masculinity characterized by individuality and control—whether real or imagined. NASA named the program to land on the moon Apollo, after the son of the gods Zeus and Leto. Apollo is known as the god of archery, much like his twin sister, Artemis. The warrior Apollo symbolized the individual strength the Americans needed to fly, land on the moon and return safely to Earth. The astronaut possessed upper body strength to walk in bulky, heavy spacesuits while contending with the moon's weak gravitational pull. The astronauts needed courage in the face of faulty hardware and software.

Despite their courage, the astronauts could not succeed alone and needed teamwork with aerospace companies that designed the technology. North American Aviation engaged in breakneck speed to create the Apollo command modules that would rendezvous with the lunar landing module (LM)—nicknamed LEM by the astronauts. The Grumman Aircraft Corporation encountered the same rushed schedule in designing the LMs. Much like with the command module, NASA needed multiple LMs because they did not possess a heat shield. The LM could not return to Earth, and the astronauts had to jettison the LM in space. The LM burned up as it entered Earth's atmosphere. Neither the command module nor LM were ready heading into 1967 and even 1968. Commencing the Apollo program to beat the Soviets to the moon epitomized President John F. Kennedy's "grab our balls and go" stance on facing uncertainty.[9] The American space program pressed on despite the insurmountable odds that the machinery would fail.

The following details the changing public discourse in the Apollo program and argues that uncertainty with technology and even domestic and international strife tested this individual hero astronaut image and beckoned a new masculinity that symbolized democratic manhood for all Americans. Americans continued their risky pace despite crises over race, ethnicity, gender, sexuality, economic uncertainty and war. The god Apollo was multifaceted. Apollo was not simply a warrior; he was also the Greek god of music, poetry, truth and healing. Americans and the world sought truth in outer space, but they also sought healing and togetherness both at home and abroad.

The multifaceted Apollo became symbolic of United States gender culture, technological progress and social tensions. The Apollo program, much like domestic and international crises, needed teamwork as never before. All individuals involved mattered and would have to trust each other's expertise to land on the moon. However, within the space race narrative, this democratic manhood did not extend to gender and race and thus became emblematic of the long civil rights era. The United States had money to go to the moon and technological capability second to none, but economic equality and inclusion were not extended to the poorest Americans, minorities, or women. Overall, the Apollo program demonstrated a lot about American technological prowess, gendered meanings of protector, heroism, individuality, teamwork and uncovered hidden figures that strove for gender rights and women's equality.

Kranz's emphasis on individual "toughness and competence" in courage and technological prowess proved essential for a successful moon landing. Apollo required three astronauts. The *Saturn* rocket blasted the three men into space. The LM sat directly underneath the command module, attached to the *Saturn V's* third upper booster. This third upper-stage booster was fired to complete the translunar injection to send the command module (with the LM secured below) into lunar orbit. As the command module reached lunar orbit, the Spacecraft-to-LM adapter released the LM. The command module pilot then rendezvoused with the LM by turning the command module around, upside down, to dock or mate with the LM. Docking was extremely difficult and did not necessarily need jet-pilot skills but a vast knowledge of orbital mechanics.[10]

The command module pilot stayed in the command module while the commander and lunar module pilot descended to the moon. Nobody really knew what would happen once the LM landed on the moon. Finding the right landing site was key to survival. Otherwise, the craft might succumb to a rocky crater or risk not having enough fuel to return to the command module. The LM's payload had to be light. A heavy LM would use too much fuel from the command module and risk not having enough fuel for a return-to-Earth sequence to get home. Fuel conservation was necessary for survival. Using too much LM fuel might mean the astronauts did not have enough fuel for an ascent—the hairiest part of the moon landing missions—back to the command module and risk being stuck on the moon until the astronauts ran out of oxygen.

The entire mission required not just individual courage and skill but also teamwork. The astronauts not only relied on each other for survival but much like Mercury and Gemini, needed mission controllers and space stations around the globe. The following chapter argues that Project Apollo encountered a refashioning with the astronauts engaging in teamwork with mission controllers and scientist-astronauts. Apollo space missions remained extremely dangerous despite the public sentiment that they became routine or even safe. Spaceflight required quick thinking and steel nerves and nobody, not an astronaut or engineer, could control gremlins (faulty hardware) or the weather. Spaceflight missions laid the foundations for flight communications. Nobody could go it alone—there was no lone wolf. NASA astronaut nurse Dee O'Hara claimed, "And, boy, if you want to see teamwork in action, the space program is the place to watch. It's not any one individual. Nobody can do it by themselves."[11]

## IT'S HIP TO BE SQUARE                                161

Like the previous spaceflight programs, the public discourse focused on astronauts wrestling control from faulty machinery, but the discourse also embraced the team effort following the *Apollo 1* fire. The mission controllers became more prevalent in the spaceflight discourse. The mission controllers appeared to be carbon copies of white men with black slacks, short-sleeve button-down shirts, complete with pocket protectors, slide rules and crew cuts. However, the discourse did not present these men as William Whyte Jr.'s organization men whether they appeared athletic like Rocco Anthony Petrone or small like flight director Christopher Kraft.[12] Those on the ground at NASA were doers and creators, with individualist ideas who implemented new technologies in a team environment. The combination of individuality and teamwork refashioned the Apollo astronaut image to one of democratic manhood. In this refashioning, the American space program became emblematic of national healing during the explosive 1960s at home and abroad. The thirty-billion-dollar program to the moon received criticism as the teamwork exhibited to land on the moon was woefully falling apart on the national stage as astronaut Neil Armstrong declared, "That's one small step for man. One giant leap for mankind."[13]

Manned spaceflights resumed in October 1968, but at a chaotic time for the nation and the Cold War. Civil rights movements gained ground and had massive setbacks. The assassinations of Martin Luther King Jr. and Bobby Kennedy, race riots, soaring numbers of dead American soldiers in Vietnam, Hispanic student walkouts, a growing equal rights movement and the disastrous and bloody Democratic National Convention in Chicago sent shockwaves of anger and pain throughout American living rooms.[14] Black workers at NASA centers were on the front lines of the civil rights movement, demanding an end to segregation and to be treated with human decency, especially in southern states.

The Soviet Union experienced its own internal struggles from a disastrously poor planned economy, lack of consumer goods, widening gaps between the elite and the average citizen, cries for freedom and revolutions in their Eastern Bloc satellite states such as Hungary, Poland and Czechoslovakia. Like the United States, the Soviet space program also experienced major setbacks and tragedies. On April 24, 1967, veteran cosmonaut Vladimir Komarov died when his *Soyuz 1* parachute failed, and he plummeted four miles to his death. Colonel Komarov became the first person to die in space. The Soviet craft had many technical failures on board.[15] Neither the Americans nor the Soviets had perfected manned spaceflight.

Both nations pressed forward, building rockets with powerful payloads. Despite an immense loss, the Soviets launched *Zond 5* aboard a *Proton-K/D* rocket on September 14, 1968. The Soviet *Proton-K/D* rocket had a smaller payload than the Apollo *Saturn V* rocket. Even with more powerful thrust and the success of *Apollo 6*'s uncrewed translunar injection flight on April 4, 1968, the *Saturn V* was still floundering through much of the previous year. *Zond 5* was uncrewed—unless you count the payload tortoises. *Zond 5* completed the world's first circumlunar trajectory. However, *Proton-K*'s upper stage booster was not strong enough to launch *Zond 5* into lunar orbit.[16]

*Zond 5* was impactful enough to motivate George Low, now the Apollo Spacecraft Program Office Manager, as the Apollo program setbacks mounted. Difficulties plagued Grumman's lunar module. Low reasoned that the LM was not necessary for Apollo lunar orbit missions. Administrator James Webb was furious with the rushed idea. The LM doubled as a lifeboat for the astronauts in case the command module experienced technical issues. NASA had just lost three astronauts, and Congress recently cut their budget. NASA Associate Administrator, Thomas O. Paine, convinced Webb of the urgency. Low's idea of scrapping the figure-eight translunar injection in favor of a lunar orbit mission would surpass the Soviets and keep the Americans on schedule for a moon landing.[17] But it was extremely risky. Astronauts were used to danger, but the risk shocked mission controllers. They pressed on anyway.[18]

NASA continued with the scheduled crewed *Apollo 7* launch before making the dangerous *Apollo 8* lunar orbit mission. Launched from the *Saturn IB* rocket, *Apollo 7* flew into Earth's orbit from October 11 to October 22, 1968. NASA chose space veteran Wally Schirra as the craft's mission commander. *Life* described Schirra's personality as exuding "authority" and "a competence which inspires people" to the point where "nothing but his hair ever gets ruffled."[19] In reality, Schirra was irate at NASA engineers and North American Rockwell for changing the flight schedule, for shoddy workmanship and at times ignoring astronaut input in the spacecraft design and systems.[20] Astronaut office manager Deke Slayton picked Donn F. Eisele as the command module pilot and R. Walter Cunningham, one of the few non-jet test-pilot astronauts, as the lunar module pilot aboard the mission.

The public discourse highlighted the teamwork between the astronauts and their onboard computer. In Apollo, the astronauts were again part of a team, with each astronaut having his own individual responsibility aboard the craft. A team at MIT's Instrumentation Laboratory (IL), headed by Margaret Hamilton, designed the computer's software.[21] The public referred to the computer as the fourth astronaut. The astronauts insisted they had control. For instance, Schirra commented on Eisele's navigational ability: "He could make that guidance and control system perform and sing to us" so well in fact that he "sang into the most precise landing that any spacecraft has

# IT'S HIP TO BE SQUARE

163

ever achieved."[22] The astronauts held fast to their image as pilots controlling their craft.

However, Eisele's own statements insisted on a shared control between the astronauts, mission control and computers. He referred to the tasks during the trip as "getting beautiful information from the ground giving us our position" and "feeding the data into the on-board computer which keeps its own knowledge of where you are and where the target is." Even with teamwork between man and machine, reporters continued to highlight the role of man's individuality as Eisele mastered the computer. At a particular moment during the mission, the astronaut quit trusting his computer and instead, relied upon his own estimation of how far *Apollo 7* was to its landing zone. According to astronaut reports, a couple of times the computer went "crazy" and Eisele said to himself, "Oh man there goes the computer" again.[23]

The *New York Times* reported tension between astronauts and mission controllers over who held flight control. At times, mission control changed the flight plan on the astronauts. According to the *Times*, Schirra finally lambasted mission control Building 30, roaring over the radio, "I have had it up here today [...] and from now on I am going to be an on-board flight director for these updates. We are not going to accept any new games like doing some crazy tests we've never heard of before." Wilford reported that Schirra's choice words for mission control were the "stormiest fits of temper ever displayed by an orbiting astronaut." He wrote that "stunned, ground controllers could manage only a soft 'Roger' in reply [...]." Schirra demanded to know "the idiot's name who thought up this test [...] and talk to him personally when I get back down."[24] Schirra's anger was warranted with the death of his close friend and neighbor Gus Grissom, not to mention he battled a head cold in orbit. Some of the astronauts did not see his behavior as becoming of the heroic astronaut.[25] The masculinity exuded by the astronaut was not hysterics but calm control. Schirra's emotions appeared human.

The public discourse focused on the craft's automation and teamwork at mission control as *Apollo 7* splashed down in the Atlantic Ocean on October 22, 1968. Apollo Program Director, Air Force Lieutenant General Samuel C. Phillips, hailed the feat as a "Perfect Mission." With news of the successful pickup of the astronauts by the USS *Essex*, the dozens of engineers inside the control center under 31-year-old flight director Glynn S. Lunney "lit the traditional post-flight cigars. Smiling Apollo officials milled among the control consoles offering congratulations to the controllers." The *New York Times* interpreted the perfection of the flight as the perfection of the automated systems that "triggered the ignition of the 20,500 pound-thrust service module engine" to slow the craft down, and the "explosive devices" fired "automatically [...] to separate the service module from the command module." The craft automatically reentered the atmosphere through the automatic firing of "small rockets on the service module."[26] Even the craft aligned itself for descent automatically by the automatic firing of the command module's thrusters.[27] The words "automatically" and "automated" appeared over and over with limited mention of astronaut maneuvers.

Advertisements used space missions to focus on the need for American teamwork during one of the most turbulent years in American history. Almost a year after the Tet Offensive turned American public opinion against the Vietnam Conflict, the American space program demonstrated American superiority in spaceflight technology. The *Apollo 8* flight was a giant risk to those within NASA, but the public discourse focused on American control, teamwork and mastery over technology at a time of flagging vigor in Southeast Asia. The flight was so significant to American prestige domestically and internationally that Charles Lindbergh and his wife Anne met with the crew before liftoff. International and domestic strife would not be solved in 1968, but the American astronauts and thousands of engineers and missileers demonstrated the superiority of the American dream, technological exceptionalism and bravery.

From December 21 to December 27, 1968, commander Frank Borman, command module pilot Jim Lovell, and lunar module pilot William Anders sat atop a solid-fueled rocket that ignited twenty tons of fuel per second and reinvigorated American masculinity by doing the impossible.[28] The *New York Times* described Colonel Borman as a "take-charge man" and "a sneaky nonconformist." Borman and his fellow astronauts "kept a firm rein on their emotions."[29] Borman interjected his jet test piloting skills, telling *Life*, "I was flying the spacecraft manually, firing our attitude-control thrusters [...]"[30] Anders viewed the trip as emblematic of the American spirit. He wrote that throughout history, American "men came to conquer" and that on the "frontier" of space, "I was in the lead wagon."[31] Teams of nineteenth-century Conestoga wagons, guns, telegraph and railroads conquered the western United States. Spaceflight also needed technology and teamwork to conquer space.

The teamwork between technology and man was evident in *Apollo 8*'s success as well as the astronauts' Christmas Eve radio message. The *Saturn V's* upper booster, the largest in the world, propelled the astronauts for their sixty-six-hour flight from the Earth to the moon's orbit. The *Apollo 8* astronauts became the first humans to see the far side of the moon. The astronauts orbited the moon ten times in twenty hours.

On Christmas Eve, ABC, CBS and NBC broadcasted the astronauts reading the first ten verses from the book of Genesis. NASA's public information officer, Julian Sheer asked Borman to come up with something to say to the world on Christmas Eve. Borman's friend Simon Bourgin and his wife gave Borman the idea for the crew to read from the book of Genesis. Bourgin added the ending line "on the good earth."[32] The astronauts believed the reading symbolized unity and the "foundation of many of the world's religions."[33] As conflict and poverty engulfed the globe, the astronauts hoped to bring healing words in a moment of peace and togetherness.[34] The astronauts were typically conservative and not vocal about political issues.[35] Their focus remained on flying the newest crafts faster and farther. However, this was one of the few times the early astronauts acknowledged publicly their power for social and technological change. The astronauts viewed spaceflight's advanced technology and the Americans conquering the moon as beneficial to cure social unrest and inequalities. Borman told reporters, "The gains to be made from Apollo 8 far outweigh the risks."[36]

Harrowing astronaut exploration was sometimes lost on the American public, as reports of the flights often made them appear routine. *Life* reported that the astronaut children were unenthusiastic about their fathers' flights and wanted to watch cartoons.[37] Their mothers, however, were in agony. The press degraded the astronaut wives' support meetings by referring to them as a "hen party."[38] The wives knew the flight's realities. For instance, the mission controllers would lose contact for approximately ten seconds while the spacecraft circled behind the moon. The lack of a properly designed waste system meant that feces and vomit flew aboard the craft, making the astronauts sick.[39] The software engineers often had to compute the trajectory to get back to Earth's orbit in real-time using IBM's Real Time Computer Complex housed at mission control.[40]

Despite the *Apollo 1* tragedy, the public discourse focused on the routinization of spaceflight and failed to recognize its continued dangers. Homer Bigart's article "New-Breed Astronauts: Scientists, Not Daredevils," insisted that unlike the courageous early astronauts, Apollo astronauts were not out to perform a "historic act" but rather cared more for an "obsessive curiosity about space travel."[41] To the *Times*, routinization had taken the danger out of spaceflight and had become "somewhat routine."[42] Likewise, the *Fresno Bee* credited the bull's-eye landing to the Sacramento rocket engine designed by Aerojet-General Motor, not the astronauts' piloting abilities.[43]

Even mission controllers referred to flying in space as safe. Before the Wings Club at the Biltmore Hotel, Director of Manned Space Flight Safety Jerome Lederer, claimed that the astronauts would be safer aboard their craft than any of the crewmen aboard one of Columbus's ships.[44] Lederer was in a unique position. He needed to demonstrate spaceflight safety to Congress to ensure future spaceflight funding. The *Apollo 7* and *8* successes presented an

166        GENDER AND THE RACE FOR SPACE

accurate depiction of man's ability to control technology both in space and on the ground but an incorrect assumption that spaceflight was safe and routine.

The public discourse in *Apollo 8* highlighted the necessity of democratic manhood between astronauts, mission controllers and onboard computer systems to leave Earth's orbit safely. Previous flights only orbited the Earth. Therefore, the astronauts' main task was to fire the craft's retro-rockets to slow down and drop back into the atmosphere. However, because *Apollo 8* was returning from another orbit, the craft would be flying about seven thousand miles an hour faster than normal. If the craft hit Earth's orbit too hard, it would bounce off it like a rock. The astronauts relied on the automatic computer to keep the craft's roll at a one hundred eighty-degree angle to prevent the craft from bouncing out of Earth's orbit. The computer also controlled the roll's angle. Borman said of his reliance on the computer:

> I was watching it closely because if it failed to function I would have to fire our engines manually to make it roll. It performed perfectly. This wonderful machine, this spacecraft, which had taken us all these miles, saved its most sophisticated performance for the final eight minutes of our flight.[45]

Also underscoring the cooperation between astronauts and mission controllers, Lovell claimed that in actually getting from the Earth to the moon "the ground would have primary responsibilities."[46] Upon *Apollo 8*'s arrival home, the *Atlanta Constitution* lauded the computer aboard the ship as "flawless," and claimed that the flight was not only a testament to man's dreams, spirit and inventiveness, but also to the "integrity of his machines."[47] Eau Claire, Wisconsin repeated the sentiments, exclaiming, the "computer takes charge."[48]

Space journalists wrote furiously about these new computer systems, their designers and controllers. The *New York Times'* piece on Rocco Anthony Petrone, the Director of Launching Operations at the Kennedy Space Center, depicted the West Point grad and former football player as performing "defensive measures" as the "the unsung hero [...]" falling in love with "the beauty of the teamwork, the precision of the men and instruments [...]."[49] The media emphasized the reactions of the controllers at Houston's Manned Spaceflight Center. One controller described the scene as: "I've seen locker rallies in locker rooms after championship games, happy politicians after elections but never—none of them do justice to the spirit pervading this room."[50]

The music from John Glenn's documentary "Eyes on the Stars" and cigar smoke filled the room. A close associate of acting NASA Director Thomas O. Paine called *Apollo 8*'s flight "a triumph of the squares—meaning the guys

## IT'S HIP TO BE SQUARE

with crewcuts and slide rules who read the Bible and get things done."[51] The focus on ground control brought a different masculine image than that of the astronaut, suggesting masculinity to not be fixed but rather continuously influx. The mission controllers represented the corporate team player but in the same pendulum swing as the astronauts, unique individuals that created and controlled technology.

The *Bulletin of the Atomic Scientists* furthered this public discourse shift in control from individual astronauts to the teamwork with the men at mission control. Editor Eugene Rabinowitch wrote of the *Apollo 8* astronauts: "Their flight was monitored by instruments of incredible sensitivity and guided by computers of lightning speed [...]. The one decision of their own was to join the program." The *Bulletin* depicted the flight as "a triumph of enormous teamwork, of scientific discovery, technical skills and organization—served by a daring and disciplined crew [...]." The authors continued to applaud the team effort behind spaceflight, underscoring the control of the engineers and scientists:

> Certainly, most, if not all, of the critical maneuvers—the separation of the command and service modules from the carrier rocket, the acceleration to leave the earth's orbit, the deceleration needed to enter the lunar orbit, the renewed acceleration employed to leave the moon and the final entry into the atmosphere—were performed with the aid of computerized, semi-robot guidance and control system programmed to do its job in advance. Its performance was continually supervised by the crew, able to resort to manual operation if the automatic controls had failed.

The *Bulletin* asserted boldly that the "true authors" of *Apollo 8*'s flight were not the astronauts alone but the scientists and engineers who built the rockets, computers, radios, cameras, heat shields, fuel cell batteries and the other mechanized pieces of equipment used during the mission.[52]

Advanced technology aided mission controllers and astronauts with equations and coding and made button-pushing masculine. Space journalist Walter Sullivan correctly speculated that in the new age of spaceflight, instruments were necessary that go beyond the scope of the human mind: "While the explorers who first ventured across the seas, tramped the Polar ice and pioneered in plane flight, were able to navigate on their own, this is not possible in space." In space navigation, the astronaut faced "complex" calculations that "depend on a computer." The computer changed the way men explored, conquered and pioneered. Television transformed the relationship of people to their explorer, allowing the public to take part in exploration as it unfolded.

Exploration's interpretation was shared between viewer and explorer, taking away the explorer's control over the narrative.[53] The audience decided whether spaceflights were routine or dangerous or whether the heroes were astronauts, mission controllers or a combination through teamwork.

*Time* paid respect to the democratic manhood needed to launch astronauts to the moon's orbit and back and viewed the feat as an example of the togetherness needed throughout the world. The *Apollo 8* astronauts were the only astronauts to make *Time*'s "man of the year." While the three men, Anders, Borman and Lovell received the top honor for their "courage, grace, and cool proficiency," *Time* also remembered the teamwork and the democratic capitalism behind the trio. The issue proclaimed:

> The mission's fantastic precision could never have been achieved without the creativity and dedication of the greatest task force ever assembled for a peaceful purpose: 300,000 engineers, technicians, and workers. 20,000 contractors backed by $33 billion spent on the nation's space effort in the past decade.

To the magazine, the astronauts became a "gift" in a rough year. The "nation's own self-confidence sank to a nadir" with war, assassinations and Johnson's decision not to not seek re-election.[54] Student protests around the globe, challenges to the racial status quo and revolts against the Soviet Union demanded change and teamwork. The world saw countless efforts of people expressing their own individual wants and needs to be seen as human. At times, the space race appeared tone-deaf to domestic and international strife. The countless jobs, technological advances and teamwork needed to get to the moon illustrated a symbolic push for togetherness but also suggested the cognitive dissonance that white middle-class Americans held the key to civilization and advancement.

The Americans continued with manned spaceflight firsts as national and world unrest mounted. The March 3 to March 13, 1969 flight of *Apollo 9* completed one hundred and fifty-one revolutions around the Earth. The media described the flight as "smooth" and "accurate." The less-than-stellar amount of print media coverage of *Apollo 9* implied that despite Nixon's comment that the flight was "10 days that thrilled the world," *Apollo 9*'s "perfection flight" did not excite the American public, but rather, seemed routine.[55] The routinization of the flight led to speculation for a summer moon landing.

The *Apollo 9* astronauts completed the first transfer of an American astronaut from one orbiting spaceship into another orbiting ship. This took place from the command ship into the LM. Previously, on January 16, 1969, the Soviets accomplished this same feat between *Soyuz 4* and *Soyuz 5*. To counter this Soviet achievement, the United States also succeeded in its first link-up of two manned spaceships and its first spaceship flown in space that could not reenter the atmosphere, the LM. However, the Americans did complete their own "first" in world history as three spacemen were simultaneously exposed to the dangers of space. Astronaut Russell L. Schweickart performed a spacewalk, Colonel David R. Scott "poked his head out of the command ship door," all while Colonel James A. McDivitt sat in the lunar module with the door open to the elements of space.[56] The Soviets on the other hand, only had two men simultaneously exposed to the elements. Finally, Schweickart performed the first spacewalk where an astronaut was free from life support lines. Instead, he used a back-pack full of oxygen for life support—a must if astronauts were to walk on the moon.[57]

While Mercury and Gemini missions almost always had an automatic system fail, space journalists emphasized the safety and routineness with teamwork between astronauts, mission control and computers during Apollo. Space reporter Wilford wrote of this cooperation during *Apollo 9*'s flight:

> As soon as Colonel Scott found the exact point in the sextant (telescope) cross-hairs, he pressed a button, feeding the information to the onboard guidance computer [...]. From this, the computer calculated the spacecraft's orbital position and velocity and, if necessary, could order rocket firings to correct the space craft's position.

Democratic manhood and masculine button-pushing continued with the *Times* reporting that during the mission "ground controllers are confident they can accurately handle all systems on the orbiting spaceship" while the astronauts slept. Originally, NASA believed that the astronauts would sleep in different shifts, giving astronauts more control over the craft. However, since most of the astronauts' jobs onboard required all three simultaneously, this proved difficult. As one astronaut put it, "We say 'mission control you've got it' and we close our eyes."[58]

Space journalist William K. Stevens even went so far as to report, "Although Apollo astronauts are among the busiest of men once they venture into space, in a sense they are just along for the ride." The space journalist insisted that "the real work of 'flying' the spacecraft is done by an ingenious electronic guidance system that is coordinated and controlled by an on-board computer about the size of a suitcase." The computing system, designed by MIT and built by General Motors and the Raytheon Company, operated as the heart of the craft, checking the speed, position and future course of the mission. The astronauts entered information into the computer through their DSKY keyboard on the control panel, checked it and held the final say in

170    GENDER AND THE RACE FOR SPACE

what to do with its output, "but," Stevens argued, "for the most part they sit back, figuratively, and let it [the computer] do its job."[59]

Veteran space reporter Wilford detailed the fallibility of the astronauts in the system of man and machine. For instance, during a March 8, 1969 firing of the main rocket to propel the craft back into a lower orbit, the astronauts noticed a "sloshing" of propellants when the rocket was to fire. Due to a lack of gravity, the liquids within the tank sometimes remained suspended. To make the liquids settle into the outlet pipes, the craft needed to be at a tilting position, especially during the firing of the main rocket. An explosion might take place if the liquids were suspended during a rocket launch. Luckily for the astronauts, the computer failed to launch the main rocket while the liquids were suspended. Mission control "suspected that the astronauts fed incorrect instructions into the auto pilot for the maneuver. Spotting the error, the auto pilot never ordered the maneuvering thrusters to fire." Mission control "instructed" the astronauts to orbit the Earth and try again as the astronauts pushed "new information" into the computer. Colonel McDivitt radioed to Houston, "Thank you from the bottom of our computer."[60]

Despite *Apollo 10* being the most dangerous mission to date, it was largely overshadowed by the *Apollo 11* build-up. NASA launched *Apollo 10* on May 18 to May 26, 1969, with commander Thomas Stafford, command module pilot John Young and lunar module pilot Gene Cernan. They were all experienced astronauts, spending a total of eight days within Earth's orbit. The mission was a "dry run" for *Apollo 11*. *Apollo 10*'s lunar module did not land on the moon, but it did come within eight nautical miles of the moon's surface.

Assuming the flight plan went smoothly, the most difficult part was ensuring that the LM (*Snoopy*) did not waste too much fuel descending five hundred thousand feet above the moon or crash.[61] The most harrowing part of the mission was during the translunar burn, as the rocket booster pressure relief valves caused uncontrollable vibrations that almost led Stafford to abort the mission—but the men believed that the entire craft might explode and continued.[62] The astronauts accepted the personal risk as mission control scrambled to provide a set of corrective procedures to release *Snoopy* from the command module, *Charlie Brown*.[63] The teamwork between astronauts and ground control led to a successful "dress rehearsal" for *Apollo 11*.

Pilot astronaut masculinity reemerged as the manned moon landing gave the public discourse a reprieve from the tumultuous 1960s. On the surface, it appeared that the moon landing strengthened the vitality of the United States. President Nixon exalted the landing as the "greatest moment of our time."[64] The *New York Times* reported that the astronauts behind this accomplishment that so many Americans idolized were

# IT'S HIP TO BE SQUARE

171

not scientists seeking fundamental truth—although astronauts on future flights will be—but supremely self-confident pilots, who like action; and highly disciplined engineers whose natural habitat is the sometimes bewildering technology of the electronic age.

The *Times* hailed the men who would be first to step foot onto the surface of the moon as "expressions of the dominant values of the broad American middle class, but each represents a different current in that mainstream of society."[65]

The men Deke Slayton picked to go to the moon represented the same ordinary and yet extraordinary qualities as the astronauts before them. Neil Armstrong, the son of an auditor and a devote Christian mother, grew up in Ohio. Armstrong put himself through college with a Naval scholarship to Purdue University. Upon commission, he flew Panther jets off the deck of the USS *Essex*. He completed seventy-eight combat missions in Korea, earning three Air Medals. After being shot down, he spent a day behind enemy lines before being rescued. After the service, he flew at Edwards Air Force Base as a civilian jet test pilot, flying the experimental X-15 alongside Scott Crossfield. Armstrong considered himself a pilot and an engineer—bringing about a new breed of pilots focused on systems engineering. As an engineer, he viewed his role as "using airplanes merely as tools, the way an astronomer uses a telescope as a tool." While describing the demeanor of Armstrong, *Life* referred to his moments of silence in conversations not as "icy" but as "controlled."[66]

In this ordinary but extraordinary narrative, *Life* created a pioneer image of the Armstrong family. *Life* described the first house that Armstrong and his wife Janet built five thousand feet into the mountains outside Edwards Air Force Base. The family mastered their surroundings in a household with few modern conveniences. Armstrong frequently fished for their dinner. The article pointed out that as a young Eagle Scout, Armstrong was never a fan of team sports. Reinforcing a rugged individual image, the "introverted" Armstrong preferred solitude within the sport of flying gliders or reading. The *Times* continued with a dialogue of control, suggesting that although Armstrong did drink [alcohol], he never appeared "visibly affected."[67]

Edwin Eugene "Buzz" Aldrin, the son of an aviator and oil man, grew up with an upper-middle-class childhood in Montclair, New Jersey. He was a particularly no-nonsense child who dreamed of flying for the military. After graduating number one in his class at West Point, Aldrin went to Korea and flew sixty-six missions. He became an Air Force instructor pilot and married Joan Archer. Aldrin received a PhD from MIT in aeronautical engineering. *Life* described Aldrin as having the best scientific mind of the astronauts because he could correct a computer. The technology did not control Aldrin;

172          GENDER AND THE RACE FOR SPACE

he controlled the technology.[68] The media also reported on his manly physique. The *Times* stated that beneath Aldrin's "suave urbanity" and "stylish clothing" hid a "well-conditioned body whose individual muscles are under disciplined control, an asset that has made him the most accomplished of the six Americans to 'walk' in space."[69]

Michael Collins held a similar background to Aldrin. His father, General James Collins, was a military attaché to the U.S. Embassy in Italy. Collins was born in Rome. The Collins household had a cosmopolitan flair and was forward thinking despite his father's rigorous military career. General Collins served as General John Jay Pershing's aide in the Philippines, against Pancho Villa, and in World War I. After moving around throughout his childhood, Michael Collins settled at the all-boys St. Albans School in Washington, D.C. He went to West Point and then entered the Air Force. Like the other astronauts, he tested jets at Edwards. Collins' choice to become a fighter pilot was because they are "independent, they say what they mean, they prove who they are by what they do."[70] Collins was not scared to go to the moon because "things that you understand fully are not really frightening."[71] Collins' ability to control emotions encompassed his ability to drink "with no apparent ill effects" and yet possessed a great compassion for others.[72]

Veteran astronaut reporter David Nevin's interview with Collins revealed that while the astronauts presented themselves as ordinary men, they were extraordinary because they feared nothing. Nevin had never personally met an astronaut before Collins. He assumed astronauts to be stiff from courage, "the faceless man who does the incredible by a marvelous but not quite human feat of engineering rote." However, Nevin viewed Collins as an ordinary suburban dad when Collins, clad in shorts and sandals, welcomed the reporter into his Houston home. For two hours, the writer and astronaut discussed, "fear and courage, fatalism and confidence, man's relationship to his machine and to himself." Despite the cutoff jeans, Nevin concluded the astronauts to be "extraordinary" not because he could adequately "articulate their reasons" for signing up for danger but because "they are without nerves or cannot imagine failure and death or have a simplistic faith in machines."[73]

Fear typically holds people back from not living up to their potential; for not realizing their dreams. Yet, here were the astronauts, ordinary men who could do the extraordinary. They provided a hope and possibility for all men to strive to face their fears and do more. As Americans created a heroic astronaut image, they failed to realize that the extraordinary was in all ordinary people. Realizing this would give way to a mythical astronaut masculinity and allow all people the chance to be extraordinary.

Perhaps that determination and grit in facing their fears and controlling technology came not from an innate fearlessness but from their mothers. All the *Apollo 11* astronauts are further connected by their close relationships with their mothers. Armstrong, Aldrin and Collins' mothers embraced intellectual pursuits such as reading, languages, music and museums and imparted these to their sons. All three men wanted to meet or exceed their mothers' expectations.[74] The public discourse at the beginning of Mercury warned of maternal overprotection, and yet these astronauts were men enough to share with the world that their strong mothers had a profound influence on their individuality, knowledge and courage.

The public discourse emphasized this fearless pilot astronaut masculinity with the moon landing. On July 16, 1969, *Apollo 11* launched into space. The most apprehensive part of the mission was landing the LM *Eagle* on the moon and flying it back to the command module, *Columbia*. Armstrong's unflappable nature, especially during *Gemini 8*, led Slayton to choose him as the moon landing mission commander. A potential repeat of *Gemini 8* as the LM approached the moon appeared imminent. The *New York Times* reported that even though the computer fired the engine and pitch-up maneuver, and the keyboard controlled the attitude, during the flight, Armstrong switched to manual control to find a safe place to land the LM.[75] The public discourse made the excruciatingly difficult landing appear almost too easy. The *Charlotte Observer* concurred, writing that "Armstrong had to seize control of the spaceship from a computer that would have dropped them" into a dangerously large crater.[76] The computer headed for the rocky crater, and Armstrong "grabbed control of his ship, sent it clear of the area where it would have met almost certain disaster." The necessity for Armstrong to switch to manual control cost the astronauts over half the fuel needed to make the ascent back to *Columbia*.[77] To the *Charlotte Observer*, "In the end, man was on his own. The wondrous machine he'd built to land him safely on the moon just wasn't as versatile as man himself."[78] Man proved extraordinary while the technology proved faulty.

Astronaut control over technology and teamwork with mission control took center stage in the public discourse. The *Birmingham News* ran the headline "To Houston, Crew, LM Moon Landing 'Hairy.'" The article highlighted the individual control of Armstrong as the astronaut switched to manual control when the automatic guidance system of the LM sought to miss the landing site and send Armstrong and Aldrin into an enormous crater.

NASA director Thomas O. Paine lauded the "cagy piloting" of Armstrong as he landed the *Eagle* safely in the Sea of Tranquility.[79] The *Los Angeles Times* quoted Paine as suggesting that the United States had been lucky with their 1966 uncrewed moon landing of *Surveyor 1*, four months behind the Soviet's *Luna* 9 unmanned moon landings, because without a "pilot," the LM might not have made a successful landing.[80]

174 GENDER AND THE RACE FOR SPACE

Mission control was anxious during the dangerous situation. Likewise, the astronauts' hearts raced, but they "kept their voices under 'tight control.'"[81] Mission control touted, "The men and equipment that are Apollo 11 have performed to perfection. Perfection is not too strong a word."[82] Headlines likened the training of the men to a "unit."[83] Praising the mission controllers, the *Los Angeles Times* reported that the men back in Houston "play[ed] it cool."[84] British historian Arnold Toynbee was quick to point out that the heroic feat of the astronauts would not have been possible without the "skill, toil, devotion, loyalty, and competitiveness of the hundreds of thousands of scientists and technicians who have made the astronaut's feat possible."[85] The astronauts were still deft pilots but not alone.

Half a billion people across the globe watched the landing.[86] Trafalgar Square erupted into cheers, and Chileans danced. The Associated Press declared, "Almost everyone on Earth was somehow touched."[87] Former President Johnson boasted that the landing proved that Americans "can do anything that needs to be done."[88] To celebrate the launching of *Apollo 11*, Nixon declared a day of national participation. Nixon ordered nonessential government employees, governors, mayors, heads of school systems and private employers to close for the day. The president proclaimed that the feat of landing on the moon was not to be enjoyed by NASA alone, but rather that all Americans should take pride in the accomplishment.[89] The Americans launched the world into a new future—what to make of it was up to everyone.

John Glenn rejoiced and reminded Americans that the astronaut did not embody rugged individualism alone, but rather that he was part of a vast network of control. Glenn remarked that the explorers of yesteryear, such as Edmund Hillary and Charles Lindbergh, "were independent agents. They had only to apply their own ingenuity and round up the necessary backing before taking off on their own to satisfy their urges to learn, accomplish, and conquer." However, Glenn invoked the democratic manhood necessary for a moon landing. Glenn wrote, "Astronauts are part of a complex, interdependent system from which they cannot separate themselves, and the very existence of which rests on the say-so of the public."[90]

Some reporters even suggested that it was not the skill of the pilot that led to the safe LM landing, but rather man and machine. Journalists maintained that a "Change of 2 Numbers on Apollo Computer" shifted the craft to a new landing location two hundred forty-seven miles farther north and east to land closer to Johnson Island.[91] Louisville's *Courier-Journal* ran a similar article that proclaimed, "Eagle's Descent to the Moon Mostly in Computer's Hands" as the astronauts pushed the buttons "Program 63" followed by the "Pro" [Proceed] key that enabled the computer to fire the engines.[92] The computer performed all the flying until Armstrong was forced to manually take over the controls to land the LM on the surface of the moon.

However, some journalists feared that Americans were losing control both domestically and internationally despite the successful moon landing. *The Christian Science Monitor's* Saville R. Davis warned that "the good name of the United States will still have to be proved. It is not enough to have its flag propped up in the Sea of Tranquility, where it can no more feel or know the gales of Earth [...]." When the enthusiasm for the astronauts died down, space headlines would once again be replaced by American war and civil rights protestors clashing with police. While the world "regards [Americans] as doers," in the end, warned Davis, the world will not judge the United States on its ability to land a man on the moon, but rather, on its "civilization." "The country that 'cannot afford to be second best in space,'" wrote Davis, "may make more friends by its frank acknowledgement, at last, that it could not achieve military victory within South Vietnam."[93]

Putting domestic and international problems aside to go to the moon would not solve the United States' or the world's problems. David Bowie's "Space Oddity" lyrics aptly described this inability of the courageous astronaut to save the world: "Here I am, floatin' 'round my tin can far above the world, Planet earth is blue and there is nothing I can do." The astronaut hero is helpless to control domestic and international conflict. The song continues:

> Ground control to major Tom, your circuits dead, there's something wrong, Can you hear me major Tom? [...]. Here I am sitting in my tin can far above the Moon, Planet Earth is blue and there's nothing I can do.[94]

Likewise, the *New York Times* called on the United States not to move into the future by abandoning Earth's problems. The *Winston-Salem Journal* ran the headline to the *Times'* editorial, "After the Moon Can We Conquer the Earth?"[95] The author meant ethnic, national and racial tensions, coupled with wars that circled the globe. An editorial appearing in the *Courier-Journal* wrote of the moon landing's "Human Paradox," one of both "hope" and "fear." If man could reach the moon, why can man not cure "hunger," "greed," "warfare" or "cruelty?" Taking the moon landing as a symbol of hope, the editorial remained optimistic, anticipating that "the day man touches the virginal moon must surely be the day man starts to purify himself, breaking free from hate and horror as the astronauts broke free from the very earth."[96] Another editorial asked, "How far can we go to satisfy scientific curiosity without making the earth a living—or dying—hell?"[97] War, poverty and race riots competed for front-page headlines with NASA. Astronaut masculinity could not cure America's problems. Instead of representing control, the astronaut represented a complete lack of control. The lone-wolf astronaut image was facing a masculinity crisis as Americans paid forty cents per citizen each week to get to the moon and back.[98]

The United States commander in Vietnam, General Creighton Abrams, did not take time out from running the war to listen to the moon landing. However, the press suggested that "everybody else" in Vietnam was listening to the footage on Armed Forces Radio.[99] Contradicting the report, journalist Keyes Beech interviewed volunteers and soldiers at the United Service Organization (USO) in Saigon, who reported that the pool game at the base never stopped during the landing. Specialist William D. Hutchison of North Dakota commented, "You might think that a country that can put a man on the moon could end a crummy war like this."[100]

Likewise, Black civil rights leaders protested the space race. As the astronauts readied for space, the poor watched at the Cape. While Paine lauded the feat as "an example of what this country can do," Southern Christian Leadership Conference (SCLC) president, Reverend Ralph D. Abernathy, watched along with one hundred and fifty poor and three mules. The spectacle created a metaphor for the challenge to pilot astronaut masculinity, not only control in the form of Black demonstrations but also control over their own Earth, and the need for democratic manhood to feed the hungry and eliminate poverty and racial inequality. NASA historian Brian C. Odom argues that Abernathy's protest demonstrated that the Apollo program marked "a turning away from the plight of the poor and, with it, the abandonment of previous gains of the civil rights movement."[101]

Abernathy congratulated NASA on such an achievement but wished for Americans to learn to live together "down here on earth." As the world watched, Abernathy pointed out America's shortcomings. Paine maintained that NASA was for "all Americans" and implored Abernathy to "hitch your wagons to our rockets." Paine said he too wished for an end to poverty and racial injustice, telling Abernathy, "if it were possible for us not to push that button tomorrow and solve the problems you are talking about, we would not push that button."[102]

*New York Times* staff writer Bernard Weintraub viewed *Apollo 11*'s launch as a microcosm of American strife. On one side of the launch sat businessmen, politicians and generals in the bleachers. On the other side, the poor gathered outside their Cape Canaveral shacks, angry, hopeless and shaken, but at the same time "yearning to break through, possibly even smash through, this very power." In between the two groups stood white middle-class engineers, teachers, farmers and housewives, "whose pride in the country, and themselves, was pure."[103] A divided America stood at the Cape.

Black Americans' response to the moon landing typically focused on social injustice. A cartoon inside the pages of Baltimore's *Afro-American* had the headline "Our Prayers Go With You." The cartoon depicted a white astronaut waving to a crowd of onlookers as he entered the spacecraft. In the picture, spectators held up cards reading "Remember the Poor" and "Please Share More with the Poor."[104] The *New York Times* reported that most Black Americans "couldn't have cared less" about the *Apollo 11* flight. In fact, fifty thousand Black Americans gathered in Harlem on the day of the moon landing to celebrate a cultural soul music festival. Upon hearing the news of the *Eagle's* landing, the crowd booed. Bars patronized by Black Americans on Chicago's Michigan Avenue reported that as the astronauts landed, the patrons watched baseball. The newspaper quoted one patron as saying, "There ain't no brothers in the program where they can get into some of that big money."[105]

Operations Director of Pride Incorporated blasted the flight, telling workers to "keep on working" as he castigated NASA and the United States government with: "Why should blacks rejoice when two white Americans land on the moon when white America's money and technology have not even reached" the poor Black populations? Journalist J. Anthony Lukas wrote that while white men were landing on the moon, poverty prevented some Americans' ability to "Discover America." Lukas interviewed a resident of James, Mississippi that only made twenty-three dollars a week working on a white man's "plantation."[106] Lukas speculated that "even relatively well-off Negroes frequently feel their hold on prosperity is precarious."

The *Chicago Defender* reported that even though, for one instant the moon landing united all Americans, it could also be considered a "cultural lag."[107] An attorney for the National Association for the Advancement of Colored People's (NAACP) Legal Defense and Education Fund commented:

> It proves that white America will do whatever it is committed to doing [...]. If America fails to end discrimination, hunger, and malnutrition then we must conclude that America is not committed to ending discrimination, hunger, and malnutrition. Walking on the moon proves that we do what we want to do as a nation.[108]

*Newsweek* reported that a young San Francisco journalist lamented that the trip to the moon did not include a minority. He wrote, "If one of the Americans setting foot on the lunar surface had been a Negro I feel that the $24 billion might have been justifiable." To the journalist, if NASA had launched a Black American, it "would have demonstrated to ourselves and to the world not only that we have the best technicians, but also we know how to live with each other."[109] Similar to NASA's inability to see the value of sending a woman into space, NASA failed to realize the prestige and cultural necessity of giving voice to minorities.

178                    GENDER AND THE RACE FOR SPACE

Black protests outside Houston's Manned Spaceflight Center led to a con-
tentious confrontation over race in American society. The *Washington Post's*
William Greider reported that "outside the white buildings of the Manned
Spacecraft Center campus, Sunday visitors strolled along the walkways with
dreamlike disregard." White families enjoyed a leisurely afternoon. However,
in the background appeared a different image of American life in the 1960s as
"an assemblage of about 40 black children and their mothers, welfare recipi-
ents from Houston, gathered on the grass terrace beside the LM [model] to
demonstrate." An organizer passed out signs that read: "Good Luck from the
hungry children of Houston" or "41 cents a day is not enough."

An employee for NASA's contractor AV Corporation, John Harrison, pulled
dollar bills from his wallet and waved them in the demonstrators' faces, yelling,
"Are you people hungry? Here's a dollar!" A Black woman cried back, "Take us
out tomorrow to one of those big cafeterias where we can't go." Harrison roared:
"Why don't you go out and work and get yourself some food?"[110] Likewise,
*Newsweek* attacked NASA as lacking any real "over-all goal" other than "flag-
waving in the xenophobes and only a moldering sense of injustice in the dis-
sidents," but there were still "promises of what the new age can be [...]."[111]

The astronaut image faced an identity crisis. America was torn between
two worlds. The astronaut was somewhere in the middle. He was a symbol of
a new man, a symbol of hope, the rugged individualist Cold War pioneer. He
symbolized a superior America, and yet he could not solve American problems. The astronaut needed to control technology, be an individualist, a team
player and represent American inclusion. It was a tall order. The astronaut
image that depicted individuality, teamwork and even hope failed to consider
more than half the United States population: women and minorities. The
space program read as a centuries-old narrative that women and minorities
would have to wait for white men to master, control and conquer before their
chance to participate.

Democratic manhood proved necessary for Apollo 11's success as well
as for a potential triumph over strife at home and abroad. The next Apollo
mission demonstrated the same need for pilot skills coupled with working
with the individuals at mission control. A Florida cold front brought thun-
derstorms and lightning to Cape Kennedy on November 13, 1969. The rainy
weather seemed "favorable," and even President Nixon and First Lady Pat
stayed on hand in the rain to watch the launch.[112] Less than fourteen seconds
to liftoff on November 14, 1969, *Apollo 12* commander Pete Conrad, command module pilot Richard F. Gordon and rookie lunar module pilot Alan
L. Bean, felt "engulfed by vibration" that continued as *Apollo 12* lifted off pad
39-A.[113] Conrad radioed Houston twenty-two seconds into the flight, "It's a
lovely liftoff."[114]

Lightning then struck the *Saturn V* launch vehicle just over thirty-six seconds after liftoff. Conrad saw a light and felt a jolt in the command module. He radioed Houston, "What the hell was that?" Conrad lost the spacecraft's orientation as the 8-ball (artificial horizon) dropped. He radioed at fifty-one seconds in, "AC BUS 1 light, all the fuel cells." A second later, "I just lost platform." It appeared to the crew that they lost electrical power. LM pilot Bean radioed Capcom, "I can't—There's nothing I can tell is wrong, Pete," as the rocket continued its trajectory with its own internal guidance system sending seven and a half million pounds of thrust under the astronauts.[115]

Young EECOM (electrical systems) engineer, 24-year-old John Aaron, noticed unreadable numbers at thirty-seven seconds into the flight. He remembered these same number patterns during a simulation. Simulations bored the astronauts, but they knew their importance as pilots and engineers, and now was the time to thank those countless hours. During one simulation, Aaron used the Signal Condition Equipment switch to bring back the spacecraft's correct telemetry or data. Leading his first mission as flight director, Gerry Griffin looked over at Aaron as *Apollo 12* continued its path. Aaron replied calmly, "Flight, try S-C-E to Aux." Seated at Capcom, astronaut Jerry Carr radioed to *Apollo 12*, "Try SCE to AUXILLARY. Over." Conrad replied, "FCE to AUXILLIARY. What the hell is that?" Astronaut Carr repeated, "SCE—SCE to AUXILLIARY." Bean reached for the switch. The astronauts checked the systems. Everything looked good from the astronauts' perspective and at mission control. Conrad half-heartedly joked, "I suggest we do a little more all weather testing." Carr responded, "Amen."[116]

Conrad's calm piloting skills and Aaron's quick thinking led to a safe flight and another successful American crewed moon landing. The public discourse reported that "static electricity" had "knocked out the spacecraft electrical system." Papers attributed the astronauts' experience as Navy test pilots to saving the day as they "acted quickly. They traced the trouble, found three circuit breakers open, and reset them, restoring power."[117] Throughout the ordeal, Conrad stayed in control as he "remained unshaken."[118] Conrad was a "pilot's pilot"; Gordon a "tough cookie," and the "balding" Bean possessed "a bold streak."[119] Seconds after the astronauts restored telemetry, mission control radioed, "We've had a couple of cardiac arrests down here, too, Pete." Conrad responded, "There wasn't any time for that up here."[120] Astronaut Thomas Stafford told reporters of the harrowing seconds, "That's why we have experienced test pilots flying these vehicles."[121] A *New York Times* editorial by Earl Ubell, science editor for WCBS News-New York, suggested controversially that *Apollo 12* was the spacecraft to prove what *Apollo 11*, *Gemini* and *Mercury* failed to prove; that man with machines have a "role beyond piloting."[122]

180 GENDER AND THE RACE FOR SPACE

*Apollo 12* demonstrated the need for ingenuity, quick thinking, and, above all, teamwork between men and machines during the unpredictability of spaceflight. *Apollo 13* proved the same. Obstacles commenced before *Apollo 13* left the ground. For the first time, an astronaut needed to be replaced only days before the mission. NASA believed that the quiet bachelor command module pilot Thomas Kenneth "Ken" Mattingly II was exposed to the German measles during training exercises. Doctors felt it best to replace him rather than risk a sick astronaut in space. NASA replaced Mattingly with the "rambunctious bachelor" astronaut John Leonard "Jack" Swigert Jr., seventy-two hours before the launch.[123] Jim Lovell commanded the mission with Fred W. Haise as the lunar module pilot.

Fifty-six hours after liftoff on April 11, 1970, *Apollo 13* experienced a "power failure."[124] Unbeknownst to Swigert, when he flipped the switch to stir the oxygen tanks, the second tank exploded. Swigert alerted mission control with, "Okay Houston, we've had a problem here." Capcom astronaut Jack R. Lousma radioed back, "This is Houston. Say again, please." This time, Lovell repeated, "Houston, we've had a problem. We've had a Main B Bus Underbolt."[125] As *Apollo 13* approached the moon's orbit, oxygen leaked out of the craft, and the command module, the *Odyssey*, went dead. The explosion triggered a chain reaction of power failures, including the onboard computer. While only fitted for two men, mission control ordered the astronauts into LM *Aquarius* to do its job as a lifeboat. The LM had working oxygen tanks and electrical power. *Aquarius* acted as a service and command module. To survive, the astronauts needed to exhibit democratic manhood above and beyond any previous spaceflight.

Lovell's piloting skills and mission control's calculations were needed to get back to Earth. The leaking oxygen prevented the astronauts from determining the spacecraft's alignment. They linked the LM with the service module platform and relied on the LM to get them back from the dark side of the moon. The astronauts quickly stepped in as pilots and reoriented the LM for a free-range trajectory back home. Lovell used his pilot skills to stop the craft from rolling. The astronauts trusted the LM's technology as they still could not see *Aquarius*'s telemetry. The astronauts were overtired, freezing and damp. Exhaustion set in, and communication with mission control, as it always had been, remained paramount for success. Lovell almost made a major error in attempting to reorient *Aquarius*'s trajectory, and thankfully, mission controllers were not nervous about correcting the commander. Swigert knew everything about the command module but knew nothing about the LM, which he was never supposed to fly. Through all of this, the men's voices remained calm.[126]

## IT'S HIP TO BE SQUARE

Carbon dioxide produced from the astronauts' breathing became another serious issue as NASA demanded the spaceflight technology and pilots do the impossible. Three men in the LM produced more carbon dioxide than the lithium hydroxide batteries could handle. Countless Apollo simulations led mission controllers to a solution during real-time missions. Mission controller Ed Smylie produced a breathing filter after a failed *Apollo 8* simulation. Scientist-astronaut Joe Kerwin, a medical doctor, instructed the *Apollo 13* astronauts to take the lithium hydroxide batteries from the command module and tape plastic bags to them. The astronauts then blew through the bags with the aid of the red hose from the astronaut suits to filter out the carbon monoxide.[127]

Democratic manhood solved the carbon dioxide problem, but the dead command module proved the next issue. The astronauts needed to return to *Odyssey* to reenter the Earth's atmosphere. Despite the fact that the command module manual stated a command module could not be powered back to life—it did, complete with a working computer and guidance system. The astronauts jettisoned the *Aquarius*. Miraculously, the *Odyssey's* heat shield was still attached, and the parachutes deployed.[128] Jet test-pilot astronauts, a scientist-astronaut, countless engineers and technicians—all with differing masculine images—worked together exercising democratic manhood to bring the *Apollo 13* crew home safely.

The press portrayed the mission controllers as heroes who saved the astronauts. Mission controllers were "at the console in the big room, men in shirtsleeves" looking over sheets of paper and instrument panels.[129] The comingled smell of smoke and sweat filled the air. The *New York Times* proclaimed, the crew lay "crippled" and flight director Lunney was "making the decisions."[130] As Slayton said, "We've got things well under control."[131] While reflecting on the 1995 movie *Apollo 13*, Roger Launius described the scene in Building 30 as an "interesting transference of masculine power from the astronauts" to the mission controllers.[132] At mission control, Americans gazed upon men of action and smarts—the same as the astronauts but this time with a different physique. White middle-class men with brains over brawn, the squares, exercised masculinity in spaceflight, protecting the astronauts from faulty technology.

*Apollo 13's* safe return required "intricate maneuvering" between the astronauts and mission controllers.[133] Three men spent four days in a cramped cockpit designed for two men. They survived on six ounces of water a day in freezing conditions with little sleep. Mission Control and the astronauts worked out the necessary steps together to detach the lunar and command modules. On April 17, 1970, *Apollo 13* returned to Earth with a "perfect" landing in the Pacific Ocean.[134] The USS *Iwo Jima* picked up the astronauts.

182 GENDER AND THE RACE FOR SPACE

Mission controllers erupted into cheers, lighting cigars and downing champagne.[135] After the safe return of the astronauts, the media and Director Paine hailed the feat as a "triumph of teamwork."[136] Low stated that never had a mission required "as much from the men flying the machines as this one has."[137] Which men he is referring to is unclear. It was the *New York Times'* Nancy Hicks who wrote that Flight Director Kranz "collates all the information on systems' operations, makes the command decision and feeds it to the crew in space so that they can execute critical maneuvers." Nicknamed "General Savage," the "extremely friendly" Kranz acted in a "selfless" manner, replacing tired mission control teams with fresh ones for the betterment of the crew safety.[138] Kranz's intelligence, individuality, leadership and generosity epitomized the democratic manhood necessary for successful missions.

Even while highlighting the quick thinking and heroism at mission control, reporters could not dismiss the astronauts' courage within this teamwork. The *New York Times'* Joseph Lelyveld summarized the uniqueness of the astronauts not for their "courage or the perils they faced," but rather that it was their "training and technical expertise" that made them part of a "unique fraternity." He suggested that transforming *Apollo 13*'s mission from one of scientific and technical importance to one that focused on simple needs such as air, oxygen and a lifeboat, transformed the astronauts into Odysseus facing the Cyclops and longing to return to Penelope.

> Of course we knew that their return would be impossible without the computers and simulators and expert technologists arrayed in their orderly rows. But in the final 14 minutes of flight, when the tiny capsule hurled back into the earth's atmosphere at last we found ourselves talking of "recovery" and "acquisition"—simple, supremely non-technical concepts [...].[139]

For their courage, President Nixon awarded the Medal of Freedom, America's highest civilian honor, to the three astronauts in Hawaii. However, before he did so, he stopped by Houston and awarded the Medal of Freedom to the *Apollo 13* ground crew. Director of Flight Operations at the Manned Space Center, Sigurd A. Sjoberg, accepted the award on behalf of mission control. Nixon declared a National Day of Prayer and thanksgiving.[140]

Despite the masculine-focused spaceflight and engineering narrative, a woman had entered this manly space. In the sea of *Apollo 13*'s white middle-class male mission controllers sat a "Pretty Mini skirted Blond Mathematician" and "former beauty contestant" named Francis Marian "Poppy" Northcutt. Northcutt worked as a return-to-Earth specialist who "talked" to the *Apollo*

**Figure 5.2** *Apollo 13* flight directors (left to right), Gerald D. Griffin, Gene Kranz and Glynn S. Luney, celebrate *Apollo 13*'s splashdown. Source: NASA. https://www.cnn.com/2019/07/19/us/apollo-11-space-mission-control-teams-scn/index.html.

*13* computer she programmed to find the safest path for the astronauts' return to Earth.[141]

This was not the first time the world heard of Poppy Northcutt, but most of her story reflects the parameters of uncovering hidden voices in the long civil rights movement. Northcutt graduated from the University of Texas with a bachelor's degree in mathematics. Thomas Ramo Woolridge (TRW), a NASA contractor located across from Houston's Manned Spaceflight Center, hired Northcutt as a "computress" right out of college.[142] Northcutt found it "weird" that TRW was "going to gender me as a computer."[143] In rooms full of men with advanced degrees from prestigious universities, Poppy believed they were not smarter than her. With individual drive and ingenuity to learn all she could about engineering at work and on her own time, TRW promoted Northcutt to engineer after six months.[144]

Despite gross gender inequalities in pay and promotion, TRW ebbed and flowed with progressive gendered roles. TRW used a picture of Northcutt for a national advertisement during *Apollo 12*, touting "TRW's Poppy Northcutt keeps bringing astronauts home."[145] TRW used a 25-year-old white woman's face to sell the prowess of its software systems. The words "bringing the astronauts home" also suggest a transference of the role of protector from the astronauts to Northcutt. The advertisement implied that Northcutt had control over spaceflight technology, not just the astronauts. A woman could control spaceflight technology from the ground. TRW understood the untapped talent and skill that women brought to computer programming at a time in which society viewed women as non-technological users.

The public discourses' fascination with Northcutt ran along the lines of shock, awe and conventional gender depictions focusing on her looks, attire, dating and feminine hobbies. The 26-year-old "tall, winsome" and "Bachelor girl" was the lone female at mission control. The mention that she was a self-professed rule breaker who loved vogue fashions, sewed, "looks like a stewardess," "bleaches her hair," "wears contacts" and "likes to swim, dance, ski, or sail," helped create the public image of how a woman in a male-dominated field would look and act.[146] As all well-behaved women should, she had "complete self-confidence but without any personal vanity."[147] While she lit up the traditional cigar with the boys following missions, one mission controller told the press that "having Poppy on the team has sure cleaned up our language."[148] She was included, but also apart from the group. This engineer cleaned up his language to either make space for her or out of cultural

**Figure 5.3** Poppy Northcutt at Mission Control, Johnson Space Center, during *Apollo 8*. Source: TRW/PhotoQuest/Getty Images. https://www.space.com/poppy-northcutt-remembers-apollo-11.html.

assumptions for how one should act around a lady. Either way, Northcutt joined the National Organization for Women (NOW) to protest gender inequalities in employment.[149] She outwardly appeared conventionally feminine but controlled technology and fought for equal rights. She presented to the public a multilayered feminine identity.

Northcutt exhibited both conventional feminine and culturally masculine characteristics that suggested gender was on a spectrum. Northcutt's individuality and teamwork symbolized the democratic manhood needed for spaceflight. Reporters noticed that she refrained from "using the word 'I' when she talks about her work, but always says 'we' to credit the other people in Mission control—all males."[150] Not using "I" reflected the engineering team atmosphere. But not giving herself personal credit or praise reflected conventional feminine gender roles in which women did not boast or brag.

Northcutt acknowledged to intrigued reporters that "I was singled out because I'm a woman," but she recognized the importance of normalizing women engineers. She believed that society "brainwashed" women to think they were unqualified for engineering careers.[151] While most American women got married and had children in young adulthood, Poppy subverted gender roles and entered spaces denied or limited to women. Northcutt chose a different path from societal expectations apart from secretary, nurse or teacher. She embodied the astronauts' individuality and mastery over technology, showing that individuals could create their own identities apart from societal constraints.

The public discourse questioned sex discrimination during Apollo. Northcutt understood that it was not simply employers that discriminated against women, but rather American culture.[152] The arguments against women in spaceflight still focused on the cost, their unpredictable bodies, marriage and motherhood. A Carroll College (Helena, Montana) coed asked scientist-astronaut Harrison Schmitt why there were not any women astronauts. He replied that women presented an "engineering problem. Women are built different than men and new pressurized suits would have to be designed."[153] NASA test pilot B. J. "Jack" Long summed up the environment of space as "not conducive to lady-like living."[154] Princeton geology professor and Chairman of the Space Science Board of the National Academy of Science, Dr. Harry Hess, argued that it would cost over "$100,000" to design a spacesuit for women. That was too costly for the billion-dollar space industry. Hess also believed women did not possess "the astronautical engineering skills of men." Furthermore, NASA had plenty of astronauts. Finally, Hess told reporters, "women tend to get married" and would not want to leave their children behind for a mission.[155] These were the same arguments to disband the WASPs and the same arguments to keep the FLATs out of spaceflight.

The continuation of these arguments generation after generation once again depicted women—even white women—as part of the long civil rights era.

The idea of women astronauts still seemed absurd. A brave girl at Cooper High School in Abilene, Texas, asked astronaut Swigert when there would be a woman astronaut. Laughter erupted in the cafeteria when he replied, "I'm a bachelor, so I certainly hope so." Women were still sex objects and not skilled individuals. Swigert reined in his humor and repeated the dominant narrative that it was too costly to design a spacesuit.[156] Even progressive Rene Carpenter, wife of astronaut Scott Carpenter, told the *Boston Globe* that the idea of a woman astronaut was "ridiculous! Besides, you'd have to have special plumbing for her!"[157] Over half the United States population would be left out of spaceflight because their bodies were different. NASA adapted to *Apollo 13*'s carbon monoxide problem by creating a device to save the astronauts but failed to create a spacesuit for a woman's body.

Marriage and motherhood continued to be a primary argument for keeping women out of the astronaut corps. "NASA consultant" Jackie Cochran argued once again that training women would be a waste of tax dollars if women dropped out to get married or have children.[158] The marriage and motherhood argument also crept up during a press conference for *Tektite II*, a NASA-funded underwater living project. For two weeks in July 1970, seventeen teams, one of them all women, lived fifty feet below the waters of Great Lameshur Bay in the Virgin Islands. The press reported that one of the teams under NASA's Richard Sprince comprised of all women (five in total) who completed the same work as men. NASA officials commented that while these "women worked as efficiently as men," women in the astronaut corps would have to wait until NASA created a floating space laboratory. Presently, wrote the press, the "pioneering venture" of spaceflight was currently one in "which man was more suited." The reason given by chief astronaut physician Charles A. Berry was that an astronaut woman had the "prerogative to change her mind and get married," leading to wasted dollars and time spent training her. Berry envisioned a time in which women would go into space but pointed out the fear of sexual impropriety if men and women were alone in space. There had to be more than one woman on a spaceflight and "they've got to be able to do useful work and contribute to the mission."[159] Women would not be propaganda. They had to have skill. Berry's reasoning highlighted the broader cognitive dissonance within American culture, which suggested that women lacked the same skills as men and could not contribute to male-dominated fields.

The public discourse emphasized that women's entrance into the astronaut corps would be as scientists after spaceflight was safe. Chief consulting pilot for Grumman, Scott MacLeod, told an Upsala College audience that "women do not have the qualifications to be astronauts because the requirements call for test pilots" but "women could go into space as scientists."[160] This questioned if scientist-astronauts were true astronauts. Colonel John Prodan argued that one day NASA would "need women" once it had "manned laboratories orbiting the earth and sitting on the moon [...]." However, in this capacity, women would be "scientists" and the "Men will be aboard to face the physical and mental rigors. And women will be along to take care of details."[161] Colonel Prodan failed to understand that all astronauts and scientists aboard faced the rigors of manned spaceflight. In its historical context, controlling technology appeared masculine, while women with technology were passive—even those selected as scientists aboard a floating space laboratory. For the moment, women continued to wait for the routinization of spaceflight technology.

The scientist-astronauts also feared they too would have to wait for spaceflight. By May 1971, there were no scientist-astronauts listed as any of the crew members for *Apollo 14*, *Apollo 15* or *Apollo 16*. Only scientist-astronaut Jack Schmitt was listed as one of the backup crew for *Apollo 15*.[162] Scientists felt betrayed. Scientists wrote a scathing opinion piece in the *Bulletin of Atomic Scientists* entitled "Requiem for the Scientists-Astronauts" maintaining the importance of space science and a scientist on crewed missions. Claiming that astronaut Gordon Cooper perceived crew selection to be part of "politics," the article defended the ability of the scientist-astronauts to pilot the spacecraft and lunar modules. Making their case for non-jet test-pilot astronauts, the article claimed that when it came to space technology, "The Apollo command module is controlled primarily by an on-board computer, and space craft activities, both routine and emergency are generally supervised and directed by ground control."[163] The mission control squares controlled the craft.

A week after the August 7, 1971 landing of *Apollo 15*, NASA announced that it would, in fact, send up a scientist-astronaut, Jack Schmitt, in *Apollo 17* as the crew's lunar module pilot. Scientist-astronaut Schmitt replaced test-pilot astronaut Joe Engle. Chuck Yeager recommended Engle for Air Force Test Pilot School.[164] *Apollo 17* commander Gene Cernan commented in his memoirs that Engle was an "outstanding aviator" but "only an adequate lunar module pilot."[165] NASA believed a scientist-astronaut—who had completed Air Force jet pilot training—could step into the shoes of a pilot astronaut. The press reported a narrative that NASA had "bowed to scientific pressures." The scientist-astronauts no longer wanted to be treated as "window dressing," and the pilot astronauts would have to make concessions.[166] The announcement elated the scientific community, especially scientist-astronaut champion, Wernher von Braun. Von Braun reflected upon the achievements

GENDER AND THE RACE FOR SPACE

of the Apollo program. Von Braun viewed Apollo as important for highlighting manned spaceflight over unmanned flight. It captured American hearts and minds. Von Braun argued, "Each Apollo mission, including the ill-fated *Apollo 13*, confirmed and expanded the role of man in space." But the scientist as an astronaut was an essential missing element.[167] The public discourse provided a fascinating insight into this new scientist space flier image as

> the end of the supremacy of the racing car drivers in space—the men who spring beyond our atmosphere for national prestige, for flexing engineering muscle, for adventure or just for getting there [...]. scientists have finally won parity with, if not ascendency over, engineers and publicists.[168]

The commercial television stations only sporadically interrupted programs with Apollo updates. Cable appeared to be a better medium for spaceflights, but still few viewers tuned in.[169] While lackluster coverage appeared on-screen, newspapers, especially the *New York Times*, continued with their barrage of spaceflight coverage. Journalists asked what Americans had learned from Apollo. While assuaging critics of the thirty-billion-dollar price tag on space exploration, historian at the Smithsonian Institute, Dr. Daniel J. Boorstin, proposed that NASA acted more as a cultural representative in space. Boorstin proposed that "the great thing about space exploration is that we don't know what its payoff will be. This symbolizes the American civilization. The people who settled America had no idea what the payoff would be. They settled it before they explored it."[170] *Times* sportswriter, Nelson Bryant, wrote passionately of the qualities of the astronaut:

> They are the most daring, dedicated and disciplined hunter-explorers mankind has ever known, willing and even eager riders of machines in the infancy of their development, performing tasks with their bodies and minds beyond the reach of technology.

Bryant described the astronauts as not only rugged but paradoxically wrote that they were surprisingly "human and fragile."[171]

Despite questions over the benefits of federal money spent on space exploration and spaceflight routinization, Americans flocked to Cape Kennedy for the last Apollo mission. About half a million spectators arrived. They saw the teamwork between humans and machines as thirty seconds before the scheduled liftoff the "computer signal halted countdown." The liquid oxygen in the third and top stage did not pressurize automatically. The ground crew switched to manual control and pressurized the liquid oxygen. The *New York Times* hailed the feat as "Experts Tricked the Computer."[172]

# IT'S HIP TO BE SQUARE

189

The countdown continued, and *Apollo 17* blasted into space on December 7, 1972. *Apollo 17* symbolized the last lunar flight and the birth of a new astronaut image.[173] Journalists saw scientist-astronaut Schmitt as different. Not only had Schmitt learned to fly "after being named an astronaut," but unlike the previous astronauts, he was not going into space for "adventure" but rather "science." Clearly, science was not adventurous to the American imagination. The wording mattered. The scientist took the moxie out of flying. According to the *New York Times*, many astronauts believed a lunar landing would be too difficult for anyone who was not a career pilot. However, through his training, Schmitt proved that "a geologist could learn to fly spacecraft as competently as a test pilot."[174]

The official NASA *Apollo 17* Mission Report concluded that Schmitt's flight "demonstrated the practicality of training scientists to become qualified astronauts and yet retain their expertise and knowledge in the scientific field."[175] The ultimate compliment came from commander Cernan who referred to Schmitt in his memoirs as an "outstanding" lunar module pilot.[176] White male scientists had the right stuff. The public astronaut image changed. Schmitt became not simply a scientist-astronaut in NASA's report, but he became a pilot astronaut. Schmitt demonstrated a fluctuating masculinity, a man belonging to the squares who passed jet pilot school and flew a spacecraft, all while retaining his scientific nerdom. He had the right stuff. The public discourse depicted this shifting masculine astronaut image as the press and those within NASA continued to create the notion of spaceflight routinization. A gendered spaceflight chapter ended, and another one commenced that focused not on rugged individualism but democratic manhood, teamwork and science in space. Spaceflight and spaceflight technology was becoming more democratic.

## Conclusion

Journalists, politicians and NASA praised the teamwork of the new scientist-astronauts, astronauts and mission control. A sense of satisfaction swept over flight director Kranz as he scanned Building 30. He wanted the one thing that every manned spaceflight since Mercury possessed. He wanted mission control to have their own mission patch. Talking with patch designer Bob McCall, Kranz "emotionally" remembered:

> We fought and won the race in space and listened to the cries of the Apollo 1 crew. With great resolve and personal anger, we picked up the pieces, pounded them together, and went on the attack again. We were

190        GENDER AND THE RACE FOR SPACE

the ones in the trenches of space and with only the tools of leadership, trust, and teamwork, we contained the risks and made the conquest of space possible.[177]

While they may not have won the initial debate over who would fly into space, the "squares" carved out a new masculine identity for themselves as scientist-astronauts and mission controllers. The scientists became astronauts, but as hyphenated members of the corps. Slowly, the public discourse viewed spaceflight as routine. Passengers could follow. Passengers meant that women could fly, and this symbolized spaceflight's domestication. The astronaut moved farther away from an individual controlling his craft, into a multilayered individual with multiple masculine archetypes. The astronaut no longer symbolized Cold War masculinity solely through his individuality; instead, he embodied a more dynamic concept that showed a man's ability to define his own masculinity through choice.

## Notes

1  Chapter title borrowed from Bill Gibson, Sean Hopper and Huey Lewis, "Hip to be Square," Track 4 on Fore!, Chrysalis Records, 1986, cassette tape.
2  John Noble Wilford, "3 Astronauts' Tape Ended With Get Us Out of Here!"; Tape of Astronauts' Last Moments Ends with Cry: "Get Us Out Of Here!"; Space Program Supported," *New York Times*, January 31, 1967, 1, 24. See also, Chaikin, *A Man on the Moon*, 24–25.
3  Wilford, "3 Astronauts'," 1, 24. See also, Chaikin, *A Man on the Moon*, 24–25.
4  Wilford, "3 Astronauts'," 24 and Chaikin, *A Man on the Moon*, 24–25.
5  Evert Clark, "Apollo Program Dealt Hard Blow," *New York Times*, January 28, 1967, 1, 10.
6  "Grief Expressed the World Over," *New York Times*, January 29, 1967, 49; The Associated Press, "Russians Broadcast Message of Sympathy after Apollo Fire," *Yuma Daily Sun*, January 29, 1967, 1.
7  Ralph Morse, "Put them High on the List of Men Who Count," *Life*, February 3, 1967, 18.
8  Gene Kranz, Interview by Roy Neal, NASA Headquarters History Office, Johnson Space Center, March 19, 1998, 17, 28–29, accessed September 12, 2023, https://historycollection.jsc.nasa.gov/JSCHistoryPortal/history/oral_histories/KranzEF/EFK_3-19-98.pdf.
9  William H. Chafe, *The Unfinished Journey: American Since World War II* (New York: Oxford University Press, 1995), 180.
10  Chaikin, *A Man on the Moon*, 142, 155.
11  Dee O'Hara, interview by Rebecca Wright, NASA Headquarters History Office, Johnson Space Center, 23 April 2002, 20–21, accessed October 19, 2022, https://historycollection.jsc.nasa.gov/JSCHistoryPortal/history/oral_histories/OHaraDB/OHaraDB_4-23-02.pdf.

12 Launius, "Heroes in a Vacuum," 204. See also, Norman Mailer, *Of a Fire on the Moon* (New York: Random House, 1969), 11–12.

13 Apollo 11 Lunar Surface Journal, "Apollo 11 Spacecraft Commentary, July 16–24, 1969," The National Aeronautics and Space Administration History Division, 378, accessed August 26, 2023, https://history.nasa.gov/alsj/a11/AS11_PAO.PDF.

14 Chaikin, *A Man on the Moon*, 56.

15 Raymond H. Anderson, "Dies in Re-entry; Komarov First Known Fatality of Any Manned Flights," *New York Times*, April 25, 1967, 1, 20.

16 Raymond H. Anderson, "Russians Confirm Flight of Zond 5 Around the Moon; Soviets Confirm a Flight to Moon," *New York Times*, September 21, 1968, 1, 14; Raymond H. Anderson, "A Soviet Space Mission Stirs World's Conjecture; Lovell Says Zond 5 Passed Moon and is Returning; U.S. Sources Suspect Failure of Round-Trip Attempt," *New York Times*, September 19, 1968, 29.

17 Chaikin, *A Man on the Moon*, 58–60.

18 Francis M. Northcutt, interview by Jennifer Ross-Nazzal, NASA Headquarters History Office, Johnson Space Center, November 14, 2018, 16, accessed August 16, 2023, https://historycollection.jsc.nasa.gov/JSCHistoryPortal/history/oral_histories/NorthcuttFM/NorthcuttFM_11-14-18.pdf.

19 "Wally Shoots for Three," *Life*, October 25, 1968, 36.

20 Chaikin, *A Man on the Moon*, 76–77.

21 Margaret Hamilton, interview by David C. Brock, Computer History Museum, April 13, 2017, 18–19, accessed August 20, 2023, https://archive.computerhistory.org/resources/access/text/2022/03/102738243-05-01-acc.pdf. Hamilton was the Director of Software Engineering. See also, Alan H. Sheehan, "Women in Business/ Margaret Hamilton Lickly; Putting "Eagle" On Course," *Boston Globe*, November 1, 1972, 24.

22 "11 Days Aboard Apollo 7," *Life*, December 6, 1968, 76.

23 "11 Days Aboard," 76, 78.

24 John Noble Wilford, "Schirra Nettled Over New Tests," *New York Times*, October 1, 1968, 7.

25 Chaikin, *A Man on the Moon*, 76–77.

26 John Noble Wilford, "U.S. Prepares Moon Shot in December," *New York Times*, October 23, 1968, 1, 23.

27 See also, *New York Times News Service*, "Apollo Flight Director is No Johnny-Come-Lately," *Press-Telegram* (Long Beach, California), October 23, 1968, 9. To note, the astronauts have strong input and do help design some of the crafts' systems.

28 Chaikin, *A Man on the Moon*, 79–80.

29 "A Crew with Brains and Experience," *New York Times*, December 22, 1968, 36. See also "The Week in Review: Triumph!" *New York Times*, December 29, 1968, 1E.

30 Frank Borman, "A Science Fiction World-Awesome, Forlorn, Beauty," *Life*, January 17, 1969, 27.

31 William Anders, "The Black Side: Pulverized, Like a Battlefield," *Life*, January 17, 1969, 30.

32 Frank Borman, interview by Catherine Harwood, NASA Headquarters History Office, Johnson Space Center, April 13, 1999, 12-28-12-29, accessed November 21, 2023, https://historycollection.jsc.nasa.gov/JSCHistoryPortal/history/oral_histories/BormanF/FFB_4-13-99.pdf.

33 James A. Lovell Jr., interview by Ron Stone, NASA Headquarters History Office, Johnson Space Center, May 25, 1999, 33-34, accessed August 23, 2023, https://historycollection.jsc.nasa.gov/JSCHistoryPortal/history/oral_histories/LovellJA/LovellJA_5-25-99.htm.

34 Homer Bigart, "New-Breed Astronauts: Scientists, Not Daredevils," *New York Times*, December 30, 1968, 18.

35 Chaikin, *A Man on the Moon*, 48.

36 William J. Perkins, "A Preview of Apollo 8—III: Three Astronauts Tell Why they Feel Set to Fly Around Moon, Now," *Evening Sun* (Baltimore, Maryland), December 18, 1968, C1.

37 Dora Jane Hamblin, "Christmas Cheers on the Apollo 8 Home Front," *Life*, January 10, 1969, 79, 81.

38 The Associated Press Wire Photo, "Gathering for a 'hen party'" *Fresno Bee* (Fresno, California), December 27, 1968, 5-A.

39 Chaikin, *A Man on the Moon*, 93–97. See also, Borman, interview, 12-48-12-51.

40 Northcutt, interview, 16.

41 Bigart, "New-Breed Astronauts," 1.

42 "Apollo's Voyage Called Safer than Columbus's," *New York Times*, December 19, 1968, 56.

43 Leo Rennert, McClatchy newspapers staff writer, "Engine Gets Credit for Apollo Bullseye," *Fresno Bee* (Fresno, California), December 27, 1968, 5-A. For more on what the paper means by a "Sacramento rocket," see, Willy Logan, "The Rocket Testing Ruins of Sacramento," podcast audio, June 15, 2021, https://www.willylogan.com/?p=2410.

44 "Apollo's Voyage Called Safer than Columbus's," 56.

45 Borman, "A Science Fiction World-Awesome," 28.

46 James Lovell, "Earth We are Forsaking You for the Moon," *Life*, January 17, 1969, 29.

47 "Home From the Moon," *Atlanta Constitution*, December 28, 1968, 5.

48 The Associate Press, "Pinpoint Return Completes Apollo Success," *Eau Claire* (Wisconsin) *Ledger*, December 28, 1968, 1.

49 "Launching Operations Chief Likes Job to Football Coach's," *New York Times*, December 22, 1968, 37.

50 "Apollo Workers Display Rare Emotions After Feat," *New York Times*, December 28, 1968, 14.

51 "Head Man at NASA: Thomas Otten Paine," *New York Times*, December 28, 1968, 14.

52 Eugene Rabinowitch, "Reflections on Apollo 8," *Bulletin of the Atomic Scientists* 24, no. 10 (March 1969): 2–3, 12, 2.

53 Walter Sullivan, "Computer Aids Navigation of Apollo 8 Crewmen," *New York Times*, December 24, 1968, 7.

54 "Men of the Year," *Time*, January 3, 1969, 9.

55 Vern Haughland, The Associated Press, "U.S. Could 'Shoot for Moon'; Apollo 9 has Opened Possibility; Astronauts Flying back to Houston," *News-Palladium* (Benton Harbor, Michigan), March 14, 1969, 1, back page; and John Noble Wilford, "Apollo 9 Splashes Down Accurately; Opens Way for Summer Moon Landing," *New York Times*, March 14, 1969, 1, 22.

## IT'S HIP TO BE SQUARE 193

56 The Associated Press, "5 Firsts and 3 Records for Flight," *New York Times*, March 14, 1969, 14.

57 Wilford, "Apollo 9 Splashes Down Accurately," 22.

58 The Associated Press, "Ground Control System Lets Apollo Crew Sleep," *New York Times*, March 4, 1969, 14.

59 William K. Stevens, "Computer on Board Apollo Does the Flying; 3 Astronauts Permit Electronic System to Run Main Task," *New York Times*, March 4, 1969, 14.

60 John Noble Wilford, "Apollo Maneuver Delayed Briefly By Sloshing Fuel," *New York Times*, March 9, 1969, 1, 52.

61 Brooks, Grimwood and Swenson Jr., *Chariots for Apollo*, 303–312. Chaikin, *A Man on the Moon*, 151–152. The Associated Press, "Apollo 10 Flight Most Dangerous," *Jacksonville Daily News* (Jacksonville, Illinois), May 20, 1969, 1.

62 Chaikin, *A Man on the Moon*, 153.

63 The United Press International, "Apollo 10 Develops Trouble," *Ledger-Enquirer* (Columbus, Georgia), May 23, 1969, 11.

64 The United Press International, "'Greatest Moment of Our Time,' Says the President," *Charlotte Observer*, July 21, 1969, 1.

65 William K. Stevens, "What Kind of Men Are They," *New York Times*, July 17, 1969, 31.

66 Dora Jane Hamblin, "Neil Armstrong Refuses to 'Waste Any Heartbeats'," *Life*, July 4, 1969, 18–19.

67 Hamblin, "Neil Armstrong Refuses," 18–19 and Stevens, "What Kind of Men Are They," 31, 39.

68 Gene Farmer, "Buzz Aldrin has 'The Best Scientific Mind We Have Send Into Space'," *Life*, July 4, 1969, 22–25.

69 Stevens, "What Kind of Men Are They," 31, 39.

70 David Nevin, "Collins has Cool to Cope With Space and the Easter Bunny," *Life*, July 4, 1969, 27, 26; and Stevens, "What Kind of Men Are They," 31, 39.

71 Nevin, "Collins Has Cool to Cope," 27.

72 Stevens, "What Kind of Men Are They," 31, 39.

73 Editor's Note, "The man behind the glass mask," *Life*, July 4, 1969, 2A.

74 Stevens, "What Kind of Men Are They," 31, 39.

75 Richard Witkin, "Shortly Before Landing, Armstrong Took Over From Computer," *New York Times*, July 21, 1969, 12.

76 Robert S. Boyd, "Crew Does its Work on Lunar Surface," *Charlotte Observer*, July 21, 1969, 1.

77 The Associated Press, "Walking Around; Armstrong Steers Eagle Away From Rough Landing," *Winston-Salem Journal* (Winston-Salem, North Carolina), July 21, 1969, 1.

78 Richard Pothier, "How Armstrong Took Over to Land LEM," *Charlotte Observer*, July 21, 1969, 12A.

79 Richard Lewis, "To Houston, Crew, LM Landing 'Hairy'," *Birmingham News* (Birmingham, Alabama), July 21, 1969, 24.

80 NASA Space Science Coordinated Archive, "Surveyor 1," The National Aeronautics and Space Administration, accessed September 5, 2023, https://nssdc.gsfc.nasa .gov/nmc/spacecraft/display.action?id=1966-045A. There were approximately 7 Surveyor missions to the moon between 1966 and 1968. For more on Luna 9, see NASA Space Science Coordinated Archive, "Luna 9," The National Aeronautics

and Space Administration, accessed September 5, 2023, https://nssdc.gsfc.nasa.gov/nmc/spacecraft/display.action?id=1966-006A.

81 Jack Nelson, "U.S. Called Fortunate in Unmanned Landings; Official Notes Rough Terrain, Says Eagle Might have had Trouble Without a Pilot," *Los Angeles Times*, July 21, 1969, 2.

82 John Noble Wilford, "LM is Jettisoned," *New York Times*, July 22, 1969.

83 Stuart Auerbach, "Crew Has Trained as a Unit For Any Space Eventuality," *Washington Post*, July 17, 1969, A7.

84 John J. Goldman and Nicholas C. Chriss, "Mission Control to Eagle: Houston Cool Heads to Spacemen Trio," *Los Angeles Times*, July 21, 1969, 3. It was Flight Director Gene Kranz who ordered Mission Control to "Play it Cool."

85 Arnold J. Toynbee, "Some Thoughts on the Moon Landing," *Charlotte Observer*, July 21, 1969, 11A.

86 The Associated Press, "America Cheers Feat With Few Dissenting," *Montgomery Advertiser* (Montgomery, Alabama), July 21, 1969, 2. See also, "Half a Billion Watch on TV: Earthlings Dance, Shout and Pray As Astronauts 'Conquer' the Moon," *Courier-Journal* (Louisville), July 21, 1969, A5.

87 The Associated Press, "Britons Screamed, Chileans Danced," *Montgomery Advertiser* (Montgomery, Alabama), July 21, 1969, 1. At the time of the American moon landing, the Soviet Union was attempting to land an unmanned satellite, Luna 15, onto the surface of the moon. See also, *New York Times* Wire Service, "Crosses Apollo Path: Russians Place Luna 10 Miles Above Moon," *Courier-Journal* (Louisville, Kentucky), July 21, 1969, A9. For other world reactions to the landing, see R. W. Apple Jr., *New York Times* Wire Service, "Landing Intrigues Africans, Who Ask About Falling Off and Moon's Size," *Courier-Journal* (Louisville), July 22, 1969; and The Associated Press, "Iroquois Fear Monsters, Praise Echoes Around Globe but Some Voices Superstitious," *Los Angeles Times*, July 22, 1969, 2.

88 "Johnson Says Feat Shows 'We Can Do Anything,'" *New York Times*, July 21, 1969, 15.

89 Carroll Kilpatrick, "Apollo 11 Holiday Set For Monday," *Washington Post*, July 17, 1969, A1, A8. See also, Walter Rugaber, "Nixon Calls for a Holiday So All Can Share in 'Glory,'" *New York Times*, July 17, 1969, 1, 22. Not all counties and cities throughout the country agreed with the holiday.

90 Rugaber, "Nixon Calls for a Holiday," 22, 26.

91 Harold M. Schmeck Jr., "The Navigation is Practically Perfect," *New York Times*, July 25, 1969, 30.

92 Richard Witkin, *New York Times* News Service, "Eagle's Descent to the Moon Mostly in Computer's Hands," *Courier-Journal* (Louisville, Kentucky), July 21, 1969, A9.

93 Suville R. Davis, "Not Just by Way of the Moon: The World Will Continue to Judge U.S. by the Quality of its Civilization," *Christian Science Monitor*, July 21, 1969, 1, 5.

94 David Bowie writer, "Space Oddity," on album *Space Oddity*. Producer Gus Dudgeon, released July 11, 1969, Philips Records (U.K.), Mercury Records (U.S.).

95 James Reston, *New York Times*, "After the Moon, Can We Conquer the Earth," *Winston-Salem Journal*, July 21, 1969, 9.

96 Flora Lewis, Editorials. "Human Paradox: A Contrast between Capacity, Deficiency," *Courier-Journal* (Louisville, Kentucky), July 22, 1969.

97 Editorials. "'A Giant Leap for Mankind' From this Precarious Planet," *Courier-Journal* (Louisville), July 22, 1969.

# IT'S HIP TO BE SQUARE     195

98   Chaikin, *A Man on the Moon*, 2.

99   The Associated Press, "Millions Around the World Hang on Astronauts' Words," *Birmingham News*, July 21, 1969, 6.

100   Keyes Beech, "Not Really Excited—Moon Walk? Good, Says GIs in Saigon," *Birmingham News*, July 21, 1969.

101   Odom, "Introduction: Exploring NASA in the Long Civil Rights Movement," 1.

102   John H. Sengstackk, "Earthly Questions," *Chicago Defender*, July 22, 1969, 13.

103   Bernard Weinraub, "At the Launching, Turbulent America in Microcosm," *New York Times*, July 20, 1969, E1.

104   "Our Prayers Go With You," *Afro-American* (Baltimore, Maryland), July 26, 1969, 3.

105   Thomas A. Johnson, "Blacks and Apollo; Most Could've Cared Less," *New York Times*, July 27, 1969, E6.

106   Vincent Paka, "Barry Slams Apollo 11 Mission," *Washington Post*, July 19, 1969, A9.

107   "Moon Shot Unites U.S. For Instant," *Chicago Defender*, July 21, 1969, 1, 3. See also, "Chicagoans Hail Historic Moon Walk ... But," *Chicago Defender*, July 22, 1969, 3.

108   Johnson, "Blacks and Apollo," E6.

109   Joseph Morgenstem, "Moon Age: New Dawn?" *Newsweek*, July 7, 1969, 41.

110   William Greider, "Houston Watches: Awe, Laughter," *Washington Post*, July 21, 1969, A8.

111   Morgenstem, "Moon Age: New Dawn?" 40, 55.

112   "Apollo Flight Journal: More than *SCE* to *Aux*—Apollo 12 Lighting Strike Incident," NASA History Division, Accessed August 25, 2023, https://history.nasa.gov/afj/ap12fj/a12-lightningstrike.html.

113   Chaikin, *A Man on the Moon*, 236. See also, Brooks, Grimwood, and Swenson Jr., *Chariots for Apollo*, 365–366.

114   David Woods and Lennox J. Waugh, Apollo Flight Journal, "Apollo 12 Lunar Surface Journal: Apollo 12 Onboard Voice Transcription, January 1970," 1, The National Aeronautics and Space Administration History Division, Accessed August 25, 2023, https://history.nasa.gov/alsj/a12/AS12_CM.PDF. See also, Chaikin, *A Man on the Moon*, 236–239.

115   "Apollo 12 Lunar Surface Journal," 3, 2.

116   "Apollo 12 Lunar Surface Journal," 3, 5.

117   Bill Stockton, The Associated Press Science Writer, "12 Seconds Agonizing at Houston," *Daily Journal* (Fergus Falls, Minnesota), November 15, 1969, 1.

118   Herald Wire Service, "Conrad Remained Unshaken Even During Tense Moments," *Miami Herald*, November 15, 1969, 16-A. See also, United Press International, "Astronauts Calm After 'Wild Ride,'" *Courier Post*, (Camden, New Jersey), November 15, 1969, 8.

119   *New York Times Service*, "Beans Boldness Streak Got Him Flying," *Billings Gazette* (Billings, Montana), November 15, 1969, 15; *New York Times Service*, "Feisty Pete Conrad Flew at Early Age," *Billings Gazette* (Billings, Montana), November 15, 1969, 9; *New York Times Service*, "Gordon Would Rather Land," *Billings Gazette* (Billings, Montana), November 15, 1969, 9. See originals in "The Astronauts 12," *New York Times*, November 15, 1969, 23.

120   Wood and Waugh, "Apollo 12 Lunar Surface Journal," 6.

121   The Associated Press, "Decision on Liftoff a Tough One to Make," *Intelligencer Journal* (Lancaster, Pennsylvania), November 15, 1969, 16.

# GENDER AND THE RACE FOR SPACE

122 Earl Ubell, "Apollo 12: Testing New Role for Man in Space," *New York Times*, November 9, 1969, E8; and The Associated Press, "Astronaut Conrad Called Expert on Moon Geology," *Hobbs-Daily News Sun* (Hobbs, New Mexico), November 9, 1969, 20.

123 David Woods and Lennox J. Waugh, "Apollo Flight Journal: Apollo 13 Pre-launch Activities and the Crewman Change," The National Aeronautics and Space Administration History Division, accessed September 7, 2023, https://history.nasa .gov/afj/ap13fj/00crewchange.html and "Substitute Swigert, 38, Has a Girl in Every (Air) Port," *New York Times*, April 12, 1970, 60. Astronaut Mattingly married Elizabeth Daily in 1970. Mattingly flew in Apollo 16 as well as aboard the shuttle in STS-4 and STS-51-C.

124 John Noble Wilford, "Power Failure Imperils Astronauts; Apollo Will Head Back to the Earth," *New York Times*, April 14, 1970, 1.

125 Woods and Waugh, "Apollo 13 Technical Air-to-Ground Voice Transcription," Apollo Lunar Journal, NASA History Division, accessed August 15, 2023, https:// history.nasa.gov/alsj/a13/AS13_TEC.PDF. The transcript gives Commander Jim Lovell credit for the first communication of a problem; however, NASA confirms that it is the voice of lunar module pilot Jack Swigert who first radioed the problem. See, "50 Years Ago: Houston, We've had a Problem," NASA, accessed August 15, 2023, https://www.nasa.gov/feature/50-years-ago-houston-we-ve-had-a-problem.

126 Chaikin, *A Man on the Moon*, 292–328. The freezing environment turned the astronauts' breath into droplets of water. The LM and Command Module became swampy.

127 Hermann Dur and Eric Jones, "Apollo 13 Lunar Surface Journal: Building an Apollo 13 LiOH Cannister," NASA History Office, accessed August 17, 2023, https://history.nasa.gov/alsj/a13/a13_LIOH_Adapter.html. See also, Robert E. "Ed" Smylie, interview by Carol Butler, NASA Headquarters History Office, Johnson Space Center, April 17, 1999, accessed August 17, 2023, https://historycollection.jsc.nasa .gov/JSCHistoryPortal/history/oral_histories/SmylieRE/SmylieRE_4-17-99.htm.

128 Chaikin, *A Man on the Moon*, 329–334.

129 John Noble Wilford, "Crew of Crippled Apollo 13 Starts Back After Rounding Moon and Firing Rocket; Men Appear Calm Despite Low Reserves," *New York Times*, April 15, 1970, 1.

130 Martin Waldron, "Flight Director is Making the Decisions," *New York Times*, April 16, 1970, 30.

131 John Noble Wilford, "Stricken Apollo Speeding Toward Earth for Pacific Splashdown this Afternoon," *New York Times*, April 17, 1970, 1.

132 Launius, "Heroes in a Vacuum," 207.

133 John Noble Wilford, "Astronauts Land Gently on Target, Unharmed by Their Four-Day Ordeal; Sea Recovery Swift After Perfect Entry; Aquarius Praised for Vital Role," *New York Times*, April 18, 1970, 1, 12; *Washington Post* Service, "Astronauts Exhausted After Ordeal in Space," *Arizona Republic* (Phoenix, Arizona), April 18, 1970, 48; and Bill Stockton, Associate Press Writer, "Astronauts Thaw Out on Carrier; NASA Not Ready to Speculate on Apollo 14 Flight," *Independent Press Telegram*, (Long Beach, California), April 18, 1970, 1.

134 Wilford, "Astronauts Land Gently," 12.

135 Martin Waldron, "Applause, Cigars and Champagne Toasts Greet Capsule's Landing," *New York Times*, April 18, 1970, 13; *Washington Post* Service, "Everything

# IT'S HIP TO BE SQUARE                              197

Fell into Place in the Last Few Minutes," *Arizona Republic* (Phoenix, Arizona), April 18, 1970, 48; and The Associated Press, "Mission Control Wins Game As Odyssey's Chutes Open," *Victoria Advocate* (Victoria, Texas), April 18, 1970, 9.

136  Harold M. Schmeck Jr., "NASA to Review Space Accident," *New York Times*, April 18, 1970, 1.

137  Wilford, "Astronauts Land Gently on Target," 1, 12. *Aquarius* was the name of the Lunar Module.

138  Nancy Hicks, "The Flight Controllers' Taskmaster: Eugene Francis Kranz," *New York Times*, April 18, 1970, 12.

139  Joseph Lelyveld, "Apollo 13: Moment of Exaltation," *New York Times*, April 18, 1970, 13.

140  Robert B. Semple Jr., "Nixon to Give Medal to Crew in Hawaii," *New York Times*, April 18, 1970, 1.

141  William McNutt, World Book Service, "Pretty Mini-skirted Blonde Mathematician Talked to Computer to Bring Apollo-13 Home," *Buffalo News* (Buffalo, New York), April 29, 1970, 11.

142  Northcutt, interview, 2.

143  Lucy Diavolo, "Career Advice from Poppy Northcutt—Activist, Lawyer, and NASA's First Female Engineer in Mission Control," *Teen Vogue*, July 10, 2019, https://www.teenvogue.com/story/career-advice-poppy-northcutt-activist-lawyer -nasa-first-female-engineer. See also, Northcutt, interview, 2–3.

144  Northcutt, interview, 2–3.

145  Poppy Northcutt, Post of TRW Advertisement, Twitter, November 21, 2019, https:// twitter.com/poppy_northcutt?lang=en.

146  McNutt, "Pretty Mini-Skirted Blonde," 11. See also, Margaret Converse, Gannett News Service, "Poppy: The pretty blonde from Texas used to be a 'dancing, drinking Mary College.' Today she's one of the six engineers who calculate timing for the Apollo astronauts ..."the first woman at mission control who wasn't just running errands," *Democrat and Chronicle* (Rochester, New York), February 22, 1970, 4H-5H. This article appears on the first page of the "Feminique" section.

147  McNutt, "Pretty Mini-Skirted Blonde," 11.

148  "What in the World!: NASA's Texas Rose," *Colorado Springs Gazette-Telegraph*, February 1, 1970, 105.

149  Northcutt, interview, 31.

150  McNutt, "Pretty Mini-Skirted Blonde," 11.

151  Converse, "Poppy," 4H–5H.

152  Northcutt, interview, 32.

153  "Women Astronauts," *Waukesha Daily Freeman* (Waukesha, Wisconsin), July 13, 1968, 12.

154  Jack Childs, "'Housekeeping' Job Not Easy In Space," *News and Observer* (Raleigh, North Carolina), August 31, 1968, 22.

155  Ruth Winters, Women's News Service, "Future Bleak For Women Astronauts," *Pensacola News*, March 7, 1968, 10A.

156  Tom Kershaw, "Top Scholars are Told: For Every Astronaut, 5,000 Helpers on Ground," *Abilene Reporter-News*, May 17, 1968, 1.

157  Gloria Negri, "Astronaut's Wife: Mod Voice of the Establishment," *Boston Globe*, October 15, 1968, 47.

158  Tom Tiede, NEA Staff Correspondent, "Famed Woman Flier Speaks on Lady Astronauts; Jackie: Stork Stops Space Girls," *Idaho Statesman* (Boise, Idaho), September 7, 1969, 40.

159 Howard Benedict, The Associated Press Aerospace Writer, "Tekite lifts barrier for first women astronauts," *Capital Journal* (Salem, Oregon), July 29, 1970, section 3, page 29.

160 The Associated Press, "No Women Astronauts," *Asbury Park Evening Press* (Asbury, New Jersey), December 5, 1970, 6.

161 Tiede, "Famed Woman Flier," 40.

162 Apollo book in office.

163 Richard S. Lewis, "Requiem for the Scientist-Astronauts," *Bulletin of the Atomic Scientists* 27, no. 5 (May 1971): 17–22; 17–18.

164 Joe H. Engle, interview by Rebecca Wright, NASA Headquarters History Office, Johnson Space Center, April 22, 2004, 11, accessed August 22, 2023, https://historycollection.jsc.nasa.gov/JSCHistoryPortal/history/oral_histories/EngleJH/EngleJH_4-22-04.pdf.

165 Eugene Cernan and Don Davis, *Last Man on the Moon: Astronaut Gene Cernan and America's Race in Space* (New York: St. Martin's Press, 1999), 331. See also, Mindell, *Digital Apollo*, 257.

166 "Purse strings might loosen for space program of U.S.," *Arizona Republic* (Phoenix, Arizona), October 2, 1971, 85.

167 Werner von Braun, "Space Pioneer Reflects on Apollo's Achievement," *New York Times*, December 3, 1972, 68.

168 Earl Ubell, "The Time of the Scientists has Come," *New York Times*, July 25, 1971, E6.

169 John L O'Connor, "Apollo 17 Coverage Gets Little Viewer Response," *New York Times*, December 14, 1972, B95.

170 "Last Apollo Wednesday; Scholars Assess Program; 23-Billion Space Project Ran 11 Years; Cape Kennedy Presses Countdown; Last Apollo Flight Sets Off Evaluation," *New York Times*, December 3, 1972, 68.

171 Nelson Bryant, "Wood, Field and Stream; Astronauts Turn a Hunter's Attention From Buckshot, to a Moonshot," *New York Times*, December 3, 1972, S11.

172 Richard Witkin, "Experts Tricked the Computer," *New York Times*, December 8, 1972, 30.

173 "Geologist Schmitt and Combat Flier Evans on Apollo," *Chicago Tribune*, December 7, 1972, 4.

174 "3 Men on Last Apollo Moon Flight; Eugene Andrew Cernan; Harrison Hagan Schmitt; Ronald Ellwin Evans," *New York Times*, December 8, 1972, 30.

175 "Apollo 17 Mission Report," NASA Headquarters History Office, Johnson Space Center, March 1973, 16–1, accessed August 22, 2023, https://history.nasa.gov/alsj/a17/A17_MissionReport.pdf. See also, Mindell, *Digital Apollo*, 257.

176 Cernan and Davis, *The Last Man on the Moon*, 331. See also, Mindell, *Digital Apollo*, 257.

177 Gene Kranz, *Failure is Not an Option: Mission Control from Mercury to Apollo and Beyond* (New York: Simon & Schuster, 2000), 376.

# Chapter 6

# WHAT MADE IT POSSIBLE FOR SALLY TO RIDE?: THE SHUTTLE'S DOMESTICATION AND DEMOCRATIZATION OF SPACEFLIGHT

Wearing T-shirts that read "Ride, Sally Ride," Americans cheered as Dr. Sally K. Ride became the first American woman in space as she blasted off aboard STS-7 on June 18, 1983.[1] *Ms. Magazine* celebrated that Ride's flight penetrated "NASA's world of 'flaming phallic rockets,'" symbolizing American women's breakthrough and visibility in male-dominated spaceflight.[2] Her flight took place as Americans attempted to navigate women's growing independence and the pop-culture world of *Three's Company, Annie Hall*, stay-at-home dads and Erma Bombeck.[3] At the same time, rugged individual masculinity reemerged in films such as *Rocky, Rambo, The Right Stuff*, and *Top Gun* as Jerry Falwell and Phyllis Schlafly blamed feminism for social ills.[4] Ride's feat came at a time of clashing American gender roles, an identity crisis following the wave of defeat in Vietnam, civil rights and a new reusable spacecraft that once again promised hope.[5]

American spaceflight needed to be reinvigorated as Americans grew increasingly bored with space feats. Between 1973 and 1979, Skylab circled the Earth. On July 15, 1975, NASA launched the first *Apollo-Soyuz* mission, and it appeared the Americans and Soviets made détente in space.[6] Jet pilot teamwork prevailed, and Americans grew tired of the "pale, male, and stale" astronauts.[7] NASA proposed a new space transportation system (STS) to "salvage human spaceflight" at a time when "ordinary passengers who might receive little training, and could be almost anyone" could fly in a reusable shuttle.[8]

Matthew H. Hersch's *Inventing the American Astronaut* argues that the shuttle, and the diversity of the astronauts aboard, democratized American spaceflight technology.[9] Bettyann Kevles' *Almost Heavan* argues that the shuttle era evoked a domesticated public discourse of "homesteaders" and "frontier settlers" not of "frontier conquerors."[10] The domesticated floating laboratory demanded astronauts conduct more complex scientific experiments in space and forced a renegotiation of the astronaut image. The astronaut image expanded to include pilot astronauts and mission specialist astronauts. Both groups made up the new astronaut corps and went through years of training together before shuttle missions. In this new home in space, the chapter argues that the shuttle acted as a vehicle for social change, with the new astronaut corps reflecting gains made in the civil rights and feminist movements. Like the previous spaceflight programs, it was not the technology alone that captured the American interest, but rather the people within the spacecraft—the astronauts willing to travel into space. Within this domesticated framework, women of 1978's Astronaut Group 8 entered the all-male space of the astronaut corps, finally making women visible in spaceflight, science and engineering.[11]

However, the following chapter also argues that the widespread sexism and anti-feminist attitudes in the media perpetuated a disconnect between perceptions of women's abilities and conventional gender roles, linking the views expressed in the WASPs' Ramspeck Report and the 1962 FLAT subcommittee hearing with the first women astronauts. The Public discourse viewed women's entrance into the astronaut corps as a product of the safety and domesticity of shuttle technology and even lamented the end of the rugged individual astronaut image as women challenged or took on culturally constructed "masculine" roles.

Women employees at NASA, including the astronauts, represented the "individual agency" that became necessary during Hall's long civil rights era and the "New Aerospace History."[12] The women astronauts railed against this cognitive dissonance within the public discourse and the astronaut corps. Within this paradigm shift in spaceflight technology and the astronaut image, women created and controlled how women astronauts looked and acted, demonstrating that women had—like pilot Janey Hart argued before Congress in 1962—a "real contribution to make."[13] The women exercised rugged individualism and self-determination. NASA chose the astronaut women because they exercised individuality as highly skilled professionals in a "high-challenge, high competition" field, not because they were women or symbolized the domesticity aboard an STS.[14]

The same combination of rugged individual masculinity and democratic manhood that it took to land men on the moon was the same combination of individuality and teamwork that was necessary between the "new breed" of astronauts and mission control.[15] The public discourse focused on depicting the women in conventional gender roles and images, suggesting a society coming to terms with liberated women. The women did not simply want to fit in with the prevailing astronaut image, nor did they remain passive and allow the public discourse to create the woman astronaut image. The women brought their unique personalities and diverse gender identities to

## WHAT MADE SALLY TO RIDE? 

the astronaut corps, transforming the image of the astronaut from masculine into one that reflected self-determination and gender as an artificial cultural construct.[16]

## A Domesticated Shuttle

As early as July 21, 1969, news reports circulated about Wernher Von Braun and Maxime Faget's future reusable space shuttle. The *Washington Post* reported that if approved by Congress, the $6 billion shuttle program would serve as a "taxi service" for the $3 billion proposed orbiting space laboratory. Von Braun and Faget also hoped that the shuttle would be able to carry passengers to the moon and back. The paper reported, "Up to now, the stress and expense of space flights have restricted them to astronauts—a carefully selected and highly motivated crew of young physically fit and rigorously trained men."[17] Von Braun and Faget envisioned a "new breed" of astronauts, thus shifting the focus of the astronaut image toward individuals with scientific backgrounds like their own, and potentially including women and minorities as well.[18]

A new chapter for astronauts appeared inevitable. On January 5, 1972, President Richard M. Nixon announced his approval of NASA's space shuttle. He declared that the new spacecraft would "revolutionize transportation into near space, by routinizing it." The reusable shuttle would not only be cost-efficient, perhaps being used "again and again—up to 100 times," but he also suggested that "the resulting changes in modes of flight and re-entry will make the ride safe, and less demanding for the passengers, so that men and women with work to do in space can 'commute' aloft, without having to spend years in training for the skills and rigors of old-style space flight."[19] Lack of skill and rigor suggested spaceflight was easier.

Furthermore, as the language of spaceflight shifted from "manned" to "human" spaceflight, NASA Administrator James C. Fletcher asked that a "plan be developed for our next selection of astronauts, with full consideration being given to minority groups and women."[20] On August 16, 1972, NASA issued a press release "Bathroom Commode Design for Space Shuttle Passengers" that detailed a system that could be used "for men and women Shuttle passengers."[21] Women were a real consideration. However, it is up for debate as to whether Fletcher intended to integrate the astronaut corps with all deliberate speed. NASA had plenty of pilot astronauts available for early flights. Fletcher assumed mission and payload specialists would wait until pilot astronauts successfully flew the shuttle. The other NASA brass were hesitant. In 1975, NASA's Deputy Administrator George Low told Associate Administrator of Manned Spaceflight, John Yardley, that the current astronaut recruitment plan does not indicate a method for insuring [*sic*] application by minorities and/or women in the new astronaut group and mission specialist group. I am sure that you are aware of the importance to NASA that every opportunity be presented to these potential candidates to encourage applications and, if qualified, selections. Please let me know how you intend to proceed to solve this problem.[22]

Maintaining the traditional male "WASPdom" image of the astronaut corps did not seem like the best approach after the passage of Title IX, and as three Black women significantly challenged and changed the prevailing spaceflight narrative.[23]

NASA was on the defensive since the administration made headlines for firing its top Black female administrator, Deputy Administrator for Equal Opportunity, Ruth Bates Harris, who blew the whistle on NASA's paltry efforts to recruit more women and minorities. New minority and women employees increased from 4.1 percent in 1966 to just 5.1 percent in 1973.[24] Harris' office declared NASA's equal employment opportunity programs to be "a near total failure" and "the worst statistically in government."[25] There was a silver lining of females in space, according to Harris. NASA had in fact flown three females: two female spiders named Arabella and Anita, and a monkey named Miss Baker.[26]

NASA blamed recent budget cuts for the lack of growth in any new hires and reportedly fired Harris because she failed to "carry out equal employment opportunity goals" and did not "get along with her superior."[27] Harris claimed recruiting efforts were stalled by her impossible position of being stuck between middle management and higher-ups who failed to commit to equal employment.[28] The press compared her firing to that of Watergate investigator Archibald Cox. After multiple congressional hearings, NASA rehired Harris after ten months of one of the most intensive battles of race and gender relations at the administration.[29] NASA named Harris the Deputy Assistant Administrator of Public Affairs for Community and Human Relations. NASA argued that Ms. Harris would have more direct contact with recruitment in this position.[30]

That same year, NASA appointed Oceola "Ocie" Hall as the coordinator of NASA's Federal Women's Program.[31] Hall aimed for the administration to hire more women in executive positions and as astronauts, promising that "NASA will look a lot different." A supporter of the Equal Rights Amendment and avid reader of *This I Can Do: The Women's Machiavelli,* Hall joined a long line of underrepresented Black women in and outside of NASA who strove to subvert artificially constructed gender and racial roles and hierarchies. Much like in the case of Harris, these women put their reputations at risk. Ms. Hall did not mind. She "detest[ed] the women who say they have no problems and who do not want to rock the boat" because those women "have already made it" and were a growing problem of women's lack of access to conventional masculine careers.[32]

Hall recognized a responsibility women owed each other. Harris and Hall spoke the same language of education and community outreach. Harris told the National Black Women's Political Caucus in Tampa, Florida, that educating people on how to change the system was the key to preventing "boatrockers" from being "kicked overboard."[33] Similar to Harris, Hall's job was to recruit women and minorities. She spoke to both professional women and women on "the streets." To become professionals, women needed training, education on how to be managers, how to negotiate contracts, the purpose of the equal employment opportunity counselor and childcare and transportation services. People needed to be active in creating these new roles for women, not simply waiting around for qualified women to show up at NASA's doorstep. There needed to be inclusion, not just integration. Educational opportunities were key, with Oceola commenting to the press, "I don't like talking about what is a male or female job [...]. We have to allow freedom of choice."[34] Unlike the FLATs, Harris and Hall were able to influence change from within as NASA decided who would be selected for the next astronaut shuttle groups.

The moon landing as a national security urgency no longer existed to prevent NASA from integrating women and minorities into the corps. Creating new bathroom facilities and spacesuits would take time, but so too would the creation of the shuttle technology. Hersch argues, "The ethnic and gender homogeneity of NASA's astronaut corps also suggested a dissonance between the goals of Apollo (its obsession with putting 'Whitey on the Moon') and the needs of a nation increasingly inclined to view persistent social discrimination as the leading cause of national concern." In fact, Hersch points out, not integrating the corps might even be illegal under new anti-sex discrimination laws.[35]

American gender and racial roles changed dramatically, both culturally and legally in the last twenty years. The context of these discussions is important. NASA might disapprove of using the term "integration" for the astronaut corps because the administration argued that they did not discriminate against women and minorities. The moon had been conquered. Colonization followed. The shuttle technology broadened the skills necessary aboard a reusable STS—essentially, changing the astronaut image and gender. The media quoted future astronaut Dr. Judith Resnik on the shuttle technology: "The shuttle program in the 1970s forced the space agency to change its definition of those with 'the right stuff.' It needed doctors, geologists, engineers, and other scientists to perform experiments and technical tasks on shuttle flights" that pilot astronauts did not have the skills or qualifications to conduct.[36]

Women in even greater numbers had acquired these skills through an increase in educational opportunities since the FLATs. Congress and President Nixon signed Title IX into law, reinforcing anti-sex discrimination, which was already codified under the 1964 Civil Rights Act, Title VII and NASA Policy Directive NPD 3713.3.[37] Adding to this, the 1958 National Defense Education Act opened doors for women's education in science and engineering, but women's visibility in STEM was far from normalized. Women represented about 4% of engineering professionals in 1981.[38] What changed was the transition from women being excluded from science and engineering programs to a gradual entry, which was hindered by a lack of inclusion.

Coupled with the women's movement and the end of the draft, women won expanded opportunities in the military, including entrance into pilot training schools and test pilot school pipelines.[39] Women even gained control over their own reproductive choices—for a few decades, anyway—with the affirmation of *Roe v. Wade* (1973).[40] Despite these changes, in 1975, NASA's intention to continue to select test pilots would severely limit its pool of women candidates and minorities. To attract more diverse applicants and to take full advantage of scientific experiments aboard the shuttle, NASA decided to recruit both pilots and mission specialists. NASA expected the candidates to meet the same standards as any previous astronaut, including T-38 training.[41] There would be one major difference in astronaut pilot training: the mission specialists would not be sent to Air Force Undergraduate Pilot Training. Rather, they would learn to fly T-38s at NASA facilities—requiring ten days of flight training per month.[42] NASA relaxed the jet piloting skills for the mission specialists, leading some Americans to mourn the end of the early Cold War rugged individualist astronaut image.

NASA sent announcements to the usual aerospace industries and public and private colleges and universities to recruit pilots and mission specialists, but this astronaut recruitment was different. NASA took affirmative action in recruiting diversity. NASA representatives visited Historically Black Colleges (HBCUs) and Hispanic-Serving Institutions (HSIs). NASA mailed hundreds of announcements to minority and women's groups such as the American Association of University Women (AAUW), the League of United Latin American Citizens (LULAC), the National Association for the Advancement of Colored People (NAACP) and the Society of Women Engineers. Astronaut recruitment announcements appeared in minority and women's magazines.[43]

A third Black woman stepped in to play an invaluable role in the astronaut corps' diversity and inclusion. In 1977, NASA hired Nichelle Nichols—known as *Star Trek's* Lieutenant Uhura to American households—to promote NASA's commitment to recruiting women and minorities. She toured the country for half a year, giving lectures on the importance of women and minorities in STEM. Nichols spoke to graduate students at public and private institutions of higher education, specifically pinpointing HBCUs and HSIs. She met with administrators, faculty and students privately and publicly.[44] Nichols gave guest lectures to space and rocketry companies and NASA installations at Cocoa Beach, Florida; Huntsville, Alabama; Hancock County, Mississippi; all the way to Lockheed Missiles & Space Company in Sunnyvale, California.

Ironically, Nichols had never been a fan of the space race, thinking that money from the program could be better spent to clean up societal inequalities such as "ghettos, and to fight poverty and disease."[45] By the 1970s, her attitude changed considerably. Like others within NASA, Nichols viewed spaceflight as a way to encourage the visibility of underrepresented groups in science and engineering—specifically through the creation of her company Women in Motion, Inc., with partner Shirley Bryant.[46] Nichols told the *Orlando Sentinel* that she had an uphill battle, "It's a very difficult task because to date we still have an all-male, all-white astronaut corps. It's very hard to promote support for a program when you don't see yourself, and you have no way of feeling involved."[47] Future astronaut Dr. Kathy Sullivan commented on the importance of visibility in the corps, "If I had watched Jane Smith walk out to the launch pad in a Mercury flight or an Apollo flight, maybe it would have registered differently to me that that could be one of the things that I could do."[48]

As Nichols correctly understood, NASA was not simply looking for women and minorities to fulfill an affirmative action quota but rather, to give the administration "a broad spectrum of which to choose their astronauts for the space shuttle program."[49] Much like the early computers at Langley, women and minorities represented untapped skill. Nichols did not always mince words, and at times would "rock the boat" with comments that NASA had a past of "being a chauvinist pig," especially when it came to the astronaut corps. Nichols charged that "NASA's astronaut selection board 'did keep women and minorities out, otherwise there wouldn't be an all-male, white astronaut corps.'"[50]

Empowering through ownership, Nichols challenged minorities to change racial segregation at NASA. After all, "It's our national space agency." She empowered women, saying, "This is your NASA. Get in, sit in, fit in and grow in it. You owe your daughters for generations to come their place as liberated human beings."[51] Nichols did not shy away from the battle of the sexes argument, suggesting that women were equipped better than men "internally," "emotionally" and "psychologically" for spaceflight.[52] Astronaut applicants

206                    GENDER AND THE RACE FOR SPACE

increased from one thousand five hundred to over eight thousand during her lectures.[53]

Whether Fletcher and other administrators were ready to integrate the corps has been argued in other scholarly works. But without a doubt, Nichols, Harris and Hall laid down the challenge to NASA from within. Black women remained hidden figures no more and acted as subversive actors, forcing a change on a dusty institution as they sought relevance for a new generation of not just integration, but diversity and inclusion that challenged gender roles and assumptions. If anything, they were at the forefront of redefining NASA's mission for the shuttle era. It was up to the astronaut selection committee to decide what to do with that new mission.

NASA was no longer using the military or the National Science Foundation (NSF) to screen applicants, giving the administration full control over the eight thousand plus applications for Group 8.[54] The process was arduous, complete with former president Eisenhower's fears of crackpots applying. For the first time, NASA chose an African American, Dr. Joseph D. Atkinson, Jr., director of Equal Employment Opportunity Programs, and a woman, Dr. Carolyn Huntoon, a physiologist, for the mission specialist astronaut selection committee. A World War II veteran, Atkinson came to NASA in 1964 after fifteen years at Kelly Air Force Base in San Antonio, Texas. He implemented affirmative action and scholarship programs at NASA.[55]

Huntoon joined NASA during Apollo. She conducted weightless experiments as Chief of the Endocrine Laboratory at Johnson Space Center. Her colleagues nicknamed her "mother hen."[56] Christopher Kraft personally asked Huntoon if she wanted to apply to the astronaut corps. She turned him down, and he put her on the astronaut selection committee, telling her, "So then I want you to work with us to select some astronauts, both men and women."[57] Choosing women and minorities was not required, but NASA highly desired the committee to find qualified candidates. NASA lowered the educational requirement to a bachelor's degree to find women and minority applicants.[58] Women and minority astronaut applicants notedly demonstrated that NASA failed to grasp women's and minorities' educational attainments.

Like her Black counterparts, Huntoon toured the country to encourage women and minorities to apply for the astronaut corps. Her recruitment efforts focused on mission specialists. These astronauts were typically engineers, scientists or doctors who conducted experiments aboard the shuttle. Recruiting women pilots in the military posed difficulties around flight schedules and access to names and bases. As other NASA histories have pointed out, women military pilots were in the pipeline for flying and testing jets, but they were few and far between. Huntoon remembers that despite the few women available, there was still a "pool" of women pilot astronaut applicants.[59]

WHAT MADE SALLY TO RIDE? 207

Huntoon speculated that the lack of women astronaut applicants early on was due to the fact that women assumed they would not get chosen.[60] Much like the passion exhibited by Harris, Hall and Nichols, Huntoon viewed inclusion as bigger than the astronaut corps. Changing the astronaut image would send shock waves across the country, affirming the intelligence and professional skill set exhibited by women and minorities. The integrated astronaut image affirmed that all Americans could strive to choose their own career path. The dedicated recruiting efforts of these four women, along with NASA's affirmative action to show that women and minorities were valued, resulted in a dramatic shift in the astronaut image to one that highlighted the worth and value of all people.

On January 16, 1978, NASA introduced Group 8's "Thirty-Five New Guys—TFNG" of fifteen pilots and twenty mission specialists, which included women, minorities, mustaches, beards and long hair.[61] Their gender, race and professional appearance were markedly different from the twenty-seven crew-cut pilot astronauts from Apollo.[62] Group 8 mission specialist astronaut Mike Mullane explains:

> The diversity of America was represented on that stage. There was a mother of three (Shannon Lucid), two astronauts of the Jewish faith (Jeff Hoffman and Judy Resnik), and one Buddhist (El Onizuka). There were Catholics and Protestants, atheists, and fundamentalists. Truth be known, there were probably gay astronauts among us. [...]. Every press camera was focused on this rainbow coalition, particularly the females.[63]

Mullane was correct as the women and minorities garnered attention in the media and in the American imagination. They included Dr. Anna L. Fisher (medicine), Dr. Shannon Lucid (biochemistry), Dr. Judith Resnik (electrical engineering), Dr. Sally K. Ride (physics), Dr. Margaret "Rhea" Seddon (medicine) and Dr. Kathryn "Kathy" Sullivan (earth sciences/oceanography). NASA chose three Black men and one Asian American male: Dr. Guin Bluford (aerospace engineering), Dr. Ronald McNair (physics), Ellison Onizuka (aerospace engineering/flight test engineer/test pilot) and Major Frederick D. Gregory of the Air Force, the only pilot astronaut among the minorities or women. However, to note, Onizuka attended Air Force Test Pilot School as a flight engineer and test pilot.[64] Two years later, NASA included two more women with Astronaut Group 9's, Dr. Mary L. Cleave (engineering) and Dr. Bonnie Dunbar (engineering and physiology). Group 9 also included the first Hispanic Chinese American astronaut, Franklin Chang-Diaz (mechanical engineering/physicist).

The first women astronaut candidates were mostly from middle-class backgrounds. Fisher was a self-professed "Army brat" of an American father and German immigrant mother.[65] Lucid's parents were missionaries, and she was born in Shanghai, China. The Japanese imprisoned the family when Shannon was six weeks old. The Lucid's later settled in Bethany, Oklahoma.[66] Resnik's father, the son of a rabbi, was an optometrist and her mother a legal secretary. She grew up in Akron, Ohio.[67] Ride and Sullivan both hailed from the suburbs of Southern California. Ride spent most of her youth in Van Nuys and Encino. Her parents were active in the Presbyterian Church. Her mother taught special education, and her father was a political science professor at Santa Monica City College.[68] Sullivan's father was in the aerospace industry.[69] Finally, Seddon, the daughter of a New York lawyer, grew up in conservative Murfreesboro, Tennessee. Her father was on a local hospital board, giving Seddon a connection to her first love of medicine.[70] Group 9's Dr. Mary Cleave's parents were teachers in Southampton, New York. Dr. Bonnie Dunbar spent her childhood on her parents' farm in Outlook, Washington, and graduated from Sunnydale High School.[71] Much like the Mercury 7, most had seemingly ordinary childhoods.

Despite their average backgrounds, their academic career paths were anything but ordinary. All these women entered academia at a time when women's faces in STEM were new if not unwanted. The discrimination and intimidation of entering an all-male space did not deter the women, and they earned advanced degrees. All but Ride and Sullivan entered the workforce upon graduation as the 1960s and early 1970s women's rights movement headed into the conservative early 1980s.[72] Their entrance into the male-dominated corps meant once again proving themselves to be more than a gender, but rather extraordinarily skilled as individuals.

The Associated Press's Paul Recer described the skills of an astronaut as "No other field demands a personal tapestry of so complex a weave, with threads of education, experience, intelligence, and proven and unflappable grit."[73] All these astronaut women "are scholastically gifted and fiercely independent," wrote Recer.[74] One writer got it. These women might not fly the shuttle, but they still exhibited the old astronaut attributes. Much to the chagrin of anti-Equal Rights Amendment crusader Phyllis Schlafly, the Group 8 and 9 women all intended to be economically independent.

The women's education benefited from both Eisenhower's National Defense Education Act and Title IX. The eldest, the five-foot, eleven-inch Lucid—the tallest of the group—earned her bachelor's in 1963, pre-dating the women's and civil rights movements. Lucid's undergraduate advisor told her, "You are not going to get a job because you are a woman. You just need to go home and get married."[75] Undeterred, Lucid received her PhD in biochemistry at the

University of Oklahoma in 1973. She wanted to be a commercial airline pilot but was turned down in 1964.[76] Like Dr. Nancy Roman's experience, Lucid remembered writing a high school essay about what she hoped to be when she grew up. Lucid wanted to become a rocket scientist. Her teacher "scolded" her "for failing to take her assignment seriously."[77] Lucid persevered, carving out her own space in chemistry. As a woman, her few employment offers were cleaning bedpans at nursing homes. She did it anyway. She eventually became a research associate after graduation at the Oklahoma Medical Research Foundation.[78]

Fisher's dream of becoming an astronaut came early. She enjoyed math and science as a young girl. She remembered listening to Shepard's flight while in school. She aspired to do something similar, but she knew pilot training was off-limits to women. Her early passion for spaceflight did not segue into her being an avid science-fiction reader because she preferred books about strong women. Science fiction lacked such characters. Fisher found it difficult to identify with male characters, demonstrating the importance of why diverse voices and narratives matter. She volunteered at a hospital where her friend's mother worked as a nurse. While going over X-ray film, Fisher whispered to the nurse, "I'd really like to be an astronaut." Nobody else knew of Fisher's dream. She hoped for a doctorate in chemistry while researching and publishing papers on X-ray crystallographic studies of metallocarboranes at the University of California, Los Angeles (UCLA), but much like Lucid, she realized job opportunities in chemistry were limited. She earned her master's degree in chemistry and then went on to UCLA's medical school, choosing to specialize in emergency medicine.[79]

The other medical doctor of the group, Seddon, left her small and conservative Murfreesboro, Tennessee town for the University of California, Berkeley. It was a cultural eye-opener for her with its campus full of antiwar protestors, liberals, "communists" and hippies. She did not necessarily agree with their stances but benefited from learning about different ideas. She explored classes and settled on her love for the sciences. Her Berkeley grades were "good enough," and while she did not identify as a feminist, she understood that the 1960s feminist movement helped further her opportunities in medical school. The University of Tennessee Medical School was active in recruiting women and minorities, and she benefited from these opened doors the "crazy" and "radical" feminists created. When Seddon entered medical school, she was one of only six women out of a total class of one hundred fifteen medical students. Seddon specialized in surgery but also worked in emergency rooms in Houston to supplement her small astronaut salary.[80]

Resnik grew up in an "academically privileged" household, attending the wealthy Harvey S. Firestone public high school. Her mother doted on her, ensuring that Judy played classical piano, studied Hebrew and learned to cook. With her parents' divorce, the "intensely private" Judy grew her hair long, drank with the boys and still received straight A's in her advanced placement classes.[81] She was brilliant and aimed to attend The Juilliard School for classical piano. Her perfect math SAT score changed Resnik's mind, and she attended Carnegie Tech (Carnegie Mellon University).[82] She earned a bachelor's degree in electrical engineering and completed her master's and doctorate in electrical engineering at the University of Maryland.

Ride hit the junior tennis circuit at a young age. She received a full scholarship to Swarthmore College, the Ivy League schools still being off-limits to undergraduate women, where she played tennis, golf and field hockey. She returned to California to become a professional tennis player. She took courses in literature and physics at the University of California at Los Angeles, spending a semester in Moscow at the Institute for High Energy Physics. Sally preferred dabbling in quantum physics over the dedication necessary to become an elite tennis player. She left for Stanford and received a bachelor's in physics and another in literature. Sally and her girlfriend, Molly Tyson, both played tennis for Stanford.[83] Sally quit the team and went on to receive her master's and doctorate in physics. She focused on X-rays, lasers and astrophysics, making her an ideal astronaut candidate.[84]

Once chosen by NASA, Ride made a point to master the Remote Manipulator System (RMS) or Canadarm, used for deploying payloads such as satellites into space. Ride spent months in Toronto creating the procedures for using the arm. She did not necessarily need or want to be the first American woman in space, but she understood that mastering the RMS would almost guarantee a mission and even a spot at CapCom. She trained the STS-2 and STS-3 crews on the RMS and became the first woman's voice at CapCom for their missions.[85] The NASA astronaut office chose Ride to be the first woman astronaut in space not because they needed a woman for the mission, but because they needed the best person to operate the RMS for STS-7.[86]

Sullivan's pre-NASA background reads like an exploration novel. She was drawn to studying foreign languages as a young teen but fell in love with oceanography. She wrote her dissertation on the Newfoundland Basin at Dalhousie University in Nova Scotia, Canada. Her goal was to dive aboard the Alvin submersible to the ocean floor. She spent most of her time on a boat off Greenland researching the fourteen thousand miles below. She believed the role of the mission specialist was very similar to these expeditions. An oceanographic crew typically consisted of an engineer, navigator, skipper and the research group. The crew normally lived aboard the boat for two to six weeks at a time. Since both parties shared one space, Sullivan understood that unpredictable sea conditions required a working relationship between the crew and researchers. The harmonious relationship was like future shuttle missions, the only difference being that the mission specialists became "deeply trained in the ship itself." Being a mission specialist was not simply knowing your experiment but being competent with the shuttle.[87] After all, in the event of a pilot-astronaut emergency, the mission specialists would be responsible for gliding the shuttle home.

When the women astronauts arrived, Johnson Space Center housed roughly four thousand engineers and scientists—almost exclusively male except for a handful of females. Ride quipped that with the six women astronauts, the female technical workspace at Johnson doubled.[88] The *New York Times* reported that women employed at NASA made up 23% in 1983 of a staff just under twenty-two thousand. A total of 6.5% were women in engineering and science, with 5% at the managerial or supervisor level. According to NASA's assistant administrator for equal opportunities program, this was higher than the almost 4.5% average across the country. The *Times* argued that women's entrance into STEM nationally and at NASA was a "transition rather than a revolution."[89] However, to women's rights supporters, this was a revolution because these women astronauts showed themselves to be individualists and rule breakers, like the Mercury astronauts. However, it was not a complete revolution but rather a transition because the public discourse still focused on women confined to conventional gender roles.

The women astronauts created systems engineering at NASA much like the old breed of astronauts. For instance, Ride was put to work on the simulators and procedures for the shuttle's RMS. She recalls, "There weren't any checklists when we started; we developed them all."[90] Fisher backs this up, recalling, "Back in those days it was just, 'Okay, you're doing this,' with no training whatsoever as to how to go about doing that. So that was hard." At the start of the shuttle program, the astronauts and flight controllers created the procedures for the shuttle CapCom ascent. NASA used these procedures for most of the shuttle program.[91]

While the women were accepted by their fellow male astronauts, at times NASA employees questioned their skills. Dr. Huntoon received complaints about the women—as if she were their supervisor—she was not. She would often respond, "Well, that sounds just like a man, doesn't it?" Complaints about the women often stemmed from actions that some men perceived as emasculating, such as women questioning or correcting their skills, especially during meetings with male colleagues.[92] Despite the women's equal contributions to the shuttle program, the public discourse focused on the women as tokens or heroes and frequently failed to recognize the women's achievements.

The public discourse did not question the astronaut men's skill, but the women had to prove themselves. *Florida Today* reasoned, "The bottom line must be: Can they do the job?"[93] Women journalists also noticed the burden to prove themselves on the women astronaut candidates' shoulders. These women would be the first professional women integrating an all-male space in the public eye. Not just any male space. The astronaut corps was *the* male space. Journalist Carolynn Lee Conley argued that "well-meaning men questioned their [women's] ability to handle stressful episodes during space missions."[94] Similarly, Harriet Van Horne summed up the moment as, "They're going to be flying with a monstrous pack on their backs, namely, the reputation of newly liberated women." The women's enormous duty was "to show the world that women astronauts are as tough, smart, and resourceful as any hero of the Space Age, real or comic book."[95] The women had spent their life proving that they could traverse gender norms and spent their academic and professional careers demonstrating that they belonged. Spaceflight, although in the public eye, proved no different.

At the 1978 press conference, NASA reiterated that they did not lower the astronaut qualifications and standards to include women and minorities. Oddly enough, the WASPs received veteran status a year before with the GI Improvement Act.[96] The WASPs had finally been recognized for their contributions, and their services, as unnecessary or somehow less than, were put to rest—for now. NASA responded to questions from the media pertaining to a "formula" that may have been included "in regard to racial, social, and ethnic distribution in making the selection" and argued that a "formula" did not exist, only "a very strong affirmative action program to get as many candidates as we could from as wide a selection of U.S. society as possible, and particularly to get both minority and women candidates."[97] NASA administrator Dr. Robert Frosch told reporters, pertaining to the

> feminizing of the astronaut corps [...]. There is no real need for reverse discrimination: if "the most competent, talented, and experienced people available to us today are chosen [...]. they will be both men and women, black and white, and yellow, because talent and ability know no barriers of color, race, or gender.[98]

Seddon understood the pressures the women faced. The male astronaut candidates had plenty of former astronauts who had careers the men could measure up to. Other than Valentina Tereshkova, the women did not have a female astronaut image, so they created one out of themselves. The first NASA women astronauts set the standard for how an astronaut woman looked and acted. Seddon remembers, "We (women candidates) didn't know if they were looking for pure scientists, those with a lot of flying experience or whether appearance, athletic ability and strength were factors." The women were to simply "present ourselves."[99] The women entered the astronaut candidacy as individuals in control of creating the astronaut woman image.

Sullivan summed up the tremendous impact on gender in the corps as, "All the guys we walked into, every woman in their life, before we arrived, was a wife, girlfriend, daughter, or secretary, period; occasionally a nurse. [...] so whether we wanted it or not, it fell to us to change their views about women." In creating their own identity within the astronaut corps, "We had to figure out and make our way in it individually and also make our way in it in a fashion that kept the ground open for other women to come behind."[100]

As the first women and minorities entered the astronaut corps, the astronaut candidates started referring to their astronaut group as "ten interesting people and twenty-five standard white guys." The media was done with asking the "white guys" questions within "4.3 minutes," and the rest had the remainder of the day to answer questions.[101] The women and minority astronaut candidates captured the media's attention and, with it, reinvigorated interest in spaceflight for the shuttle era. American fascination with the new breed of astronauts meant more funding for NASA. The fascination with the women seemed to shift between comparing them to the early jet test-pilot astronauts, a focus on conventional gender roles and simultaneously acknowledging the women as both ordinary and extraordinary.[102]

## Piloting

The entrance of women into the astronaut corps highlighted the significance of gender roles as many Americans lamented the loss of the old astronaut image of a "rugged-individualist-hero" or "flying-ace." Head of the Astronaut Office, former astronaut and Air Force jet pilot, George Abbey, told reporters he looked for "a team player" in the astronaut candidates.[103] This was strikingly different from the original individualist astronaut narrative. NASA charged astronaut Alan Bean with integrating women into the "super-male society" of the corps.[104] Bean reiterated that the nearly twenty-year delay in integrating women into the astronaut corps was not due to "conscious discrimination," but rather because NASA was still learning the skillset necessary for spaceflight, and prioritized jet test-pilot experience above all else. The military banned women from military pilot training and thus women's exclusion was more "practical" and "logical" at the time.[105]

Despite the Group 8 women's skillset, the public discourse focused on the women doing "everything but the flying."[106] When *Science News* introduced

Group 8 to its readers, it divided the astronauts into the pilot astronauts who NASA "charged with actually flying the rocket-cure-glider to and from its orbital positions" and those who were "space shuttle riders"—the mission specialists and the future "payload specialists."[107] The term "riders" helped domesticate the public spaceflight image, making it seem safer and more routine, implying that the people on board were passive participants, simply along for the ride with the technology or pilot astronauts handling most of the work. The *Sydney Morning Herald* charged that the women would be "passengers, as the Russian Valentina Tereshkova, was" in 1963.[108] This was confirmed by the *New York Times* as they wrote that the astronaut women "will be trained to conduct scientific, engineering, and medical duties, but probably will not pilot the space shuttle."[109]

NASA paired each mission specialist with a pilot astronaut during T-38 training. The mission specialists were the "backseat riders."[110] Mary Cleave's Instructor Pilot was given strict instructions to not "get the new scientist sick," much to Cleave's dismay, as she wanted to fly higher and faster.[111] Most of the women wanted to pilot the plane. They were individualist daredevils breaking gender constructs daily and wanted to pilot the T-38. Lucid was so fond of the T-38 that Kraft told the press of the "torture" Lucid felt not being able to "fly" the jet.[112] All six of the Group 8 women eventually earned private pilot licenses.[113] The women performed so well in T-38 training that even astronaut Bean was shocked.[114]

While motherhood was a large argument to keep women out of the cockpit since the beginning of flight, Fisher continued to fly in the back seat of a T-38 while she was four months pregnant.[115] The same was true later for Seddon. Cleave got a kick out of watching the gaping mouths of male pilots as Seddon walked the El Paso flight line "slightly showing." Seddon convinced NASA to allow pregnant women to fly in their first trimester.[116] Despite their visibility in flight, Resnik relayed her job to the press as "flight engineering, managing space systems, deploying satellites and walking in space [...] anything on the shuttle that the pilot doesn't do."[117] Since mission specialists were not piloting the shuttle, it led to the belief that spaceflight was safe. This perception softened the once challenging and complex technology used from Mercury through Apollo.

*The Saturday Evening Post's* "Make Way For The Ladies In Space" by Janis Williams generally applauded women's entrance into the astronaut fraternity. She pointed out that the "new kind of astronaut" was chosen from eight-thousand-plus candidates of the country's best engineering, technical and medical minds—which is extraordinary for women. However, she pinpointed that the changing nature of spaceflight technology was largely responsible for the integration of women into the corps, maintaining that

# WHAT MADE SALLY TO RIDE?

the spacecraft itself has been developed to the point that it's operated largely by computer from the ground. Therefore, those finely honed pilot skills formerly so critical to an astronaut are no longer vital. What is needed more than upper-body strength or flying experience are the technical skills to monitor and interpret the on-board scientific experiments.[118]

Her assessment that ground computers controlled the shuttle reinforced the outdated idea of an astronaut hero in control of the spacecraft, even though computers and monkeys could control a spacecraft.

*Newsweek* followed along similar lines, professing of the shuttle astronaut image: the "original astronaut corps is slowly being diluted by those to whom having the 'right stuff' means being able to solve quadric equations in their heads."[119] Bean told reporters of the less rigorous 1.5-3 G shuttle forces, "Hell, anybody can take that."[120] Likewise, after Ride's flight, *Time* insisted that "much of the daredevil aspect has gone out of space travel. No longer are astronauts subject to bone-crunching liftoffs [...]. The shuttle has made the going easy. NASA is even talking of inviting ordinary folks along for the ride."[121]

The *Gannett News Service*'s Ellen Hale argued that the old Tom Wolfe "right stuff" or the "shine" and the "mystique" of "manliness" and "bravery" had been taken out of the astronaut. Astronauts used to fly higher, faster and farther than anyone. Jungle and desert survival school had been axed from astronaut training, but water survival school remained in case of an emergency ejection from the T-38 or shuttle.[122] Hale reminisced about a mythical astronaut masculinity when she wrote, "In the old days, astronauts were run through survival courses only superhumans could survive; dropped on deserted desert islands"; they made their way "through jungles" and "climbed mountains." However, the "new breed of astronauts" do not have to be physically strong. New requirements destroyed rugged individualist masculinity, "After all, if men can do it, and now women can do it, then maybe just about anyone can be an astronaut?"[123]

The new astronaut as a focus of difference and safety continued in the public discourse. Pilot astronaut Robert "Hoot" Gibson echoed Hale, acknowledging that while the pilot astronauts and mission specialists were a "tight group," you will not find the women throwing back a "flaming hooker." The fighter pilot Gibson explained of the new shuttle astronaut image, "That whole muscle-men image, well, just having eight women here changes it. They already have softened the image of the astronaut."[124] The *Chicago Tribune* argued of the shuttle's safety, "We can talk casually about her [Ride] because there's no doubt that she's coming back safely. That's one thing that has changed since the John Glenn days."[125] The shuttle was indestructible.

**Figure 6.1** Sally Ride, Judith Resnik, Anna Fisher, Kathryn Sullivan and Rhea Seddon undergo water survival training at Homestead Air Force Base. Source: NASA.

Astronaut mission specialist Mullane's evaluation of the astronaut image added further complexity to the changing perceptions of masculine and feminine roles in spaceflight. Of the Group 8 astronauts, seven were from the military and thirteen were civilians. Mullane served as a flight surgeon in combat during Vietnam. Mullane was tested in battle. Enemy fire forced Mullane to eject out of his aircraft. He earned his masculinity. While not "stick and rudder" pilots, Mullane viewed the military mission specialists as presenting a masculinity that had been hardened by wartime and life experience. They were "self-reliant." Whereas the civilian mission specialists exhibited "a softness, an innocence in their demeanor [...]." They had not experienced the real world and certainly not the world of combat readiness. The other mission specialists were

> people who had probably protested the Vietnam War [...] who had marched for gay rights, abortion rights, civil rights, and animal rights. For the first time in history, the astronaut title was being bestowed on tree-huggers, dolphin-friendly fish eaters, vegetarians, and subscribers to the *New York Times*.

Mullane tied his preferred astronaut image back to that of the original astronauts who served in combat. The space race was an extension of that combat. He lamented that the astronaut image no longer included "conservative" military men alone.[126] The astronaut image presented masculinity and femininity as fluctuating on a pendulum swinging back and forth between conservative and progressive political spectrums.

The inclusion of women and male mission specialists in the astronaut corps challenged American cultural stereotypes that associated physical strength with bravery and a slight build with weakness. One did not have to be an athletic astronaut, but Ride was a former nationally ranked junior tennis player who ran twenty to thirty miles a week and worked out at the astronaut gym regularly. The male astronauts had difficulty keeping up with her pace.[127] Cultural assumptions take generations to change, but the women's presence in the once male-dominated profession defied American gender constructs, especially bravery. Early astronauts exhibited bravery through risk-taking and button-pushing. The astronaut women also pushed buttons, risked their lives atop a twin rocket that none of the astronauts, including the pilots, could control.[128] Acknowledging this meant acknowledging that gender roles were more cultural than natural—perhaps even artificial. Recognizing women as brave would disrupt perceptions of men as providers and protectors. However, the public discourse failed to see women astronauts as courageous. Instead, the public discourse continued to view women's use of technology as a symbol of safety in the STS.

Bean insisted that spaceflight technology was "male things" before he worked with the astronaut women.[129] Sullivan fired back at this cultural understanding that only men control technology with, "Kepler's laws are not spontaneously violated, the spacecraft will not spontaneously fall from the sky [...]. Believe it or not, the instrument panel does not know if it is a male or female hand that flips the switches."[130] The first Black astronaut woman, Dr. Mae Jemison (1987's Astronaut Group 12), grew tired of such gender discrimination and eloquently stated to the press, "The shuttle instruments can't give a damn whether you are a man or woman."[131] But, as the first American women integrated into the astronaut corps, Americans assumed the shuttle to be so safe that it aroused average Americans' aspirations of spaceflight.

Americans with no piloting or STEM experience eagerly awaited news of the Citizen Astronaut Program. As early as 1978, articles filled magazines and journals dedicated to spaceflight predicting who the first civilian flier would be and the price of space fare. The introduction of the citizen program took away from all that the women and men had achieved through academics or piloting to earn a place in space. Even astronaut Mullane believed the academic non-military mission specialists "hadn't paid their dues" to be astronauts.[132]

In 1981, *Newsweek* reported of the shuttle as "the most practical, efficient, down-to-earth space vehicle ever designed, a 'space truck' whose mission is

218                    GENDER AND THE RACE FOR SPACE

not exploration but the exploitation of the familiar region of nearby space."[133] NASA hoped to have over forty shuttle missions per year. The following year, Space Camp opened to children throughout the country, again representing a domesticated image of space. On the eve of Ride's flight, *Newsweek* speculated that by 1986, NASA would carry at least eight citizen passengers yearly on board shuttle missions. These passengers would range from foreign diplomats and scientists to Walter Cronkite and John Denver.[134]

Preparations for Ride's first flight reflected the passive role of mission specialists. Papers reported Ride as sitting "just behind the two pilots."[135] The language suggests Ride was a passenger, passive and not active with the technology, although she was chosen for her expertise with the RMS.[136] Even when discussing the astronauts' "day of leisure" before the launch of STS-7, Ride was likened to a passenger as fellow STS-7 astronauts Robert Crippen, Frederick Hauk, John Fabian and Norman Thagard spent the day flying "in their jet trainers over Central Florida [...] the first American woman in space, just went along for the ride." Fabian and Thagard were mission specialists, but also former military pilots. However, they did not use their skills as pilots in the position of astronaut. The article reported—erroneously of course—that "she [Ride] doesn't fly. The other crew members are either former test pilots or veteran combat fliers."[137]

Astronaut Sullivan encountered a similar situation while spending the day in a T-38 near the Mojave Airport. A male astronaut asked famed jet test pilot Chuck Yeager if he wanted to meet Sullivan, who was "flying chase." Yeager quipped, "Riding, maybe. Ain't flying."[138] Astronaut Wally Schirra commented that the old breed of astronauts were "'test pilots,' and the lack of piloting by mission specialists took 'some of the shine off.'" In fact, "A lot of this new group who will fly are not really astronauts."[139] Did the mission specialists need to fly to be astronauts? Schirra's comment lends itself to women and men as mission specialists as a direct threat to rugged individualist masculinity.

By downplaying the dangers of launching with massive solid rocket boosters—dangers so great that even pilot astronauts could not control them—the idea that being an astronaut required bravery was still valid. Mission specialists, in this view, had that bravery in abundance. Twenty years after the 1962 subcommittee hearings, the public discourse continued the exclusion of women as the pilot or equal partner aboard the spacecraft. The women astronauts would not have commanding authority aboard the shuttle since they were all mission specialists. Ride found this "irksome" and said, "If I had the ability to change any part of our training program I would get us qualified as (jet) pilots."[140] Ride understood this left the Group 8 and 9 women out of positions of authority aboard the shuttle.

# WHAT MADE SALLY TO RIDE?

*Ms.* magazine was one of the few media outlets that depicted the dangers of flying the shuttle. *Ms.* reported that there were not enough ejection seats aboard the shuttle for every member of the crew. If the launch went horribly wrong, and it appeared that the rocket or orbiter might crash into populated areas, NASA would blow up the shuttle. Astronaut Mullane backs this up but correctly points out that the ejection seats were removed after the first four shuttle missions that consisted of only the commander and pilot astronauts. The twin solid rocket boosters made the shuttle missions even more dangerous, with the astronauts attached to over two million pounds of thrust. The rockets were in four pieces held together by rubber O-rings. Mercury, Gemini and Apollo all had escape hatches, complete with parachutes for the astronauts—even with those, things could and did go wrong. Mullane blames the "safety" narrative on NASA's "post-Apollo hubris." NASA employees engineered and controlled the most technologically advanced of all machines—ever! The shuttle was an extension of that, having Mullane professing:

> While no member of the shuttle design team would have ever made the blasphemous claim, "We're gods. We can do anything," the reality was this: The space shuttle itself *was* such a statement. Mere mortals might not be able to design and safely operate a reusable spacecraft boosted by the world's largest, segmented, uncontrollable solid-fueled rockets, but gods certainly could.[141]

The success of the post-*Apollo 1* mission flights, including bringing *Apollo 13* safely home, fostered the belief that men could master spaceflight technology, even with minority and women passengers aboard.

Conversely, spaceflight nurse Dee O'Hara argued, "spaceflight is certain [*sic*] not for sissies." Despite the changing narrative in the shuttle era, "Spaceflight is dangerous, and I think we lose sight of that because we've been so successful, very successful."[142] Americans lost sight of the dangers even after both STS-41-D and STS-51-F aborted a few seconds before liftoff. STS-41-D's hydrogen fuel valve in the third engine failed to open, triggering *Discovery*'s computers to shut down and abort. STS-41-D commander astronaut Henry Hartsfield reassured the press that "at no time did I not feel protected."[143] *Challenger's* computers shut the launch down on STS-51-F, saving the crew when a faulty coolant valve in the second engine malfunctioned and caught fire.[144] The danger appeared lost on the press with the comfort that shuttle computers "are sophisticated enough to shut down when things go awry."[145] The Associated Press wired that the abort demonstrated "a prime example of the extremely careful approach" of NASA shuttle missions.[146]

220 GENDER AND THE RACE FOR SPACE

Even in the face of danger, with tail ends and launch pads catching fire, spaceflight under shuttle technology appeared safe until the harsh reality of the 1986 *Challenger* (STS-51-L) disaster that killed all astronauts aboard, including Judith Resnik, Ellison S. Onizuka and the first citizen astronaut, teacher Christa McAuliffe.[147] The dangers of spaceflight from the 1960s largely left women out because of the masculine need to protect women, especially mothers. Woman as astronaut demonstrated the same safety and ease of spaceflight as the flight attendant demonstrated for commercial flight.

## Makeup and Motherhood

Taking her title from a popular Virginia Slims feminist advertisement campaign, Jennifer Ross-Nazzal argues in "You've Come a Long Way, Maybe: The First Six Women Astronauts and the Media" that the public discourse focused on the women astronauts' "weight, appearance, diet, exercise, domesticity, dating, marriage, and motherhood."[148] The public discourse's treatment of the astronaut women as skilled professionals often conflicted with conventional feminine roles. During the later Cold War years, the role of wife and mother remained central to the domestic and international security of both the United States and the Soviet Union, even amid calls for gender equality at home.

Not wanting to be outdone by the Americans, the Soviets launched the second woman into space, 34-year-old Svetlana Y. Savitskaya, aboard Soyuz T-7 on August 19, 1982. Savitskaya and fellow cosmonauts, pilot Commander Leonid Popov and engineer Alexander Serebrov, flew to station Soyuz T-7. The three docked to meet cosmonauts Valentin Lebedev and Anatoly Berezovy. TASS's goal in terms of Savitskaya was to test women's performance in a zero-gravity environment.[149] The Soviet agency did not find any differences between male and female bodies in flight.[150] The Soviets reveled that they once again beat the Americans in sending a woman into space. The Soviets continued to claim gender equality, but the same conflicting gender attitudes present during Tereshkova's 1963 flight were still evident during Savitskaya's flight.

A world-renowned aerobatic pilot, Savitskaya came from a fighter-pilot pedigree with her father serving as Soviet Air Force Marshal, Yevgeny Savitsky. Her husband was also a military pilot.[151] She was admitted to the Moscow College of Aviation, where she first got her pilot's license. She then entered test-pilot school for the Soviet Air Force. In her career, Savitskaya successfully logged over five hundred parachute jumps and flew twenty different aerial platforms.[152] Despite TASS celebrating "the triumph of the emancipation of women," Savitskaya's fellow cosmonauts quipped during her capsule's

# WHAT MADE SALLY TO RIDE?

link-up with the Soviet space station, "'We've Got an Apron Ready'—'we have a kitchen for you; that'd be where you work.'"[153] While the cosmonauts said they were only "joshing," they did enjoy that Savitskaya was not a typical female "chatter-box."[154] The banter was enough to make "a feminist cringe," but it got worse. Instead of ribbing between comrades, the "joshing" appeared almost serious in nature, especially from a high-ranking cosmonaut.[155] The media described pilot-cosmonaut Savitskaya as "young, slim, and petite"—a woman who was "charming and soft, a hospitable hostess" who liked to "sew her own clothes," and actually enjoyed "housekeeping."[156]

The Chief of Soviet Training Program, General Georgi Beregovoy, beamed about Svetlana's "tightly fitting space suit, accentuating her figure." The general went on to refer to Svetlana as "the weaker sex" and stated, "Women's emancipation was never meant to mean an end to chivalry."[157] Despite her celebrity status, TASS assured the world that Savitskaya would be performing "serious and responsible work in outer space."[158] The United Press International appeared so taken aback by this that some newspapers ran headlines that Savitskaya performed "in masculine orbit."[159]

American journalists responded to the Soviet achievement by highlighting sexism within Soviet society. Reporter Kirsten O. Lundberg argued that while the Soviets may have had laws that professed some sort of "legal equality," joking about women's "housekeeping tasks" was not "liberated."[160] The Associated Press wrote that Lenin's dream of the abolition of "domestic slavery" was anything but over. The communist leader believed that if women were engaged in jobs and industry outside of the home, they would be freed from "stupefying and humiliating subjugation to the eternal drudgery of the kitchen and the nursery." However, women still found themselves laboring inside the home, picking up "dirty clothes" while their husbands relaxed with "the aid of a bottle of vodka."[161] This was something that even Savitskaya was attuned to, even relaying to the press that she had to put up a "fight" to get into test pilot school.[162]

Despite the fact that the Americans pointed out inequality in the Soviet Union, Americans still believed neither Soviet woman cosmonaut had the skill to fly, but rather served as a spectacle. For instance, an American reporter declared that "the Russian women were picked because they were women. It was absolute tokenism."[163] Even the American public discourse still viewed women as affirmative action hires—not as equally skilled colleagues.

Unlike the early Cold War astronauts, the American astronaut women navigated their qualifications and celebrity status without the shelter of NASA public affairs officers John Anthony "Shorty" Powers or Walter T. Bonney. The women presented womanhood on their terms—all individual women, each with a different story to tell. Much like the Mercury 7, the women were not necessarily close friends, but they banded together as a team, presenting "a united front." Sullivan recalls that the women were different in their "style, manner, personality, personal history—married, single, dating; whatever [...]." The women met about four to six times a year with Huntoon to discuss issues specific to the women.[164] When Huntoon traveled with the Group 8 women, she was often identified as the women's "chaperone."[165] This echoed the sheltering of military women from the lures of promiscuity. The term "chaperone" insinuated a woman's inability to control their bodies.

Despite the misunderstanding of Huntoon's role in the press, she was an important role model for the young women—and men—who were "straight out of grad school" and very unfamiliar with the world outside academia.[166] As Fisher, Ride and Seddon recalled, Huntoon guided the women and helped them navigate an all-male space at NASA. She often asked the women, when faced with criticism or a challenge over their gender, "Okay, what do we want to do? What do you all want to do?"[167] NASA permitted the women to "use their own judgement" when it came to talking to the press—demonstrating a tremendous amount of progress to trust women.[168] After all, if the women failed, NASA failed. The women astronauts understood that however one of them individually answered a question in the press, the press might assume "that to be an answer for all time, for all women, the complete image and declaration of what women astronauts are."[169] As the women teamed together, they found their experience in spaceflight followed a similar narrative to that of Savitskaya and gender roles pre-1960s.

Straight out of the 1950s, the women's appearance took center stage with the term "Glamornauts" as opposed to astronauts.[170] One of the psychologists during the astronaut selection process, Dr. Stuart Bergman, told reporters: "We were looking for women who were comfortable being female but who weren't intimidated by men or easily brushed aside."[171] He went on to say that the committee could not select women interested in a "'battle of the sexes,' nor the 'female chauvinist cow' or a 'southern belle.'" Both Fisher and Seddon were often referred to as "pretty" or "sexy" and women that you wanted to "protect."[172] Reporter Pat Casey Daley referred to Seddon as a "princess" in a "modern American fairytale."[173] According to Ride, "the engineers at NASA, in their infinite wisdom, decided that women astronauts would want makeup—so they designed a makeup kit."[174] Ride would have enjoyed being around for the engineers' discussions on women's makeup. Other than Seddon, the women astronauts rarely wore makeup and did not on the shuttle. Even Fisher described herself as "one of these no-makeup kind of people."[175] Ride wanted no part of the project, and it fell to Fisher and Seddon to design the female hygiene kit.

NASA engineers continued to demonstrate a lack of knowledge of feminine hygiene. Engineers asked Ride if one hundred tampons would be enough for her six-day flight. The stunned Ride replied, "No, that would not be the right number." In their ignorance of women's bodies, the engineers responded, "Well, we want to be safe." Ride laughed, "Well, you can cut that in half with no problem at all."[176]

While the press and NASA focused on conventional femininity, the astronaut women created modern feminine roles that at times blended with what was conventionally masculine. This did not make the women any less feminine but demonstrated gender on a spectrum. Sullivan commented that she was not the "cover girl" type, but with Seddon:

> You know, Rhea shows up, blonde surgeon driving a red corvette. Bam, there you go. Okay, let's guess who will get the attention. It's about fitting the mental models that the writers or the reporters have and I've never fit very well into people's standard bins. [...]. Too tomboy, too smart, too strong, too all of those things. Not the archetypal little girl.[177]

Ride's California girl "elfin face" and "body" transfixed the *Miami Herald*.[178] Ride preferred rugby shirts and khakis, while Fisher enjoyed wearing suits with wedges.[179] Like Sullivan and Seddon, both women presented different feminine constructs. The *Philadelphia Inquirer* and *Santa Cruz Sentinel* ran stories of Ride's career as a junior-ranked tennis player—the student to coach Billie Jean King. The *Santa Cruz Sentinel* called Ride "a pint-sized dynamo, with an awesome mind and an athletic ability that made her first choice when teams were picked for neighborhood ball games." She was especially good "when she played football in the street with the boys."[180] Ride hated being referred to as a "tom-boy" because it "applied to a girl when acting like a boy as opposed to a girl acting like a girl [...]."[181] Within this California girl's petite frame, the *Miami Herald* championed Ride's individuality: "She is self-possessed. Eventempered. In control. Detached."[182]

Despite praising her athleticism, the paper still focused on the burning questions of women in spaceflight. Pertaining to stressful situations, the press asked Ride, "During your training exercises, when there is a problem, how do you take it as a human being? Do you weep?" to which "Ride paused long enough to laugh, roll her eyes and collapse on the table in mock exasperation," asking "Why doesn't anyone ever ask Crip [STS-7 Shuttle Commander Robert Crippen] those questions?"[183] Reporters fixated on whether Ride would wear a bra and makeup during her flight, and how she thought zero gravity would affect her reproductive organs. Ride responded at a NASA news conference, "It's too bad our society isn't further along."[184] The press likened Ride to having to "plead, and even bristle at times, to convince the press and public that she preferred to be thought of as one of a team rather than a unique heroine."[185] Sullivan supported Ride's frustration fielding gendered questions while the press overlooked her contributions to the space mission. Sullivan believed Americans to be "discomforted" about women in roles outside caregivers and teachers, "whether it's driving a school bus or flying a spacecraft."[186] Reporters' gendered assumptions spoke volumes to an American public discourse coming to terms with economically liberated career women.

Along with looks and motherhood, sex and marriage took center stage in the public discourse. At the January 1978 NASA Press Release introducing Group 8, Bill Hines of the *Chicago Sun-Times* asked what "consideration went into Shannon Lucid's responsibilities to her children versus her responsibilities to the program and how these were resolved?" Kraft answered: "none" and told the press that "women and men would be treated and trained just the same for space flights [...]. The only differences between astronauts would be because of their professional specialties, not their sex or race."[187]

Despite Kraft's attempt to focus on individualized skillsets as opposed to gender, the media persisted with its focus on the creation of conventional gender roles within spaceflight. *People Weekly* focused on the women's accomplishments inside the home, assuming they would be used in spaceflight.[188] Newspapers ran a cartoon of a female astronaut joining male astronauts aboard the shuttle. A male astronaut turned to the woman astronaut and said, "Well, Ms. Higgins, let's run through your duties as a woman astronaut—Wainwright here is coffee no cream, Nicholls there is tea, and I'm plain milk."[189] Other cartoons mocked that the women would be doing laundry, the dishes and that some astronauts' wives were jealous.[190] The mockery assumed a hostess or stewardess role for the women aboard the shuttle.

When the astronaut women were not on the shuttle, their home lives were as paramount to spaceflight as those of the original astronauts. However, unusual for NASA was that the astronaut candidates were women and at times single. Ride's boyfriend Bill Colson, also a Stanford physics graduate student, moved in with her during astronaut training. NASA did not have a problem with one of the women candidates living out of wedlock. When she broke up with Colson, Ride briefly dated fellow astronaut Hoot Gibson.[191] Fears of women's astronaut sexuality run amok did not appear in the public discourse.

The women became celebrities and, much like the male astronauts, did not seem to have a problem "getting dates."[192] A member of NASA's astronaut selection committee asked Seddon, "Suppose on the plane going back home you were to meet a man that you fell in love with, and he didn't want you to do this kind of work. What would you do?"[193] Women's roles as preparing

# WHAT MADE SALLY TO RIDE? 225

for wife and mother once again made their way into the press and at NASA. London's *Sunday Mirror* ran the headline: "A Date In Space? But What on Earth Will a Girl Wear?"[194]

Like Tereshkova, some of the women were married to astronauts. Dr. Anna Fisher (Sims) married Dr. William "Bill" Fisher before they applied to become astronauts. She was chosen by NASA first as part of Group 8. NASA chose Bill two years later as part of Group 9 in 1980. The media fawned over the pair as they became NASA's first astronaut couple in what the *Times* called "A Marriage That Was Made for The Heavens."[195] But this match had all the makings of a post-Title IX marriage. As Fisher went to astronaut candidate training at Johnson Spaceflight Center, it was Bill who stayed behind and looked for a home they would buy together.[196] This created a dramatic change in domestic roles as Bill, the husband, would be the one left behind while his wife worked in space.

Other astronaut marriages took place, presenting a domesticated image of spaceflight. Seddon married astronaut Gibson in 1981. In July 1982, Ride married fellow mission specialist astronaut Steve Hawley (also of Group 8) in a very small and unconventional ceremony—the bride wore jeans and a rugby shirt.[197] According to the *New York Times*, "NASA posters, shuttle dishware, and a large photograph of the astronauts on the moon in the master bedroom filled Ride and Hawley's home."[198] The chosen décor suggested that spaceflight had been brought to the home and that the home had been brought to spaceflight. Before her flight into space, Ride declined to answer a female reporter's question: "Do you have any plans to be the first mother who has traveled in space?"[199] In her refusal to answer, Ride was setting the precedent that gendered questions such as this would not be answered. This is also in line with Ride's refusal to accept a bouquet of flowers upon STS-7's return from space.[200]

Likewise, Lucid's attitude toward parental roles reflected changing gender norms. Tired of answering dozens of questions on how she would juggle motherhood with spaceflight, she responded that nobody ever asked the male astronauts how they would handle their responsibilities as fathers with spaceflight. Overall, "there's no reason for the children to hold me back. I had two baby girls to look after while I was going through graduate school. My husband has always helped. After all, they are half his."[201]

Fisher had no problem telling the selection committee during her initial interviews that she wanted children. In fact, NASA chose Fisher for her first spaceflight two weeks before she delivered her first child, a daughter named Kristin. A few weeks after giving birth, Fisher returned to work thinking, "I'm here and nothing's going to change."[202] Fisher never took formal leave. She had a nanny when she needed one; they became as close as family. On the American fascination with her being the first mother in space, the astronaut told reporters, "It intrigues me the way people think."[203] Bill Fisher responded, "We still work among a bunch of people who believe that pregnancy is a disease state."[204] Fisher's daughter, Kristin, was brought into mission control to listen to "Mommy" on a transistor and watch her on the control screen as Fisher "worked" in space.[205]

Further imparting a domesticated image of the shuttle, astronaut Joseph Allen's *Entering Space: An Astronaut's Odyssey* remarked on the transition from the old astronaut image to the shuttle's creature comforts: "The astronauts who now enter space wear sport shirts and slacks during their days in orbit [...] eat shrimp cocktail and barbecued beef and sleep in private bunks," finding themselves "increasingly at home in the new frontier."[206] Similarly, when Ride was in space, the media reported her wearing a "blue—and white T-shirt carrying the message 'We Deliver,'" as she "punched the button yesterday morning that sent a $24 million Indonesian communications satellite spinning into orbit."[207]

Americans marveled in not only this new work and sleep environment for astronauts, but they certainly wanted to know what and how astronauts ate. The *Philadelphia Inquirer* wrote that Ride "bantered with crewmates while munching sandwiches at lunch, joking that there were 'three turkeys and two hams' aboard. The lunch was prepared by Ride's fellow mission specialist John M. Fabian. Ride will get that chore tomorrow."[208]

Finally, in the same month as Ride's flight, the cover of *Space World* suggested that the shuttle was "Designing a Home in Space."[209] Creating a home in space domesticated the once dangerous feat of spaceflight. The popular spaceflight media outlet created the image that Sally was helping to build a home in space, not attempting to control spaceflight technology. Creating a home in space domesticated the once dangerous image of spaceflight. Robert Voas's comment after Tereshkova's flight that a woman's presence in space would mean that man had found a "home" in space seemed to come to fruition.

Overall, media reports surrounding the Group 8 women fashioned the shuttle's image as not only a beacon of American Cold War democracy but also, as a symbol of the domestication of space travel. Not only did the shuttle represent the comforts of home, but in "designing a home," the trope of conventional gender roles and domesticity once again entered the public discourse surrounding the Group 8 women. The women's roles as wives and mothers appeared as important as they were to the wives of the original astronauts. The American interest in conventional gender roles connected them to the early 1960s female fliers who sought their chance to fly and were denied due to fears of motherhood and women's bodies during spaceflight.

**Figure 6.2** Sally Ride takes off aboard a T-38 from Houston, Texas, to Kennedy Space Center, Florida, three days before STS-7. Source: NASA. https://sallyridescience.ucsd.edu/20-things-you-might-not-know-about-sally-ride/.

Despite the domesticated spaceflight image, NASA still allowed the women to control their own astronaut image. Sullivan remembers of the immense pressure the women faced:

> I think if something had really gone badly, if one of us had really, really muffed an assignment, their personality clashed with someone, or the lack of personal strength of character to stand up to the combination of scrutiny, joshing, and public exposure, if any of that had fractured any one of us, I don't know that it would have reversed the process, but certainly it would have probably created a deep, long detour and just left more debris for the next wave of folks to have to pick through before they could really regain the path and start making the kind of progress that we would want.[210]

In essence, failure was not an option. The women did not succumb to the pressures of sexism or arguments of tokenism, and through teamwork successfully created the astronaut woman as an individualist. Much like Harris, Hall, Nichols and Huntoon, the women astronauts forced a conversation about women's professionalism and skill—their individuality—thus subverting any assumptions about fixed gender roles.

## Conclusion

With hindsight and the tragic deaths of astronauts aboard both *Challenger* (1986) and *Columbia* (2003), shuttle technology was not passive, and with the physical and intellectual rigors involved, could be anything but democratic. However, looking back from the early years of spaceflight in the 1960s to the early 1980s, definitions of democratic technology and domestic technology have both evolved and stayed the same. This demonstrates that the shuttle communicated conflicting ideas of American democracy and gender culture. The astronaut image and the shuttle became an artifact of women's entrance into the public sphere of science, technology, engineering, mathematics, medicine and aviation.

The shuttle also acted as an artifact that connected tropes of domesticity and liberation within the rhetoric of American technology from the early Cold War to the later Cold War era. Spaceflight itself was seen as routine, and women and minorities were helping to make a home in space. Culturally, women's presence insinuated a degree of ease within spaceflight technology. The emphasis on routinization domesticated the dangers of spaceflight in the popular culture narrative. As engineers and designers integrated women into the astronaut corps, Americans, specifically the media, exhibited a keen interest in how female bodies would interact with spaceflight technology and what their presence symbolized for the future of space exploration or colonization.

Evocative of the Kitchen Debate's rhetoric of the freeing powers of washing machines and automatic ovens, the new shuttle technology was believed to release men, women and minorities from not only the confines of Earth but from spaceflight's former requirements of physicality and rigor into a technology that could be used by passengers aboard a reusable and routine craft. Thus, the language of ease and passenger status created the new technology as a domestic technology that liberated women into American spaceflight. While that language of domesticity and Title IX paved the way for astronaut women, unlike the Mercury 7, the astronaut woman image was not molded or controlled by NASA. The women crafted their image by authentically being themselves. They did not succumb to the pressures of being in an all-male space, nor did they back away from the pressures within the press to appear as doting wives, mothers or sex objects. They did not fall to the pressures of appearing to be heroes or feminists. They were astronauts. The women did it their way as individualists and part of a team. The first women of American spaceflight crafted the image of the astronaut not as one that was conventionally masculine nor feminine, or even some fantasy of what American culture assumed heroes to act, look or dress. Rather, the women exercised the ultimate in terms of power and control, creating an astronaut image as symbolic of American freedom of individuality, self-determination, choice and gender expression.

# Notes

1 Mike Leary, "Sally K. Ride Is In Orbit," *Philadelphia Inquirer,* June 19, 1983, A01, and John Noble Wilford, "Shuttle Rockets to Orbit with 5 Aboard," *New York Times,* June 19, 1983, 1.

2 Sara Sanborn, "Sally Ride, Astronaut: The World is Watching," *Ms. Magazine,* June 1983, 45 and "Sally's Joy Ride into the Sky," *Time,* 13 June 1983, 56.

3 "Men are Changing," *Newsweek,* January 16, 1978, 52–.61 and Harry F. Waters, Martin Kasindorf, and Betsy Carter, "Sex and TV," *Newsweek,* February 27, 1978, 54–63.

4 Kenneth J. Heineman, *The Reagan Revolution and the Rise of the New Right: A Reference Guide* (New York, Bloomsbury USA, 2001).

5 Foster, *Integrating Women into the Astronaut* Corps, 7.

6 Hersch, *Inventing the American Astronaut,* 142.

7 T.A. Heppenheimer, *Development of the Shuttle, 1972–1981* (Washington, DC: Smithsonian Institute Press, 2002), 387.

8 Hersch, *Inventing the American Astronaut,* 157.

9 Hersch, *Inventing the American Astronaut,* 157.

10 Kevles, *Almost Heaven,* 56. See also, James Spiller, "Nostalgia for the Right Stuff: Astronauts and Public Anxiety about a Changing Nation," in *Spacefarers: Images of Astronauts and Cosmonauts in the Heroic Era of Spaceflight,* ed. Michael Neufeld (Washington, DC: Smithsonian Institution Scholarly Press, 2013), 61.

11 For a look into the personal and professional life of Ride by a space reporter—and close friend—see Lynn Sherr's *Sally Ride: America's First Woman in Space* (New York: Simon and Schuster Paperbacks, 2014).

12 Odom, "Introduction: Exploring NASA in the Long Civil Rights Movement," 3.

13 Congress, House, *Qualifications for Astronauts: Subcommittee Hearings,* 7.

14 Kathryn D. Sullivan, interview by Jennifer Ross-Nazzal, NASA Headquarters History Office, Johnson Space Center, May 10, 2007, 32, accessed October 22, 2022, https://historycollection.jsc.nasa.gov/JSCHistoryPortal/history/oral_histories/SullivanKD/SullivanKD_5-10-07.pdf.

15 Ellen Hale, Gamnnett News Service, "Today's Astronauts are a New Breed," *Poughkeepsie Journal* (Poughkeepsie, New York), April 6, 1981, 1, 6, 6.

16 The idea of gender as an artificial gender construct is taken from Merryman's *Clipped Wings,* 168.

17 "Von Braun and Colleagues Designing Space Shuttle," *Washington Post,* July 25, 1969, A13

18 Thomas O'Toole, *Washington Post,* "Careers, Wealth Sacrificed For Lure Of Space: An Old Fever Burns in New Generation of Astronauts," *Los Angeles Times,* September 3, 1982, 93.

19 "The Statement by President Nixon, 5 January 1972," The National Aeronautics and Space Administration, accessed October 12, 2023, http://history.nasa.gov/sts-nixon.htm. Parts of the speech also appear in Hersch, *Inventing the American Astronaut,* 144.

20 George M. Low, NASA Deputy Administrator, memorandum for the record, on Center Directors' meeting, Peaks of Otter Lodge, September 11–12, 1972, found in Atkinson Jr. and Shafritz, *The Real Stuff,* 138. Hersch, *Inventing the American Astronaut,*

155. James C. Fletcher became NASA administrator on April 27, 1971, to May 1, 1977.

21 NASA Press Release 72–163, "Bathroom Commode Design For Space Shuttle Passengers," August 16, 1972, 1, Folder 008994, NASA Historical Reference Collection, NASA Headquarters, Washington, DC.

22 Atkinson Jr. and Shafritz, *The Real Stuff*, 143. Also quoted in Heppenheimer, *Development of the Space Shuttle*, 388.

23 Vincent Canby, *New York Times* News Service, "The movie that has 'The Right Stuff'; Film History of U.S. Mercury Program Scheduled to Open Nationwide Today," *Daily Press* (Victorville, California), October 21, 1983, 21.

24 Paul Delaney, "Top Black Woman is Ousted by NASA," *New York Times*, October 28, 1973.

25 Carl Hiaasen, "Fired, Hired, Still Speaking," *Florida Today* (Cocoa Beach, Florida), August 21, 1974, 10 and Associated Press, "Ruth Bates Harris gets new NASA Job," *Anniston Star* (Anniston, Alabama), August 18, 1974, 6.

26 Hiaasen, "Fired, Hired, Still Speaking," 10.

27 Washington Associated Press, "Ruth Bates Harris," 6.

28 Constance Holden, "NASA: Sacking of Top Black Woman Stirs Concern for Equal Employment," *Science* 182, no. 4114 (November 23, 1973): 804–805, 805.

29 The Associated Press, "NASA Commits an Outrage: Add 'Ruth Bates Harris' to Misfired List," *Dayton Daily News* (Dayton, Ohio), January 2, 1974, 29; Hiaasen, "Fired, Hired, Still Speaking," 10.

30 "Fired Woman Receives New Post at NASA," *Pittsburgh Courier*, September 7, 1974, 13.

31 "Oceola (Ocie) Hall—NASA's Federal Women's Program Coordinator," Marshall Spaceflight Center, The National Aeronautics and Space Administration, accessed October 4, 2022, https://www.nasa.gov/centers/marshall/history/oceola-ocie-hall -nasa-s-federal-women-s-program-coordinator.html. See also, "NASA Officials," *Louisiana Weekly* (New Orleans, Louisiana), November 30, 1974, 12.

32 Lora Mackie, Media General News Service, "One Giant Step for Womankind Is Aim of NASA Coordinator," *Times Dispatch* (Richmond, Virginia), August 4, 1974, 92.

33 Jaclyn Dalrymple, "Minority Involvement in Politics is Urged," *Tampa Tribune*, December 29, 1974, 30.

34 Mackie, "One Giant Step for Womankind," 92.

35 Hersch, *Inventing the American Astronaut*, 154.

36 Olive Talley, United Press International, "Women Astronauts get their Place in Space," *Indianapolis News*, June 8, 1983, 24.

37 "Title IX and Sex Discrimination," Office for Civil Rights, The United States Department of Education, accessed October 12, 2023, https://www2.ed.gov/about /offices/list/ocr/docs/tix_dis.html.

38 Robert Reinhold, "Behind Each Astronaut Stand the 'Other' Women of NASA," *New York Times*, August 28, 1983, 20. See also, Foster, *Integrating Women into the Astronaut Corps*, 17.

39 Robert C. Toth, *Los Angeles Times*, "Female Pilots are High Fliers Altering the Wild Blue Yonder," *Harford Courant* (Hartford, Connecticut), October 6, 1981, 48.

40 Warren Weaver Jr., "National Guidelines Set by 7-to-2 Vote," *New York Times*, January 23, 1973.

41 Hersch *Inventing the American Astronaut* 156.

42 Sherr, *Sally Ride*, 102–103.

## WHAT MADE SALLY TO RIDE?

43 Heppenheimer, *Development of the Space Shuttle*, 389.

44 "Lt. Uhura finds a new 'enterprise,'" *Orlando Sentinel*, May 4, 1977, 17.

45 Dick Keliner, Hollywood NEA, "Actress Space Fan After Trek," *Indianapolis Star*, December 11, 1977, 185.

46 Alice Jackson, "Nichelle Nichols (Lt. Uhura) wants to make science of Star Trek Reality," *Sun Herald* (Biloxi, Mississippi), June 4, 1977, 1, A12, 1, and Virginia Rankin, "Star Trek's Lt. Uhura Plans Future in Space," *Corvallis Gazette-Times* (Corvallis, Oregon), March 12, 1977, 2. Women in Motion, Inc. made educational and motivational films to encourage students in STEM.

47 "Lt. Uhura finds," 17.

48 Sullivan, interview, 47.

49 "Lt. Uhura finds," 17.

50 Ellen Norman, "'Star Trek' Star Recruits Women for NASA Program," *Peninsula Times Tribune* (Palo Alto, California), June 22, 1977, 27.

51 Al Rossiter, United Press International, "Actress is Shadowed by 'Star Trek' Character," *Bangor Daily News* (Bangor, Maine), April 9, 1977, 52. Another version of the UPI's article can be found credited to Al Rossiter, United Press International, "Life Changed 'Holds' Nichelle," *El-Paso Herald Post*, March 12, 1977, 35.

52 Norman, "'Star Trek' Star Recruits," 27.

53 Foster, *Integrating Women into the Astronaut Corps*, 91. According to Ellen Norman of *Peninsula Times Tribune*, of that 1,500 number, fewer than 70 applicants were women and fewer than 30 minorities. See, Norman, "'Star Trek' Star Recruits," 27.

54 Hersch, *Inventing the American Astronaut*, 156.

55 Salatheia Bryant, "A Diligent Advocate for Diversity at the Johnson Space Center, Joseph D. Atkinson, Jr. dies in Houston at the age of 79," *Houston Chronicle*, November 6, 2005, accessed July 17, 2023, https://www.chron.com/news/houston-deaths /article/A-diligent-advocate-for-diversity-at-the-Johnson-1915030.php. See also Heppenheimer, *Development of the Shuttle*, 387.

56 "President Ford Applauds Awardees," *Hill Top Times*, October 13, 2022, December 6, 1974, 4. See also, Foster, *Integrating Women into the Astronaut Corps*, 100.

57 Carolyn L. Huntoon, interview by Rebecca Wright, NASA Headquarters History Office, Johnson Space Center, June 5, 2002, 12, accessed October 13, 2023, https://historycollection.jsc.nasa.gov/JSCHistoryPortal/history/oral_histories/ HuntoonCL/HuntoonCL_6-05-02.pdf.

58 Heppenheimer, *Development of the Space Shuttle*, 389

59 Carolyn L. Huntoon, interview by Jennifer Ross-Nazzel, NASA Headquarters History Office, Johnson Space Center, April 21, 2008, 2, accessed October 13, 2023, https://historycollection.jsc.nasa.gov/JSCHistoryPortal/history/oral_histories/ HuntoonCL/HuntoonCL_4-21-08.pdf.

60 Huntoon, interview, 3.

61 Richard Lyons, "35 Chosen Astronaut Candidates; Six are Women and 3 Blacks," *New York Times*, January 17, 1978, 14.

62 Bruce Nichols, United Press International, "New Astronauts Welcomed," *Daily News Journal* (Murfreesboro, Tennessee), February 2, 1978, 10.

63 Mike Mullane, *Riding Rockets: The Outrageous Tales of a Space Shuttle Astronaut* (New York: Scribner, 2006), 29.

64 Lyons, "35 Chosen Astronaut Candidates," Six are Women and 3 Blacks," 14.

65 Anna Fisher, interview by Jennifer Ross-Nazzal, NASA Headquarters History Office, Johnson Space Center, 17 February 2009, 1, accessed February 17, 2023, https://historycollection.jsc.nasa.gov/JSCHistoryPortal/history/oral_histories/FisherAL/FisherAL_2-17-09.pdf.

66 Jeanne Forbis, "Space Spirited: For this Pioneering Sooner, the Quest for Flight Discovery began a Long Time Ago," *Tulsa World*, September 21, 1980, 77.

67 James Hoffman and Mathew Tekulsky, "Adventurers in Space: Six Extraordinary Women Look to the Stars and see their Futures," *Pensacola News Journal*, March 19, 1978, 197.

68 Sherr, *Sally's Ride*, 9–10.

69 Sullivan, interview, 1.

70 Rhea Seddon, interview by Jennifer Ross-Nazzal, NASA Headquarters History Office, Johnson Space Center, May 20, 2010, 4–5, accessed October 12, 2023, https://historycollection.jsc.nasa.gov/JSCHistoryPortal/history/oral_histories/SeddonMR/SeddonMR_5-20-10.pdf.

71 Mike Murphy, Yakima-Herald Republic, "Woman Sees Dream of Becoming an Astronaut Come True," *Columbian* (Vancouver, Washington), July 7, 1980, 10.

72 Sally Ride entered astronaut candidate training directly after finishing her PhD.

73 Paul Recer, Associated Press, "Wings of Change will Carry First US Woman into Space," *Fort Worth Star-Telegram*, June 12, 1983, 15A.

74 Paul Recer, Associated Press, "Next In Line: 7 Women Waiting For Turn Aboard Shuttle," *Anderson Independent-Mail* (Anderson, South Carolina), June 22, 1983, 4B.

75 Foster, *Integrating Women into the Astronaut Corps*, 18.

76 Kevels, *Almost Heaven*, 67–68.

77 Pat Rowe, "Into Space: Pat Rowe meets America's Women Astronauts in Training at the Houston Center," *Guardian* (London, Greater London, United Kingdom), February 1, 1979, 13.

78 Foster, *Integrating Women into the Astronaut Corps*, 18.

79 Fisher, interview, 1–3. See also, David J. Shayler and Colin Burgess, *NASA's First Space Shuttle Astronaut Selection: Redefining the Right Stuff* (Chichester: Springer-Praxis, 2020), 105.

80 Seddon, interview, 5, 7, 6, and 42.

81 Kevles, *Almost Heaven*, 96.

82 Society for Women Engineers' Magazine (SWE), "Judith Resnik's Living Legacy," Winter 2021, https://alltogether.swe.org/2021/01/judith-resniks-living-legacy/.

83 The book does not go into detail about Ride's sexuality since she was not open at NASA. "Open" is probably not the correct word if we contextualize Sally's romantic relationships—all men—during her time at NASA. I will also not label Ride's sexuality in the book. Like gender, sexuality in Ride's case was on a spectrum.

84 Sherr, *Sally Ride*, 32–42.

85 Sally K. Ride, interview by Rebecca Wright, NASA Headquarters History Office, Johnson Space Center, 22 October 2002, 8–9, 12, accessed October 20, 2022, https://historycollection.jsc.nasa.gov/JSCHistoryPortal/history/oral_histories/RideSK/RideSK_10-22-02.pdf.

86 Sherr, *Sally Ride*, 128–129, 135.

87 Sullivan, interview, 21–23.

88 Ride, interview, 5.

89 Reinhold, "Behind Each Astronaut," 20.

90 Ride, interview, 9.

91 Fisher, interview, 23, 20.

92 Huntoon, interview, 13–14.

93 "New Breed of Astronauts," *Florida Today*, January 18, 1978, 6A.

94 Reinhold, "Behind Each Astronaut," 20.

95 Harriet Van Horne, "A Long Way, Baby: The Sky is No Limit for Today's Woman," *Philadelphia Inquirer* February 2, 1978, 7-A.

96 Merryman, *Clipped Wings*, 156.

97 Jennifer Ross-Nazzal, "You've Come a Long Way, Maybe: The First Six Women Astronauts and the Media," in *Spacefarers: Images of Astronauts and Cosmonauts in the Heroic Era of Spaceflight*, ed. Michael J. Neufeld (Washington, DC: Smithsonian Institution Scholarly Press, 2013), 182. Find the pages of chapter.

98 "New Breed," 6A.

99 Sharon Herbaugh, Associated Press, "Women Astronauts see Future beyond Clouds," *Herald and Review* (Decatur, Illinois), April 10, 1980, 19.

100 Sullivan, interview, 48, 50.

101 Sullivan, interview, 36.

102 Kevles, *Almost Heaven*, 105. Kevels notes that citizen astronaut Christa McAuliffe referred to herself as "extraordinarily ordinary."

103 Carole Agus, "Nothing Flighty about this Lady," *Victoria Advocate* (Victoria, Texas), December 27, 1982, 18.

104 Wright, *Texas Monthly*, "Tribulations and Elations," 15.

105 Sharon Herbaugh, Associated Press, "First Women Astronauts Aim High," *Honolulu Star Bulletin*, March 19, 1980, 28.

106 "New Breed of Astronauts," *Athol Daily News* (Athol, Massachusetts), July 14, 1978, 4.

107 "Women, Blacks Join Astronaut Corps," *Science News*, January 21, 1978, 36.

108 Ann Kent, "Look!: For America's Women Astronauts it's a Space Countdown," *Sydney Morning Herald* (Sydney, Australia), September 7, 1978, 14.

109 Lyons, "35 Chosen Astronaut," 14.

110 Fisher, interview, 16.

111 Mary L. Cleave, interview by Rebecca Wright, NASA Headquarters History Office, Johnson Space Center, March 5, 2002, 8, accessed July 19, 2023, https://historycollection.jsc.nasa.gov/JSCHistoryPortal/history/oral_histories/CleaveML/CleaveML_3-5-02.htm.

112 Lyons, "35 Chosen Astronaut," 14.

113 Herbaugh, Associated Press, "Women Astronauts see Future," 19.

114 Thomas O'Toole, *Washington Post Service*, "Space Shuttle gets set to Launch a New Generation of Astronauts," *Tampa Times*, January 1, 1981, 14.

115 Fisher, interview, 32.

116 Cleave, interview, 7.

117 Edwina Rankin, "CMU Grad Is Ready For Liftoff," *Pittsburgh Press*, December 7, 1978, 21.

118 Janis Williams, "Making Way for the Ladies in Space," *Saturday Evening Post*, September 1982, 42–45, 108, 44, 45.

119 "Sally Ride: Ready for Liftoff," *Newsweek*, June 13, 1983, 38.

120 Thomas O'Toole, *Washington Post*, "Space Claims a New Breed," *Sun* (Biloxi, Mississippi), September 4, 1980, C-4.

121 "Sally's Joy Ride," 56.

122 Hale, "Today's Astronauts are a New Breed," 6; See also, O'Tool, "Space Claims New Breed," C-4 and Fisher, interview, 16–17.

123 Hale, "Today's Astronauts are a New Breed," 6.

124 Hale, "Today's Astronauts are a New Breed," 6.

125 Bob Greene, "Women Ride Wave of Sally's Heroism," *Chicago Tribune*, June 21, 1983, 49.

126 Mullane, *Riding Rockets*, 29, 30, 29.

127 Sherr, *Sally Ride*, 118.

128 O'Toole, "Space Claims a New Breed," C-4.

129 Kevles, *Almost Heaven*, 71.

130 Paul Recer, Associated Press, "Seven More Women Waiting for Ride into Space," *Anniston Star* (Anniston, Alabama), June 21, 1983, 8B.

131 Lynn Simross, *Los Angeles Times*, "An Astronaut or a Multi-role Model? 1st Black Woman in Space Corps Surprised at New Image," *Philadelphia Inquirer*, August 9, 1987, 9.

132 Mullane, *Riding Rockets*, 30.

133 "In Space to Stay," *Newsweek*, April 27, 1981, 28.

134 "No Joy Riding Allowed," *Newsweek*, June 13, 1983, 40.

135 Wilford, "Shuttle Rockets to Orbit," 1.

136 Ride, interview, 9–10.

137 Mike Toner, "Shuttle Crew has a Day of Leisure Before the Challenge," *Miami Herald*, June 17, 1983, 18A.

138 Sherr, *Sally Ride*, 108.

139 Hale, "Today's Astronauts are a New Breed," 6.

140 Agus, "Nothing Flighty about this Lady," 18.

141 Mullan, *Riding Rockets*, 33–34. The shuttle astronauts did have parachutes.

142 O'Hara, interview, 20.

143 The United Press International, "Foul-up aborts Discovery's launch," *Birmingham Post-Herald* (Birmingham, Alabama), June 27, 1984, 12.

144 Chet Lunner, "Challenger starts, stalls: engine valve halts liftoff at 3 seconds," *Florida Today*, July 13, 1985, 1, 3. See also, United Press International, "Space Shuttle Flight Aborted: Challengers Computers Command Engines to Shut Down," *York Dispatch* (York, Pennsylvania), July 13, 1985, 1.

145 Veronica T. Jennings, "Expectations Rose Higher than Shuttle," *Florida Today*, July 13, 1985, 3.

146 The Associated Press, "A Tyranny of Perfection: Committee of Computers does its Job on Shuttle," *Tyler Morning Telegraph* (Tyler, Texas), July 13, 1985, 2.

147 William J. Broad, "The Shuttle Explodes; 6 In Crew and High-School Teacher Killed 74 Seconds After Liftoff; Thousands Watch a Rain of Debris," *New York Times*, January 29, 1986, 1, A5.

148 Ross-Nazzal, "You've Come a Long Way, Maybe," 175–176.

149 United Press International, "Soviets Invent New Male Bastion—Then Breach it," *Hartford Currant* (Hartford, Connecticut), August 21, 1982, 7.

150 The United Press International, "Female Cosmonaut is Praised," *St. Louis Post-Dispatch*, August 29, 1982, 37.

151 The Associated Press, "Soviets Launch Second Female in Space," *Tampa Tribune*, August 29, 1982, 13.

152 "Soviet Pilot, 34, Becomes Second Woman in Space," *New York Times*, August 20, 1982, A001.

# WHAT MADE SALLY TO RIDE?

153 John F. Burns, "An Apron For Soviet Woman in Space," *New York Times*, August 29, 1982, 3. See also, The Associated Press, "Female Cosmonaut Finds Chauvinism in Space," *Montgomery Advertiser* (Montgomery, Alabama), August 22, 1982, 9.

154 The United Press International, "Reports on Female Cosmonaut Smack of Sexism," *St. Louis Post-Dispatch*, August 29, 1982, 37.

155 The Associated Press, "Female Cosmonaut Finds Chauvinism," 9.

156 Burns, "An Apron for Soviet Woman," 3. See also, Kirsten O. Lundberg, United Press International, "Women's Liberation Different in the Soviet Union," *Spokane Chronicle* (Spokane, Washington), August 28, 1982, 9.

157 Lundberg, "Women's Liberation Different," 9. See also, United Press International, "Reports on Female Cosmonaut," 37 and United Press International, "Soviets Invent New Male Bastion," 7.

158 *New York Times* News Services, "Soviet Spacewoman Hailed, but Feminine Stereotypes Remain," *Wisconsin State Journal* (Madison, Wisconsin), September 1, 1982, 25.

159 The United Press International, "Soviets Invent New Male Bastion," 7.

160 Lundberg, "Women's Liberation Different," 9.

161 The Associated Press, "Here's the Kitchen, Cosmonette," *Daily Tribune* (Wisconsin Rapids, Wisconsin), August 23, 1982, 7.

162 Lundberg, "Women's Liberation Different," 9.

163 Talley, United Press International, "Women Astronauts," 24.

164 Sullivan, interview, 39, 37, 41.

165 Huntoon, interview, 11.

166 Huntoon, interview, 13.

167 Seddon, interview, 56, 58.

168 Fisher, interview, 10.

169 Sullivan, interview, 37.

170 Bart Hart, "The Glamornauts: America's Eye-popping Space Gals are Really Flying High," *Globe*, March 18, 1980, 176.

171 Kent, "Look!," 14.

172 John Knight, "A Date in Space? But what on Earth will a Girl Wear?" *Sunday Mirror* (London, United Kingdom), October 8, 1978, 33.

173 Pat Casey Daley, "Astro-Doctor: Rhea Seddon—Down to Earth but Counting," *Tennessean* (Nashville, Tennessee), September 9, 1984, 35.

174 Ride, interview, 35–36.

175 Fisher, interview, 22.

176 Ride, interview, 35–36.

177 Sullivan, interview, 40.

178 Mary Voboril, "Ride Keeps Cool about Breaking a Gender Barrier," *Miami Herald*, June 17, 1983, 18A.

179 Fisher, interview, 8.

180 The Associated Press, "Sally Kristen Ride: First American Woman to Fly into Space," *Santa Cruz Sentinel* (Santa Cruz, California), June 12, 1983, 42. See also, Leary, "Sally K. Ride," A01.

181 Ron Laytner and Donald MacLachlin, freelance reporters, "Sally Ride Finds Hassles Part of Spaceflight," *Star-Phoenix* (Saskatoon, Saskatchewan, Canada), August 20, 1983, 58.

182 Voboril, "Ride Keeps Cool," 18A.

183 Voboril, "Ride Keeps Cool," 18A.

184 William J. Broad, "Woman in the News; Cool, Versatile Astronaut: Sally Kristen Ride," *New York Times*, June 19, 1983.

185 Rusty Brown, "As No. 2; Resnik is just one of the Crew," *Telegraph Forum* (Bucryus, Ohio), July 19, 1984, 6.

186 Recer, The Associated Press Aerospace Writer, "Seven More Women Waiting," 8B.

187 Vivian Vahlberg, "State's Astronaut Highly Visible," *Daily Oklahoman* (Oklahoma City, Oklahoma), January 17, 1978, 15.

188 *People Weekly*, "NASA Picks Six Women Astronauts with the Message: You're Going a Long Way Baby," February 6, 1978.

189 Cartoon, *Orlando Sentinel*, February 13, 1978, 31.

190 Valerie Neil, *Spaceflight in the Shuttle Era and Beyond: Redefining Humanity's Purpose in Space* (New Haven: Yale University Press, 2017), Chapter 3, footnote 24.

191 Sherr, *Sally Ride*, 118.

192 Wright, *Texas Monthly*, "Tribulations and Elations," 15.

193 Seddon, interview, 12.

194 Knight, "A Date in Space," 33.

195 Judy Klemsrud, "A Marriage that was Made for the Heavens," *New York Times*, June 3, 1980, B12. The couple welcomed their first baby, a girl, shortly after Ride's flight. See "Astronauts Have New Daughter," *Miami Herald*, August 11, 1983, 2A.

196 Fisher, interview, 9.

197 Williams, "Making Way for the Ladies," 45.

198 Klemsrud, "A Marriage that was Made," B12.

199 Mary Voboril, "Astronaut Says Women Can do it all," *Miami Herald*, May 25, 1983, 1A.

200 Sherr, 169.

201 Kent, "Look!" 14.

202 Fisher, interview, 9, 34.

203 "Anna Fisher to become First Mother to Travel into Space," *Belleville News-Democrat* (Belleville, Illinois), November 5, 1984, 5.

204 "In NASA training, she carried a Stowaway," *Newsday, Suffolk Edition*, (Melville, New York), October 26, 1984, 9.

205 The Associated Press, "Shuttle Closing in On Errant Satellite; Spacewalk May Lead to Rescue," *Intelligencer Journal* (Lancaster, Pennsylvania), November 12, 1984, 1.

206 Joseph Allen, *Entering Space: An Astronaut's Odyssey* (New York: Stewart, Tabori and Chang, 1984), 21, 31.

207 Mike Leary, "Challenger Launches 2D Satellite—Shuttle's Crew has a 'Super Day,'" *Philadelphia Inquirer*, June 20, 1983, A01.

208 Leary, "Challenger Launches," A01 and Leary, "Sally K. Ride," A01.

209 *Space World*, June/July 1983, Front Cover.

210 Sullivan, interview, 50.

# CONCLUSION: TO INFINITY AND BEYOND

In September 1989, Billy Joel's lyrics "Wheel of Fortune, Sally Ride, Heavy Metal Suicide" blasted through stereos across the United States.[1] The lyrics were from his pop hit "We Didn't Start the Fire."[2] The song represented Joel's passion for history and societal angst within progressive and destructive Cold War events. Ride made the cut along with *Sputnik*, space monkey and John Glenn. Astronaut Mullane joked with Joel about why Mullane was not chosen for the song. Perhaps there was a little jealousy. Ride had always stayed clear of Mullane and his self-professed sexist jokes. The two mission specialist astronauts were opposites. Mullane grew up in a culture that viewed women strictly as passive, sex objects. He epitomized early Cold War masculinity, being hardened by combat in Vietnam and his belief that women were undeserving of the astronaut title for their lack of combat experience. Ride was new to him—and the world. She was a feminist with a sticker on her office wall that read "A woman's place is in the cockpit." Mullane's pilot astronaut friend remarked to Ride, "A woman *is* a COCKPIT."[3] Aviation and aerospace history acted as artifacts for social change, both progressive and regressive. The private discourse within the astronaut corps at times mirrored that within the public discourse as the shuttle introduced conventional masculinity to the women's rights movement.

Early aviation pioneers viewed the airplane as a tool for social change. A man who conquered the sky could surely rid the world of inequalities and inhumanity. History is wrought with uncomfortable lessons, and the plane became a weapon for war and the continuation of social and gender norms. Rotating turrets and dogfights weaponized the airplane during World War I. Segregation laws banned people of color from earning pilot's licenses. Airline companies used female images as sky hostesses to sell the safety of flight.[4] Conventional masculinity took to the skies to destroy the Axis powers and brought an arsenal of democratic capitalism to the Western world. The pilot as protector again shaped aviation technology and flight—certainly the cockpit—along accepted gender norms as the government refused to militarize

238 GENDER AND THE RACE FOR SPACE

the WASPs. The WASPs' disbandment and continued racial inequalities at the end of the war secured conventional masculinity as provider and protector over the cockpit.

The Cold War strengthened conventional roles—equating gender norms of masculinity and femininity as necessary for national security. Technological change threatened to tear down gender roles with the rise of automation, armies of corporate organization men and feminists that softened masculinity. Outside the home, intercontinental ballistic missiles soared into the heavens, creating a quasi-push-button war in space that challenged masculine control over technology and combat. A perceived masculinity crisis took hold across the country, and Americans looked for a reinvigorated masculine image for the space age.

NASA presented a solution. Space needed an explorer to capture the American imagination and funding. President Eisenhower chose jet test pilots as astronauts for practical reasons and effectively shut the door to women on this new dangerous space adventure. The American spacecraft provided another opportunity for social change. If man could conquer space, surely man could conquer social ills that plagued the Cold War landscape. While the American space program appeared outwardly democratic, with thousands of opportunities for all Americans to take part in this great scientific adventure for all mankind, the spacecraft cockpit was a limited space, only available to those with the right stuff. The white male astronaut railed against the perceived Cold War masculinity crisis' automation fear as the public discourse highlighted pilot astronaut control over the spacecraft while demeaning the Soviet cosmonaut as a feminized passenger.

Women were left out of controlling spacecraft technology and instead pioneered on the ground, creating and controlling technology as computers, mathematicians, engineers and scientists. The women remained hidden figures in the public discourse as the white male astronaut became the face of NASA and spaceflight. The space race public discourse developed a conventional gender role narrative as the white male astronauts controlled their spacecraft technology and their wives remained at home with automatic domestic appliances to liberate them from household drudgeries. In the private discourse, the astronaut wives took on dual gender roles as both mother and father. In the public discourse, women pilots fought against conventional gender roles, forcing the public discourse to discuss sex discrimination in the astronaut corps.

The FLATs wanted to contribute to national security needs—a conventional masculine space—but were denied entrance into the astronaut corps based on the military's ban on women pilots. The FLATs did not make the traditional argument that spaceflight would make them better wives or mothers. Instead, they paved the way for a new public discourse narrative that

# CONCLUSION

focused on women as having an equal contribution to make, especially to national security.

Famed pilot Jackie Cochran preferred that women wait for the right moment for spaceflight. NASA and Cochran made arguments before Congress and the press that women's bodies and motherhood complicated spaceflight and proved too costly on a fixed budget. There was no national need for women's contributions, and NASA was at breakneck speed to beat the Soviets to the moon. While the Soviets sent a woman into space, the American public discourse responded that a woman in the craft was merely a publicity stunt that represented the lack of piloting skills in a Soviet craft. Creating a spacecraft suitable for American women would only slow the program down and weaken the American resolve to reach the moon. Finally, a woman in the cockpit represented the routinization of spaceflight technology, which was at odds with the public narrative of astronaut control over spaceflight and a reinvigoration of American masculinity at home and abroad. Cochran told the FLATs to exercise their feminine virtue of patience for space to be conquered and space travel to be safe for their chance to fly.

Scientists and engineers without piloting experience pushed for their chance at spaceflight and to be part of the astronaut image, effectively shifting who controlled spaceflight technology. Holding true to the conventional astronaut image, NASA required these new hyphenated scientist-astronauts to complete Air Force Undergraduate Pilot School upon entrance into the astronaut corps. The scientist-astronauts would get their chance to fly the spacecraft, unlike the Soviet scientist-cosmonauts, who remained passive with the technology. The scientist-astronaut presented an opening wedge for astronaut women.

However, NASA did not choose a woman in either of the two scientist-astronaut groups. NASA responded to reporters that none of the women applicants were qualified, despite that women with advanced degrees and research publications had applied. Doctors, engineers and astronauts told reporters that women's bodies, lack of physical strength and privacy barred women from the spacecraft. The scientist-astronaut requirement to pass Air Force Undergraduate Pilot training still effectively prevented women from joining the astronaut corps.

Even though NASA prevented women from joining this masculine space, masculinity and masculine performance with spaceflight technology acted as if on a spectrum. As NASA introduced more technology into the spacecraft, the astronauts gained more ability to control the craft by pushing buttons, making pushing buttons appear masculine. Likewise, increased automation and longer spaceflights demanded greater teamwork between astronauts and mission controllers. The public discourse's self-reliant, individualist astronaut shared the work of spaceflight with mission controllers and computers. The astronaut image shifted to democratic manhood, representing a new masculine image that fluctuated between individual self-reliance and teamwork as Apollo conquered the moon. The shifting astronaut images, the archetype of American manhood, could be renegotiated, demonstrating that masculinity was not inherently fixed.

NASA transitioned to a new space transportation system after claiming victory in the space race. The routinized shuttle became an orbiter of great social change as it created a home in space for working scientists, engineers and pilot astronauts. NASA considered women as both passengers and astronauts when they designed the shuttle. This decision came at a time when women secured the federal right to not be discriminated against in education and the workplace.

Doors opened but remained heavy for women's entrance into the hard sciences and even non-combat military pilot programs.[5] The Navy admitted eight women to their pilot training program in January 1973. The Navy's first female pilot candidate was Lieutenant Judith Anne Neuffer, a computer scientist and daughter of a World War II combat pilot.[6] She went on to become the first woman P-3 aircraft commander and the first woman to fly through a hurricane as part of the infamous Navy hurricane hunters.[7] She accepted danger and daring. Women like Neuffer exercised self-determination—conventional masculinity—as they entered all-male spaces to fulfill their dreams in STEM and piloting. In accordance with Title IX, NASA created an affirmative action program led by strong women to recruit women and minorities into the astronaut corps. NASA did not simply want a woman or person of color in the corps. NASA wanted to ensure they had done everything to secure the best minds in the country into the astronaut corps.

NASA's decision to choose six women astronauts in 1978's Group 8 introduced Americans and the world to women as skilled professionals working as equals with men. Americans and the world viewed this post-women's liberation change publicly through astronaut interviews and shuttle missions. The public discourse clamored for information relating to the astronaut women, not the men. Early Cold War white conventional masculinity—for a moment—appeared a past relic, nostalgic. White male astronauts had been replaced in the discourse. These men could have blamed reverse discrimination for their lack of attention—publicly or privately. Instead, training and working in the diverse astronaut corps environment led to their education about women's abilities that took place both in the private and public discourse. Astronaut women were not simply integrated into the astronaut corps. The Group 8 women's skill and the necessity for teamwork in space led to inclusivity within the astronaut corps and image.

CONCLUSION 241

The women's acceptance by their male colleagues was paramount to the women's success. The press widely quoted astronaut Dr. Mae Jemison rolling her eyes at the idea of being a role model. She knew Black female visibility did not rest on her shoulders alone. She told the press, "It's important not only for a little black girl growing up to know, yeah, you can become an astronaut because here's Mae Jemison [...]. But, it's important for older white males who sometimes make decisions on those careers of those little black girls."[8] Those with power in Cold War society—white males—benefited from listening to the plight of women and minorities and understanding their ability to contribute equally if change was to take place. Mullane acknowledges this transformation within him—realizing the privilege he had as a white male. He worked extremely hard and obtained the unimaginable with his own grit and skill, but he understood the opened doors and visibility the world presented to white males were often closed for others. The astronauts needed to work together as individuals in a teamwork environment for mission success and for the success of American gender and racial progress. Everyone was part of the equation.

The change was not perfect. The public discourse created a cognitive dissonance that held fast to conventional gender stereotypes, as early focus pertained to motherhood, makeup and menstruation. The Group 8 women fought back and presented femininity on their own terms—not fixed, but on a spectrum that depended on the individual. Women exercised conventional masculine traits and remained feminine. Feminine traits did not have to be defined by sex, societal norms or motherhood, but gender roles became individually defined by whatever made the person fully human. The Group 8 astronaut women's presence became less like "viewing animals at the zoo" and more normalized as "skilled specialists" with all the "sparkle and originality of a suburban coffee morning in Sticksville."[9]

Like NASA history, American society ebbed and flowed with the acceptance of changing conventional gender roles. Jemison became the first African American woman astronaut in 1987. Her need to defy both gender and racial cultural norms differed from the Group 8 women. On the heels of Title IX, 16-year-old Jemison entered Stanford in 1973. She knew she wanted to be a scientist since the age of nine.[10] Like the Group 8 women, she entered a career path in which women who looked like her remained hidden figures. Her parents encouraged her education. She was one of the few Black women on campus, let alone in her classes. She remembers professor bias against her as a chemical engineering student. Professors mocked or discarded her questions in class, "But when a white boy down the row would ask the very same question they'd say, 'astute observation.'"[11] It took great courage to stay in a department unwelcoming of her presence.

242 GENDER AND THE RACE FOR SPACE

Jemison double majored in chemical engineering and African American Studies. She embraced dance, demonstrating a multilayered feminine image—or individual image much like Sally Ride, Kathy Sullivan and Judith Resnik. Jemison's studies at Cornell University Medical School took her to Cuba, Thailand and a Cambodia refugee camp. Upon graduation, she entered the Peace Corps. Jemison embodied the explorer spirit like Sullivan and sought adventure and self-fulfillment in all-white male spaces with no role models. NASA chose Jemison for 1987's Astronaut Group 12, the first group selected after the *Challenger* accident. From September 12 to September 20, 1992, Jemison flew aboard *Endeavor* STS-47. The mission was a joint venture with Japan's space agency. Aboard the flight, Jemison induced four female frogs to test weightlessness on tadpoles.[12] She took a photograph of Bessie Coleman with her aboard the mission.[13]

Ellen Ochoa became the first Hispanic woman astronaut in 1990. Her father's parents were Mexican immigrants, and her mother was an Anglo American. She grew up in San Diego, California, the middle of five children. Her parents divorced when she was in middle school. Her mother encouraged education and modeled that by taking one college class per semester until she received her degree.

Ochoa had an interest in electrical engineering when she entered San Diego State University. A professor in the department discouraged her, saying, "Well, we did have a woman come through here once, but it's a really difficult course of study and I just don't know that you'd be interested." The physics department proved more welcoming. Fellow Stanford physics alum, Ride, became the first American woman in space while Ochoa was working on her doctorate in physics at Stanford. Franklin Chang-Diaz flew three years later. Ochoa felt she, "really needed to see those kinds of comparisons for me to think about it."[14]

NASA chose Ochoa as part of Astronaut Group 13, "The Hairballs" and she faced similar bias in the private discourse that the Group 8 women faced. She had to prove herself, probably in a way that most white men did not. Like the Group 8 women, Ochoa received her pilot's license as she recognized the extra knowledge and skillset were beneficial to flying aboard the shuttle orbiter. She remembered that the "other astronauts" wanted "people who can make decisions on the fly and operate in high-stress and high-visibility environments."[15] It was assumed the male astronauts had these qualities, but the women had to prove they could operate successfully. Despite inclusion in previous spaceflight missions, new male astronauts coming into the corps had probably never worked with women—or flown with women.

One of Ochoa's Group 13 teammates was the first American woman pilot astronaut, Eileen Collins. Collins grew up in a toxic household. Her father's

CONCLUSION                                                                 243

alcoholism and abandonment led to her mother's institutionalization. Collins was often the parent at home to her younger siblings. She decided she did not want her parents' life. Collins took control of her own life and charted her own course like the astronaut women before her. These were conventionally masculine attributes, but as time progressed, they became normalized for women.

Nine-year-old Collins made the decision in 1965 that she wanted to be a military pilot and astronaut—again, with no role models. She worked extremely hard, always having to be better than the men. She graduated from the United States Air Force Undergraduate Pilot School in 1979 and became a T-38 instructor pilot until 1982. Knowing that flying different platforms was necessary for astronaut credentials, she segued to the C-141 Starlifter as a commander and instructor pilot. Collins knew the C-141 would be useful on an astronaut application since it had a similar mixed crew team of pilots and non-pilots aboard to perform the mission, much like the shuttle. The military still banned women in aerial combat, but Collins did fly troops from California during the United States invasion of Grenada.[16]

Collins earned her master's degree in operations research and a second in space systems management. She worked as an assistant professor of mathematics and T-41 instructor pilot for the United States Air Force Academy. She then went on to become one of the first women test pilots at Edwards. In 1993, the military removed their ban on women in aerial combat despite arguments from conservatives pertaining to marriage and motherhood. Like Sally Ride's friend Gloria Steinem, Amelia Earhart, Jackie Cochran, the WASPs, Dr. Nancy Roman, Dottie Lee, the FLATs, Katherine Johnson, Betty Friedan, Poppy Northcutt, Ruth Bates Harris, Nichelle Nichols, Carolyn Huntoon, the Group 8 women and thousands of other successful feminists, pilots and STEM women paved and pioneered the path for Collins. Collins understood this on February 3, 1995, as she sat in *Discovery*'s cockpit for three hours waiting for STS-63's liftoff. She did not only have an eighty-pound pressure suit strapped to her back, but she also had the future of women as pilots, jet pilots and astronauts on her shoulders.[17]

STS-63's mission was to rendezvous with the Russian Space Station, Mir, and pick up Russian cosmonaut Vladimir Titov. The Cold War had ended, and a woman sat at the orbiter's controls, ready to pick up an early Cold War rival. NASA invited the WASPs and the FLATs to watch the launch.[18] While taking deep breaths, Collins repeated the Astronaut's Prayer: "Dear God, please don't let me screw up!"[19] She did not. Collins controlled aerospace technology as a pilot. FLAT Wally Funk summed up the importance of Collins' flight: "We've got a girl in the left seat and that is just absolutely

**Figure 7.1** Astronaut Eileen Collins in the pilot's station aboard STS-63. Source: NASA. https://www.nasa.gov/image-article/feb-3-1995-astronaut-eileen-collins-pilots-station-shuttle-discovery/.

incredible. And this is going to show youngsters and young ladies […] that you can do anything you want with your life."[20]

Visibility within the space race narrative mattered. However, like most women's gains in history, their inclusion was far from perfect. This continued complexity and national discussions over gender and sex roles demonstrate women's rights and gender rights as part of Hall's long civil rights era. Sexism continued within aviation and aerospace fields. The public discourse today congratulates women's breakthroughs, whether it be an all-female flyover at Super Bowl LVII or NASA's proposed *Artemis* all-female moon landing.[21] However, social media has added another layer to the public discourse. People around the world can comment their opinions on platforms openly or in complete anonymity. This new public discourse platform differs from Cold War editorials, as content and language are not edited or rejected for publication. While I champion free speech, the toxic comments continue to create a cacophony of public opinions that reinforce sexism and racism as still alive and well.

Conventional narratives, along with racial, sexist and gendered rhetoric, were a focal point in the 2024 United States presidential election. Vice President J. D. Vance depicted women working outside the home as unfulfilled "childless cat ladies."[22] Renewed voices wanting to remove women from

# CONCLUSION

military combat have reentered the public discourse. The main argument once again for taking women out of combat is that the standards for women combatants have been lowered and their presence does not contribute to an effecting fighting force, and they make things more "complicated."[23] These were the same arguments used to oppose the militarization of the WASPs, the same arguments to keep women out of the 1960s astronaut corps—and for a small few—the arguments against the shuttle astronaut women. Women and minorities in powerful positions are mockingly called "diversity, equity, and inclusion" hires in the press and by powerful politicians and business leaders.[24] The arguments are the same tokenism acceptable since Tereshkova's flight. Gender discussions, specifically centered on the military and combat, are a tale as old as time. Discussions continue as to whether societal focus on female or minority firsts reinforces sexism or empowers marginalized groups. These public discussions also demonstrate that gender still matters, as challenging conventional masculine and feminine roles or viewing gender on a spectrum elicit a response, whether excitement or rage from the American public. Women and minorities, unfortunately, are used to this type of criticism and yet continue to push the edge of the envelope demonstrating themselves as not a quota to be filled but as human beings with real contributions to make.

## Notes

1  The quote is taken from the character Buzz Lightyear in the movie *Toy Story*, directed by John Lasseter, Pixar/Walt Disney Pictures, 1995.
2  Billy Joel, writer, "We Didn't Start the Fire," Track 2 on *Storm Front*, Columbia, 1989, record.
3  Mullane, *Riding Rockets*, 295, 41–42, 36, and 39.
4  Barry, *Femininity in Flight*, 36. "Glamour Girls of the Air: For the Lucky Ones Being Hostess is the Mostest," *Life*, August 25, 1953, 68–75.
5  Linda Charlton, Special to the *New York Times*, "Almost all the Noncombat Jobs in the Air Force Opened to Women," *New York Times*, November 23, 1972, 38.
6  Eric Pace, Special to the *New York Times*, "Navy Puts First Woman in Pilot Training," *New York Times*, January 11, 1973, 77. For more on the first women Navy aviators, see Beverly Weintraub, *Wings of Gold: The Story of the First Women Naval Aviators* (New York: Lyons Press, 2021).
7  Obituary for Judith Neuffer Bruner at Wm. Reese & Sons Mortuary, P.A., accessed on January 10, 2024, https://www.wmreeseandsons.com/obituary/judith-neuffer-bruner?lud=D3119E250801545D5C3AAA8943DF0AD6. See also, "Women with Wings: LT. Judith Anne Neuffer," *All Hands*, January 1975, 35.
8  Warren E. Leary, "Woman in the News; A Determined Breaker of Boundaries—Mae Carol Jemison," *New York Times*, September 13, 1992, 42.
9  "Into Space: Pat Rowe Meets America's Women Astronauts in Training at the Houston Center," *Guardian* (London, United Kingdom), February 1, 1979, 13.

10  Joyce Saenz Harris, *Dallas Morning News*, 29. "Trek to Stars a Bold Dream Come True," *Akron Beacon Journal* (Akron, Ohio), March 15, 1993, C5.
11  Tamar Lewin, "Bias Called Persistent Hurdle for Women in Sciences," *New York Times*, March 22, 2010, A14.
12  Marcia Dunn, The Associated Press, "Equality boosted by Launch; Shuttle will Carry First Black Woman," *Corpus Christi Caller-Times*, September 8, 1989, 4.
13  Christy Jones, "No Fear of Flying Here: 12 Women Aviators to Celebrate," American Association of University Women, August 19, 2014, accessed January 9, 2024, https://web.archive.org/web/20190509162202/https://www.aauw.org/2014/08/19/aviation-day/.
14  Jade Scipioni, "How Ellen Ochoa, the First Hispanic Woman in Space, Deals with 'People Who Didn't Think I Should be There,'" *CNBC*, September 21, 2021, accessed January 9, 2024, https://www.cnbc.com/2021/09/21/ellen-ochoa-first-hispanic-woman-in-space-on-challenges-leadership.html.
15  Scipioni, "How Ellen Ochoa."
16  Eileen M. Collins and Jonathan H. Ward, *Through the Glass Ceiling to the Stars: The Story of the First American Woman to Command a Space Mission* (New York: Arcade Publishing, 2021), 12, 18-20, 83, 79-81.
17  Collins and War, *Through the Glass Ceiling to the Stars*, 89, 96, 1, 6.
18  Ellen M. Hallerman, "WASPs fliers inspired Collins to make history," *Florida Today*, February 4, 1995, 4, and Marcia Dunn, The Associated Press, "After 34 years, the right stuff, Women astronauts ready in '61," *Arizona Republic* (Phoenix, Arizona), February 3, 1995, A1, A16.
19  Collins and Ward, *Through the Glass Ceiling to the Stars*, 2.
20  Wally Funk, interview by Carol Butler, NASA Headquarters History Office, Johnson Space Center, July 18, 1999, 3–4, accessed January 9, 2024, https://historycollection.jsc.nasa.gov/JSCHistoryPortal/history/oral_histories/NASA_HQ/Aviatrix/FunkW/WF_7-18-99.pdf.
21  Kanya Whitworth, Lissette Rodriguez, and Katie Kindelan, "All-female Super Bowl flyover team makes history," ABC News, February 20, 2023, https://abcnews.go.com/GMA/Living/female-super-bowl-flyover-team-speaks-making-history/story?id=96983944#:~:text=In%20a%20Super%20Bowl%20first,the%20flyover%20at%20Sunday's%20game.&text=For%20the%20first%20time%20ever,group%20of%20women%20made%20history and Samantha Kubota, "NASA wants to land Americans back on the moon. These women are making it happen; These leaders are behind NASA's massive Artemis program that's hoping to make even more ground-breaking lunar discoveries," *Today*, February 2, 2022, https://www.today.com/news/women-behind-nasa-trip-moon-rcna14509.
22  The use of the phrase "childless cat lady" was meant to be disparaging. Rachel Treisman, "JD Vance went viral for 'cat lady' comments. The centuries-old trope has a long tail," National Public Radio, July 29, 2024, https://www.npr.org/2024/07/29/nx-s1-5055616/jd-vance-childless-cat-lady-history .
23  Lolita C. Baldor, "Should women be allowed to fight on the front lines? Trump's defense pick reignites the debate," The Associated Press, November 18, 2024, https://apnews.com/article/military-women-defense-hegseth-combat-916d50a7b465ccfea1aeb13bb91064b3.
24  Susan Harmeling, "What Might It Mean When Critics Call Someone A DEI Hire?," *Forbes*, July 26, 2024, https://www.forbes.com/sites/susanharmeling/2024/07/26/what-might-it-mean-when-critics-call-someone-a-dei-hire/.

# BIBLIOGRAPHY

## Archives

Congressional and Political Research Center, University Archives, Mitchell Memorial Library, Mississippi State University.
John F. Kennedy Presidential Library and Museum, Boston, Massachusetts.
NASA Historical Reference Collection, NASA Headquarters, Washington, D.C.

## Primary Sources

"Adams, Abigail to John Adams, 31 March–5 April 1776." In *Adams Family Correspondence, Volume 1 and 2: December 1761–March 1778*, edited by L. H. Butterfield. Cambridge, M.A.: The Belknap Press of Harvard University Press, 1963.
Apollo 11 Lunar Surface Journal. "Apollo 11 Spacecraft Commentary, July 16–24, 1969." The National Aeronautics and Space Administration History Division. Accessed August 26, 2023. https://history.nasa.gov/alsj/a11/AS11_PAO.PDF.
"Apollo 17 Mission Report." NASA Headquarters History Office, Johnson Space Center, March 1973. Accessed December 7, 2023. https://history.nasa.gov/alsj/a17/A17_MissionReport.pdf.
Balke, Bruno and Ray W. Ware. "The Present Status of Physical Fitness in the Air Force." School of Aviation Medicine, ASF, Randolph Air Force Base, Defense Technical Information Center, May 1959. Accessed October 20, 2023. https://apps.dtic.mil/sti/pdfs/ADA036235.pdf.
Betson, M.D., Johnnie R., and Robert R. Secrest, M.D., "Prospective Women Astronauts Selection Program: Rationale and Comments." *American Journal of Obstetrics and Gynecology* 88 (February 1, 1964): 421–423.
Boreman, Frank. Interview by Catherine Harwood. NASA Headquarters History Office, Johnson Space Center, April 13, 1999. Accessed November 21, 2023. https://historycollection.jsc.nasa.gov/JSCHistoryPortal/history/oral_histories/BormanF/FFB_4-13-99.pdf.
Bowie, David, writer. "Space Oddity." Track 1 on *David Bowie*, Phillips, 1969, record.
Carl, Ann. *A WASP Among Eagles: A Woman Military Test Pilot in World War II*. Washington, D.C.: Smithsonian Books, 2010.
Carpenter, Scott M. et al. *We Seven*. New York: Simon and Schuster, 1962; January 2010 edition.
Cernan, Eugene and Don Davis. *Last Man on the Moon: Astronaut Gene Cernan and America's Race in Space*. New York: St. Martin's Press, 1999.

Cleave, Mary L. Interview by Rebecca Wright. NASA Headquarters History Office, Johnson Space Center, March 5, 2002. Accessed July 19, 2023. https://historycollection.jsc.nasa.gov/JSCHistoryPortal/history/oral_histories/CleaveML/CleaveML_3-5-02.htm.

Cobb, Jerrie and Jane Rieker. *Woman into Space: The Jerrie Cobb Story*. Englewood Cliffs, N.J.: Prentice-Hall International, Inc., 1963.

Cochran, Jacqueline and Maryann Bucknum Brinley. *Jackie Cochran: An Autobiography*. New York: Bantam Books, 1987.

Collins, Eileen M. and Jonathan H. Ward. *Through the Glass Ceiling to the Stars: The Story of the First American Woman to Command a Space Mission*. New York: Arcade Publishing, 2021.

Collins, Michael. *Carrying the Fire: An Astronaut's Journey's* with a forward by Charles A. Lindbergh. New York: Farrar, Straus, and Giroux, 1975, 4th ed., 2009.

Congress, House, Committee on Science and Astronautics. *Qualifications for Astronauts: Hearings before the Special Subcommittee on the Selection of Astronauts of the Committee on Science and Astronautics*, 87th Cong., 2d sess., July 17–18, 1962.

Cuordileone, K. A. "'Politics in an Age of Anxiety': Cold War Political Culture and the Crisis of American Masculinity, 1949–1960." *The Journal of American History* 87, no. 2 (September 2000): 515–545.

De Beauvoir, Simone. *The Second Sex*, edited by H. M. Parshley. New York: Vintage Books, 1989.

De Tocqueville, Alexander. *Democracy in America*. London: Saunders & Otley, 1840.

Diavolo, Lucy. "Career Advice from Poppy Northcutt—Activist, Lawyer, and NASA's First Female Engineer in Mission Control." *Teen Vogue*, July 10, 2019. https://www.teenvogue.com/story/career-advice-poppy-northcutt-activist-lawyer-nasa-first-female-engineer.

Faulkner, William. *Requiem for a Nun*. New York: Vintage International, reprint 2011.

Fisher, Anna. Interview by Jennifer Ross-Nazzal. NASA Headquarters History Office, Johnson Space Center, February 17, 2009. Accessed February 17, 2023. https://historycollection.jsc.nasa.gov/JSCHistoryPortal/history/oral_histories/FisherAL/FisherAL_2-17-09.pdf.

*The Fountainhead*. Directed by King Vidor, Warner Bros, 1949.

Friedan, Betty. *The Feminine Mystique*, Fiftieth anniversary ed. New York: W.W. Norton & Company, 2013.

Funk, Wally. Interview by Carol Butler. NASA Headquarters History Office, Johnson Space Center, July 18, 1999. Accessed January 9, 2024, https://historycollection.jsc.nasa.gov/JSCHistoryPortal/history/oral_histories/NASA_HQ/Aviatrix/FunkW/WF_7-18-99.pdf.

"Gemini VIII Voice Communications (Air-To-Ground, Ground-To-Air, and On-Board Transcription, MAC Control No. C-115471." History Collection, Mission Transcripts, Johnson Spaceflight Center, Accessed September 7, 2022. https://historycollection.jsc.nasa.gov/JSCHistoryPortal/history/mission_trans/GT08_TEC.PDF.

Hamilton, Margaret. Interview by David C. Brock. Computer History Museum, April 13, 2017. Accessed August 20, 2023. https://archive.computerhistory.org/resources/access/text/2022/03/102738243-05-01-acc.pdf.

Hammock, Jerome B. et al. "NASA Project Mercury Working Paper No. 192: Postlaunch Report for Mercury-Redston-3 (MR-3), June 16, 1961." NASA Johnson Space Center

# BIBLIOGRAPHY

Historical Collection. Accessed June 20, 2023. https://historycollection.jsc.nasa.gov/JSCHistoryPortal/history/mission_trans/MR03_TEC.PDF.

Horner, Richard. "Banquet Address before the First Annual Awards Banquet of the Society of Experimental Test Pilots." *SETP Quarterly Review* 2, no. 1 (Fall 1957): 1–10.

Huntoon, Carolyn L. Interview by Jennifer Ross-Nazzel. NASA Headquarters History Office, Johnson Space Center. April 21, 2008. Accessed October 13, 2023. https://historycollection.jsc.nasa.gov/JSCHistoryPortal/history/oral_histories/HuntoonCL/HuntoonCL_4-21-08.pdf.

Jefferson, Thomas. *Notes on the State of Virginia*, intro. Thomas Perkins Abernathy. New York: Harper Torch Books, 1964.

Joel, Billy, writer. "We didn't Start the Fire." Track 2 on *Storm Front*, Columbia, 1989, record.

Kennedy, John F. "Acceptance of Democratic Nomination for President, July 15, 1960." The John F. Kennedy Presidential Library and Museum. Accessed June 7, 2022. https://www.jfklibrary.org/learn/about-jfk/historic-speeches/acceptance-of-democratic-nomination-for-president.

Kennedy, John F. "Address Before the American Society of Newspaper Editors, April 20, 1961." The John F. Kennedy Library Presidential Library and Museum. Accessed August 17, 2021. https://www.jfklibrary.org/archives/other-resources/john-f-kennedy-speeches/american-society-of-newspaper-editors-19610420.

Kennedy, John F. "General Science: Candidates on Science—The Presidential Candidates Give their Views on Science and Technology." In *Freedom of Communications: Final Report of the Committee On Commerce, United States Senate, Part 3, The Joint Appearances of Senator John F. Kennedy and Vice President Richard M. Nixon and Other 1960 Campaign Presentations.* Washington, D.C.: The United States Government Printing Office, 1961.

Kennedy, John F. "President John F. Kennedy Moon Speech—Rice Stadium, September 12, 1962." The National Aeronautics and Space Administration, Johnson Spaceflight Center. Accessed June 14, 2022. https://er.jsc.nasa.gov/seh/ricetalk.htm#:~:text=We%20choose%20to%20go%20to%20the%20moon%20in%20this%20decade,to%20postpone%2C%20and%20one%20which.

Kennedy, John F. "Special Message to the Congress on Urgent National Needs, May 25, 1961." The John F. Kennedy Presidential Library and Museum. Accessed October 24, 2023. https://www.jfklibrary.org/archives/other-resources/john-f-kennedy-speeches/united-states-congress-special-message-19610525.

Kennedy, John F. *The Strategy of Peace*, edited by Allan Nevins. New York: Harper & Row, 1960.

King, Charleton J. House of Representatives. April 16, 1962, 87th Cong., 2d sess., *Cong. Rec.* 108, pt15.

King, Dr. Martin Luther Jr. "Our God is Marching On." Speech delivered in Montgomery, Alabama on 25 March 1965. The Martin Luther King, Jr. Research and Education Institute, Stanford University. Accessed September 19, 2023. https://kinginstitute.stanford.edu/our-god-marching.

"The Kitchen Debate Transcript." The Central Intelligence Agency. Accessed June 6, 2023. https://www.cia.gov/readingroom/docs/1959-07-24.pdf.

Kranz, Gene. *Failure is Not an Option: Mission Control from Mercury to Apollo and Beyond.* New York: Simon & Schuster, 2000.

Kranz, Gene. Interview by Roy Neal. NASA Headquarters History Office, Johnson Space Center, March 19, 1998. Accessed September 12, 2023. https://historycollection.jsc.nasa.gov/JSCHistoryPortal/history/oral_histories/KranzEF/EFK_3-19-98.pdf.

Lee, Dorothy "Dottie" B. Interview by Rebecca Wright. NASA Headquarters History Office, Johnson Space Center, November 10, 1999. Accessed April 20, 2023. https://historycollection.jsc.nasa.gov/JSCHistoryPortal/history/oral_histories/LeeDB/DBL_11-10-99.pdf.

Lister, D. M. "Digital Computation of Downstream Modes Generated by the Interaction of a Shock Wave with an Upstream Containing the Three Disturbance Modes." Wyle Laboratories—Research Staff, Technical Memorandum 69-1. Work Performed Under Contract No. NAS8-21100. Accessed August 3, 2023. https://ntrs.nasa.gov/api/citations/19690026452/downloads/19690026452.pdf.

*Look Magazine. The Decline of the American Male.* New York: Random House, 1958.

Lovell, James A. Jr. Interview by Ron Stone. NASA Headquarters History Office, Johnson Space Center, May 25, 1999. Accessed August 23, 2023. https://historycollection.jsc.nasa.gov/JSCHistoryPortal/history/oral_histories/LovellJA/LovellJA_5-25-99.htm.

Mahan, Alfred Thayer. *The Influence of Sea Power upon History: Securing International Markets in the 1890s.* New York: Little Brown & Company, 1890.

Mailer, Norman. *The Naked and the Dead.* New York: Holt, Rinehart, and Winston, 1948.

Mailer, Norman. *Of a Fire on the Moon.* New York: Random House, 1969.

Mailer, Norman. "The White Negro." *Dissent*, Fall 1957. Accessed October 17, 2023. https://www.dissentmagazine.org/online_articles/the-white-negro-fall-1957/.

Mills, C. Wright. *White Collar: The American Middle Class.* New York: Oxford University Press, 1951.

Mullane, Mike. *Riding Rockets: The Outrageous Tales of a Space Shuttle Astronaut.* New York: Scribner, 2006.

NASA History Program Office. "Address By Dr. George E. Mueller, Associate Administrator for Manned Space Flight, The National Aeronautics and Space Administration, at the Dedication of the Science Center Cedar Crest College, Allentown, Pennsylvania, October 19, 1966." The National Aeronautics and Space Administration. Accessed June 21, 2023. https://historydms.hq.nasa.gov/sites/default/files/DMS/e000040149.pdf.

"NASA Release No. 59-113: Mercury Astronaut Selection Factsheet, April 9, 1959." The Ohio State University. Accessed October 22, 2023. https://library.osu.edu/site/friendship7/files/2017/06/SelectionFactSheet.pdf.

Northcutt, Francis M. Interview by Jennifer Ross-Nazzal. NASA Headquarters History Office, Johnson Space Center, November 14, 2018. Accessed August 16, 2023, https://historycollection.jsc.nasa.gov/JSCHistoryPortal/history/oral_histories/NorthcuttFM/NorthcuttFM_11-14-18.pdf

Northcutt, Francis M. Post of TRW Advertisement. *Twitter*, November 21, 2019. https://twitter.com/poppy_northcutt?lang=en.

Office of the Historian. "Report to the President by the Security Resources Panel of the ODM Science Advisory Committee on Deterrence and Survival in the Nuclear Age, NSC5724." The United States Department of State. Accessed August 30, 2023. https://history.state.gov/historicaldocuments/frus1955-57v19/d158.

O'Hara, Dee. Interview by Rebecca Wright. NASA Headquarters History Office, Johnson Space Center, April 23, 2002. Accessed October 19, 2022. https://historycollection

# BIBLIOGRAPHY

.jsc.nasa.gov/JSCHistoryPortal/history/oral_histories/OHaraDB/OHaraDB_4-23 -02.pdf.

Osgood, Catherine T. Interview by Rebecca Wright. NASA Headquarters History Office, Johnson Space Center, November 15, 1999. Accessed June 13, 2023. https:// historycollection.jsc.nasa.gov/JSCHistoryPortal/history/oral_histories/OsgoodCT/ CTO_11-15-99.pdf.

Potter, David M. "American Women and the American Character." In *American Character and Culture*, edited by John A Hague. Deland, F.L.: Everett Edwards Press, Inc, 1964.

Presidential Recordings Program. "John F. Kennedy, Tape 63A: 'Fly Me to the Moon.'" Courtesy of the John F. Kennedy Library and Museum, University of Virginia, Miller Center. Accessed November 10, 2023, https://millercenter.org/the-presidency /educational-resources/fly-me-to-the-moon.

"Press Conference, Mercury Astronaut Team, April 9, 1959." NASA Historical Reference Collection. Accessed October 22, 2023. https://history.nasa.gov/40thmerc7/ presscon.pdf.

Pyle, Ernie. *Brave Men*. 1944. repr. Lincoln, N.E.: University of Nebraska Press, 2001.

Pyle, Ernie. *Here is Your War: The Story of G. I. Joe*. 1944; repr. Lincoln, N.E.: University of Nebraska Press, 2001.

Rand, Ayn. *The Fountainhead*. Indianapolis, I.N.: The Bobbs-Merrill Company, 1943.

Ride, Sally K. Interview by Rebecca Wright. NASA Headquarters History Office, Johnson Space Center, October 22, 2002. Accessed October 20, 2022. https:// historycollection.jsc.nasa.gov/JSCHistoryPortal/history/oral_histories/RideSK/ RideSK_10-22-02.pdf.

Riesman, David, Nathan Glazer, and Raul Denney. *The Lonely Crowd: A Study of the Changing American Character*, abr. edition. New Haven: Yale University Press, 1974.

Roman, Nancy G. Interview by Rebecca Wright. NASA Headquarters History Office, Johnson Space Center, September 15, 2000. Accessed July 18, 2022. https:// historycollection.jsc.nasa.gov/JSCHistoryPortal/history/oral_histories/NASA_HQ /Herstory/RomanNG/NGR_9-15-00.pdf.

Ruff, George E. and Edwin Z. Levy. "Psychiatric Evaluation of Candidates for Space Flight." *American Journal of Psychiatry* 116 (1959): 385–391.

Schirra, Wally and Richard N. Billings. *Schirra's Space*. Annapolis, M.D.: Naval Institute Press, 1995.

Schlesinger, Arthur Jr. "The Crisis of American Masculinity." In *The Politics of Hope*. Boston: Houghton Mifflin Company, 1963.

Schlesinger, Arthur Jr. *The Vital Center*. Boston: Houghton Mifflin Company, 1949.

Scott-Heron, Gill. "Whitey on the Moon." Track 9 on *Small Talk at 125th and Lenox*. Flying Dutchman Records, 1970, record.

Seddon, Rhea. Interview by Jennifer Ross-Nazzal. NASA Headquarters History Office, Johnson Space Center, May 20, 2010. Accessed October 12, 2023. https:// historycollection.jsc.nasa.gov/JSCHistoryPortal/history/oral_histories/SeddonMR /SeddonMR_5-20-10.pdf.

Shelley, Mary. *Frankenstein*. New York: Penguin Books, 1985; first published in London, 1818.

Shepard, Alan Bartlett Jr., and Deke Slayton, with Jay Barbree and Howard Benedict. *Moon Shot: The Inside Story of America's Race to the Moon*. New York: Turner Publishing, 1994.

Smith, Ephraim K. "'A Question from Which We Could Not Escape." *Diplomatic History* 9, no. 4 (Fall 1985): 365–375.

Smylie, Robert E. 'Ed'. Interview by Carol Butler. NASA Headquarters History Office. Johnson Space Center, April 17, 1999. Accessed August 17, 2023. https://historycollection.jsc.nasa.gov/JSCHistoryPortal/history/oral_histories/SmylieRE/SmylieRE_4-17-99.htm.

Sobel, Raymond. "The Battalion Surgeons as Psychiatrist," *Bulletin of the U.S. Army Medical Department.* Washington, D.C.: War Dept., Office of the Surgeon General, 1949.

"The Statement by President Nixon, 5 January 1972." The National Aeronautics and Space Administration History Division. Accessed October 12, 2023. http://history.nasa.gov/stsnixon.htm.

Stevenson, Adlai. "A Purpose for Modern Woman (1955)." W.W. Norton & Company. Accessed October 17, 2023. https://wwnorton.com/college/history/archive/resources/documents/ch32_04.htm.

Strecker, Edward., M.D. *Their Mother's Sons.* Philadelphia: Lippincott, 1946.

Sullivan, Kathryn D. *Handprints on Hubble: An Astronaut's Story of Invention.* Cambridge, M.A.: The Massachusetts Institute of Technology Press, 2019.

Sullivan, Kathryn D. Interview by Jennifer Ross-Nazzal. NASA Headquarters History Office, Johnson Space Center, May 10, 2007. Accessed October 22, 2022. https://historycollection.jsc.nasa.gov/JSCHistoryPortal/history/oral_histories/SullivanKD/SullivanKD_5-10-07.pdf.

"Title IX and Sex Discrimination." Office for Civil Rights, The United States Department of Education. Accessed October 12, 2023. https://www2.ed.gov/about/offices/list/ocr/docs/tix_dis.html.

Turner, Frederick Jackson. "The Significance of the Frontier in American History." The American Historical Association. Accessed May 31, 2022. https://www.historians.org/about-aha-and-membership/aha-history-and-archives/historical-archives/the-significance-of-the-frontier-in-american-history-(1893).

United States Capitol Visitor Center. "The Women's Armed Services Integration Act: Letter from Edith L. Stallings to the Chairman of the House Armed Forces Services Committee, March 11, 1948." United States Capitol Visitor Center. Accessed July 25, 2022. https://www.visitthecapitol.gov/exhibitions/artifact/letter-edith-l-stallings-chairman-house-armed-forces-service-committee-march.

United States, Congress, Senate, *Hearings before the Special Committee on Space and Astronautics.* H.R. 1181, 85th Cong., 2d sess., 1958.

United States Federal Civil Defense Service. *Bert the Turtle Says Duck and Cover.* Washington, D.C.: Federal Civil Defense Administration, 1951.

United States, Senate, Committee on Aeronautical and Space Sciences, *Soviet Space Programs, 1962–1965; Goals and Purposes, Achievements, Plans, and International Implications.* 89th Cong., 2d sess., 1966. Washington, D.C.: U.S. Government Printing Office, 1966.

Voas, Robert V., M.D. Interviewed by Summer Chick Bergen. NASA Headquarters History Office, Johnson Space Center, May 19, 2002. Accessed October 21, 2023. https://historycollection.jsc.nasa.gov/JSCHistoryPortal/history/oral_histories/VoasRB/VoasRB_5-19-02.pdf.

Whitman, Walt. "Pioneers! Oh, Pioneers!" *Leaves of Grass.* Accessed May 31, 2022. https://whitmanarchive.org/published/LG/1891/poems/99.

Whyte, William. *The Organization Man.* New York: Simon and Schuster, 1956.

# BIBLIOGRAPHY

Wilson, Woodrow. "Address of President Woodrow Wilson to Joint Session of Congress, April 2, 1917." The Library of Congress. Accessed November 12, 2023. https://www.loc.gov/exhibitions/world-war-i-american-experiences/about-this-exhibition/arguing-over-war/for-or-against-war/wilson-before-congress/.

Wolfe, Tom. *The Right Stuff.* New York, Bantam Books, 1980.

Wollstonecraft, Mary. "A Vindication of the Rights of Woman." In *A Mary Wollstonecraft Reader,* edited by Barbara H. Solomon and Paula S. Berggren. New York: New Amsterdam Library, 1983.

Wylie, Philip. *A Generation of Vipers.* New York: Farrar & Rinehart, 1942.

## Secondary Sources

Ackmann, Martha. *The Mercury 13: The True Story of Thirteen Women and the Dream of Space Flight.* New York: Random House Trade Paperbacks, 2003.

Allen, Joseph. *Entering Space: An Astronaut's Odyssey.* New York: Stewart, Tabori and Chang, 1984.

Andrews, James T. and Asif A. Siddiqi, eds. *Into the Cosmos: Space Exploration and Soviet Culture.* Pittsburgh: University of Pittsburgh Press, 2011.

Atkinson Joseph D. and Jay M. Shafritz. *The Real Stuff: A History of NASA's Astronaut Recruitment Program.* New York: Praeger, 1985.

Barry, Kathleen Morgan. *Femininity and Flight: A History of Flight Attendants.* Durham, N.C.: Duke University Press, 2007.

Beattie, Donald. *Taking Science to the Moon: Lunar Experiments and the Apollo Program.* Baltimore: Johns Hopkins University Press, 2001.

Bederman, Gail. *Manliness and Civilization: A Cultural History of Gender and Race in the United States, 1880–1917.* Chicago: The University of Chicago Press, 1995.

Bertschi, Jenna. "Barbie: An Astronaut for the Ages." The National Air and Space Museum. July 18, 2023. https://airandspace.si.edu/stories/editorial/barbie-astronaut-ages.

Bijker, Wiebe K., Thomas P. Hughes, and Trevor Pinch, eds. "Forward by Debbie Douglas." In *The Social Construction of Technological Systems: New Directions in the Sociology and History of Technology.* Cambridge, M.A.: The Massachusetts Institute of Technology Press, 2012.

Bix, Amy Sue. *Girls Coming to Tech: A History of American Engineering Education for Women.* Cambridge, M.A.: MIT Press, 2014.

Bridger, Sue. "The Cold War and the Cosmos: Valentina Tereshkova and the First Woman's Space Flight," In *Women in the Khrushchev Era,* edited by Melanie Ilic, Susan Reid, and Lynn Atwood. New York: Palgrave Macmillan, 2004.

Brock, Julia, Jennifer W. Dickey, and Richard Harker, eds. *Beyond Rosie: A Documentary History of Women in World War II.* Fayetteville, A.K. The University of Arkansas Press, 2015.

Brooks, Courtney G., James M. Grimwood, and Loyd S. Swenson. *Chariots for Apollo: A History of Manned Lunar Spacecraft.* Washington, D.C.: NASA-4205, 1979.

Burgess, Colin. *Selecting the Mercury Seven: The Search for America's First Astronauts.* New York: Springer-Praxis, 2011.

Butler, Judith. *Gender Trouble: Feminism and the Subversion Identity.* New York: Routledge, 2000.

Butler, Judith. "Performative Acts and Gender Constitution: An Essay in Phenomenology and Feminist Theory." *Theater Journal* 40, no. 4 (1988): 519–531.

Campbell, D'Ann. *Women at War with America: Private Lives in a Patriotic Era*. Boston: Harvard University Press, 1984.

Chafe, William H. *The Unfinished Journey: American Since World War II*. New York: Oxford University Press, 1995.

Chaikin, Andrew. *A Man on the Moon: The Voyages of the Apollo Astronauts*. New York: Penguin Books, 1998.

Clinton, Catherine and Nina Silber, eds. *Divided Houses: Gender and the Civil War*. New York: Oxford University Press, 1992.

Cohen, Lizbeth. *A Consumer's Republic: The Politics of Mass Consumption in Postwar America*. New York: Vintage Books, 2003.

Cole, Jean Hascall. *Women Pilots of World War II*. Salt Lake City: University of Utah Press, 1992.

Compton, William David. *Where No Man Has Gone Before: A History of Apollo Lunar Exploration Missions*. Washington, D.C.: The National Aeronautics and Space Administration, 1989.

Connell, R. W. and James W. Messerschmidt. "Hegemonic Masculinity: Rethinking the Concept." *Gender and Society* 19, no. 6 (2005): 829–59.

Cooney, Dan, System Administrator, TWAPilot.Org. "Grandma Leads a Fast Life and Loves It!" TWAPILOT.Org. Accessed June 6, 2023. http://www.twapilot.org/images/Grandma%20Leads%20a%20fast%20life%20and%20loves%20it.jpg.

Cooper, Patricia. "Cigarmaking." in *Gender and Technology: A Reader*, edited by Nina Lerman, Arwen Mohun, and Ruth Oldenzial. Baltimore: The Johns Hopkins University Press, 2003).

Corn, Joseph. *The Winged Gospel: America's Romance with Aviation, 2nd Printing*. Baltimore: Johns Hopkins University Press, 2002.

Courtwright, David T. "The Routine Stuff: How Flying became a Form of Mass Transportation." In *Reconsidering a Century of Flight*, edited by Roger D. Launius and Janet R. Daly Bednarek. Chapel Hill, N.C.: The University of North Carolina Press, 2003.

Cowan, Ruth Schwartz. *More Work for Mother: The Ironies of Household Technology from the Open Hearth to the Microwave*. New York: Basic Books, 1985.

Daddis, Gregory A. *Pulp Vietnam: War and Gender in Cold War Men's Adventure Magazines*. Cambridge: Cambridge University Press, 2021.

Dean, Robert D. "Masculinity as Ideology: John F. Kennedy and the Domestic Politics of Foreign Policy." *Diplomatic History* 22, no. 1 (Winter 1998): 29–62.

De Groot, Gerard J. *Dark Side of the Moon: The Magnificent Madness of the American Lunar Quest*. New York: New York University Press, 2006.

Dick, Steven and Roger D. Launius, eds. *Societal Impact of Spaceflight*. Washington, D.C.: NASA SP-4801, 2009.

Divine, Robert A. *The Sputnik Challenge*. New York: Oxford University Press, 1994.

Douglas, Deborah G. *American Women and Flight Since 1940*. Lexington, K.Y.: University of Kentucky Press, 2004.

Dunne, Matthew W. *A Cold War State of Mind: Brainwashing and Postwar American Society*. Amherst, M.A.: University of Massachusetts Press, 2013.

Dur, Hermann and Eric Jones. "Apollo 13 Lunar Surface Journal: Building an Apollo 13 LiOH Cannister." NASA History Division. Accessed August 17, 2023. https://history.nasa.gov/alsj/a13/a13_LIOH_Adapter.html.

## BIBLIOGRAPHY

"Ellison Onizuka: First Asian American in Space." The National Aeronautics and Space Administration. Accessed December 20, 2024. https://www.nasa.gov/image-article/ellison-onizuka-first-asian-american-space/.

Faludi, Susan. *Stiffed: The Betrayal of the American Man*. New York: Harper Collins, 1999.

Fausto-Sterling, Anne. *Sexing the Body: Gender Politics and the Construction of Sexuality*. New York: Basic Books, 2000.

Fenner, Lorry M. and Marie De Young, *Women in Combat: Civic Duty or Military Liability?* Georgetown: Georgetown University Press, 2001.

Fino, Steven A. *Tiger Check: Automating the US Air Force Fighter Pilot in Air-to-Air Combat, 1950–1980*. Baltimore: Johns Hopkins University Press, 2017.

Foner, Eric. ed. *The New American History*. Philadelphia: Temple University Press, 1990.

Foster, Amy Elizabeth. *Integrating Women into the Astronaut Corps: Politics and Logistics, 1972–2004*. Baltimore: University of Johns Hopkins Press, 2011.

Fox-Genovese, Elizabeth. *Within the Plantation Household: Black and White Women of the Old South*. Chapel Hill: The University of North Carolina Press, 1988.

Francke, Linda Bird. *Ground Zero: The Gender Wars in the Military*. New York: Simon & Schuster, 1997.

Gaddis, John Lewis. *Strategies of Containment: A Critical Appraisal of American National Security Policy During the Cold War*, Rev. ed. New York: Oxford University Press, 2005.

Gavin, Lettie. *They Also Served: American Women in World War I*. Boulder: The University of Colorado Press, 1997.

Gerovitch, Slava. "'New Soviet Man' Inside Machine: Human Engineering, Spacecraft Design, and the Construction of Communism." *OSIRIS* 22, no. 1 (2007): 135–157.

Gibson, Bill, Sean Hopper, and Huey Lewis. "Hip to be Square." Track 4 on Fore!. Chrysalis Records. 1986, cassette tape.

Gilbert, James. *Men in the Middle: Searching for Masculinity in the 1950s*. Chicago: The University of Chicago Press, 2005.

Gillispie, Val. "Eleanor C. Pressly: A Duke Alumna at NASA." Duke University. Accessed June 13, 2023. https://blogs.library.duke.edu/rubenstein/2019/07/12/pressly/.

Gilmore, David. *Manhood in the Making: Cultural Concepts of Masculinity*. New Haven: Yale University Press, 1990.

Granger, Byrd H. *On Final Approach: The Women Air Force Service Pilots of World War II*. Kingwood, T.X.: Falcon Publishing Company, 1991.

Greenwald, Maurine Weiner. *Women, War, and Work: The Impact of World War I on Women Workers in the United States*. Ithaca, N.Y. Cornell University Press, 1990.

Hacker, Barton C. and James M. Grimwood. *On the Shoulders of Titans: A History of Project Gemini*. Washington, D.C.: NASA, SP-4203, 1977.

Hacker, Sally. *Pleasure, Power, and Technology: Some Tales of Gender, Engineering, and the Cooperative Workplace*. Boston: Unwin Hyman, 1989.

Hall, Jaquelyn Dowd. "The Long Civil Rights Movement and the Political Uses of the Past." *The Journal of American History* 91, no. 4 (2005): 1233–1263.

Hall, Rex D., Shayler David, and Bert Vis. *Russia's Cosmonauts: Inside the Yuri Gagarin Training Center*. Chichester: Springer, 2007.

Hankins, Michael W. *Flying Camelot: The F-15, The F-16, and the Weaponization of Fighter Pilot Nostalgia*. Ithaca, N.Y.: Cornell University Press, 2021.

Hansen, James R. *Engineer In Charge: A History of Langley Aeronautical Laboratory, 1917–1958*. Washington, D.C.: The National Aeronautics and Space Administration, 1987.

Hansen, James R. *First Man: The Life of Neil A. Armstrong.* New York: Simon & Schuster, 2012.

Hansen, James R. *Spaceflight Revolution: NASA Langley Research Center from Sputnik to Apollo.* Washington, D.C.: The National Aeronautics and Space Administration, 1995.

Haynsworth, Leslie and David Toomey, *Amelia Earhart's Daughters: The Wild and Glorious Story of American Women Aviators from World War Two to the Dawn of the Space Age.* New York: Perennial, 1998.

Heineman, Kenneth J. *The Reagan Revolution and the Rise of the New Right: A Reference Guide.* New York: Bloomsbury USA, 2001.

Heppenheimer, T. A. *Development of the Shuttle, 1972–1981.* Washington, D.C.: Smithsonian Institute Press, 2002.

Hersch, Matthew H. *Inventing the American Astronaut.* New York: Palgrave, 2012.

Hersch, Matthew H. "Return of the Lost Spaceman: America's Astronauts in Popular Culture." *Journal of Popular Culture* 4, no. 1 (February 2011): 73–92.

Holt, Nathalia. *Rise of the Rocket Girls: The Women Who Propelled Us, from Missiles to the Moon and Mars.* New York: Little, Brown and Company, 2016.

Johnson, David K. *The Lavender Scare: The Cold War Persecution of Gays and Lesbians in the Federal Government.* Chicago: The University of Chicago Press, 2004.

Kauffman, James L. *Selling Outer Space: Kennedy, the Media, and Funding for Project Apollo, 1961–1963.* Tuscaloosa, A.L.: The University of Alabama Press, 1994.

Kerber, Linda. *Women of the Republic: Intellect and Ideology in Revolutionary America.* Chapel Hill, N.C.: The University of North Carolina Press, 1980.

Kevles, Bettyann Holtzmann. *Almost Heaven: The Story of Women in Space.* Cambridge: The MIT Press, 2006.

Kimmel, Michael. *Manhood in America: A Cultural History.* New York: The Free Press, 1996.

Kinsey, Alfred C. *Sexual Behavior in the Human Male.* Philadelphia: W.B. Saunders & Company, 1948.

Koppal, Lily. *The Astronaut Wives' Club: A True Story.* New York: Grand Central Publishing, 2013.

Krug, Linda T. *Presidential Perspectives on Space Exploration: Guiding Metaphors from Eisenhower to Bush.* New York: Praeger, 1991.

Landrum-Mangus, Susan. "Conestoga Wagons to the Moon: The Frontier, The American Space Program, and National Identity." PhD diss. The Ohio State University, 1999.

Lathers, Marie. "'No Official Requirement': Women, History, Time, and the U.S. Space Program." *Feminist Studies* 35, no. 1 (Spring 2009): 14–40.

Launius, Roger D. "Heroes in a Vacuum: The Apollo Astronaut as Cultural Icon." *Florida Historical Quarterly: Special Issue Celebrating 50th Anniversary NASA in Florida (1958–2008)* 87, no. 2 (Fall 2008): 174–209.

Launius, Roger D. "The Historical Dimension of Space Exploration: Reflections and Possibilities." *Space Policy* 16 (2000): 23–38.

Levy, David. *Maternal Overprotection.* New York: Columbia University Press, 1943.

Lewis, Cathleen S. *Cosmonaut: A Cultural History.* Gainesville, F.L.: University of Florida Press, 2023.

Logan, Willy. "The Rocket Testing Ruins of Sacramento." Podcast audio. June 15, 2021. https://www.willylogan.com/?p=2410.

Mackersey, Ian. *The Wright Brothers: The Remarkable Story of the Aviation Pioneers Who Changed the World.* London: Little, Brown, 2003.

# BIBLIOGRAPHY

257

Maher, Neil M. *Apollo in the Age of Aquarius*. Cambridge, M.A.: Harvard University Press, 2017.

May, Elaine Tyler. *Homeward Bound: American Families in the Cold War Era*. New York: Basic Books, 1988.

McComb, Erinn. "Push-Button Masculinity: Democratic Manhood and Operation Paperclip's Transnational Transfer of German Aerospace Technology, 1946–1959." In *Yearbook of Transnational History, Volume 4*, edited by Thomas Adam, assisted by Austin E. Loignon. Madison, N.J.: Farleigh Dickinson University Press, 2021.

McCurdy, Howard E. *Space and the American Imagination*, 2nd ed. Baltimore: The Johns Hopkins University Press, 1997.

McCurry, Stephanie. *Women's War: Fighting and Surviving the American Civil War*. Boston: Harvard University Press, 2019.

McDougall, Walter. *...The Heavens and The Earth: A Political History of Space Flight*. New York: Basic Books, 1985.

McLennan, Sarah and Mary Gainer. "When the Computer Wore a Skirt: Langley's Computers, 1935–1970." *News & Notes, NASA History Office* 21, no. 1 (December 2017). Accessed October 17, 2023. https://history.nasa.gov/nltr29-1.pdf.

Meadows, William C. *The Comanche Code Talkers of World War II*. Austin, T.X.: University of Texas Press, 2002.

Merryman, Molly. *Clipped Wings: The Rise and Fall of the Woman Airforce Service Pilots (WASPS) of World War II*. New York: New York University Press, 2001.

Meyer, Alan. *Weekend Pilots: Technology, Masculinity, and Private Aviation in Postwar America*. Baltimore: The Johns Hopkins University Press, 2013.

Meyer, Leisa D. *Creating G.I. Jane: Sexuality and Power in the Women's Army Corps during World War II*. New York: Columbia University Press, 1996.

Milkman, Ruth. *Gender at Work: The Dynamics of Job Segregation by Sex during World War II*. Urbana, I.L.: The University of Illinois Press, 1987.

Mindell, David A. *Digital Apollo: Human and Machine in Spaceflight*. Cambridge, M.A.: The MIT Press, 2008.

Monahan, Evelyn and Rosemary Neidel-Greenlee. *And if I Perish: Frontline U.S. Army Nurses in World War II*. New York: Anchor Books, 2003.

Muehlenbeck, P. E. *Gender, Sexuality, and the Cold War: A Global Perspective*. Nashville: Vanderbilt University Press, 2017.

Muir-Harmony, Teasel. *Operation Moonglow: A Political History of Project Apollo*. New York: Basic Books, 2020.

Myers, Sarah Parry. *Earning Their Wings: The WASPS of World War II and the Fight for Veteran Recognition*. Chapel Hill, N.C.: The University of North Carolina Press, 2023.

NASA History Division, "Key Moments in Human Spaceflight, April 26–27, 2011." The National Aeronautics and Space Administration. Accessed November 14, 2023. http://history.nasa.gov/1961-1981conf/index.html.

NASA Space Science Coordinated Archive. "Luna 9." The National Aeronautics and Space Administration. Accessed September 5, 2023. https://nssdc.gsfc.nasa.gov/nmc/spacecraft/display.action?id=1966-006A.

NASA Space Science Coordinated Archive. "Surveyor 1." The National Aeronautics and Space Administration. Accessed September 5, 2023. https://nssdc.gsfc.nasa.gov/nmc/spacecraft/display.action?id=1966-045A.

Neil, Valerie. *Spaceflight in the Shuttle Era and Beyond: Redefining Humanity's Purpose in Space*. New Haven: Yale University Press, 2017.

Neufeld, Michael J. "First American in Space: The Flight of Alan B. Shepard." The National Air and Space Museum. Accessed May 31, 2022. https://airandspace.si .edu/stories/editorial/first-american-space-flight-alan-b-shepard#:~:text=Shepard, -Posted%20on%20May&text=Sixty%20years%20ago%2C%20on%20May,downra nge%20from%20Cape%20Canaveral%2C%20Florida.

Neufeld, Michael J. "The Sinking of *Liberty Bell 7:* Gus Grissom's Near Fatal Mission." The National Air and Space Museum. July 21, 2021. Accessed October 25, 2023. https://airandspace.si.edu/stories/editorial/sinking-liberty-bell-7-gus-grissoms-near -fatal-mission.

Neufeld, Michael J. *Von Braun: Dreamer of Space, Engineer of War.* New York: Vintage Books, 2008.

Norton, Mary Beth. *Liberty's Daughters: The Revolutionary Experience of American Women, 1750–1800.* Ithaca, N.Y.: Cornell University Press, 1996.

"Oceola (Ocie) Hall—NASA's Federal Women's Program Coordinator." Marshall Spaceflight Center, The National Aeronautics and Space Administration. Accessed October 4, 2022. https://www.nasa.gov/centers/marshall/history/oceola-ocie-hall -nasa-s-federal-women-s-program-coordinator.html.

Odom, Brian C. and Stephen P. Waring, eds. *NASA and the Long Civil Rights Movement.* Gainesville, F.L.: University of Florida Press, 2019.

Oldenziel, Ruth. *Making Technology Masculine: Men, Women, and Modern Machines in America, 1870–1945.* Amsterdam: Amsterdam University Press, 1999.

Paechter, Carrie. "Rethinking the Possibilities for Hegemonic Femininity: Exploring a Gramscian Framework." *Women's Studies International Forum* 68 (2018): 121–128.

Paul, Doris A. *The Navajo Code Talkers.* Philadelphia: Dorrance & Company, 1973.

Paul, Richard and Steven Moss. *We Could Not Fail: The First African Americans in the Space Program.* Austin: University of Texas Press, 2015.

Pennington, Reina. *Wings, Women, and War: Soviet Airwomen in World War II Combat.* Lawrence, K.S.: University Press of Kansas, 2002.

Powers, Sheryll Goecke. *Women in Flight Research at NASA Dryden Flight Research Center from 1946 to 1995.* Washington, D.C.: The National Aeronautics and Space Administration, 1997.

Prelinger, Megan. *Another Science Fiction: Advertising the Space Race, 1957–1962.* New York. Blast Books, 2010.

Puaca, Laura Micheletti. *Searching for Scientific Womanpower: Technocratic Feminism and the Politics of National Security, 1940–1980.* Chapel Hill, N.C.: The University of North Carolina Press, 2014.

Robertson, Linda R. *The Dream of Civilized Warfare: World War I Flying Aces and the American Imagination.* Minneapolis: University of Minnesota Press, 2003.

Roman, Peter J. *Eisenhower and the Missile Gap.* Ithaca, N.Y.: Cornel University Press, 1995.

Ross-Nazzal, Jennifer M. *Making Space for Women: Stories from Trailblazing Women of NASA's Johnson Space Center.* College Station, T.X.: Texas A&M University Press, 2022.

Ross-Nazzal, Jennifer M. "You've Come a Long Way, Maybe: The First Six Women Astronauts and the Media." In *Spacefarers: Images of Astronauts and Cosmonauts in the Heroic Era of Spaceflight,* edited by Michael J. Neufeld, Washington, D.C.: Smithsonian Institution Scholarly Press, 2013.

Rossiter, Margaret W. *Women Scientists in America: Before Affirmative Action 1940–1972.* Baltimore: Johns Hopkins University Press, 1995.

# BIBLIOGRAPHY

Schoettle, Enid Curtis Bok. "The Establishment of NASA." In *Knowledge and Power: Essays on Science and Government*, edited by Sanford A. Lakoff. New York: The Free Press, 1966.

Scott, Joan Wallach. *Gender and the Politics of History*, Rev. ed. New York: Columbia University Press, 1999.

Shayler, David J. and Collin Burgess. *NASA's First Space Shuttle Astronaut Selection: Redefining the Right Stuff*. Chichester: Springer-Praxis, 2020.

Shayler, David J. and Collin Burgess. *NASA's Scientist-Astronauts*. New York: Springer-Praxis, 2006.

Sherr, Lynn. *Sally Ride: America's First Woman in Space*. New York: Simon and Schuster Paperbacks, 2014.

Sherry, Michael. *The Rise of American Air Power: The Creation of Armageddon*. New Haven, C.T.: Yale University Press, 1987.

Sherwood, John Darrell. *Officers in Flight Suits: The Story of American Air Force Fighter Pilots in the Korean War*. New York: New York University Press, 1996, 6.

Shetterley, Margot Lee. "Dorothy Vaughn Biography." National Aeronautics and Space Administration. Accessed June 14, 2023. https://www.nasa.gov/content/dorothy-vaughan-biography.

Shetterley, Margot Lee. *Hidden Figures: The American Dream and the Untold Story of the Black Women Mathematicians Who Helped Win the Space Race*. New York: Harper Collins, 2016.

Siddiqi, Asif A. *Challenge to Apollo: The Soviet Union and the Space Race, 1945–1974*. Washington, D.C.: NASA SP-4408, 2000.

Siddiqi, Asif A. *Sputnik and the Soviet Space Challenge*. Gainesville: University Press of Florida, 2004.

Snead, David. *The Gaither Committee, Eisenhower, and the Cold War*. Columbus, O.H: The Ohio State University Press, 1998.

Society for Women Engineer's Magazine (SWE). "Judith Resnik's Living Legacy." Winter 2021, https://alltogether.swe.org/2021/01/judith-resniks-living-legacy/.

Spiller, James. "Nostalgia for the Right Stuff: Astronauts and Public Anxiety about a Changing Nation." In *Spacefarers: Images of Astronauts and Cosmonauts in the Heroic Era of Spaceflight*, edited by Michael Neufeld. Washington, D.C.: Smithsonian Institution Scholarly Press, 2013.

Swenson, Loyd S., James M. Grimwood, and Charles C. Alexander, *This New Ocean: A History of Project Mercury*. Washington, D.C.: NASA SP-4201, 1966.

Teitel, Amy Shira. *Fighting for Space: Two Pilots and their Historic Battle for Female Spaceflight*. New York: Grand Central Publishing, 2020.

Thompson, Neal. *Light This Candle: The Life and Times of Alan Shepard, America's First Spaceman*. New York: Crown Publishers, 2004.

*Toy Story*. Directed by John Lasseter, Pixar/Walt Disney Pictures, 1995.

Treadwell, Mattie. *The Women's Army Corps*, Vol. 8, *The United States Army in World War II, Special Studies*. Washington, D.C.: United States Government Printing Office, 1954.

Tribbe, Matthew D. *No Requiem for the Space Age: The Apollo Moon Landings and American Culture*. New York: Oxford University Press, 2014.

Van Vleck, Jennifer. *Empire of the Air: Aviation and the American Ascendancy*. Cambridge, M.A.: Harvard University Press, 2013.

Verges, Marianne. *On Silver Wings: The Women Airforce Service Pilots of World War II*. New York: Ballantine Books, 1991.

Wajcman, Judy. "Feminist Theories of Technology." *Cambridge Journal of Economics* 34 (2010): 143–152.

Ward, John W. "The Meaning of Lindbergh's Flight." *American Quarterly* 10, no. 1 (Spring, 1958): 3–16.

Watts, Steven. *JFK and the Masculine Mystique: Sex and Power on the New Frontier.* New York: St. Martin's Press, 2016.

Weitekamp, Margaret A. *Right Stuff, Wrong Sex: America's First Women in Space Program.* Baltimore: Johns Hopkins University Press, 2005.

Weintraub, Beverly. *Wings of Gold: The Story of the First Women Naval Aviators.* Lyons Press: N.Y.: 2021.

Wellesley College. "1970 Alumni Achievement Awards: Dr. Jocelyn R. Gill." Accessed July 13, 2023. https://www.wellesley.edu/alumnae/awards/achievementawards/allrecipients/jocelyn_r._gill_38.

Yellin, Emily. *Our Mother's War: American Women at Home and at the Front during World War II.* New York: Simon & Schuster, 2010.

"50 Years Ago: Houston, We've Had a Problem." The National Aeronautics and Space Administration. Accessed August 15, 2023. https://www.nasa.gov/feature/50-years-ago-houston-we-ve-had-a-problem.

## Articles

Agus, Carole. "Nothing Flighty About this Lady." *Victoria Advocate* (Victoria, Texas), December 27, 1982.

Alsop, Stewart. "Crossfield Aims for the Stars!" *Tennessean* (Nashville, Tennessee), December 29, 1957.

"America Puts on a Brave Face: President's Congratulations on 'Outstanding' Feat." *Times* (London, United Kingdom), April 13, 1961.

American Airlines. Advertisement. *Colliers*, November 15, 1947.

American Airlines. Advertisement. *Life*, July 8, 1946.

American Airlines. "The Scheduled Airlines of the United States." Advertisement. *Colliers*, November 1, 1947.

Anders, William. "'The Black Side: Pulverized, Like a Battlefield'." *Life*, January 17, 1969.

Anderson, Jack. "Would-be Astronauts: Legions of Angry Women." *Boston Globe*, November 19, 1967.

Anderson, Raymond H. "A Soviet Space Mission Stirs World's Conjecture; Lovell Says Zond 5 Passed Moon and is Returning; U.S. Sources Suspect Failure of Round-Trip Attempt." *New York Times*, September 19, 1968.

Anderson, Raymond H. "Dies in Re-entry; Komarov First Known Fatality of Any Manned Flights." *New York Times*, April 25, 1967.

Anderson, Raymond H. "Russians Confirm Flight of Zoned 5 Around the Moon; Soviets Confirm a Flight to Moon." *New York Times*, September 21, 1968.

"Anna Fisher to become First Mother to Travel into Space." *Belleville News-Democrat* (Belleville, Illinois), November 5, 1984.

Annin, Katherine H. "Let Us Now Praise Famous Men." *Berkshire Eagle* (Pittsfield, Massachusetts), February 18, 1958.

"Apollo Flight Journal: More than *SCE* to *Aux*—Apollo 12 Lighting Strike Incident." NASA History Division. Accessed August 25, 2023. https://history.nasa.gov/afj/ap12fj/a12-lightningstrike.html.

"Apollo's Voyage Called Safer than Columbus's." *New York Times*, December 19, 1968.

"Apollo Workers Display Rare Emotions After Feat." *New York Times*, December 28, 1968.

# BIBLIOGRAPHY

Apple, R. W. Jr., *New York Times* Wire Service. "Landing Intrigues Africans, Who Ask About Falling Off and Moon's Size." *Courier-Journal* (Louisville), July 22, 1969.

Arnold, Henry H. "Text of Final Section of Arnold's Report Blueprinting Needs for Maintaining Air Power." *New York Times*, November 12, 1945.

The Associated Press. "America Cheers Feat With Few Dissenting." *Montgomery Advertiser* (Montgomery, Alabama), July 21, 1969.

The Associated Press. "Another Chapter Written." *Kingsport Times-News* (Kingsport Tennessee), May 27, 1962.

The Associated Press. "Apollo 10 Flight Most Dangerous." *Jacksonville Daily News* (Jacksonville, Illinois), May 20, 1969.

The Associated Press. "Astronauts Healthy; Gemini Hits Ocean Safely on Target." *Wisconsin State Journal* (Madison, Wisconsin), September 16, 1966.

The Associated Press. "Astronaut Recruiting Plan Slated; Soviet Gains Spur NASA?" *Spokesman-Review* (Spokane, Washington), October 20, 1964.

The Associated Press. "Astronaut Seeks Flight Freedom." *Abilene Reporter-News*, May 28, 1961.

The Associated Press. "Britons Screamed, Chileans Danced." *Montgomery Advertiser* (Montgomery, Alabama), July 21, 1969.

The Associated Press. "The Carpenter Drama: 3 Orbits, Overshoot, Disappearance Reveal New Dangers, Solutions, Vistas." *Fitchburg Sentinel* (Fitchburg, Massachusetts), May 25, 1962.

The Associated Press. "CMDR. Shepard's Plea; Said to have Asked Kennedy for Freedom in Space." *New York Times*, May 28, 1961.

The Associated Press. "Cosmonette Lacking in Piloting Skills; Attempt to Launch Third Flier Rumored." *Lubbock-Avalanche Journal*, June 17, 1963.

The Associated Press. "Decision on Liftoff a Tough One to Make." *Intelligencer Journal* (Lancaster, Pennsylvania), November 15, 1969.

The Associated Press. "Deke won't be Making Solo Flight." *Tucson Daily Citizen*, July 12, 1962.

The Associated Press. "Displaying Calm Mastery: Women are Finding Place in Sun in Space Program." *Columbia Record* (Columbia, South Carolina), December 14, 1964.

The Associated Press. "Female Cosmonaut Finds Chauvinism in Space." *Montgomery Advertiser* (Montgomery, Alabama), August 22, 1982.

The Associated Press. "5 Firsts and 3 Records for Flight." *New York Times*, March 14, 1969.

The Associated Press. "Gathering for a 'hen party.'" *Fresno Bee* (Fresno, California), December 27, 1968.

The Associated Press. "Gemini 9 Astronauts Die as Jet Hits Building Housing Capsule; Elliot See and Charles Bassett are Killed at St. Louis; Stafford and Cernan to Fill In." *Rutland Daily Herald* (Rutland, Vermont), March 1, 19661.

The Associated Press. "Gemini: Space Pilots' Blood Tests Appear Fine; Astronauts Begin Telling Experts of 3-Orbit Journey." *Emporia Gazette* (Emporia, Kansas), March 24, 1965.

The Associated Press. "The Gemini Success." *Lawrence Daily Journal-World* (Lawrence, Kansas), March 24, 1965.

The Associated Press. "Ground Control System Lets Apollo Crew Sleep." *New York Times*, March 4, 1969.

262  GENDER AND THE RACE FOR SPACE

The Associated Press. "Here's the Kitchen, Cosmonette." *Daily Tribune* (Wisconsin Rapids, Wisconsin), August 23, 1982.

The Associated Press. "Hero's Welcome Awaits Astronaut Shepard as U.S. Charts Plans to Put Spaceman in Orbit." *Reno Gazette Journal*, May 6, 1961.

The Associated Press. "'Iroquois Fear Monsters,' Praise Echoes Around Globe but Some Voices Superstitious," *Los Angeles Times*, July 22, 1969.

The Associated Press. "John Glenn Tried to Keep Himself, Family in Background of Mission." *Danville Register* (Danville, Virginia), February 22, 1962.

The Associated Press. "'Just Let Us Go!' Shepard told Kennedy." *Gazette-Mail* (Charleston, West Virginia), May 28, 1961.

The Associated Press. "Lady 'Astro' Hopefuls Blast NASA Brushoff; Red Girls Success doesn't Shift U.S. Policy Despite 'Equal Rights.'" *Pittsburgh-Post Gazette*, June 17, 1963.

The Associated Press. "Lady Astronauts: 3 Blondes Ask Equality-In Space." *Corpus Christi Times*, July 17, 1962.

The Associated Press. "Mercury Flight Chief, Christopher Columbus Kraft Jr." *New York Times*, May 26, 1962.

The Associated Press. "Millions Around the World Hang on Astronauts' Words." *Birmingham News*, July 21, 1969.

The Associated Press. "Mission Control Wins Game as Odyssey's Chutes Open." *Victoria Advocate* (Victoria, Texas), April 18, 1970.

The Associated Press. "NASA Commits an Outrage: Add 'Ruth Bates Harris' to Misfired List." *Dayton Daily News* (Dayton, Ohio), January 2, 1974.

The Associated Press. "Nation Lauds Courage of Spaceman Shepard." *Albuquerque Journal*, May 6, 1961.

The Associated Press. "The New Six: Scientist-Spacemen View their Jobs." *San Antonio Express*, June 30, 1965.

The Associated Press. "No Women Astronauts." *Asbury Park Evening Press* (Asbury, New Jersey), December 5, 1970.

The Associated Press. "Paper Reports Goose Hits Astronaut's Plane." *Tampa Tribune*, November 8, 1964.

The Associated Press. "Pinpoint Return Completes Apollo Success." *Eau Claire* (Wisconsin) *Ledger*, December 28, 1968.

The Associated Press. "Pioneer's Story of Space!" *Chicago Tribune*, April 13, 1961.

The Associated Press. "Reaction is Mixed: Four Women Rejected as Scientist-Astronauts." *Belleville News-Democrat* (Belleville, Illinois), April 27, 1965.

The Associated Press. "Red Describes Eerie Space Flight." *Hammond Times* (Hammond, Indiana), April 13, 1961.

The Associated Press. "Ruth Bates Harris gets New NASA Job." *Anniston Star* (Anniston, Alabama), August 18, 1974.

The Associated Press. "Russians Broadcast Message of Sympathy after Apollo Fire." *Yuma Daily Sun*, January 29, 1967.

The Associated Press. "Sally Kristen Ride: First American Woman to Fly into Space." *Santa Cruz Sentinel* (Santa Cruz, California), June 12, 1983.

The Associated Press. "Scientist-Astronaut Sees Moon as 'Unclimbed Mountain.'" *Orlando Sentinel*, June 28, 1965.

The Associated Press. "11 Scientists Join Team of Astronauts." *Spokane-Review*, August 5, 1967.

# BIBLIOGRAPHY

The Associated Press. "Shepard Pilot's Capsule on Sky Flight; U.S. Astronaut Reaches Height of 115 Miles; Spaceman Termed in Good Condition After Historic Hop." *Albuquerque Journal*, May 6, 1961.

The Associated Press. "Shuttle Closing in on Errant Satellite; Spacewalk May Lead to Rescue." *Intelligencer Journal* (Lancaster, Pennsylvania), November 12, 1984.

The Associated Press. "Six Scientist-Astronauts Declare: Instruments Leave Space Gaps Only Man Can Fill." *Independent*, (Long Beach, California), June 30, 1965.

The Associated Press. "Soviet Lands Man After Orbit of World; K [Khrushchev] Challenges West to Duplicate Feat." *Washington Post*, April 13, 1961.

The Associated Press. "Soviet Union's Latest Space Feat Evokes Little Concern in Washington." *Record Searchlight* (Redding, California), June 17, 1963.

The Associated Press. "Soviets Hail Space Hero." *Logansport Press* (Logansport, Indiana), August 16, 1962.

The Associated Press. "Soviets Launch Second Female in Space." *Tampa Tribune*, August 29, 1982.

The Associated Press. "Space Chiefs Brush Aside Female Issue." *Waco-News Tribune* (Waco, Texas), June 30, 1965.

The Associated Press. "Space Chiefs Claim U.S. Program Still Superior." *Independent* (Pasadena, C.A.), March 19, 1965.

The Associated Press. "TASS Accuses U.S. of Risking Gemini 5 to Outstrip Soviet." *New York Times*, August 23, 1965.

The Associated Press. "Ted Freeman, Astronaut Dies in Plane Crash." *Miami Herald*, November 1, 1964.

The Associated Press. "Their Men Landed Safely; Astronauts' Families are Sad but Glad." *Knoxville News-Sentinel*, March 17, 1966.

The Associated Press. "A Tyranny of Perfection: Committee Of Computers Does its Job on Shuttle." *Tyler Morning Telegraph* (Tyler, Texas), July 13, 1985.

The Associated Press. "U.S. Cosmonette will have to Earn her Place in Space: Myths of Superiority of Physical Endurance Hit by Scientists." *Record* (Hackensack, New Jersey), June 17, 1963.

The Associated Press. "U.S. Gals Green at Red Feat." *Philadelphia Inquirer*, June 17, 1963.

The Associated Press. "Val, Valery Land Safely; His 82 Orbits; Hers 49; Both Feeling Well; Moscow Radio Blares." *Dayton Daily News*, June 19, 1963.

The Associated Press. "Valentina has a Good Background for a Russian Heroine." *Philadelphia Inquirer*, June 17, 1963.

The Associated Press. "Valentina Meets Soviet Reporters." *Philadelphia Inquirer*, June 17, 1963.

The Associated Press. "Valya: Blonde With Muscles." *Newsday* (Nassau Edition, Hampstead, New York), June 17, 1963.

The Associated Press. "Veteran Pilot Victim in Landing Accident," *Indianapolis Star*, November 1, 1964.

The Associated Press. "Walking Around; Armstrong Steers Eagle Away From Rough Landing." *Winston-Salem Journal* (Winston-Salem, North Carolina), July 21, 1969.

The Associated Press. "We Got Serious Problems." *Democrat and Chronicle*, (Rochester, New York), March 18, 1966.

The Associated Press. "White House in a Message to Soviet Union Expresses Hope for a Space Accord; Soviet Shot Viewed by World as a Big Advance in Space Race." *New York Times*, August 7, 1961.

The Associated Press. "Wife of Astronaut Sues for Divorce, Charging Cruelty." *New York Times*, July 22, 1965.

The Associated Press. Wire Photo. *Journal Times* (Racine, Wisconsin), June 17, 1963.

The Associated Press. "Woman in 'Space': She Star Gazes With the Astronauts." *Columbia Record* (Columbia, South Carolina), December 14, 1964.

The Associated Press. "Woman Space Pioneer." *Philadelphia Inquirer*, January 15, 1959.

"Astronaut is Former Lumberjack." *New York Times*, August 12, 1962.

"Astronauts' Aide?" *Washington Post*, April 30, 1959.

"Astronauts have New Daughter." *Miami Herald*, August 11, 1983, 2A.

"The Astronauts—Ready to Make History." *Life*, September 14, 1959.

"The Astronauts 12." *New York Times*, November 15, 1969.

Auerbach, Stuart. "Crew has Trained as a Unit for Any Space Eventuality." *Washington Post*, July 17, 1969.

Azrara, Sara, and Richard Stacks. "Women Behind the Spacemen and the Satellites." *Sun Magazine*, May 17, 1964.

Bailey, Ronald. "Gemini's Last Mission is a Lulu—Now On to the Moon." *Life*, December 2, 1966.

Baldor, Lolita C. "Should Women be Allowed to Fight on the Front Lines? Trump's Defense Pick Reignites the Debate." The Associated Press. November 18, 2024. https://apnews.com/article/military-women-defense-hegseth-combat-916d50a7b46 5ccfea1aeb13bb91064b3.

Baldwin, Hanson W. "The 'Drone': Portent of Push-Button War; Recent Operations Point to the Pilotless Plane as a Formidable Weapon in War's New Armory." *New York Times*, August 25, 1946.

Baldwin, Hanson W. "Missiles in Push-Button War; Frightening Import of these Weapons is Heightened by Varieties Made Possible by a Fusing of Principles." *New York Times*, July 8, 1946.

Baldwin, Hanson W. "Nazi V-2 Climbs Almost 75 Miles as 'Push-Button War' Tests Begin." *New York Times*, May 11, 1946.

Baldwin, Hanson W. "Our Fighting Men have Gone Soft." *Saturday Evening Post*, August 8, 1959.

Barbour, John. The Associated Press. "Jubilant Astros Back Home after Near-Perfect Landing; 'Jinxed' Gemini Ends in Success." *Salt Lake Tribune*, June 7, 1966.

Barbour, John. "Spacemen Head For Okinawa in Good Condition." *Philadelphia Inquirer*, March 17, 1963.

Barclay, Dorothy. "Trousered Mothers and Dishwashing Dads." *New York Times*, April 28, 1957.

"Bayard Girl Departs for Avenger Field; Miss Lois Bristol Will Train in Texas for Ferry Command." *Bayard Transcript* (Bayard, Nebraska), September 30, 1943.

BBC News. "Jeff Bezos and Sir Richard Branson Not Astronauts Yet, US Says." July 23, 2021. https://www.bbc.com/news/world-us-canada-57950149.

Beech, Keyes. "Not Really Excited—Moon Walk? Good, Says GIs in Saigon." *Birmingham News*, July 21, 1969.

Bell, Joseph N. "Scott Crossfield's Story: X-15—Past and Future." *Detroit Free Press*, December 24, 1960.

Belser, Lee. "Blond Would go into Orbit." *Los Angeles Mirror*, May 22, 1959.

Benedict, Howard. Associated Press Aerospace Writer. "Tekite Lifts Barrier for First Women Astronauts." *Capital Journal* (Salem, Oregon), July 29, 1970.

# BIBLIOGRAPHY 265

Bigart, Homer. "New-Breed Astronauts: Scientists, Not Daredevils." *New York Times*, December 30, 1968.

Bird, David. "A Hand-Held Gun is used to Maneuver in Space." *New York Times*, July 21, 1966.

Boreman, Frank "'A Science Fiction World-Awesome, Forlorn, Beauty'." *Life*, January 17, 1969.

Bowie, July 11, 1969. "Space Oddity," on album *Space Oddity*. Producer Gus Dudgeon. Phillips Records (U.K.), Mercury Records (U.S.), record.

Boyd, Robert S. "Crew does it's Work on Lunar Surface." *Charlotte Observer*, July 21, 1969.

"British Press Hails Whites Space Feat." *New York Times*, June 4, 1965.

Broad, William J. "The Shuttle Explodes; 6 In Crew and High-School Teacher Killed 74 Seconds After Liftoff; Thousands Watch A Rain of Debris." *New York Times*, January 29, 1986.

Broad, William J. "Woman in the News; Cool, Versatile Astronaut: Sally Kristen Ride." *New York Times*, June 19, 1983.

Brock, H. "The Flying Man is Etched in Court." *New York Times Magazine*, December 6, 1925.

Brown, Murray, United Press International. "Satellite Flop May Force Ike to Attend Conference." *Yuma Daily Sun* (Yuma, Arizona), December 8, 1957.

Brown, Rusty. "As No. 2; Resnik is just one of the Crew." *Telegraph Forum* (Bucryus, Ohio), July 19, 1984.

Bryant, Nelson. "Wood, Field and Stream; Astronauts Turn a Hunter's Attention From Buckshot, to a Moonshot." *New York Times*, December 3, 1972.

Bryant, Salathei. "A Diligent Advocate for Diversity at the Johnson Space Center, Joseph D. Atkinson, Jr. dies in Houston at the Age of 79." *Houston Chronicle*, November 6, 2005. Accessed July 17, 2023. https://www.chron.com/news/houston-deaths/article /A-diligent-advocate-for-diversity-at-the-Johnson-1915030.php.

Burns, John F. "An Apron For Soviet Woman in Space." *New York Times*, August 29, 1982.

"Cadettes Guests of R.P.I. Head." *Troy Record* (Troy, New York), September 1, 1943.

Canby, Vincent. *New York Times* News Service. "The Movie that has 'The Right Stuff; Film History of U.S. Mercury Program Scheduled to Open Nationwide Today." *Daily Press* (Victorville, California), October 21, 1983.

Cannel, Ward. "The American Male of 1958: Experts Wonder How He Survives Beset by Fear, Bereft of Strength." *Knoxville News-Sentinel*, July 27, 1959.

"Capital Calls Flight a Good Omen." *New York Times*, July 22, 1961.

Carpenter, Scott. "A Sensitive Man's Exhilaration on a Rugged Ride: 'I Got Let in on the Great Secret'." *Life*, June 8, 1962.

Carruthers, Osgood. "Pilot Could Fire Braking Rockets." *New York Times*, April 13, 1961.

Cartoon. *Orlando Sentinel*, February 13, 1978.

"A Case of 'Constructive Alarm'." *Life*, April 8, 1966.

Charlton, Linda, Special to the *New York Times*. "Almost all the Noncombat Jobs in the Air Force Opened to Women." *New York Times*, November 23, 1972.

*Chicago Daily News Service*. "New Astronaut Unit to be Vets of Jets: High-Speed Test Pilots are Regarded as Ideal for Perils of Space." *Record* (Hackensack, New Jersey), March 15, 1962.

*Chicago Tribune Press Service*. "Scientist-Astronaut Crewman are Sought." *Spokesman-Review* (Spokane, Washington), November 29, 1964.

"Chicagoans Hail Historic Moon Walk... But." *Chicago Defender*, July 22, 1969.

266 GENDER AND THE RACE FOR SPACE

Childs, Jack. "'Housekeeping' Job not Easy in Space." *News and Observer* (Raleigh, North Carolina), August 31, 1968.

"Chimp Boosted 550 Miles Aloft in Test for Man-in-Space Try; Capsule Spotted on Bahama Isle After Fifteen Minutes." *Santa Maria Times* (Santa Maria, California) January 31, 1961.

"Chimp Found Ok After Space Hop." *Los Angeles Mirror*, February 3, 1961.

"Chimp Ready to Blaze Trail in Space for U.S. Astronauts; Hope of Manned Flight this Year Tied to Test." *Spokesman Review* (Spokane, Washington), January 28, 1961.

"Chosen as Curtis-Wright Cadette." *Milan Standard* (Milan, Missouri), March 4, 1943.

Clark, Evert. "Apollo Program Dealt Hard Blow." *New York Times*, January 28, 1967.

Clark, Ever. "Gemini Cleared for 32 Circuits; It May Go 8 days; Power Restored; Astronauts return to Original Flight Plan—New Tests Set." *New York Times*, August 23, 1965.

"Closing in on the Moon." *Newsweek*, August 1, 1966.

Coleman, Fred. "Soviet Capsule Spins On, On After Russ 'Swims' in Space: Red Millions Witness Moon-Stride on TV." *Salt Lake Tribune*, March 19, 1965.

"Collins Very Quiet but Pukish, When Schoolboy at St. Albans." *Washington Post*, July 21, 1966.

Combined News Services. "U.S. Reaction?: It's All a Matter of Sex." *Newsday* (Nassau edition, Hampstead, New York), June 17, 1963.

Conrad, Pete. "'Astronauts' Personal Stories about their Gemini 5 Flight." *Life*, September 24, 1965.

Considine, Bob. "The Untold Story of Amelia's Tragedy." *The Minneapolis Journal*, August 8, 1937, 60.

Converse, Margaret. Gannett News Service. "Poppy: The Pretty Blonde from Texas used to be a 'Dancing, Drinking Mary College.' Today she's one of the Six Engineers Who Calculate Timing for the Apollo Astronauts…' the First Woman at Mission Control Who wasn't just Running Errands." *Democrat and Chronicle* (Rochester, New York), February 22, 1970.

Cooper, Gordon. "Everyone was in a Sweat, I was Secretly Pleased." *Life*, June 7, 1963.

"Cosmonaut May Land Tonight." *Knoxville News-Sentinel*, June 17, 1963.

"Cosmonettes a Cutie." *El Paso Herald-Post*, June 17, 1963.

Cox, Donald. "NASA Refutes Space Girl Story." *New York World Telegram*, September 29, 1960.

Crane, Dr. George W. "Worry Clinic: Men Prefer Feminine Girls—Not Attracted by Masculine Characteristics." *Herald and Review* (Decatur, Illinois), August 27, 1951.

"A Crew With Brains and Experience." *New York Times*, December 22, 1968.

Cromie, William J. World Book Encyclopedia Sciences Services. "Early Training is Over; Moon Explorers Anxious for Mission." *Daily Times News* (Burlington, North Carolina), December 19, 1966.

Cromie, William J. World Book Encyclopedia Science Services. "Look forward to Flights; Scientist Astronauts Near End of First Year in Space Training." *Tucson Daily Citizen*, July 4, 1965.

Curtiss-Wright. Advertisement. *New York Times*, January 2, 1947.

Daley, Pat Casey. "Astro-Doctor: Rhea Seddon—Down to Earth but Counting." *Tennessean* (Nashville, Tennessee), September 9, 1984.

Dalrymple, Jaclyn. "Minority Involvement In Politics Is Urged." *Tampa Tribune*, December 29, 1974.

# BIBLIOGRAPHY

Davis, Suville R. "Not Just by Way of the Moon: The World Will Continue to Judge U.S. by the Quality of its Civilization." *Christian Science Monitor*, July 21, 1969.

Davis, Virginia. "Need Encouragement in Science: Women Astronauts? Maybe." *Tampa Times*, July 18, 1962.

"11 Days Aboard Apollo 7." *Life*, December 6, 1968.

Delaney, Paul. "Top Black Woman is Ousted by NASA." *New York Times*, October 28, 1973.

Dietz, David. "ADVENTURES IN SPACE: The Story of Radar; No. 8: Push-Button Warfare," *Mount Carmel Item* (Mount Carmel, Pennsylvania), April 9, 1946.

Dille, John. "At the End of a Great Flight, Big Bull's-Eye." *Life*, October 12, 1962.

Dodd, Phillip. "Behind in Space Race: Kennedy Denies Weakness in Struggle on Ideology." *Chicago Tribune*, April 13, 1961.

Dodd, Phillip. "To Space—And Back!" *Chicago Tribune*, May 6, 1961.

Douglas Super DC-3. Advertisement. *Saturday Evening Post*, July 23, 1949.

Drake, Donald. "NASA Strains to Find Scientist-Astronauts." *Newsday* (Nassau Edition, Hudson, New York), June 30, 1965.

Dunn, Marcia, The Associated Press. "After 34 years, the Right Stuff, Women Astronauts Ready in '61." *Arizona Republic* (Phoenix, Arizona), February 3, 1995.

Dunn, Marcia, The Associated Press. "Equality Boosted by Launch; Shuttle will Carry First Black Woman." *Corpus Christi Caller-Times*, September 8, 1989.

Editorial. "Gemini Confirmed Mankind's Ability to Fly In Space." *Washington Post*, March 24, 1965.

Editorial. "'A Giant Leap for Mankind' From this Precarious Planet." *Courier-Journal* (Louisville), July 22, 1969.

Editor's Note, "The Man Behind the Glass Mask." *Life*, July 4, 1969.

"Emotions of the Nation Ride in Astronaut's Capsule, So…Shepard and U.S.A. Feel 'AOK.'" *Life*, May 12, 1961.

Engle, Joe H. interview by Rebecca Wright. NASA Headquarters History Office, Johnson Space Center. April 22, 2004. Accessed August 22, 2023. https://historycollection .jsc.nasa.gov/JSCHistoryPortal/history/oral_histories/EngleJH/EngleJH_4-22-04 .pdf.

Farmer, Gene. "Buzz Aldrin has 'The Best Scientific Mind we have Send into Space.'" *Life*, July 4, 1969.

"Fattening the Record Book." *Time*, July 29, 1966.

Federal Aviation Administration. "FAA Ends Commercial Space Astronaut Wings Program, Will Recognize Individuals Reaching Space on Website." Accessed May 31, 2022. https://www.faa.gov/newsroom/faa-ends-commercial-space-astronaut-wings -program-will-recognize-individuals-reaching#:~:text=The%20Wings%20program %20was%20created,to%20carry%20humans%20into%20space.

"Feminine First." *York Dispatch* (York, Pennsylvania), June 21, 1963.

Ferguson, Walter Mrs. "Gallantry Overdone." *Evansville Press* (Evansville, Indiana), December 10, 1959.

"5th Russian Orbit; Girl May Be Next; Space Influence in Long Flight Under Study." *Chicago Tribune*, June 15, 1963.

Finney, John W. "2 Astronauts Put on Diet for Flight; Grissom Believed Choice for Space Shot this Week." *New York Times*, July 16, 1961.

Finney, John W. "Glenn's Condition Good." *New York Times*, February 22, 1962.

Finney, John W. "Glenn Feels Pilot Can Replace Much of Spaceship Automation; Glenn Enhances Astronaut Role." *New York Times*, February 23, 1962.

Finney, John W. "Pentagon Shrugs at Titov's Flight." *New York Times*, August 8, 1961.

Finney, John W. "Pilots will Control Gemini Spacecraft." *New York Times*, October 15, 1962.

"Fired Woman Receives New Post at NASA." *Pittsburgh Courier*, September 7, 1974.

"Five Key Groundlings." *Time*, March 2, 1962.

Fontaine, Andre. "Are We Staking Our Future on a Crop of Sissies?" *Better Homes and Gardens*, December 1950.

Forbis, Jeanne. "Space Spirited: For this Pioneering Sooner, the Quest for Flight Discovery began a Long Time Ago." *Tulsa World*, September 21, 1980.

Gabbatt, Adam. "Wally Funk Fulfills Lifelong Dream to go to Space with Blue Origin Flight." *Guardian*. July 20, 2021. https://www.theguardian.com/science/2021/jul/20/wally-funk-space-blue-origin-flight.

"Gemini: 'It Didn't Last Long Enough.'" *Newsweek*, April 5, 1965.

"Gemini-8 Tumble Mystery Probed; Astronauts Safe on Rescue Ship; Capsule Recovered; Headed to Okinawa." *Knoxville News-Sentinel*, March 17, 1963.

"Geologist Schmitt and Combat Flier Evans on Apollo." *Chicago Tribune*, December 7, 1972.

"Girl Holding Down One Man's Job Seeks Another—As Army Pilot." *Democrat and Chronicle* (Rochester, New York), April 19, 1944.

"Girl in the Moon." *Birmingham Post and Gazette* (Birmingham, West Midlands, England), January 16, 1959.

"Girl Pilots: Air Force Trains them at Avenger Field, Texas." *Life*, July 19, 1943.

"3000 Girls Want Air: Pilots are Grounded by Men Only Rule." *Buffalo Evening News* (Buffalo, New York), April 4, 1942.

"Glamour Girls of the Air: For the Lucky Ones Being Hostess is the Mostest." *Life*, August 25, 1953, 68–75.

Glenn Annie, et al, "Seven Brave Women Behind the Astronauts; Spacemen's Wives Tell of their Inner Thoughts and Worries." *Life*, September 21, 1959.

"The Glorious Walk in the Cosmos." *Life*, June 16, 1965.

Golden, Harry Jr. "Jane Hart Seethes: 'Why No US Space Girl?'" *Detroit Free Press*, June 17, 1963.

Goldman, John J. and Nicholas C. Chriss. "Mission Control to Eagle: Houston Cool Heads to Spacemen Trio." *Los Angeles Times*, July 21, 1969.

"The Great Adventure Moves Ahead." *Newsweek*, June 14, 1965.

Greene, Bob. "Women Ride Wave of Sally's Heroism." *Chicago Tribune*, June 21, 1983.

Greider, William "Houston Watches: Awe, Laughter." *Washington Post*, July 21, 1969.

"Grief Expressed the World Over." *New York Times*, January 29, 1967.

Grissom, Gus and John Young. "Lift-Off to a New Era in Space." *Life*, April 2, 1965.

Grissom, Gus. "Talk Delivered by Major Virgil Grissom at an SETP East Coast Section Meeting, November 9, 1962." *SETP Newsletter* (November-December 1962), 5-12.

Grover, Preston, The Associated Press. "Russ Orbit Spaceman No. 3, 'Might Stay Up for a Week;' K. Airs Shot, Asks: No A-Test Please." *Salt Lake Tribune*, August 13, 1962.

Grover, Preston, The Associated Press. "Soviet Astronaut Still Up; Khrushchev Says Quite a Number of Orbits Slated." *Lake Charles American Press* (Lake Charles, Louisiana), August 12, 1962.

# BIBLIOGRAPHY
269

Hale, Ellen. Gamnnett News Service. "Today's Astronauts are a New Breed." *Poughkeepsie Journal* (Poughkeepsie, New York), April 6, 1981.

"Half a Billion Watch on TV: Earthlings Dance, Shout and Pray As Astronauts 'Conquer' the Moon." *Courier-Journal* (Louisville), July 21, 1969.

Hallerman, Ellen M. "WASPs Fliers Inspired Collins to make History." *Florida Today*, February 4, 1995.

Hamblin, Dora Jane. "Christmas Cheers on the Apollo 8 Home front." *Life*, January 10, 1969.

Hamblin, Dora Jane. "Neil Armstrong Refuses to 'Waste Any Heartbeats'." *Life*, July 4, 1969.

Hand, Phil. "IBM Computer to Be the 'Third Man' on Gemini Flight." *Press and Sun-Bulletin* (Binghamton, New York), March 22, 1965.

Harmeling, Susan. "What Might It Mean When Critics Call Someone a DEI Hire?" *Forbes*, July 26, 2024, https://www.forbes.com/sites/susanharmeling/2024/07/26/what-might-it-mean-when-critics-call-someone-a-dei-hire/.

Harris, Joyce Saenz, *Dallas Morning News*. "Trek to Stars a Bold Dream Come True." *Akron Beacon Journal* (Akron, Ohio), March 15, 1993.

Hart, Bart. "The Glamornauts: America's Eye-popping Space Gals are Really Flying High." *Globe*, March 18, 1980.

Haseltine, Nate. "Russian is First Man to Leave Craft in Orbit." *Washington Post*, March 19, 1965.

Haughland, Vern, Associated Press. "U.S. Could 'Shoot for Moon'; Apollo 9 has Opened Possibility; Astronauts Flying back to Houston." *News-Pallidium* (Benton Harbor, Michigan), March 14, 1969.

Havemann, Ernest. "The Emptiness of too Much Leisure, Part 1." *Life*, February 14, 1964.

Havemann, Ernest. "The Task Ahead: How to Take Life Easy." *Life*, February 21, 1964.

Hayworth, Mary. "Mary Hayworth's Mail: Much Neurotic Tension Today is Caused by Individuals Trying to Adhere to Ideals of King Arthur's Time." *Tampa Tribune*, February 11, 1952.

"He Brings it in 'Right on the Old Bazoo.'" *Life*, May 24, 1963.

"He Hit the Keyhole in the Sky." *Life*, March 2, 1962.

"Head Man at NASA: Thomas Otten Paine." *New York Times*, December 28, 1968.

Hearst, Joseph. "Give Us Space Role, Women Pilots Urge." *Chicago Tribune*, July 18, 1962.

Herald Wire Service. "Conrad Remained Unshaken Even During Tense Moments." *Miami Herald*, November 15, 1969.

Herbaugh, Sharon. Associated Press. "First Women Astronauts Aim High." *Honolulu Star Bulletin*, March 19, 1980.

Herbaugh, Sharon. "Women Astronauts See Future Beyond Clouds." *Herald and Review* (Decatur, Illinois), April 10, 1980.

Hiaasen, Carl. "Fired, Hired, Still Speaking." *Florida Today* (Cocoa Beach, Florida), August 21, 1974.

Hicks, Nancy. "The Flight Controllers' Taskmaster: Eugene Francis Kranz." *New York Times*, April 18, 1970.

"High Tension Over the Astronauts." *Life* March 25, 1966.

Hill, Gladwin. "Now Even Rocket Waits For Woman; A Slide-Rule Expert Decides if Weather is Right for Tests at White Sands." *New York Times*, April 14, 1957.

270 GENDER AND THE RACE FOR SPACE

Hill, Gladwin. "Test Pilots Get Some Good News; Group is Assured Machines Won't Supplant Humans on Probes in Space." *New York Times*, October 9, 1959.

Hiner, Lou Jr. The Washington Bureau, "14 Women Pass Astronaut Test," *Indianapolis News*, July 18, 1962.

Hoffman, James, and Mathew Tekulsky. "Adventurers in Space: Six Extraordinary Women Look to the Stars and See their Futures." *Pensacola News Journal*, March 19, 1978.

Holden, Constance. "NASA: Sacking of Top Black Woman Stirs Concern for Equal Employment." *Science* 182, no. 4114 (November 23, 1973): 804–805.

"Home From the Moon." *Atlanta Constitution*, December 28, 1968.

Horn, Henry. "Acid Test of the Airman; Seventy-five Monitors at Issoudon Selected on Practical Grounds Met All the Theoretical Medical Requirements." *New York Times Magazine*, April 20, 1919.

"How Seven Were Chosen." *Newsweek*, April 20, 1959.

"In Moscow, a Welcome to the Space Walker." *Life*, August 2, 1965.

"In NASA training, she Carried a Stowaway." *Newsday, Suffolk Edition*, (Melville, New York), October 26, 1984.

"In Space to Stay." *Newsweek*, April 27, 1981.

International News Service (INS). "No Flight of Fancy; Tourists are Assured Jet Travel to Moon by 'Guided Missiles.'" *Atlanta Constitution*, August 12, 1946.

"Into Space: Pat Rowe meets America's Women Astronauts in Training at the Houston Center." *Guardian* (London, Greater London, United Kingdom), February 1, 1979.

Irwin, Everett B. "Reds Can Beat us to the Moon." *Hopewell News* (Hopewell, Virginia), April 13, 1959.

Jackson, Alice. "Nichelle Nichols (Lt. Uhura) wants to make science of Star Trek reality." *Sun Herald* (Biloxi, Mississippi), June 4, 1977.

Jennings, Veronica T. "Expectations Rose Higher than Shuttle." *Florida Today*, July 13, 1985.

"Johnson Says Feat Shows 'We Can do Anything.'" *New York Times*, July 21, 1969.

Johnson, Thomas A. "Blacks and Apollo; Most Could've Cared Less." *New York Times*, July 27, 1969.

Jones, Christy. "No Fear of Flying Here: 12 Women Aviators to Celebrate." American Association of University Women, August 19, 2014. Accessed January 9, 2024, https://web.archive.org/web/20190509162202/https://www.aauw.org/2014/08/19 /aviation-day/

Keliner, Dick. Hollywood NEA. "Actress Space Fan After Trek." *Indianapolis Star*, December 11, 1977.

Kennedy, John F. "We Must Climb to the Hilltop." *Life*, August 22, 1960.

Kent, Ann. "Look!: For America's Women Astronauts it's a Space Countdown." *Sydney Morning Herald* (Sydney, Australia), September 7, 1978.

Kershaw, Tom. "Top Scholars are Told: For Every Astronaut, 5,000 Helpers on Ground." *Abilene Reporter-News*, May 17, 1968.

Kilpatrick, Carroll. "Apollo 11 Holiday Set For Monday." *Washington Post*, July 17, 1969.

Kilpatrick, Carroll. "Johnson Phones his 'Well Done' to Gemini Pair." *Washington Post*, March 24, 1965.

Kitson, Lela Cole. "El Paso Girl Prepares for Arduous War Work; Mary Leola Freeman Soon to Complete Training as Cadette." *El Paso Herald-Post*, September 22, 1943.

# BIBLIOGRAPHY

Klemsrud, Judy. "A Marriage that was Made for the Heavens." *New York Times*, June 3, 1980.

Knight, John. "A Date In Space? But What on Earth will a Girl Wear?" *Sunday Mirror* (London, United Kingdom), October 8, 1978.

Kocivar, Ben. "The Lady Wants to Orbit." *Look*, February 2, 1960.

Kraus, Alyssa. "Here's How Jeff Bazos's Spaceflight Unfolded this Morning." *CNN*, July 20, 2021. https://www.cnn.com/business/live-news/jeff-bezos-space-flight-07-20-21/index.html.

Kubota, Samantha. "NASA Wants to Land Americans Back on the Moon. These Women are Making it Happen; These Leaders are Behind Nasa's Massive Artemis Program that's Hoping to Make Even More Groundbreaking Lunar Discoveries." *Today*. February 2, 2022. https://www.today.com/news/women-behind-nasa-trip-moon-rcna14509.

## Ladies Home Journal

"A Lady Proves She's Fit for Space Flight." *Life*, August 29, 1960.

"Last Apollo Wednesday; Scholars Assess Program; 23-Billion Space Project Ran 11 Years; Cape Kennedy Presses Countdown; Last Apollo Flight Sets Off Evaluation." *New York Times*, December 3, 1972.

Lathan, Bill. "V-2 Rocket Sets Altitude Record of 72 Miles in White Sands Test." *El Paso Times*, May 11, 1946.

Lati, Marisa. "In 1962, She lost her chance to go to space. Today, at 82, she finally got her shot." *Washington Post*. July 20, 2021. https://www.washingtonpost.com/history/2021/07/20/wally-funk-astronaut-mercury-13/.

"Launching Operations Chief Likes Job to Football Coach's." *New York Times*, December 22, 1968.

Laurence, William L. "Science in Review: Little Dog in Sputnik II May Show Animals Can Adjust to Weightlessness." *New York Times*, November 10, 1957.

Laytner, Ron and Donald MacLachlin, free-lance reporters. "Sally Ride finds Hassles Part of Spaceflight." *Star-Phoenix* (Saskatoon, Saskatchewan, Canada), August 20, 1983.

Leary, Mike. "Challenger Launches 2D Satellite—Shuttle's Crew has a 'Super Day.'" *Philadelphia Inquirer*, June 20, 1983.

Leary, Mike. "Sally K. Ride is in Orbit." *Philadelphia Inquirer*, June 19, 1983.

Leary, Warren E. "Woman in the News; A Determined Breaker of Boundaries—Mae Carol Jemison." *New York Times*, September 13, 1992.

Lelyveld, Joseph. "Apollo 13: Moment of Exaltation." *New York Times*, April 18, 1970.

Lewin, Tamar. "Bias Called persistent Hurdle for Women in Sciences." *New York Times*, March 22, 2010.

Lewis, Flora. Editorial. "Human Paradox: A Contrast between Capacity, Deficiency." *Courier-Journal* (Louisville, Kentucky), July 22, 1969.

Lewis, Richard S. "Requiem for the Scientist-Astronauts." *Bulletin of the Atomic Scientists* 27, no. 5 (May 1971): 17–22.

Lewis, Richard S. "To Houston, Crew, LM Landing 'Hairy'." *Birmingham News* (Birmingham, Alabama), July 21, 1969.

"Lift-Off to a New Era in Space." *Life*, August 2, 1965.

"Lindbergh Says Man Must Balance Science with Morality to Survive; LINDBERGH LINKS SCIENCE WITH MORALITY." *New York Times*, December 18, 1949.

"The Loquacious Astronaut and the Taciturn One." *New York Times*, August 23, 1965.

Lovell, James. "'Earth We are Forsaking You for the Moon.'" *Life*, January 17, 1969.

Luce, Clare Boothe. "But Some People Simply Never Get the Message." *Life*, June 28, 1963.

Luce, Henry. "The American Century." *Life*, February 17, 1941.

Lukas, Anthony J. *New York Times* News Service. "Back On Earth, Many U.S. Citizens Still Seeking to Discover America." *Courier-Journal* (Louisville, Kentucky), July 21, 1969.

Lundberg, Kirsten O. United Press International. "Women's Liberation Different in the Soviet Union." *Spokane Chronicle* (Spokane, Washington), August 28, 1982.

Lunner, Chet. "Challenger Starts, Stalls: Engine Valve Halts Liftoff at 3 Seconds." *Florida Today*, July 13, 1985.

Lyons, Richard. "35 Chosen Astronaut Candidates; Six are Women and 3 Blacks." *New York Times*, January 17, 1978.

Lyons, Richard. "12 Countries Offer to Help In Recovery of Astronauts." *New York Times*, April 16, 1970.

Mackie, Lora. Media General News Service. "One Giant Step for Womankind Is Aim of NASA Coordinator." *Times Dispatch* (Richmond, Virginia), August 4, 1974.

Mandel, Paul. "The Ominous Failures that Haunted Friendship's Flight." *Life*, March 2, 1962.

"Marines Seek Exes Only, Army and Air Force in Market for Fem Recruits." *San Angelo Evening Standard* (San Angelo, Texas) August 13, 1948.

Martin Aircraft. Advertisement. *Colliers*. November 8, 1947.

"May Launch One Tuesday; Six Chimps Undergoing Last Tests Before Blazing Trail into Space." *Journal and Courier* (Lafayette, Indiana) January 28, 1961.

McDivitt, James A. "The Astronauts' Own Stories about Gemini 4." *Life*, June 25, 1965.

McGaffin, William. News World Service. "NASA Needs Scientists, Women Eligible for Moon Trip." *Charlotte News* (Charlotte, North Carolina), May 4, 1964.

McNutt, William. World Book Service. "Pretty Mini-skirted Blonde Mathematician Talked to Computer to Bring Apollo-13 Home." *Buffalo News* (Buffalo, New York), April 29, 1970.

"Men are Changing." *Newsweek*, January 16, 1978.

"Men of the Year." *Time*, January 3, 1969.

"3 Men on Last Apollo Moon Flight; Eugene Andrew Cernan; Harrison Hagan Schmitt; Ronald Ellwin Evans." *New York Times*, December 8, 1972.

Meyer, Agnes E. "Woman aren't Men." *Atlantic Monthly* 186 (1950): 32–33.

"Moment of the First Docking in Space." *Life*, April 1, 1966.

"Moon Shot Unites U.S. For Instant." *Chicago Defender*, July 21, 1969.

Morgenstem, Joseph. "Moon Age: New Dawn?" *Newsweek*, July 7, 1969.

Morse, Ralph. "Put Them High on the List of Men Who Count." *Life*, February 3, 1967.

"A Mrs. in the Missile?" *Los Angeles Times*, September 7, 1958.

Murphy, Mike. Yakima-Herald Republic. "Woman Sees Dream of Becoming an Astronaut Come True." *Columbian* (Vancouver, Washington), July 7, 1980.

Myler, John L. "No US Space Woman Planned—Yet." *San Francisco Examiner*, June 17, 1963.

"NASA Officials." *Louisiana Weekly* (New Orleans, Louisiana), November 30, 1974.

# BIBLIOGRAPHY

"NASA Says No to American Woman in Orbit." *Sault Star* (Sault St. Marie, Ontario, Canada) October 21, 1963.

Negri, Gloria. "Astronaut's Wife: Mod Voice of the Establishment." *Boston Globe*, October 15, 1968.

Nelson, Jack. "U.S. Called Fortunate in Unmanned Landings; Official Notes Rough Terrain, Says Eagle Might have had Trouble Without a Pilot." *Los Angeles Times*, July 21, 1969.

Nevin, David. "Collins Has Cool to Cope with Space and the Easter Bunny." *Life*, July 4, 1969.

"New Breed of Astronauts." *Athol Daily News* (Athol, Massachusetts), July 14, 1978.

"New Breed of Astronauts." *Florida Today*, January 18, 1978.

New York (HTNS). "What the Women Say." *Tampa Tribune*, June 17, 1963.

*New York Times* Wire Service. "Apollo Flight Director is No Johnny-Come-Lately." *Press-Telegram* (Longbeach, California), October 23, 1968.

*New York Times* Wire Service. "Beans Boldness Streak got him Flying." *Billings Gazette* (Billings, Montana), November 15, 1969.

*New York Times* Wire Service. "Crosses Apollo Path: Russians Place Luna 10 Miles above Moon." *Courier-Journal* (Louisville, Kentucky), July 21, 1969.

*New York Times* Wire Service. "Feisty Pete Conrad Flew at Early Age." *Billings Gazette* (Billings, Montana), November 15, 1969.

*New York Times* Wire Service. "Gordon Would Rather Land." *Billings Gazette* (Billings, Montana), November 15, 1969.

*New York Times* Wire Service. "The Moon Comes Second: George Paul Miller." *Chattanooga Times*, March 23, 1962.

*New York Times* Wire Service. "Soviet Spacewoman Hailed, but Feminine Stereotypes Remain." *Wisconsin State Journal* (Madison, Wisconsin), September 1, 1982.

Nichols, Bruce. The United Press International. "New Astronauts Welcomed." *Daily News Journal* (Murfreesboro, Tennessee), February 2, 1978.

"No Joy Riding Allowed." *Newsweek*, June 13, 1983.

Norman, Ellen. "'Star Trek' Star Recruits Women for NASA Program." *Peninsula Times Tribune* (Palo Alto, California), June 22, 1977.

Norris, John G. "Flight Proves Man Can Control Space Ship Outside Gravity Pull." *Washington Post*, May 6, 1961.

North American News Alliance. "Air Force Tests Seek 'Superman': Experiments Seek to Prove Hard Labor Can be done 3 Miles Above Sea Level." *New York Times*, October 18, 1959.

Obituary for Judith Neuffer Bruner at Wm. Reese & Sons Mortuary, P.A. Accessed on January 10, 2024, https://www.wmreeseandsons.com/obituary/judith-neuffer-bruner?lud=D3119E250801545D5C3AAA8943DF0AD6.

O'Connor. "Apollo 17 Coverage Gets Little Viewer Response," *New York Times*, December 14, 1972

"On the Bazoo." *Newsweek*, May 27, 1963.

"Opinion of the Week: At Home and Abroad; Major Topics: The John Glenn Flight." *New York Times* February 25, 1962.

O'Toole, Thomas, *Washington Post*, "Careers, Wealth Sacrificed For Lure of Space: An Old Fever Burns in New Generation of Astronauts." *Los Angeles Times*, September 3, 1982.

274 GENDER AND THE RACE FOR SPACE

O'Toole, Thomas. "Gemini Drops Almost on Target." *Washington Post*, November 16, 1966.

O'Toole, Thomas. *Washington Post*, "Space Claims a New Breed." *Sun* (Biloxi, Mississippi), September 4, 1980.

O'Toole, Thomas. *Washington Post Service*, "Space Shuttle Gets Set to Launch a New Generation of Astronauts." *Tampa Times*, January 1, 1981.

"Our Prayers Go With You." *Afro-American* (Baltimore, Maryland), July 26, 1969.

Pace, Eric, Special to the *New York Times*. "Navy Puts First Woman in Pilot Training." *New York Times*, January 11, 1973.

Paka, Vincent. "Barry Slams Apollo 11 Mission." *Washington Post*, July 19, 1969.

Pangalos, Mary. "Newsday Reporter takes Astronaut Tests." *Newsday* (Nassau Edition, Hempstead, New York), June 19, 1959.

Pauley, Gay, United Press International, Women's Editor. "Famous Aviatrix Ruth Nichols Dies Before Completion of Dream." *San Bernardino County Sun* (San Bernadino, California), October 6, 1960.

*People Weekly*. "NASA Picks Six Women Astronauts with the Message: You're Going a Long Way Baby." February 6, 1978.

Perkins, William J. "A Preview of Apollo 8—III: Three Astronauts Tell Why they Feel Set to Fly Around Moon, Now." *The Evening Sun* (Baltimore, Maryland), December 18, 1968.

Piper Cub. Advertisement. *Life*, August 13, 1945.

Piper Cub. Advertisement. *Time*, March 26, 1965.

"The Point of No Return for Everybody." *Life*, July 19, 1963.

Pothier, Richard. "How Armstrong Took Over to Land LEM." *Charlotte Observer*, July 21, 1969.

"Pravda Hails Glenn for 'Great Courage'." *New York Times*, February 23, 1962.

"Premier Mission Pilot Prepares." *New York Times*, December 10, 1961.

"President Ford Applauds Awardees." *Hill Top Times*, October 13, 2022, December 6, 1974.

Price, Ben. "'Moment of Doubt' Reported by Glenn." *Abilene Reporter-News*, February 24, 1962.

Prompet, John D. "President Hails Crew's Coolness." *New York Times*, June 7, 1966.

"Purse Strings Might Loosen for Space Program of U.S." *Arizona Republic* (Phoenix, Arizona), October 2, 1971.

"Push-Button, War Talk Draws Blast." *Salt Lake Tribune*, January 9, 1947.

"Quiet Man in Space; Michael Collins." *New York Times*, July 21, 1966.

Rabinowitch, Eugene. "Reflections on Apollo 8." *Bulletin of the Atomic Scientists* 24, no. 10 (March 1969): 2–3, 12.

Rankin, Allen. "Gun Vanity, 'A Lost Voter,' and Plain English." *Alabama Journal* (Montgomery, AL), January 12, 1950.

Rankin, Edwina. "CMU Grad is Ready for Liftoff." *Pittsburgh Press*, December 7, 1978.

Rankin, Virginia. "Star Trek's Lt. Uhura Plans Future in Space." *Corvallis Gazette Times* (Corvallis, Oregon), March 12, 1977.

Recer, Paul. Associated Press. "Next in Line: 7 Women Waiting for Turn Aboard Shuttle." *Anderson Independent-Mail* (Anderson, South Carolina), June 22, 1983.

Recer, Paul "Seven More Women Waiting for Ride into Space." *Anniston Star* (Anniston, Alabama), June 21, 1983.

# BIBLIOGRAPHY 275

Recer, Paul. "Wings of Change will Carry First US Woman into Space." *Fort Worth Star-Telegram,* June 12, 1983.

"Regular Navy to Enlist 6,000 Women by '50." *Brooklyn Daily Eagle* (Brooklyn, New York), July 31, 1948.

Reinhold, Robert. "Behind Each Astronaut Stand the 'Other' Women of NASA." *New York Times,* August 28, 1983.

Reistrup, J. V. "Astronauts Enter Orbit after Target; Outlook for Dual Rendezvous is Good; Gemini X Liftoff Hailed as 3-Day Space Mission Starts in Perfect Timing." *Washington Post,* July 19, 1966.

"Rendezvous with Destiny." *Time,* April 20, 1959.

Rennert, Leo, McClatchy newspapers staff writer. "Engine Gets Credit for Apollo Bullseye." *Fresno Bee* (Fresno, California), December 27, 1968.

Reston, James. *New York Times News Service.* "After the Moon, Can we Conquer the Earth." *Winston-Salem Journal,* July 21, 1969.

Reston, James. "Cape Canaveral; Is the Moon Really Worth John Glenn?" *New York Times,* February 25, 1962.

Reynolds, Tex. "Between the Lines: A Woman in Orbit; HAAPA Statement; Bid for Air Rights." *Journal Times* (Racine, Wisconsin), June 17, 1963.

Rossiter, Al. United Press International. "Actress is Shadowed by 'Star Trek' Character." *Bangor Daily News* (Bangor, Maine), April 9, 1977.

Rossiter, Al. "Gemini Space Twin Takes Laughing Stroll into History: Medic Says Pair Doing 'Real Great'." *Independent* (Long Beach, California), June 4, 1965.

Rossiter, Al. "Life Changed 'Holds' Nichelle." *El-Paso Herald Post,* March 12, 1977.

Rowe, Pat. "Into Space: Pat Rowe Meets America's Women Astronauts in Training at the Houston Center." *Guardian* (London, Greater London, United Kingdom), February 1, 1979.

Rugaber, Walter. "Nixon Calls for a Holiday So All Can Share in 'Glory.'" *New York Times,* July 17, 1969.

"Sally Ride: Ready for Liftoff." *Newsweek,* June 13, 1983.

"Sally's Joy Ride into the Sky." *Time* 13 June 1983.

Sanborn, Sara. "Sally Ride, Astronaut: The World is Watching." *Ms. Magazine* June 1983.

Schirra, Wally. "A Real Breakthrough—The Capsule was All Mine." *Life,* October 26, 1962.

Schmeck Harold M. Jr. "Gemini 5 Orbited but a Power Loss Threatens Duration of Planned 8-Day Mission Uncertain; 2 Astronauts Strive to Continue." *New York Times,* August 22, 1965.

Schmeck Harold M. Jr. "NASA to Review Space Accident." *New York Times,* April 18, 1970.

Schmeck Harold M. Jr. "The Navigation is Practically Perfect." *New York Times,* July 25, 1969.

Schmeck Harold M. Jr. "Pilots Maneuver to Meet 'Rocket': Gemini Tests Rendezvous Technique with Computer," *New York Times,* August 24, 1965.

Schmeck Harold M. Jr. "The Scientist to Play Vital Role on Lunar Flight." *New York Times,* July 4, 1966.

Schwartz, Harry. "Moscow: Flight is taken as Another Sign that Communism is the Conquering Wave." *New York Times,* April 16, 1961.

Scipioni, Jade. "How Ellen Ochoa, the first Hispanic Woman in Space, Deal with 'People who didn't think I should be there.'" *CNBC,* September 21, 2021. Accessed January

9, 2024, https://www.cnbc.com/2021/09/21/ellen-ochoa-first-hispanic-woman-in-space-on-challenges-leadership.html

"Scott and Armstrong Extend Horizons Of Colorful Flying Careers." *Philadelphia Inquirer*, March 17, 1966.

Semple, Robert B. Jr. "Nixon to Give Medal to Crew in Hawaii." *New York Times*, April 18, 1970.

Sengstackk, John H. "Earthly Questions," *Chicago Defender*, July 22, 1969.

Shabad, Theodore. "Russians Acclaim Astronaut After Flight of 435,000 Miles." *New York Times*, August 8, 1961.

Shabad, Theodore. "Titov Describes his Space Flight." *New York Times*, August 9, 1961.

Shapiro, Henry. United Press International. "Russia Cheers its Cosmonaut." *Atlanta Constitution*, April 13, 1961.

Shapiro, Henry. United Press International. "Soviet Craft Carrying Three Launched into Earth Orbit." *Anniston* (Alabama) *Star*, October 12, 1964.

Shaw, Joy Reese. "Even Newspaperman Weeps as Redstone Takes to Air," *Miami Herald*, May 6, 1961.

"She Orbits Over the Sex Barrier." *Life*, June 28, 1963.

Sheehan, Alan H. "Women in Business/Margaret Hamilton Lickly; Putting 'Eagle' On Course." *Boston Globe*, November 1, 1972.

Shepard Alan Jr. "The Astronaut's Story of the Thrust into Space: Personal Account: 'Butterflies, a Feeling of Go, They're Yelling for Me'." *Life*, May 19, 1961.

Sidey, Hugh. "How the News Hit Washington—With Some Reactions Overseas." *Life*, April 21, 1961.

Simmons, Howard. "Astronauts Relax after 3d Rendezvous, Reschedule Space Walk this Morning; Docking Maneuver is Dropped; Space Pilots Told Not to Attempt Release of Shroud." *Washington Post*, June 5, 1966.

Simmons, Howard. "Cernan Walks in Space for Two Hours; Fogged-Up Visor Cuts Activity Short; Splashdown of Gemini 9 Set Today; Pilots maneuver Craft Into Orbit for Re-Entry." *Washington Post*, June 6, 1966.

Simmons, Howard. "Failure of Oxygen Warmer Appears to be Cause of Trouble on Gemini 5." *Washington Post*, August 22, 1965.

Simross, Lynn. *Los Angeles Times*, "An Astronaut or a Multi-role Model? 1st Black Woman in Space Corps Surprised at New Image." *Philadelphia Inquirer*, August 9, 1987.

"Sisters Tell Why they want to be Astronauts." *Medford Mail Tribune* (Medford, Oregon), July 20, 1962.

"Six Perfect Orbits; Safe." *Chicago Tribune*, October 4, 1962.

"Soviet Pilot, 34, Becomes Second Woman in Space." *New York Times*, August 20, 1982.

"Space: Adventure into Emptiness." *Time*, March 26, 1965.

"Space: Closing the Gap." *Time*, June 11, 1965.

"Space: Gemini's Wild Ride." *Time*, March 25, 1966.

"Space Pilot Training." *Greenwood Commonwealth* (Greenwood, Mississippi), June 24, 1963.

"Space Suffragette." *Daily Oklahoman* (Oklahoma City), July 17, 1962.

*Space World*, June/July 1983.

"Spaceman Ordeal." *Newsweek*, February 5, 1962.

"Speed Master Cleaner." Advertisement. *Life*, September 21, 1959.

Stafford, Charles. "Gemini's Maneuvers Start Era of History." *Washington Post*, March 24, 1965.

# BIBLIOGRAPHY                                                      277

Stanford, Neal. "Women as Astronauts." *Star Phoenix* (Saskatoon, Saskatchewan, Canada), July 28, 1962.

Start, Clarissa. "Why Just Tut-Tut Girl Astronauts?" *St. Louis Post-Dispatch*, October 2, 1962.

"State Coach on War Jobs." *Pittsburgh-Sun Telegraph* (Pittsburgh, Pennsylvania), July 16, 1943.

Stevens, William K. "Computer on Board Apollo Does the Flying; 3 Astronauts Permit Electronic System to Run Main Task." *New York Times*, March 4, 1969.

Stevens, William K. "What Kind of Men are they." *New York Times*, July 17, 1969.

"Still Struggling to Get a Chance at Space." *Kansas City Star*, September 28, 1962.

Stinson. Advertisement. *Life*, November 17, 1947.

Stockton, Bill. Associate Press Science Writer. "Astronauts Thaw Out on Carrier; NASA Not Ready to Speculate on Apollo 14 Flight." *Independent Press Telegram*, (Long Beach, California), April 18, 1970.

Stockton, Bill. "12 Seconds Agonizing at Houston." *Daily Journal* (Fergus Falls, Minnesota), November 15, 1969.

"Substitute Swigert, 38, Has a Girl in Every (Air) Port." *New York Times*, April 12, 1970.

Sullivan, Walter. "Apollo's Craft's Water Shortage Will Limit Astronauts' Use of Guidance System," *New York Times*, April 15, 1970

Sullivan, Walter. "Computer Aids Navigation of Apollo 8 Crewmen." *New York Times*, December 24, 1968.

Sullivan, Walter. "Jokes in the Void; Talk of Two Astronauts is Heard by Millions on Radio and TV." *New York Times*, June 4, 1965.

Sweeney, Louis. "Why Valentina and Not Our Gal?" *Berkshire Eagle* (Pittsfield, Massachusetts), June 21, 1962.

Syversten, George, Associated Press. "One of the 'Boys': Woman Cosmonaut is Athlete." *Decatur Daily Review* (Decatur, Illinois), June 17, 1963.

"Take a Giant Step—Into Space." *Newsweek*, March 29, 1965.

Talley, Olive. United Press International. "Women Astronauts get their Place in Space." *Indianapolis News*, June 8, 1983.

Tanner, Henry. "Soviet Spaceship is Landed Safely after 16 Circuits; 3 Astronauts Stay in Cabin During Descent—Use of Braking Rockets Hinted 437,000 MILES Covered Crew Wanted to Remain Aloft for 24 More Hours, but Plea was Refused Soviet Spaceship is Landed Safely After 16 Circuits of the Earth in 24 Hours Crew in Capsule as it Hits Ground; 3 Men Look Tired as they Leave Cabin on Farm—Interior is Described." *New York Times*, October 14, 1964.

Tiede, Tom. NEA Staff Correspondent. "Famed Woman Flier Speaks on Lady Astronauts; Jackie: Stork Stops Space Girls." *Idaho Statesman* (Boise, Idaho), September 7, 1969.

"Time For Baby Before Space." *Miami News* (Miami, Florida), July 26, 1963.

*Time* Wire Service. "Recordings Provide No Clue: Astronauts Head for Home; Mishap Remains A Mystery." *Tampa Bay Times*, March 18, 1966.

"Titov's Triumph in 17 Orbits." *Life*, August 18, 1961.

Thompson, Alice. "How to be a Woman." *Seventeen*, July 1951.

Thompson, Anne V. World Book Science Service. "Why No Women Astronauts? Equality of Sexes Ends Where Outer Space Begins." *Tribune* (Coshocton, Ohio), October 8, 1967.

Thompson, Ronald. The Associated Press. "Crew Dedicated Lives to Flying." *Rutland Daily Herald* (Rutland, Vermont), March 1, 1966.

Thompson, Ronald. The Associated Press Aerospace Writer. "The New Breed." *Cincinnati Enquirer*, September 24, 1967.

Thompson, Ronald. "Spacemen Make Perfect Landing in Sight of Ship; Call Flight of 3 Days Lots of Fun; Spacemen Make Perfect Landing." *Atlanta Constitution*, July 22, 1966.

Toner, Mike. "Shuttle Crew has a Day of Leisure Before the Challenge." *Miami Herald*, June 17, 1983.

Topping, Seymour. "Soviet Astronaut Down Safely After Orbiting Earth 17 Times; Exercised, Ate, and Slept Aloft." *New York Times*, August 7, 1961.

Topping, Seymour. "Soviet Orbits Woman Astronaut Near Bykovsky for Dual Flight; They Talk by Radio, Are Put on TV, Premier is Joyful Phones Spacewoman—She Tells World She Feels Fine." *New York Times*, June 17, 1963.

Topping, Seymour. "Soviet Pilots Spin On in Orbit; One has Flown Million Miles; He is Tired but Still Efficient; Astronauts Busy; They Work and Chat-Time of Landing is Still Undisclosed." *New York Times*, August 14, 1962.

Topping, Seymour. "Third Russian Orbiting the Earth in Flight Expected to Set Record; Soviet Watches him on TV Screen; He Sleeps 7 Hours; 'Feel Fine,' Astronaut Informs Khrushchev in Talk by Radio; Third Soviet Astronaut is Launched into Orbital Flight Expected to Outlasts Titov; Fliers TV Report Says he is Well; Khrushchev Praises Pilot as They Chat by Radio on 4th Trip Around Earth." *New York Times*, August 12, 1962.

Topping, Seymour. "Two Soviet Space Craft Circling Earth in Adjacent Orbits After New Launching; Pilots Keep in Touch by Sight and Radio; Astronauts on TV; Both Report All is Well; Nikolayev Breaks Titov's Record." *New York Times*, August 13, 1962.

Toth, Robert C. *Los Angeles Times*. "Female Pilots are High Fliers Altering the Wild Blue Yonder." *Harford Courant* (Hartford, Connecticut), October 6, 1981.

Toth, Robert C. "U.S. Took a Gamble in Planning Rendezvous of Spacecraft, Booster." *Los Angeles Times*, June 4, 1965.

Toynbee, Arnold J. "Some Thoughts on the Moon Landing." *Charlotte Observer*, July 21, 1969.

Treisman, Rachel. "JD Vance went Viral for "Cat Lady" Comments. The Centuries-old Trope has a Long Tail." National Public Radio. July 29, 2024. https://www.npr.org /2024/07/29/nx-s1-5055616/jd-vance-childless-cat-lady-history .

Troan, John. Scripps-Howard Science Writer. "Space Race Pace Hinges on 'Trouble'; Finding Cause of Tumbling is Key to Schedule." *Knoxville-News Sentinel*, March 17, 1966.

TWA. Advertisement. *Colliers*, November 22, 1947.

Ubell, Earl. "Apollo 12: Testing New Role for Man in Space." *New York Times*, November 9, 1969.

Ubell, Earl. "The Time of the Scientists has Come." *New York Times*, July 25, 1971.

The United Press International. "America Reacts to Space Feat with Woman Driver Wheezes." *Macon News* (Macon, Georgia), July 17, 1963.

The United Press International. "Apollo 10 Develops Trouble." *Ledger-Enquirer* (Columbus, Georgia), May 23, 1969.

The United Press International. "Astronauts Calm After 'Wild Ride.'" *Courier Post*, (Camden, New Jersey), November 15, 1969.

# BIBLIOGRAPHY 279

The United Press International. "The Best One Ever; Gemini Astronauts Return Triumphantly to Earth; Bring Back Batch [*sic*] New Space Records." *Aiken Standard and Review* (Aiken, South Carolina), September 16, 1966.

The United Press International. "Cosmonette—The Gal's Delight." *Record* (Hackensack, New Jersey), June 17, 1963.

The United Press International. "Female Astronauts Lose Again." *Fresno Bee* (Fresno, California), March 31, 1967.

The United Press International. "Female Cosmonaut is Praised." *St. Louis Post-Dispatch*, August 29, 1982.

The United Press International. "Foul-up aborts Discovery's Launch." *Birmingham Post-Herald* (Birmingham, Alabama), June 27, 1984.

The United Press International. "Gagarin Flies Home to Moscow After Learning of Soviet Shot." *New York Times*, August 6, 1961.

The United Press International. "'Greatest Moment of Our Time,' Says the President." *Charlotte Observer*, July 21, 1969.

The United Press International. "Grissom and Young Undergo Tests After Successful Gemini Journey." *Coshocton Tribune* (Coshocton, Ohio), March 24, 1965.

The United Press International. "Heartbeats Double During Crisis in Space." *Tampa Bay Times*, March 18, 1966.

The United Press International. "Her Weakness: Spiked Heels and Beethoven; New Soviet Heroine." *San Francisco Examiner*, June 17, 1963.

The United Press International. "Invited to Whitehouse; Two Astronauts Hear Johnson 'Well Done.'" *Albuquerque Journal*, March 24, 1965.

The United Press International. "Irony from African Tracking Station: Armstrong Vocally Calm, Cool." *Morning Call* (Paterson, New Jersey), March 17, 1966.

The United Press International. "5 Men on the Ground are Hailed by NASA." *New York Times*, February 28, 1971.

The United Press International. "NASA Selects 11 to be Astronauts; Civilian Spacemen Include Two Naturalized Citizens." *New York Times*, August 5, 1967.

The United Press International. "Rendezvous Key in Moon Plans." *Kingsport News* (Kingsport, Tennessee), June 4, 1966.

The United Press International. "Reports On Female Cosmonaut Smack of Sexism." *St. Louis Post-Dispatch*, August 29, 1982.

The United Press International. "Ruth Nichols Says: Women Ideal Astronauts." *Akron Beacon Journal* (Akron, Ohio), November 19, 1959.

The United Press International. "Skill to Decided U.S. Astronauts." *Macon News* (Macon, Georgia), July 17, 1963.

The United Press International. "Soviet Ship Returns Safely." *Athens Messenger* (Athens, Ohio), March 19, 1965.

The United Press International. "Soviets Apparently will not Attempt Space Ship Link-Up; Moscow Rumor Reports Third Shot Planned." *Macon News* (Macon, Georgia), June 17, 1963.

The United Press International. "Soviets Drop Back to Earth; Spacemen End 4-Day Spectacle; Both Men Said to be Healthy." *Bakersfield Californian*, August 15, 1962.

The United Press International. "Soviets Invent New Male Bastion—Then Breach It." *Hartford Currant* (Hartford, Connecticut), August 21, 1982.

The United Press International. "Soviets Join Other Nations in Pledging Aid." *Bedford Gazette* (Bedford, Pennsylvania), April 16, 1970.

280 GENDER AND THE RACE FOR SPACE

The United Press International. "Space Shuttle Flight Aborted: Challengers Computers Command Engines to Shut Down." *York Dispatch* (York, Pennsylvania), July 13, 1985.

The United Press International. "Sun-Splashed Return for Gemini; Spacemen Even Kept Feet Dry." *Post-Standard* (Syracuse, New York), September 16, 1966.

The United Press International. "Lt. Uhura Finds a New 'Enterprise.'" *Orlando Sentinel*, May 4, 1977.

The United Press International. "Valentina Goes For Spike Heels, Long-Haired Music." *Tampa Tribune*, June 17, 1963.

The United Press International. "Valentina Pioneer for Moon Colony?" *Dayton Daily News* (Dayton, Ohio), June 19, 1963.

The United Press International. "'We've Had a Lot of Fun'—Alan B. Shepard; Apollo 14 Home Safely With Perfect Landing." *San Bernadino County Sun* (San Bernardino, California), February 10, 1971.

The United Press International. "Women Cry 'Unfair!'—Ask Congress for Equal Rights in Space." *Memphis Press-Scimitar*, July 17, 1962.

"U.S.-Soviet Box Score on Astronauts' Flights." *New York Times*, July 22, 1966.

Vahlberg, Vivian. "State's Astronaut Highly Visible." *Daily Oklahoman* (Oklahoma City, Oklahoma), January 17, 1978.

Van Horne, Harriet. "A Long Way, Baby: the Sky is no Limit for Today's Woman." *Philadelphia Inquirer*, February 2, 1978.

"Vive la difference!" *Popular Mechanics*, October 1963.

Voboril, Mary. "Astronaut Says Women Can do it All." *Miami Herald*, May 25, 1983.

Voboril, Mary. "Ride Keeps Cool About Breaking a Gender Barrier." *Miami Herald*, June 17, 1983.

"Von Braun and Colleagues Designing Space Shuttle." *Washington Post*, July 25, 1969.

Von Braun, Wernher. "Man on the Moon: The Journey." *Colliers*, October 18, 1952.

Von Braun, Wernher. "Space Pioneer Reflects on Apollo's Achievement." *New York Times*, December 3, 1972.

Wainwright, Loudon. "All Systems are Ho-Hum." *Life*, December 2, 1966.

Wainwright, Loudon. "From a Mountain Boyhood Full of Roaming and Recklessness Comes a Quiet Man to Ride Aurora 7." *Life*, May 18, 1962.

Waldron, Martin. "Applause, Cigars and Champagne Toasts Greet Capsule's Landing." *New York Times*, April 18, 1970.

Waldron, Martin. "Flight Director is Making the Decisions." *New York Times*, April 16, 1970.

"Wally Shoots for Three." *Life*, October 25, 1968.

"War and Economics of the Push Button Variety." *Montana Standard* (Butte, Montana), November 29, 1946.

Washington Post Service. "Astronauts Exhausted After Ordeal in Space." *Arizona Republic* (Phoenix, Arizona), April 18, 1970.

Washington Post Service. "Everything Fell into Place in the Last Few Minutes." *Arizona Republic* (Phoenix, Arizona), April 18, 1970.

Waterhouse, Helen. "They're Irked: Gals want a Shot at Space Ride." *Akron Beacon Journal* (Akron, Ohio), April 22, 1962.

Waters, Harry F., Martin Kasindorf, and Betsy Carter. "Sex and TV." *Newsweek*, February 27, 1978.

# BIBLIOGRAPHY 281

Watson, Elmo Scott, Western Newspaper Union, "American Women Pilots Helped Deliver Planes Which Enabled Red Armies to Launch Offensive that May have been Turning Point of the War." *Midland Journal* (Rising Sun, Maryland), January 5, 1945.

Weaver, Warren Jr. "National Guidelines Set by 7-to-2 Vote." *New York Times*, January 23, 1973.

Webb, Alvin Jr. United Press International. "Fuel Shortage Cuts Collins' Stroll in Space." *Billings Gazette* (Billings, Montana), July 21, 1966.

Webb, Alvin Jr. "U.S. Astronaut will have Partial Control of Capsule." *Tyrone Daily Herald* (Tyrone, Pennsylvania), May 1, 1961.

Webb, Alvin Jr. "Women Irked, too: 'Cosmonette' Puts U.S. Men On Spot." *Dailey Press* (Newport News, Virginia), June 17, 1963.

"The Week in Review: Triumph!" *New York Times*, December 29, 1968.

Weinraub, Bernard. "At the Launching, Turbulent America in Microcosm." *New York Times*, July 20, 1969.

West, Dick, United Press International, "The Lighter Side: House Space Committee Ponders Problems of Pregnant Astronauts." *News-Review* (Roseburg, Oregon), July 18, 1962.

"What Flopnik! Britons Blare." *Chicago Tribune*, December 7, 1957.

"What in the World!: NASA's Texas Rose." *Colorado Springs Gazette-Telegraph*, February 1, 1970.

Wheeler, Keith. "Big Labor Hunts for the Hard Answers." *Life*, July 19, 1963.

Whitworth, Kanya, Lissette Rodriguez, and Katie Kindelan, "All-female Super Bowl Flyover Team makes History." *ABC News*, February 20, 2023. https://abcnews.go .com/GMA/Living/female-super-bowl-flyover-team-speaks-making-history/story ?id=96983944#:~:text=In%20a%20Super%20Bowl%20first,the%20flyover%20at %20Sunday's%20game.&text=For%20the%20first%20time%20ever,group%20 of%20women%20made%20history

"Why Half Our Combat Soldiers Fail to Shoot," *Colliers*, November 8, 1952.

Wilford, John Noble. "The Apollo 9 Astronauts Take a Restful Cruise Through Space." *New York Times*, March 10, 1969.

Wilford, John Noble. "Apollo 9 Splashes Down Accurately; Opens Way for Summer Moon Landing." *New York Times*, March 14, 1969.

Wilford, John Noble. "Apollo Maneuver Delayed Briefly by Sloshing Fuel." *New York Times*, March 9, 1969.

Wilford, John Noble. "Astronauts' Capsule Hits the Atlantic in Full View of Recovery Ship; Computer Guides Gemini's Re-entry and Splashdown; Automatic Landing is First for U.S.—Astronauts Go Aboard Carrier Guam; 3-Day Mission Saw the First Single-Orbit Rendezvous and Tethered Flight; Computer Guides Gemini Re-Entry and Splashdown Near Carrier Guam in Atlantic; Copter Picks Up Two Astronauts; 3-Day Mission Saw the First Single-Orbit Rendezvous and Tethered Flight." *New York Times*, September 16, 1966.

Wilford, John Noble. "Astronauts Land Gently on Target, Unharmed by their Four-Day Ordeal; Sea Recovery Swift After Perfect Entry; Aquarius Praised for Vital Role." *New York Times*, April 18, 1970.

Wilford, John Noble. "Astronauts Soar 850 Miles, Spin Tethered With Agena; Gemini 11 Reaches 850-Mile Altitude." *New York Times*, September 15, 1966.

Wilford, John Noble. "3 Astronauts' Tape Ended With Get Us Out of Here!'; Tape of Astronauts' Last Moments Ends with Cry: 'Get Us Out of Here!'; Space Program Supported." *New York Times*, January 31, 1967.

Wilford, John Noble. "Crew of Crippled Apollo 13 Starts Back After Rounding Moon and Firing Rocket; Men Appear Calm Despite Low Reserves." *New York Times*, April 15, 1970.

Wilford, John Noble. "Gemini 9 Delayed Until Tomorrow." *New York Times*, June 2, 1966.

Wilford, John Noble. "Gemini Docks With Agena and then Joined Vehicles Rocket into Higher Orbit." *New York Times*, July 19, 1966.

Wilford, John Noble. "Gemini, in Its First Orbit, Docks with Agena Target in a 94-Minute Maneuver; Link-Up is on Time Main Object Of 3-Day Mission is Achieved with Seeming Ease Gemini, in First Orbit, Docks with Agena Target Satellite in 94-Minute Maneuver Link-Up is Made without Mishap Object of the 3-Day Mission is Achieved on Schedule and with Seeming Ease." *New York Times*, September 13, 1966.

Wilford, John Noble. "Gemini 9 Lands Safely Near Bullseye; Astronauts Flow to Cape For Debriefing on Mission." *New York* Times, June 7, 1966.

Wilford, John Noble. "Gemini 7's Pilot Return From Record 14 Day Trip; Both Reported Healthy; Land on Target." *New York Times*, December 19, 1965.

Wilford, John Noble. "Gemini Postpones a 'Walk' in Space; Docking Canceled." *New York Times*, June 5, 1966.

Wilford, John Noble. "Gemini Program Ends in Success." *New York Times*, November 16, 1966.

Wilford, John Noble. "LM is Jettisoned," *New York Times*, July 22, 1969.

Wilford, John Noble. "Loose Shield Blocks Gemini Docking; Mission Continuing—Astronaut Floats in Space Today Loose Shield Blocks Gemini Docking but Flight is to Continue for Scheduled 3 Days ASTRONAUTS GAIN ORBIT ON 3D TRY Are to Practice rendezvous—2 Hour Sojourn in Space Set for Today Problem is Studied Jagged Edges a Danger Makes First Adjustment." *New York Times*, June 4, 1966.

Wilford, John Noble. "Maj. Collins 'Walks' to Nearby Agena And Retrieves a Space Dust Detector." *New York Times*, July 21, 1966.

Wilford, John Noble. "Power Failure Imperils Astronauts; Apollo Will Head Back to the Earth." *New York Times*, April 14, 1970.

Wilford, John Noble. "Schirra Nettled Over New Tests." *New York Times*, October 1, 1968.

Wilford, John Noble. "Shuttle Rockets to Orbit with 5 Aboard," *New York Times*, June 19, 1983.

Wilford, John Noble. "Stricken Apollo Speeding Toward Earth for Pacific Splashdown this Afternoon." *New York Times*, April 17, 1970.

Wilford, John Noble. "U.S. Prepares Moon Shot in December." *New York Times*, October 23, 1968.

Wilhoit, Herbert D. Associated Press. "Test Pilot: He May Fly 4,000 m.p.h." *Corpus Christi Times*, April 26, 1957.

Williams, Janis. "Making Way for the Ladies in Space." *Saturday Evening Post*, September 1982.

Winters, Ruth. Women's News Service. "Future Bleak For Women Astronauts." *Pensacola News*, March 7, 1968.

Wire Services. "Historic Space Step Taken by Cosmonaut: Feat Puts Russia Months Ahead of U.S. in Moon Race." *Independent* (Pasadena, California), March 19, 1965.

# BIBLIOGRAPHY 283

Witkin, Richard. "Cooper Maneuvers to a Bullseye Landing with Manual Control as Automatic Fails; 'I'm in Fine Shape,' He Says After 22 Orbits; Dramatic Return, Astronaut was Aloft Over 34 Hours—Aided By Glenn." *New York Times*, May 17, 1963.

Witkin, Richard. *New York Times* News Service. "Eagle's Descent to the Moon Mostly in Computer's Hands." *Courier-Journal* (Louisville, Kentucky), July 21, 1969.

Witkin, Richard. "Error By Carpenter Made Craft use too Much Fuel; He used Two Systems During Last Phase of Flight—Officials are Considering Seven Orbits for Next Astronaut." *New York Times*, May 27, 1962.

Witkin, Richard. "Experts Tricked the Computer." *New York Times*, December 8, 1972.

Witkin, Richard. "Flight by Schirra Viewed as Proving Pilots' Space Role," *New York Times*, October 5, 1962.

Witkin, Richard. "Mercury Flight Debate: Question of Another One-Man Trip Poses Technical and Cost Problems." *New York Times*, March 25, 1963.

Witkin, Richard. "Shepard had Periscope: 'What a Beautiful View'; 'What a Beautiful View,' Shepard Exclaims from Capsule at 115 Miles in Space; Astronaut Calm During his Flight; Reports Data Methodically to Center at Canaveral—Ground Crews Cheer." *New York Times*, May 6, 1961.

Witkin, Richard. "Shortly Before Landing, Armstrong Took Over From Computer." *New York Times*, July 21, 1969.

Witkin, Richard. "Space Chimpanzee is Safe After Soaring 420 Miles." *New York Times*, February 1, 1961.

Witkin, Richard. "U.S. Hurls Man 115 Miles into Space; Shepard Works Controls in Capsule, Reports by Radio in 15-Minute Flight; In Fine Condition Astronaut Drops into the Sea Four Miles from Carrier; Astronaut Sends Data from Craft; Shepard's Condition is Fine After 15-Minute Trip from Cape Canaveral." *New York Times*, May 6, 1961.

Wolfenden, Jeremy. "Russia's Woman Pioneer in Space; Valentina a Day Late for Rendezvous; Second Man May Go Up Today." *Dailey Telegraph* (London, Greater London, England), June 17, 1963.

"Women Astronaut Trainee." *Calgary Albertan*, February 27, 1962.

"Women Astronauts?" *Times and Democrat* (Orangeburg, South Carolina), August, 20, 1962.

"Women Astronauts." *Waukesha Daily Freeman* (Waukesha, Wisconsin), July 13, 1968

"Women Best Suited For Space Travel, According to Ivan Tors, TV Producer." *Times-Mail* (Bedford, Indiana), December 22, 1959.

"Women, Blacks Join Astronaut Corps." *Science News*, January 21, 1978.

"Women Fail to Qualify for Space Journeys, House Committee Told." *Akron Beacon Journal* (Akron, Ohio), July 18, 1962.

"Women Forces Seek Recruits: Four Distaff Military Services Open Drive for New Enlistees." *Arizona Daily Star* (Tucson, Arizona), June 17, 1948.

"12 Women to Take Astronaut Tests." *New York Times*, January 26, 1961.

"Women with Wings: LT. Judith Anne Neuffer." *All Hands*, January 1975.

Woods, David and Lennox J. Waugh. "Apollo 12 Lunar Surface Journal: Apollo 12 Onboard Voice Transcription, January 1970." *Apollo Flight Journal*. The National Aeronautics and Space Administration History Division. Accessed August 25, 2023. https://history.nasa.gov/alsj/a12/AS12_CM.PDF.

Woods, David and Lennox J. Waugh. "Apollo 13 Pre-launch Activities and the Crewman Change." *Apollo Flight Journal*. The National Aeronautics and Space Administration History Division. Accessed September 7, 2023. https://history.nasa.gov/afj/ap13fj/00crewchange.html.

Woods, David and Lennox J. Waugh. "Apollo 13 Technical Air-to-Ground Voice Transcription." Apollo Lunar Journal, NASA History Division. Accessed August 15, 2023. https://history.nasa.gov/alsj/a13/AS13_TEC.PDF.

"World Will Be Ruled from Skies Above." *Life*, 17 May 1963.

Wright, Lawrence, *Texas Monthly*, "Tribulations and Elations of a Woman Astronaut." *Charlotte News* (Charlotte, North Carolina), August 31, 1981.

# INDEX

**Note**: Please locators followed by 'n' refer to notes. Locators in bold refer to figures.

1951 *Seventeen Magazine* 93
1953 Powder Puff Derby 149
1957 Child Study Association of America conference 26–27
1957 Gaither Report 37
1958 NASA Act 54
1958 National Defense Education Act 204, 208
1962 Subcommittee on the Selection of Astronauts 15
1963 Equal Pay Act 100, 143
1978 NASA Press Release 224
1986 *Challenger* (STS-51-L) 220

Aaron, John 179
Abbey, George 213
Abernathy, Ralph D. 176
Ackmann, Martha 122n83
aerospace scholarship 10
*Afro-American* 176
*Agena* 135–36, 138
Air Force Test Pilot School 207
Air Research and Development Command (ARDC) 95, 96
*Air Scoop* 27
*Akron Beacon Journal* 112
*Alabama Journal* 41
*Albuquerque Journal* 67
Aldrin, Edwin "Buzz" 139–40, 171–73
Allen, Joseph 226
*Almost Heavan* (Kevles) 199
*Amelia Earhart's Daughters* (Toomey and Haynesworth) 7
American: astronaut 6, 11, 53, 55, 60, 70, 72, 77, 164, 168; automated technology 34, 39; character 34, 35, 38; culture 5, 9, 23, 44, 87, 228; discourse 46, 64; kitchen 26; male 36, 113, 115;

masculinity 2, 6, 10, 14, 16, 39, 64, 129, 239; pilot masculinity 42; public discourse 1, 14, 24, 35, 53, 64, 87, 221, 239; society 2, 241; space program 2, 161, 164, 238; spacecraft 238; woman into space 16, 36, 88, 101
American Mercury project 10–11
American Psychological Association 94
Anders, William 164, 168
Anderson, Jack 143, 148, 149
Anfuso, Victor 102–6, 110–11, 143
Annin, Katherine H. 41
*Anthem* (Rand) 33
*Apollo* 15, 108, 146, 149, 159, 240
*Apollo 1* 15, 157–58, 160–61, 165
*Apollo 7* 162–63
*Apollo 8* 162, 164–68, 181
*Apollo 9* 168–69
*Apollo 10* 170
*Apollo 11* 16, 170, 173–74, 176–79
*Apollo 12* 178–80
*Apollo 13* 16, 180–83, **183**, 186, 188, 219
*Apollo 15* 187
*Apollo 17* 16, 187, 189
Apollo Guidance Computer (AGC) 13
*Apollo in the Age of Aquarius* (Maher) 11
Apollo program 11, 141, 159–60, 162, 176, 185
*Apollo-Soyuz* mission 16, 199
*Aquarius* 180, 181
Archer, Joan 171
Armstrong, Neil 135–37, 161, 171, 173–74
Army Air Corps 8
Arnold, Henry H. "Hap" 40, 41, 89
*Artemis* 244
The Associated Press 64–66, 71, 73–74, 95–96, 113–14, 130, 139, 174, 208, 219, 221

# 286 GENDER AND THE RACE FOR SPACE

Atkinson, Joseph D. 78n11, 206
*Atlanta Constitution* 65, 166
*Atlantic Monthly* (magazine) 93
*Atlas Shrugged* (Rand) 33
Augerson, William S. 54
*Aurora 7* 72
auto-pilot 63, 170
automation 9, 14, 34, 39, 40

Baldwin, Hanson W. 41
Balke, Bruno 39–40
Baltimore 176
Bassett, Charles 137
Bassett, Preston 44
Bean, Alan L. 178, 179, 213–15, 217
Becker, P.C.C. 71
Beech, Keyes 176
Belkovsky, Valery 114
Belyayev, Pavel 129
Beregovoy, Georgi 221
Berezovy, Anatoly 220
Bergman, Stuart 222
*Berkshire Eagle* 41
Berry, Charles A. 136, 186
Betson, Johnnie R. Jr. 117
*Better Homes and Gardens* (magazine) 36
Bezos, Jeff 1
*Birmingham News* 173
*Blue Origin* 1
Bluford, Guin 207
Bong, Richard 9
Bonney, Walter T. 10
Boorstin, Daniel J. 188
Borman, Frank Jr. 135, 147, 164–66, 168
*Boston Globe* 186
Bourgin, Simon 165
Bowie, David 175
Brown, Molly 130
Bryant, Nelson 188
Bryant, Shirley 205
*Bulletin of the Atomic Scientists* 167, 187
Burgess, Colin 79n16
Bush, Vannevar 41
Butler, Abigail 148
Butler, Judith 4
Butler, Melvin 27
Bykovsky, Valery F. 76, 134

Cagle, Myrtle 97, 106
Camp Lejeune 148
Carl, Ann B. 99
Carpenter, Malcolm Scott 60–61, **61**,
72–74, 76, 102, 104, 110, 111, 140, 186

Carpenter, Rene 186
Carr, Jerry 179
Carter, Jimmy 11
Cernan, Gene 137–38, 170, 187, 189
Chaffee, Roger B. 157, **158**
*Challenger* 219, 228, 242
Chang-Diaz, Franklin 207, 242
*Charlotte Observer* 173
*Chicago Daily News* 112, 132
*Chicago Defender* 177
*Chicago Sun-Times* 224
*Chicago Tribune* 65, 74, 111, 215
Chicago's Institute of Psychoanalysis 27
*The Christian Science Monitor* 175
Citizen Astronaut Program 16, 217
Civil Rights Act 143, 144, 204
civil rights movements 144, 161
Claire, Eau 166
Cleave, Mary L. 207–8, 214
*Clipped Wings: The Rise and Fall of the Women
Air Force Service Pilots (WASPs) of World
War II* (Merryman) 5, 8, 89, 92
Cobb, Jerrie 18n13, 96–105, **97**, 107–10,
112, 115, 116, 120n55, 121n76
Cochran, Jacqueline "Jackie" 2, 66, 87,
89, **90**, 91–92, 96, 99, 101–3, 105–8,
111–12, 186, 239, 243
Cold War 14, 46, 238, 243; gender roles
5–6, 14–15, 23, 46, 117; masculinity
14, 24, 35–37, 46, 128, 149, 190, 237;
public discourse 6
Coleman, Bessie 87, 242
Collins, Eileen 242–43, **244**
Collins, James 172
Collins, Michael 58, 138, 172, 173
Colson, Bill 224
*Columbia* 173, 228
"Commercial Astronaut Wings Program"
1
commercial aviation 43, 87
Congress 37, 67, 89–92, 144, 165, 201
Congress of the Soviet Union (CPSU) 69
Congressional Armed Services
Committee 92
Congressman Phil Weaver (R-NE) 66
Conley, Carolynn Lee 212
Connor, Joseph 117
Conrad, Charles "Pete" Jr. 134–35, 139,
178–79
Considine, Bob 7
Cooper, Gordon 58, 60–61, **61**, 75, 76,
85n159–85n160, 134–35, 144, 187
Cooper, Patricia 4

## INDEX

Corman, James C. 107
Corn, Joseph 6
cosmonauts 11, 69–70, 77, 139, 221
*Courier-Journal* 174, 175
Cox, Archibald 202
Cox, Donald 98
Cox, George 69
Crane, George 26
Crippen, Robert 218
"crisis of masculinity" 4, 6
Cronkite, Walter 218
Crossfield, Scott 44–45, 56, 171
Cuadro, Elizabeth 149
Cunningham, R. Walter 162
Curtiss Cadette university programs 91
Curtiss-Wright 43

*Daily Express* 115, 132
*Daily Oklahoman* 98
*Daily Press* 27
*Daily Record* 71
Davis, Saville R. 175
de Beauvoir, Simone 4
"The Decline of the American Male" 26, 36
Deep Space Instrumentation Facility-51 12
Defense Advisory Committee on Women in the Services (DACOWITS) 92
*Democrat and Chronicle* 91
Democratic Party 100
Denver, John 218
Deputy Associate Administrator for Manned Space Flight 29
*Detroit Free Press* 45
Dietz, David 41
*Digital Apollo: Human and Machine in Space Flight* (Mindell) 13, 44
Dille, John 62
The Director of the Air Force Aeronautical Laboratory 95
*Discovery* 219, 243
Doolittle, James 54
Douglas, Debbie 93
*The Dream of Civilized Warfare: World War I Flying Aces and the American Imagination* (Robertson) 7, 42
Dryden, Hugh 99–101, 131, 144
Dunbar, Bonnie 207–8

*Eagle* 173, 177
Earhart, Amelia 7, 87

*Earning Their Wings: The WASPs of World War II and the Fight for Veteran Recognition* (Myers) 8, 88, 89
*Echo* satellite 31
Eisele, Donn F. 162–63
Eisenhower, Dwight 24, 37, 55, 78n11, 141, 206, 208, 238
*El Paso Times* 40
*Empire of the Air: Aviation and the American Ascendancy* (Van Vleck) 8
Engle, Joe 187
*Entering Space: An Astronaut's Odyssey* (Allen) 226
Equal Employment Opportunity Commission (EEOC) 144
Equal Pay Act 100, 143, 144
*Explorer 1* 37

F-104 Starfighter 44
Fabian, John M. 218, 226
Faget, Maxime 23, 201
*Faith 7* 75
Federal Aviation Administration 1
*The Feminine Mystique* (Friedan) 27, 93
Feoktistov, Konstantin 129
Ferguson, Walter 95
Finney, John W. 68, 131
Fino, Steven A. 9, 42
Firestone, Harvey S. 209
First Lady Astronaut Trainees (FLATs) 1, 8, 14, 88, 97–99, 101, 104, 111, 129, 185, 203, 238–39, 243
Fisher, Anna L. 207–9, 214, **216**, 222–23, 225–26
Fisher, William "Bill" 225
Fletcher, James C. 16, 201, 206
Flickinger, Donald "Flick" 55, 59, 95–96
*Florida Today* 212
*Flying Camelot: The F-15, the F-16, and the Weaponization of Fighter Pilot Nostalgia* (Hankins) 5, 9, 42
Fontaine, Andre 36
Foster, Amy 144
*The Fountainhead* (Rand) 33
*Freedom 7* 53, 70
Freeman, Theodore 137
*Fresno Bee* 165
Friedan, Betty 5, 27, 93
*Friendship 7* 70–71
Frosch, Robert 212
Fulton, James G. 104–5, 107–8, 110–11
Funk, Wally 1, 3, 17n4, 243

288  GENDER AND THE RACE FOR SPACE

Gagarin, Yuri 53, 64–67, 69, 113
*Gannett News Service* 215
Garriott, Owen Kay 145
Gehman, Richard 35
*Gemini* 128, 131, 140–42, 149, 159, 179
*Gemini 1* 128
*Gemini 2* 128
*Gemini 3* 15, 130
*Gemini 4* 131–33
*Gemini 5* 134
*Gemini 6A* 135
*Gemini 7* 135
*Gemini 8* 135–37, 173
*Gemini 9* 137
*Gemini 9A* 138
*Gemini 10* 138
*Gemini 11* 139
*Gemini 12* 139
Gemini missions 128–29, 138, 169
*Gender and Technology: A Reader* (Cooper) 4
gender equality 2, 112, 115, 220
gender roles 5, 7, 14–16, 24, 32, 35–36, 43, 45, 87, 91, 93, 105, 185, 241
General Motors 169
*Generation of Vipers* (Wylie) 33
Gerovitch, Slava 11
Gibson, Edward George 145, 146
Gibson, Robert "Hoot" 215, 225
Gill, Jocelyn 127
Gilmore, David 37
Gilruth, Robert "Bob" 23, 54–56, 87
"Girl Pilots" 91
Glenn, Annie 93
Glenn, John H. 9, 28, 45, 60–62, **61**, 65, 70–72, 74–75, 102, 109–11, 115, 140, 166, 174, 215, 237
Glennan, Keith 78n11
Goble, Jimmy 30
Goble, Katherine 28, 30
Goddard 30–32
Gordon, Richard F. 139, 178–79
Graveline, Duane E. 145, 155n124
The Great Depression 7
Gregory, Frederick D. 207
Greider, William 178
Griffin, Gerry 179, **183**
Grissom, Gus 60–61, **61**, 63–64, 68–69, 128, 130–31, 157, **158**, 163
Group 8 astronauts 200, 206–8, 213–14, 218, 224, 226, 240–42
Group 9 astronauts 207, 225
Group 13 astronauts 242
Grumman Aircraft Corporation 159

Guggenheim Aeronautical Laboratory 12

Hale, Ellen 215
Hall, Jacquelyn Dowd 1, 7, 12
Hall, Oceola "Ocie" 202–3, 206–7, 244
Ham (Holloman Aero Medical) 64–65, 69
Hamilton, Margaret 162
Hankins, Michael W. 5, 9, 42, 53
Harris, Ruth Bates 202–3, 206
Harris, Tom 96
Harrison, John 178
Hart, Janey 99, 100, 102–5, 107, 200
Hart, Phillip A. 99, 115, 121n76
Hartsfield, Henry 219
Hauk, Frederick 218
Hawley, Steve 225
Haynes, Marjorie "Charlie" 148
Haynesworth, Leslie 7
Hearst, Joseph 112
Hechler, Ken 107
Hellman, Lillian 115
Hernandez, Aileen 144
"Heroes in a Vacuum: The Apollo Astronaut as Cultural Icon" 10
Hersch, Matthew H. 13, 199, 203
Hess, Harry 146, 185
Hicks, Nancy 182
*Hidden Figures: The American Dream and the Untold Story of the Black Women Mathematicians Who Helped Win the Space Race* (Shetterly) 12
Hills, Beverly 94
Hines, Bill 224
Hispanic-Serving Institutions (HSIs) 204–5
Historically Black Colleges (HBCUs) 204–5
Hodges, John 134
Holt, Nathalia 12
Horner, Richard 43
House Committee on Science and Astronautics 102
House Subcommittee 110
Hubble Telescope 31
Hunter, Linda Maria 148
Huntoon, Carolyn 206–7, 211, 222
Husbands' Advancement and Protective Assn. (HAAPA) 113
Hutchison, William D. 176

IBM 133, 165
inclusion 203, 206–7, 217, 242, 244

## INDEX

289

*inner-directed* man 34
Instructor Pilot 214, 243
*Inventing the American Astronaut* (Hersch) 13, 199
*Izvestia* 113

Jayson, Pamela 94
Jefferson, Thomas 38
Jemison, Mae 217, 241–42
Jet Propulsion Laboratory (JPL) 12, 40
jet test pilot 2, 3, 44, 55–57, 72, 88, 100, 108–9, 117, 141
Joel, Billy 237
Johnson, Clarence "Kelly" 44
Johnson, Jim 30
Johnson, Katherine 28, **29**, 243
Johnson, Lyndon 93, 99–101, 121n76, 131, 138, 141, 144, 168, 174
Johnson Space Center 31, **184**, 206, 211
Josselyn, Irene 27

Kamanin, Nikolai 77
Kamin, Nikolai 112
Karth, Joseph E. 104
Kauffman, David 13
Kennan, George 4
Kennedy, Bobby 161
Kennedy, John F. 17n4, 37–39, 64, 67–68, 108, 116, 141, 144, 159, 188
Kenneth, Thomas 180
Kerwin, Joseph P. 145–46, 148, 181
Kevles, Bettyann 4, 199
Khrushchev, Nikita 2, 25, 70, 115
Kimmel, Michael 14
King, Martin Luther Jr. 129–30, 161
Kinsey, Alfred 33
Kitchen Debate 25, 228
Kitson, Lela Cole 91
Komarov, Vladimir M. 129, 161
Korolev, Sergei 10–11
Kozakoff, Emily G. 143
Kraft, Christopher 73, 75, 134, 161, 206, 214, 224
Kranz, Gene 138, 158, 160, 182, **183**, 189

*La Nacion* 132
landing module (LM) 159–60, 162, 168–70, 173–74, 178–81
Langley 14, 23, 27–30, 45
Langley Memorial Aeronautical Laboratory 23, 27–28
Launius, Roger 10, 181
Leavy, Ed 59

Lebedev, Valentin 220
Lederer, Jerome 165
Lee, Dorothy "Dottie" 23, 31, 243
Lee, William A. 142
Lelyveld, Joseph 182
Leonov, Alexei 129–30, 132
Levy, David 33
*Liberty Bell* 68, 130
*Liberty Bell 7* 68
*Life* (magazine) 15, 32, 38, 62–64, 66–67, 69–75, 91, 93, 98, 114–15, 120n39, 129–31, 133, 135–36, 139–40, 158, 162, 164, 171
Life Science Programs 98
Lindbergh, Charles 42, 95, 140, 149, 164, 174
*The Lonely Crowd: A Study of the Changing American Character* (Riesman) 34
Long, B. J. "Jack" 185
Long Civil Rights Movement 1, 12, 23–24, 183
*Look* (magazine) 26, 36, 95–96
*Los Angeles Times* 94, 173–74
Lousma, Jack R. 180
Lovelace, Randolph William Jr. 2–3, 59, 95–99, 101, 103, 106–7, 114
Lovelace Albuquerque clinic 2, 96
Lovell, Bernard 76, 166, 168
Lovell, James "Jim" A. Jr. 135, 139–40, 164, 180, 196n125
Low, George 55, 108, 110, 130, 162, 182, 201
Luce, Clare Boothe 115–16
Luce, Henry 32
Lucid, Shannon 207–9, 214, 224–25
Lukas, J. Anthony 177
*Luna* 9 173
Lundberg, Kirsten O. 221
Lunde, Barbara 32
Lunney, Glynn S. 163, 181
Lutsky, V. 69

MacLeod, Scott 186
McCall, Bob 189
McCarthy, Joseph 33
McDivitt, James A. 132–33, 147, 169–70
McDonnell Aircraft 63
McDougall, Walter 2
McNair, Ronald 207
Maher, Neil M. 11
Mailer, Norman 33, 35
"Make Way For The Ladies In Space" 214

290 GENDER AND THE RACE FOR SPACE

*Making Space for Women: Stories of Trailblazing Women from NASA's Johnson Space Center* (Ross-Nazal) 13
Malina, Frank 12
Manned Spacecraft Center 117, 146, 178
Marshall, George C. 92
Marshall Spaceflight Center 12
Martin *Titan II* 134
masculinity 14, 26, 33, 59, 131, 133, 158, 163; American masculinity 4, 6, 8, 10, 16, 39, 129; astronaut masculinity 5, 64, 67, 147, 175; Cold War masculinity 14, 24, 35–37, 46, 128, 141, 237; pendulum 70; pilot masculinity 42, 170, 173; push-button masculinity 13, 68
masculinity crisis 6, 23, 33, 36, 46, 87, 238
Massachusetts Institute of Technology (MIT) 32, 127
*Maternal Overprotection* (Levy) 33
May, Geraldine 92
Méndez, Arnaldo Tamayo 12
Mercury 57, 59, 71, 76, 109, 128, 130–31, 134, 140, 149, 159, 173, 179
Mercury 7 10, 14, **61**, 63, 70, 93, 101, 221
The Mercury 13 18n13
Mercury ballistic capsule **55**
Mercury Program 75, 127
Mercury Redstone rocket 30
Merryman, Molly 5, 8, 89, 92
Meyer, Agnes E. 93, 119n37
Meyer, Alan 93
*Miami Herald* 223
*Miami News* 106
Michael, Frank Curtis 145–46
military pilot 6, 56, 109
Miller, George P. 102, 115, 130
Mills, C. Wright 35
Mindell, David A. 13, 44–45, 133
mission control 64, 131, 134, 163, 170, 173, 180–82, 185
Moss, Steven 11–12
*Ms. Magazine* 199, 219
Mueller, George E. 29
Mullane, Mike 207, 216–17, 219, 237, 241
Muller, George 142
Myers, Sarah Parry 8, 88, 91–92

NACA Muroc Test Unit 91
*The Naked and the Dead* (Mailer) 33
*NASA and the Long Civil Rights Movement* (Odom and Waring) 12
NASA Langley Research Center 45

NASA Space Flight Activity, Langley Field 59
National Academy of Sciences (NAS) 141
National Advisory Committee for Aeronautics (NACA) 14, 23–24, 27–28, 30–32, 36, 44, 45
National Aeronautics and Space Administration (NASA) 1, 6, 15, 37, 45, 88, 92–93, 99, 103, 106, 108, 110–11, 115, 127–28, 136, 141–42, 169, 177, 199, 238–40, 243; *Apollo 7* launch 162; astronaut 60, 160, 210; contractors 63; Deep Space Instrumentation Facility-51 12; *Gemini 8* 135–37, 173; Gemini missions 128–29, 138; gender roles 32; Group 6 148–49; Group 8 mission 207; Jet Propulsion Laboratory 12; job announcement 127; Life Science Programs 98; Marshall Spaceflight Center 12; Mercury 57, 59, 71, 76, 109, 128, 130–31, 134, 140, 149, 159, 173, 179; Mercury 7 10, 14, **61**, 63, 70, 93, 101, 221; Project A 54; Project Gemini 15, 128, 131, 138; refused to launch woman astronaut 3; scientific-six 146; scientist-astronauts 143–45, **145**, 146–47; Space Task Group 54–56, 141; STG 57, 59; symposium 19n32; women workers 24
National Defense Education Act 204, 208
National Organization for Women (NOW) 185
National Safety Council 104
National Science Foundation (NSF) 206
Naval Research Library, United States 30
Navy Electronics Laboratory 57
Neuberger, Maurine 114
Neufeld, Michael J. 11
Neuffer, Judith Anne 240
Nevin, David 172
"New Frontier" 39
*The New Shepard* 1
*New York Times* 30, 41–42, 60, 64–65, 67–68, 70–71, 73, 75, 85n160, 98, 116, 132, 134–35, 139, 163–64, 166, 170, 173, 175–77, 179, 181–82, 188–89, 211, 214, 216, 225
Newell, Homer 142
*Newsweek* 71, 75, 130, 132, 177–78, 215, 217–18
Nichols, Nichelle 204–6
Nichols, Ruth 95
Nikolayev, Andrian 73–74, 76, 113

# INDEX

Ninety-Nines 95, 112
Nixon, Richard M. 25–26, 87, 168, 170, 174, 178, 182, 201
*No Requiem for the Space Age: The Apollo Moon Landings and American Culture* (Tribbe) 11
North American Aviation 157, 159
North Atlantic Treaty Organization (NATO) 24

Ochoa, Ellen 242
Odlum, Floyd 96
Odom, Brian C. 12, 176
*Odyssey* 180, 181
*Officers in Flight Suits: The Story of American Air Force Fighter Pilots in the Korean War* (Sherwood) 9
O'Hara, Dee 160, 219
Olds, Robin 9
Onizuka, Ellison 207, 220
Orbital Flight 100
*Orlando Sentinel* 205
Osberg, James 121n76
Osgood, Catherine 30
*other-directed* man 34–35
*Outlook* (magazine) 42

P-38 Lightning 44
P-40 Warhawk 90
Paine, Thomas O. 162, 166, 173, 176, 182
Parent-Teacher Association (PTA) 93
Paul, Richard 11–12
*People Weekly* 224
Pershing, John Jay 172
Petrone, Rocco Anthony 161, 166
*Philadelphia Inquirer* 115, 137, 223, 226
Phillips, Samuel C. 163
Philpott, Gladys 148
pilot astronauts 62, 142, 147–49, 187, 201, 207, 214–15
pilot masculinity 42
Pilotless Aircraft Research Division (PARD) 23
Pirie, Robert B. 99
Planck, Charles 91
Popov, Leonid 220
Popovich, Pavel 74
Poppy Northcutt, Francis Marian 182–84, **184**, 185
post-World War II 4–5, 36, 43
Potter, David M. 35
Pressly, Eleanor Crockett 30
Prodan, John 187
"Program 63" 174

Project Gemini 15, 128, 131, 138
Project Mercury **55**, 76, 131
*Proton-K/D* rocket 161–62
push-button masculinity 13, 16, 40
Pyle, Ernie 32

Rabinowitch, Eugene 167
Radio Research Laboratory, Harvard 30
Ramspeck Congressional Report 8, 101, 200
Rand, Ayn 33
Randolph, William 58
Randt, Clark T. 98
Rankin, Allen 41
Raytheon Company 169
Remote Manipulator System (RMS) 210
Resnik, Judith 203, 207–10, 214, **216**
Rickenbacker, Eddie 9
Ride, Sally K. 16, 199, 207–8, 210–11, **216**, 217–18, 222–24, 226, **227**, 232n83
Riesman, David 34, 35
*The Right Stuff* (Wolfe) 5
*Right Stuff, Wrong Sex: America's First Women in Space Program* (Weitekamp) 3
Riley, Corinne Boyd 102, 122n83
*The Rise of American Air Power: The Creation of Armageddon* (Sherry) 8
*The Rise of the Rocket Girls: The Women Who Propelled Us, from Missiles to the Moon to Mars* (Holt) 12
Roark, Howard 33
Robertson, Linda R. 7, 42
Robinson, Lina L. 148
*Roe v. Wade* 204
Roman, Nancy 31, 209
Roosevelt, Eleanor 89
Roosevelt, Franklin 27
Roosevelt, Teddy 38
Ross-Nazal, Jennifer M. 13, 220
Roush, J. Edward 104, 106
Roy, Melba 31, **31**
Ruff, George 59

*Santa Cruz Sentinel* 223
*The Saturday Evening Post* 214
*Saturn* rocket 160
*Saturn V* 160, 162, 164, 179
Savitskaya, Svetlana Y. 220–22
Savitsky, Yevgeny 220
SB2 Helldiver 91
Schirra, Walter "Wally" Marty Jr. 59–61, **61**, 63, 74–76, 80n42, 135, 147, 162–63, 218

Schlafly, Phyllis 199, 208
Schlesinger, Arthur M. Jr. 33, 36
Schmitt, Harrison Hagan "Jack" 145, 185, 187, 189
School of Aviation Medicine (SAM) 40
Schweickart, Russell L. 169
*Science News* 213
scientific-six 146
scientist-astronaut 15–16, 127, 141–46, **145**, 146–49, 187, 189, 239
Scott, David "Dave" 135–37, 169
Scott, Joan Wallach 6
Scout, Eagle 158, 171
Seamans, Robert C. 142
*The Second Sex* (de Beauvoir) 4
Secrest, Robert R. 117
Seddon, Margaret "Rhea" 207–9, 212–14, **216**, 222–25
See, Elliot 137
Selection of Astronauts of the Committee on Science and Astronautics 3
*Selling Outer Space: Kennedy, the Media, and Funding for Project Apollo, 1961-1963* (Kauffman) 13
Serebrov, Alexander 220
sexism 28, 227, 244
*Sexual Behavior in the Human Male* (Kinsey) 33
Shafritz, Jay M. 78n11
Shayler, David J. 79n16
Sheer, Julian 165
Shepard, Alan B. 1, 53, 60, **61**, 62, 65–69, 80n42, 116, 128, 145, 209
Sherry, Michael 8
Sherwood, John Darrell 9
Shetterly, Margot Lee 12
Shoemaker, Gene 147
Siddiqi, Asif A. 10–11
*Sigma 7* 74
Sjoberg, Sigurd A. 182
Skelton, Betty 95
Slayton, Deke 60–61, **61**, 72, 145–47, 162, 171, 173, 181
Smith, Jane 205
Smylie, Ed 181
social media 44
Society for Experimental Test Pilots (SETP) 61, 128
The Society of the Experimental Test Pilots 42
Soviet 2–4, 6, 11, 59, 64, 69, 74, 78–79n16, 88, 129–30, 139, 168, 221
Soviet Premier 26

Soviet space program 10, 115, 132, 161
Soviet Union 2, 4, 14–15, 23–24, 35, 76, 79n16, 112, 115–16, 129, 161
*Soyuz 1* 161
Soyuz T-7 220
SP-8 Chief Computer 28
SP-3 Junior Computer 28
Space Camp 218
Space Task Group (STG) 54–57, 59, 141
space transportation system (STS) 199, 240
*Space World* 98, 226
Spacecraft Systems and Projects Division 32
spaceflight 3, 11, 12, 15, 45, 53, 58, 73, 94, 98, 133, 139, 140, 142–44, 149, 160, 189
"Spam in a can" 11, 56, 63, 128
sports cars 62
Sprince, Richard 186
*Sputnik* 4, 14, 23, 25, 35–36, 237
Stafford, Charles 131
Stafford, Thomas 135, 137–38, 170, 179
Stapp, John 96
*Star Trek* 205
*Stepford Wives* 93
Stevens, William K. 169–70
Stevenson, Adlai 25
Stockholm 132
Strecker, Edward 33, 35
STS-63 243
STS-41-D 219
STS-51-F 219
Sullivan, Kathryn "Kathy" 205, 207–8, 210, 213, **216**, 217–18, 222–24, 226, 242
Sullivan, Walter 167
*Sun Magazine* 30
*Sunday Mirror* 225
*Surveyor 1* 173
*Svenska Dagbladet* 132
Swigert, John Leonard "Jack", Jr. 180, 186
*Sydney Morning Herald* 214
*Syracuse Post-Standard* 139
Syversten, George 113

T-38 137, 145, 204, 214, 218
TASS 74, 129, 134, 220, 221
Tereshkova, Valentina "Vayla" 2–3, 112–16, 132, 144, 212, 214, 220, 225, 226
Tex Reynolds 113
Thaden, Louise 7–8, 100

# INDEX

293

Thagard, Norman 218
*Their Mother's Sons* (Strecker) 33
*This I Can Do: The Women's Machiavelli* 202
Thomas Ramo Woolridge (TRW) 183
Thompson, Clara 26
*Tiger Check: Automating the U.S. Air Force
    Fighter Pilot for Air-to- Air Combat, 1950-
    1980* (Fino) 9, 42
*Time(s)* 62–63, 65, 70, 74, 129, 132, 136,
    139, 165, 168–72, 188, 211, 215
*Titanic* 130
Title IX 202, 204, 208, 228, 241
Titov, Gherman S. 69–70, 74, 76–77
Titov, Vladimir 243
Toomey, David 7
"Toupees, Girdles, and Sun Lamps" 35
Townshend, Charles 32
*tradition-directed* man 34
Tribbe, Matthew D. 11
Trubach, Janet 148
*Tucson Daily Citizen* 146
*Tyrone Daily Herald* 65
Tyson, Molly 210

U-2 spy plane 44
Ubell, Earl 179
United Press International 106, 113, 115,
    130, 138–39, 221
United Service Organization (USO) 176
United States 2–4, 25, 26, 33, 37, 39, 41,
    60, 67–68, 79, 100, 116, 117, 129, 131,
    177; Air Force Undergraduate Pilot
    School 243; astronaut masculinity 5,
    64, 67, 175; "crisis of masculinity"
    4; culture and gender 6; domestic
    technology 5; domesticated household
    technology 26; gender culture 159;
    masculinity crisis 6; military weapon
    25; public discourse 5; space linkups
    139; women pilots 2
United States Navy 41
University of California, Los Angeles
    (UCLA) 209, 210
University of South Florida 112
University of Tennessee Medical School
    209
U.S. Naval Test Pilot School 61
*U.S. Women in Aviation* (Douglas) 93
USS *Essex* 163, 171
USS *Iwo Jima* 181
USS *Wasp* 132

*V-2* rockets 11

Van Horne, Harriet 212
Van Vleck, Jennifer 8
Vance, J. D. 244
*Vanguard* satellite 35
Vaughn, Dorothy 28–29
*The Vital Center* 33
Voas, Robert B. 54, 57–58, 73, 78n6,
    80n62, 117, 226
*Von Braun: Dreamer of Space, Engineer of War*
    (Neufeld) 11
von Braun, Wernher 11, 39, 54, 57, 62, 87,
    94, 187–88, 201
*Voskhod* 129
*Voskhod 1* 129
*Voskhod 2* 129, 138
*Vostok* 77, 134
*Vostok I* 53
*Vostok 2* 69
*Vostok 3* 73
*Vostok 4* 74
*Vostok 5* 114
*Vostok 6* 2, 114

Wainwright, Loudon 139–40, 224
Walker, Joseph A. 56
Waring, Stephen P. 12
Warsaw Pact 24
Washington DC Aero Club 42
*Washington Post* 66, 131, 139, 178, 201
Watson, Elmo Scott 91
*We Could Not Fail: The First African
    Americans in the Space Program* (Paul and
    Moss) 11
*We Seven* (Glenn) 109
Webb, Alvin B. 113
Webb, James E. 65, 68, 98, 100, 101, 144,
    162
Webb, Jim 130, 142, 144–45
Webb, Wilse B. 94
*Weekend Pilots: Technology, Masculinity, and
    Private Aviation in Postwar* (Meyer) 93–94
Weintraub, Bernard 176
Weise, Jessica A. McCullough 102, 110
Weitekamp, Margaret A. 3, 96
White, Edward "Ed" Higgins Jr. 131–32,
    **133**, 157, **158**
White, Stanley C. 54
"The White Negro" 35
Whyte, William H. Jr. 13, 35, 37–38, 161
Wilford, John Noble 139, 157, 163, 169–70
Williams, Alfred Joseph 92
Williams, Janis 214
Williams, Walter C. 76

*The Winged Gospel: America's Romance with Aviation* (Corn) 6
*Winston-Salem Journal* 175
Witkin, Richard 75
Wolfe, Tom 5, 72, 147, 215
Women in Space Earliest (WISE) 95–96
*Women with Wings* (Planck) 91
Women's Armed Services Integration Act 92
Women's Army Service Pilots (WASPs) 2, 8, 89–90, **90**, 91–92, 99, 105–7, 114, 185, 200, 212, 238, 243, 245
Women's Auxiliary Flying Squadron (WAFS) 89
World War I 7, 9, 42, 172
World War II 2, 4, 23–24, 27, 32, 36–37, 40, 43–45, 57, 61, 87–88, 92
Wright brothers 131

Wright Brothers Memorial Trophy, 1949 42
Wright-Patterson Air Force Base 58, 59, 99
Wylie, Philip 33

X-15 flights 44–45, 77, 137
X-planes 56, 77

Yardley, John 201
Yeager, Charles "Chuck" 11, 17n4, 43, 56, 63, 99, 187, 218
Yegorov, Boris Borisovich 129
Young, John 130–31, 138, 170

Zhukovsky Air Force Academy 113
*Zond 5* 161–62

www.ingramcontent.com/pod-product-compliance
Ingram Content Group UK Ltd.
Pitfield, Milton Keynes, MK11 3LW, UK
UKHW012215040625
459144UK00004B/21